More Praise for *Management Dynamics*

"Students of the Theory of Constraints who want a detailed review of how TOC concepts apply to accounting will not want to miss this book. Business people will benefit from insights on how to apply TOC oriented thinking to pinpoint the *real* sources of waste and inefficiency in an enterprise. The Casparis have made a significant contribution to the body of knowledge in this area; moreover, their work should stimulate further discussion and advancement!"

> —Paul H. Selden, PhD, President, Performance Management, Inc.

"This book combines clear thinking and research into the purpose and role of accounting in organizations. Coupled with a deep understanding of Goldratt's Theory of Constraints, the Casparis' methodology focuses the enormous power of practical systems thinking in organizations. This book finally brings together the elements needed to truly implement and sustain a genuine process of ongoing improvement. Along with Elliott Jaques' *Requisite Organization,* we now have the blueprints for creating the right structure *and* the right operational methodology to achieve unprecedented organizational performance."

> —Romey Ross, PMP, CPE, President, Technical Project Services, Inc.

"Financial officers and accountants in profit making organizations have always struggled to understand how I, OE, and T can be applied in their world. This struggle of TOC accounting versus cost accounting in the financial record-keeping domain has inhibited many a successful TOC project. The authors have been able to lift the veil for the financial community! Now let's hope the accountants get on with it!"

> —William A. Woehr, Executive Partner, Delta Institute, S.A.,
> Board member Angel Iglesias, S.A.

"The Casparis provide a step-by-step strategy for integrating the components of Goldratt's Theory of Constraints into a highly effective system for achieving success in business. The book's roadmap describes how to structure a high-performance business by the thoughtful integration of the components of Goldratt's theory. I highly recommend this valuable work."

> —John Sambrook, President, Common Sense Systems, Inc.

MANAGEMENT
DYNAMICS

MANAGEMENT DYNAMICS

Merging Constraints Accounting to Drive Improvement

John A. Caspari

Pamela Caspari

WILEY

John Wiley & Sons, Inc.

This book is printed on acid-free paper.

Copyright © 2004 by John Wiley & Sons, Inc. All rights reserved.

Published by John Wiley & Sons, Inc., Hoboken, New Jersey.
Published simultaneously in Canada.

For general information on our other products and services, or technical support, please
contact our Customer Care Department within the United States at 800-762-2974, outside
the United States at 317-572-3993 or fax 317-572-4002.

Wiley also publishes its books in a variety of electronic formats. Some content that appears
in print may not be available in electronic books.

For more information about Wiley products, visit our Web site at *www.wiley.com*.

Library of Congress Cataloging-in-Publication Data:

ISBN 0-471-67231-9

Printed in the United States of America

10 9 8 7 6 5 4 3 2 1

In memory of our fathers,

Charles Edward Caspari, Jr.

and

John Taliesin David,

who taught us about ethical behavior and fair treatment of people.

Contents

Foreword

Reconciliation

Practitioners of the theory of constraints (TOC) have been waiting for this book for a long time. Many of you reading this now have had substantial exposure to TOC and perhaps even experience with it. Those who have not will benefit by knowing a little background.

TOC, as a management approach, has been around for almost two decades, and its creator, Eliyahu M. Goldratt, has been applying the basic principles even longer than that. Consultants have been expending a lot of effort in helping their clients use TOC to effect real change—quantum improvements—in the performance of their organizations. Visionary people within client organizations have been trying to apply what they have learned about TOC toward the same end. For both groups, the results have been mixed. For every success, there have been more failures. (Failure can be defined as TOC producing "underwhelming" results, being abandoned altogether, or the organization reverting to the way things were before the change.) The question is: *Why?*

Interestingly, that basic question—*Why?*—is at the heart of TOC itself. The thinking process created by Goldratt is designed to answer "why" types of questions. And when the "why" question is posed about an undesirable system outcome using the thinking process, the inevitable answer—whatever that may be—is the system's core problem, or critical root cause. So what is the critical root cause behind the failure of organizations (those that have tried and failed) to realize the tremendous benefits that TOC has to offer? I would suggest it's a missing element.

So what *is* that missing element? The answer is inherent in the paradigm shift that the Casparis talk about in Chapter 2: the transition—one might say a giant leap of faith—from cost-world thinking to throughput-world thinking. And that transition—or the absence of it—is what makes the difference between theory and successful rubber-meets-the-road management.

Nearly every company is heavily imbued with cost-world thinking. TOC challenges that thinking by requiring its practitioners to abandon the "old-time religion" of the cost world that virtually every executive (and chief financial officer) has grown up with.

In the movie *Indiana Jones and the Last Crusade*, Jones finds himself facing a chasm he feels he can't possibly jump over safely. Yet the instructions for him to reach his goal call for a "leap of faith." It's a life-or-death situation, so he steels himself, takes that leap, only to discover that there *was* a solid, dependable bridge beneath his feet after all. But Indiana Jones is a fictional character. Risk-takers in the business world are few, and risk-averters abound. So, tempted as they might be by the Holy Grail on the other side of the chasm, many (most?) chief executives and chief financial officers are loath to step off the security of the platform they currently stand on, make that leap of faith, and try to reach the performance improvement that TOC promises. They intuitively know that throughput-world thinking is the right thing to pursue, but they can't bring themselves to turn loose from the comfort zone provided by their cost-world history. In the vernacular of the bashful country girl at her first dance, "I'm gonna dance with the one what brung me." Cost-world thinking got them where they are today, so why mess with a winning formula?

A big reason why they're reluctant to tinker with the existing paradigm is that they can't see the invisible bridge that Indiana Jones discovered—but only by taking a huge risk—and they won't take the risk that Jones did because for most of them it's *not* a life-or-death situation.

And therein lies an important point: even among the normally risk-averse decision makers, some will make that leap, even though it runs counter to their normal thinking, behavior, or desires—but only under a particular set of circumstances: when the danger of not surviving is so great that they see risk-taking as the least undesirable option. In other words, when the survival of the company, or the executive in his or her job, is clearly at stake, decision makers will often do things they would otherwise eschew. Some, of course, will dither and fail to decide to leap until it's too late. W. Edwards Deming said it best: "It is not necessary to change; survival is not mandatory."

Wouldn't it be better, however, if organizations didn't have to be in a life-or-death situation in order to be willing to embrace a new way of fundamental thinking about how their systems should operate? Executives have such a difficult time letting go of cost-world thinking because, like Indiana Jones, they can't see the invisible bridge to the throughput world. But as in *The Last Crusade*, that bridge *is* there. They just need a way to make it visible, so that they can have the confidence to do what's required to shift their paradigms to the throughput world. That bridge might be called reconciliation.

And that's what the Casparis have in this book: they have reconciled the apparent dichotomy between cost-world and throughput-world thinking. Only someone with John Caspari's thorough understanding of both paradigms—and his penchant for independent thinking—could have conceived of that reconciliation.

The big knock on throughput accounting, as Goldratt conceived it, has always been that, although it has "accounting" in the name, it isn't truly a functional accounting system. It's more of a decision support system. It can't fully substitute for generally accepted accounting principles (GAAP) in the business world because, for one thing, it isn't rigorous enough in the details. But that criticism is based on an erroneous underlying assumption: that the existing way of calculating and reporting financials must be replaced in order for TOC to succeed. Clearly, that would be an extremely "hard sell" under any circumstances. But even harder to sell is the idea that costs are irrelevant and only throughput matters. That's an erroneous impression that many people come away with after their first exposure to TOC. And that's unfortunate because not even Goldratt would maintain that costs are irrelevant—only that they should not be the first, or even the most influential consideration.

The Casparis have done the TOC community, and the business community at large, a great service in writing this book. In presenting the concept of constraints accounting, they reveal the relationship—the bridge, if you will—between the cost world and the throughput world. It's this bridge that distinguishes true constraint management from the theory that led to it. And the authors make it clear that succeeding at TOC and embracing a throughput orientation does not require giving up traditional accounting systems. The same data are collected and compiled; they're just interpreted in a new way for the purposes of sound operational and strategic decision making—in other words, for effective *constraint management*. The Casparis explain all this, with liberal use of examples, in a way that identifies the faulty assumptions—and explains why they're faulty—underlying traditional use of financial numbers to guide management behavior.

Perhaps best of all, in this book the Casparis have put "bean counting" in the proper context of the entire organization and its activities. They relate throughput and cost financial metrics to the people of the organization and their activities. Most financially oriented books don't do this. How does constraints accounting relate to product pricing? to manufacturing production decisions? to project management? or to sales? How do financial measures affect people's motivation and priorities in doing their jobs? All of these issues are addressed here. Pay special attention to their unique concept of a bonus plan for reinforcing a process of ongoing improvement (POOGI Bonus Plan).

So what are you waiting for? You didn't pick up this book because you wanted to know what I think about the constraint management and the relationship of constraints accounting to success. An intriguing intellectual journey awaits you . . . start reading!

H. William Dettmer

Port Angeles, Washington
April 9, 2004

Preface

In their quest for success, some organizations seem to dip their hands into a bag of programs, hoping that the one they extract will bring them glowing results that turn up on the bottom line. After the first few months of implementing the new flavor, optimism is high, bottom-line results are glowing, and sighs of relief are felt rippling through the organizations— and the accolades of analysts can be heard throughout the land. Then suddenly Murphy strikes with back-to-back home runs—suppliers are late with a shipment, computers crash, the economy goes into a nosedive. The accolades give way to critical analysis of the problems, grave doubts about the financial health of the organization, and loss of confidence in top management's ability to take control and lead the organization back to robust health. Financial numbers are crunched, manipulated, massaged, and sometimes put into hibernation. People are downsized, right-sized, tossed into the roiling ocean of unemployment. And when favorable results are slow to reappear on the bottom line, the roar and accusations of the analysts become deafening and the leadership door revolves.

The new leadership, wanting to achieve bottom-line results that will not be just a flash in the pan, eagerly reach into their own bag of flavorful programs, choosing one, which they are confident, will bring lasting results. Another day at the office begins.

With this scenario playing over and over like a broken record in our minds, our journey began. First, we needed to make sense out of our thoughts. If a robust process of ongoing improvement is a desirable state for any organization to be in, why does it seem so hard to achieve? Second, we devoted ourselves to making words out of our sense and finally actions out of our words. This book is an in-depth, step-by-step analysis of our journey. What we discovered was the amazing consistency of the logical analysis of what ingredients organizations need for them to experience ongoing improvement and thus achieve a robust bottom line.

We firmly believe that when owners, leaders, and workers of an organization are held to the same ethical standards, feel the honor of fairness, hear the beat of their feet marching in the same direction, a robust process of ongoing improvement becomes the very fabric of the organization.

This book will take you on a profound journey, chapter by chapter, where you will explore the dynamic nature of constraint management and the power of a supporting transparent constraints accounting and measurement system, weaving each aspect of the implementation to reflect an organization's global goal. It will challenge you to examine your existing paradigms, take you out of comfort zones, deepen your knowledge, and awaken your common sense and intuitions. We strongly suggest that you read it in sequence, for each chapter holds a key to the next. And when you do, the keys to controlling the process of ongoing improvement which flows through to the bottom line will be in your hands.

John Caspari
Pamela Caspari

Grand Rapids, MI
August 2004

Acknowledgments

This book is an international effort worthy of the third millennium. Its content is based on observations and conversations concerning the theory of constraints (TOC), management accounting, constraint management, corporate governance, ethics, logic, corporate capital markets, and social dynamics. These conversations took place with a large international group of people interested in constraint management dynamics through multi-day symposia and training programs from 1985, when John first encountered Eli Goldratt and Bob Fox at the Institute of Management Accountants (IMA) annual convention. At that convention Dr. Goldratt, as keynote speaker, presented a paper entitled "Cost Accounting: Public Enemy Number 1 of Productivity." The conversation continued in that form until about 1996, when a group attending the APICS Constraint Management Special Interest Group (CMSIG) established an Internet discussion group, the TOC-L, hosted by Walter Bristow. The TOC-L quickly became an active and broad-based forum. It became the Goldratt discussion list, and, in 1998, it was moved to the CMSIG, where it is being hosted as this volume is being written. Each of these lists has had thousands of members, with many participating anonymously. About the same time, Dave Sucavage established the *Crazy about Constraints!* web site as a central repository for general constraint management data. So to the many, but often unknown, participants in this grand discussion we are grateful for your questions, observations, answers, and sharing of experiences.

Our undergraduate and graduate students at Bradley University, Grand Valley State University, Aquinas College, and Wayne State University have proved to be a source of honest critical analysis that is so important when redefining a field. We are grateful to them and to the bold administrators at those institutions who supported our experimentation.

We also offered an open constraints accounting seminar in Grand Rapids for several years. The basis of much of our material was developed in those courses, which attracted about 70% of their participants from outside the United States. In particular, Nelson McEwan (New Zealand) was instrumental in bringing us to the realization that we had coined the term *constraints accounting* and in specifying its attributes and definition. Dave Williams (Canada) both asked the question about a process of ongoing improvement (POOGI) bonus and stayed to help formulate a solution that stands today with only a few injections to eliminate some negative branches.

We have heard that one can tell the pioneers in an area by the arrows in their backs. The employees of Vail Rubber Company qualify for such a distinction. Bill Hanley (CEO) dared to delay implementing Vail's TOC drum-buffer-rope scheduling system for nine months in order to have a holistic implementation, including a full POOGI Bonus plan. Mike Hanley (vice president for marketing), Dave Alder (utility), Larry Regan (superintendent), Buff Goss (machine operator), Charlie Engler (manager of information systems), Tim Hanley (superintendent), Bill Boyer (union president), and Dennis Milnickle (machine operator) are just some of those who contributed to the effort.

Bob Fox, Eli Goldratt, Dale Houle, Donn Novotny, and the other partners of the Avraham Y. Goldratt Institute were extremely generous in making their Jonah training available to academics at an academic rate in the 1980s and then offered special academic courses in the 1990s.

Eli Goldratt also established and funded a not-for-profit organization, TOC for Education (TOCFE), which focuses on making the TOC thinking processes available to educators throughout the world. Both authors had the benefit of attending a TOCFE course that addressed the idea of using the three-cloud technique to define the subject matter of a particular area. During that seminar, we also benefited from Ramush Goldratt's logical discussions and Efrat Goldratt-Ashlag's psychological insights.

In addition to the above-named, many other people have generously shared their experiences with constraint measurement, constraint dynamics, and other business implementations. This group includes Mike Cahoon, John Daly, Brendon Fox, John Haberlee, Patrick Henry III, Jerry Hoffman, James Holt, Larry Leach, Jean-Claude Miermont (France), Bob Pritzker, Larry Shoemaker, Bruce Vennema, Scott Ward, Mark Woeppel, Chris Wysong, and Larry Wysong.

Jim Bowles (United Kingdom), Rudi Burkhard (Switzerland), Charles Caspari, Rick Denison, Bill Dettmer, Bill Hunt, Don Klein, Hannan Lechman (Israel), Harvey Opps, Chris Rabideau, Tony Rizzo, and Kelvyn Youngman (New Zealand) all read major portions of the manuscript and offered valuable comments. Dick Vengermeersch read and commented on the historical section included in the appendix.

Bill Hodgdon and Bill Woehr (Spain) contributed to our understanding of the marketing ramifications of constraint management.

The following also provided assistance: Susan Carnwath, David Davies (Brazil), John Parr (New Zealand), Howard Meeks, Craig Wilcox, Bill McCelland, Jack Warchalowski (Canada), Dick Frenz (South Africa), Bill Law (Hong Kong).

Material taken from John A. Caspari, "Theory of Constraints," Section 8a in the 1993 and 1994 Supplements to the *Management Accountants' Handbook*, 4th edition, Donald E. Keller, James Bulloch, and Robert L. Shultis, editors, Copyright © 1993, John Wiley and Sons, Inc., appears throughout the book as appropriate. This material is used by permission of John Wiley and Sons, Inc.

The *Management Accountants' Handbook* material on the theory of constraints, when taken in conjunction with the Noreen, Smith, and Mackey IMA research study, represent the state of throughput accounting circa 1990. This was generally accepted as all that was needed in the way of accounting knowledge. We are grateful to Bob Fox for encouraging us to pursue the subject to its logical consequences.

We would also like to thank the wonderful staff at Weber's Inn, Ann Arbor, Michigan, for providing a warm, healthy, and calming atmosphere in which to work.

Finally, we are grateful for the intuitive intellect, sharp eye, and infinite patience of Sheck Cho, our editor at John Wiley and Sons, Inc.

MANAGEMENT
DYNAMICS

1

Thinking Bridges

EVALUATING DECISION ALTERNATIVES

How do we evaluate the economic effect of potential courses of action? The anticipated economic effect is a compelling aspect of decision making. In this book we deal with profit-oriented organizations, so we will evaluate potential actions specifically in terms of their effects on **bottom-line** profitability. Our exploration of a **constraint management** approach using **constraints accounting** as a catalyst to lock in a process of ongoing improvement begins by probing strategies for evaluating common decision alternatives. We need reliable and easily applied decision rules to guide our daily actions. A **thinking bridge** links a rule of thumb with bottom-line profitability through cause-and-effect relationships.

Let us examine two such cause-and-effect thinking bridges. The first thinking bridge, *least product cost*, takes a product-cost accounting approach to evaluation. The second thinking bridge establishes *global measurements* for assessment.

Least Product Cost

How do we respond to manufacturing variety in our organizations? The typical response to manufacturing variety is to decouple operations from each other. This is accomplished by staging partially completed product inventories between linked operations and then treating each decoupled area as a separate entity for analytical purposes.[1] But managers need a means to tie the anticipated effect of actions taken in local and decoupled areas to the bottom line of the global organization.

Product-cost accounting techniques provided the solution. The basic profit measurement of an organization is provided by its **earnings statement,** which is expressed as:

Sales less *Expenses* equals *Net Profit*

1

Recognizing the reality of the equation, managers responsible for **cost centers** assume that the least-cost alternative translates into increased bottom-line profitability. The equation, restated to distinguish decoupled functional areas, is viewed as:

Sales less (*Manufacturing* and *Nonmanufacturing Expenses*) equals *Net Profit*,

emphasizing the independence of the individual areas of responsibility.

Many cost centers are very large organizational units, having hundreds of employees. Even so, the responsibility is for costs only; revenues are the responsibility of a different functional area. There is often a significant lag between the time of expenditure and the expenditure's appearance as part of the bottom line since the costs of products being produced are held as inventories at various stages of completion.

Cost center managers and their corporate controllers, needing a more timely measurement, turn to the notion of standard (or estimated) **product cost** as a surrogate for linkage to the bottom line. Here the assumption is that lower unit product cost is reflected as reduced manufacturing expense, thus leading to greater profitability. Sometimes, managers establish **pseudo-profit centers** for which the revenues reported are based on an internal transfer using what the accountants call a **transfer price.**

Of course, costs do not tell the whole story. Managers recognize the contrived nature of the measurements and rely on their intuition to protect against the effects of misleading information provided by the accounting system. *Least product cost* traditionally provides a thinking bridge that spans the gap between managerial actions and bottom-line results.[2]

Global Measurements

Viewing the organization analytically as a single comprehensive system, Eliyahu Goldratt and Jeff Cox observed that essentially three things could happen to cash with respect to operations.[3] They defined three measurements—**throughput (T), inventory/investment (I),**[4] and **operational expense (OE),** to reflect these events.

Throughput

An organization may undertake an activity, such as providing a service or producing and selling a product, that results in cash inflows. The activity typically reflects the operating strategy of the organization. Some related cash expenditures—the truly variable expenses or **throughput expense**—are associated with the sale. The difference between the sales and throughput expenses, taken over a specified period, is the rate at which the system generates money through sales and is known as throughput (T).[5] Throughput corresponds to what management accountants know as **contribution margin.** Later, we will see that some differences exist between throughput and contribution margin in practical application. Therefore, when referring to contribution margin in association with constraint management, we will use the term *throughput.*

Inventory/Investment

Some cash is expended to acquire the resources necessary to establish the operating capability for carrying out the organization's business strategy. These expenditures were originally called inventory (I).[6] In addition to raw materials, work-in-process, and finished goods inventories, this category includes property, plant, and equipment as well as intangible rights such as patents, trademarks, and computer software. In a broad sense, accountants refer to such costs as **assets.**

Since inventory has a well-established meaning in the accounting literature (raw materials, work-in-process, and finished goods), the term is expanded to inventory/investment to reflect the more comprehensive concept. Inventory/investment includes the capabilities of the system as well as raw materials and purchased parts, but it does not include direct labor or manufacturing overhead.[7]

Operational Expense

Cash is expended on a periodic basis to provide the ongoing capability to carry out the operating strategy. These expenses relate to the time period, rather than to specific sales, and accountants call them **period costs.** Property taxes and natural gas for heating are examples of such expenses. This category also includes all personnel costs at continuing positions. These period expenditures are known as operational expense (OE).[8]

T, I, and OE Taken Together

T, I, and OE describe the alternative thinking bridge. Again, the validity of the earnings statement equation is affirmed:

Sales less *Expenses* equals *Net Profit*

But now, rather than breaking the expenses down into functional categories of manufacturing and nonmanufacturing expense, the expenses are classified as being either truly variable with sales or as belonging to the time period. The profit equation now is viewed as

Throughput less *Operational Expenses* equals *Net Profit*

or the equivalent:

Sales less *Variable Expense* less *Period Expenses* equals *Net Profit*

Actions that are expected to result in increased T or decreased I or OE lead to increased profitability and are desirable actions. By asking about the expected effect of a potential action on each of the three variables, T, I, and OE, a manager can quickly, easily, and accurately predict the effect of many proposed actions on global net profit, even in a complex organization.

THINKING BRIDGES EXAMPLE

A simple example will demonstrate the extent of the difference between the two thinking bridges for decision making. First, we will present some initial data. Then, we will offer four independent, but similar, proposed changes to the operation as four scenarios. Each scenario will first be analyzed using the least product cost thinking bridge, and then the same scenario will be analyzed using the global measurements thinking bridge. Although each of the four proposed changes is similar to the others, we shall see that the bottom-line impacts of the changes are different.

Initial Data

Consider the following data relating to a company.[9]

The company is currently selling 3,500 widgets per year at a price of $400 each. The widget manufacturing process uses four workstations as shown in Exhibit 1.1.

Widgets are processed sequentially through all four stations. At the completion of processing, the product is either transferred to a finished goods storage area or shipped to the customer.

Each widget requires raw materials costing $80. An individual employee earning $18 per hour staffs each workstation. Each employee works 2,080 hours per year (40 hours per week for 52 weeks per year), and the employees are not cross trained. The company has other expenses of

Exhibit 1.1   Widget Manufacturing Process

Workstation	Processing Time
101	15 minutes
102	25 minutes
103	10 minutes
104	5 minutes
Total Time	55 minutes

Exhibit 1.2   Labor and Overhead Charging Rates

Cost Element	Calculation		Rate per Direct Labor Minute
Direct Labor	$18.00 / hour / 60 minutes / hour	=	$ 0.3000
Overhead	(4 direct labor employees) * (2,080 hours / year) = 8,320 direct labor hours per year (8,320 direct labor hours per year) * (60 minutes / hour) = 499,200 direct labor minutes per year $900,000 / (499,200 direct labor minutes)	=	$ 1.8029
Combined			2.1029

$900,000 per year. The company's cost accountant has calculated **charging rates** for direct labor and overhead. These calculations and the resulting rates are shown in Exhibit 1.2.

The costs of materials, labor, and overhead were then combined as shown in Exhibit 1.3 to form the $195.66 **standard cost** of a widget.

The plant engineer has been hard at work and has determined that, with the addition of a fixture that costs only $5,000, the processing times can be modified at the various workstations.

Scenario 1

In the first scenario, the engineer proposes acquiring the fixture and reducing the total processing time by three minutes per unit. Here is how the time savings of three minutes per unit is to be accomplished. The new fixture would allow some work to be transferred from workstation 101 to workstation 102. As shown in Exhibit 1.4, the processing time at workstation 102 would increase by two minutes, but the processing time at workstation 101 would decrease by five minutes. Thus, the total time to produce a widget is reduced from 55 minutes to 52 minutes, a net time savings of three minutes for each widget produced. This same proposal will also be analyzed for scenarios 2 and 4.

Exhibit 1.3   Standard Cost of One Widget

Cost Element	Cost
Raw Materials	$ 80.00
Direct Labor (55 minutes @ $0.3000)	16.50
Overhead (55 minutes @ $1.8029)	99.16
Standard Unit Cost	$195.66

Exhibit 1.4   Proposed Change to Widget Manufacturing Process (Scenarios 1, 2, and 4)

Workstation	Original Processing Time	Proposed Processing Time
101	15 minutes	10 minutes
102	25 minutes	27 minutes
103	10 minutes	10 minutes
104	5 minutes	5 minutes
Total Time	55 minutes	52 minutes

Scenario 1: Least Product Cost Analysis

Intuitively, the engineer knows that it is beneficial to reduce the amount of time needed to produce a product. The new unit cost of a widget, reflecting the three-minute processing time reduction, is $189.35 as shown in Exhibit 1.5.

When the revised unit standard cost is compared to the original standard cost, as is done in Exhibit 1.6, it confirms that the engineer's proposal reduces the cost of a widget by $6.31 per unit.

The expected annual cost savings resulting from this proposal are calculated in Exhibit 1.7. The engineer feels good about this proposed change, which saves the company $17,085 in the first year.

Since this proposal involves a **capital expenditure,** or an additional investment amount, we will check its rate of return on the additional invested capital. The **internal rate of return** of this proposal, calculated in Exhibit 1.8 using the estimated annual cost savings from Exhibit 1.7, is more than 400%. The payback period is less than three months. This appears to be an excellent proposal.

What do you think? *Is this proposal an improvement?* Is the example typical of how decisions are made in your organization? Does your organization pursue production efficiencies with the purpose of increasing the bottom line?

Exhibit 1.5   Revised Unit Cost after Implementing Proposal (Scenarios 1, 2, and 4)

Cost Element	Unit Cost
Raw Materials	$ 80.00
Direct Labor (52 minutes @ $0.3000)	15.60
Overhead (52 minutes @ $1.8029)	93.75
Standard Unit Cost	$189.35

Exhibit 1.6 Reduction in Standard Cost (Scenarios 1, 2, and 4)

Original standard unit cost	$195.66
New standard unit cost	189.35
Cost savings per unit	$ 6.31

Global Measurements Thinking Bridge Analysis

When using the global measurements (T, I, and OE) technique for the financial analysis of a proposed expenditure, we ask a series of five questions about the proposal:

1. What prevents the firm from increasing throughput?
2. Will the total amount of throughput (T) change?
3. Will the operational expenses (OE) of the firm change?
4. Will the amount of inventory/investment (I) in the firm change?
5. What is the real economic effect of this proposal?

Scenario 1: Global Measurements Thinking Bridge Analysis

Let us examine the engineer's proposal through the lens of the second thinking bridge, the global measurements technique. Perhaps we will gain additional insight as we ask, and answer, the T, I, and OE global measurements questions for the example.

What prevents the firm from increasing throughput? Before answering this question, we will note that this question did not arise in the least product cost analysis. It is not part of the least product cost thinking bridge.

Do we have an internal production limitation, or does the greater opportunity for improvement lie in the relationship between our customers and us? That is, does our perceived market limit us? Or is something else blocking us?

Although the production capability is limited by workstation 102, which requires more time to work on the product than any other, if we

Exhibit 1.7 Annual Cost Savings (Scenario 1)

Cost savings per unit	$ 6.31	
Annual volume	x 3,500	units
Total annual cost saving	$ 22,085	
Less: Cost of fixture	5,000	
First year cost saving	$ 17,085	

Exhibit 1.8   Internal Rate of Return

Cost savings (the presumed net cash inflow resulting from the investment)	$22,085	per year
Initial investment required	$5,000	
Approximate value of, and upper limit on, the internal rate of return** (cost savings / investment) (The payback* reciprocal)	4.417 ≈	442 %
* The payback period of this investment is about 3 months (5000 / 22085 = 0.226 years). **The reciprocal of the payback period approximates the internal rate of return when both returns are high (greater than 50%) and economic life is long (greater than twice the payback period).		

check the capacity usage, we will see that there is plenty of productive capacity. Each workstation has 40 hours available each week for 52 weeks during the year. That makes 2,080 hours or, multiplying by 60 minutes in an hour, 124,800 minutes of available production time for a year. Since each widget requires 25 minutes at workstation 102, the company could produce 4,992 widgets per year (124,800 / 25 = 4,992), well above the currently used capacity of 3,500 units. Even with the proposed change, which increased the time required at workstation 102 to 27 minutes, the company still would have the capacity to produce 4,622 widgets each year (124,800 / 27 = 4,622).

The real limitation lies in the market demand for widgets. We are only selling 3,500 widgets a year, and we have the capacity to produce more than 4,500 widgets before and even after the engineer's proposal is implemented. Thus, we must look to our marketing and sales operations in order to create greater throughput.

Will the total amount of throughput (T) change? No, since the engineer's proposal has no effect on the volume of sales, neither the sales revenue nor the variable cost of sales (raw materials) changes. There is no reason to believe that the company would sell either more or less because of this change. It already has the capacity to produce more than it can sell. Hence, the proposal is unlikely to have an effect on throughput.[10]

Will the operational expenses (OE) of the firm change? Do we have the same number of employees? Has our overhead changed? No, these all remain the same. Some small changes may take place, however. For example, we might be charging an additional amount of depreciation expense for the new fixture, or the fixture may use some additional power. But for the most part, the operational expenses remain unchanged.

Will the amount of inventory/investment (I) in the firm change? The inventory/investment increases by $5,000, the cost of the new fixture.

What is the real economic effect of this proposal? The real economic effect is that the company spends $5,000 and has a real economic loss of $5,000.

Exhibit 1.9   Summary of Changes in Global Measurements (Scenario 1)

Global Measurement	First Year	Subsequent Years
T	no change	no change
I	+$5,000	no change
OE	no change	no change
Cash Flow (=T-I-OE)	-$5,000	no change

The T, I, and OE global measurements for the first scenario are summarized in Exhibit 1.9. Throughput remains the same, inventory/investment increases by $5,000, and operational expense does not change. The overall cash flow is reduced by $5,000 in the first year.

Ask yourself again, *is this proposal an improvement?*

Scenario 2

In scenario 2 we assume that everything is the same as in scenario 1, except that the firm is currently producing and selling at its capacity of 4,992 units. The engineer makes the same proposal as in scenario 1. Production times before and after the proposed change are as shown previously in Exhibit 1.4.

Scenario 2: Least Product Cost Thinking Bridge

The reduction in standard cost is the same in the second scenario as it was for the first, so Exhibits 1.5 and 1.6 apply equally to scenario 2. After all, none of the variables that we used in calculating the $6.31 reduction in the standard cost of the product has changed. The first year cost savings, however, have increased by 55% from $17,085 to $26,500 because of the significantly higher volume. The cost savings for scenario 2 are tabulated in Exhibit 1.10.

The payback and rate of return analysis based on the cost savings in Exhibit 1.10 are summarized in Exhibit 1.11. The proposal looks even better than it did before.[11]

Exhibit 1.10   Annual Cost Savings (Scenario 2)

Cost savings per unit	$ 6.31	
Annual volume	x 4,992	units
Total annual cost savings	$31,500	
Cost of fixture	5,000	
First year cost savings	$26,500	

Exhibit 1.11   Internal Rate of Return (Scenario 2)

Cost savings (the presumed net cash inflow resulting from the investment, $6.31 * 4,992)	$31,500	per year
Initial investment required	$5,000	
Approximate value of, and upper limit on, the internal rate of return (cost savings / investment) (The payback* reciprocal)	6.3 ≈ 630%	
* The payback period of this investment is about 2 months (5000 / 31,500 = 0.159 years).		

Scenario 2: Global Measurements Thinking Bridge Analysis

Let's ask the T, I, and OE global measurement questions about scenario 2 and see if anything has changed there.

What prevents the firm from increasing throughput? The answer to this question *has* changed. The company is currently producing and selling at its capacity of 4,992 units, a limitation that is established by workstation 102. The engineer's proposal increases the time required at workstation 102 to produce a widget from 25 minutes to 27 minutes. As previously shown, the number of widgets that *now* can be produced actually drops by 370 widgets from 4,992 to 4,622. In this case there are plenty of sales; the ability of the overall system to generate greater throughput is limited by the capability of workstation 102.

Will the total amount of throughput (T) change? Yes, as shown in Exhibit 1.12, the throughput is actually reduced in the second scenario.

Exhibit 1.12   Throughput Lost (Scenario 2)

Lost Sales Volume:			
Original capacity		4,992	units per year
Capacity if proposal is implemented		– 4,622	units per year
Reduction in productive capability		370	units per year
Throughput per unit:			
Price	$400.00	per unit	
Variable Expense	– 80.00	per unit	
Throughput	$320.00	per unit	
Throughput lost	(The throughput per unit	$320.00	per unit
	multiplied by the number	x 370	units per year
	of units lost)	$118,400.00	per year

The proposal reduces the available capacity below that which is currently being sold. This means that the organization will be late delivering (or not be able to fill) about 370 of the existing orders (4,992 widgets) for which it has contracted. For each unit that is not delivered, the company will not receive the $400.00 sales price. However, for each unit not delivered the company will not need to incur its variable cost (raw materials costing $80.00). Hence, $320.00 throughput per unit ($400.00 – $80.00), when extended by the lost volume, provides a measure of the lost throughput. The current period throughput lost, as shown in Exhibit 1.12, is $118,400. This may be used as an estimate of future losses also, although there may be an additional adverse effect in the future resulting from the poor delivery performance. We just don't know at this point. We also should recognize that as a result of such situations the organization's employees, who have to answer for late shipments, feel the pressure of being trapped by policies outside their control.

Will the operational expenses (OE) of the firm change? No, as in scenario 1, the operating expenses do not appear to change.

Will the amount of inventory/investment (I) in the firm change? As in scenario 1, the inventory/investment increases by $5,000, the cost of the new fixture.

What is the real economic effect of this proposal? The real economic effect of the proposal in scenario 2, where the effect was to reduce the capacity available on an existing fully utilized resource, combines the $5,000 additional investment with the $118,400 throughput reduction for a total economic loss of $123,400 in the first year and a continuing amount of $118,400 or more until something else changes.

The measurements for scenario 2 are summarized in Exhibit 1.13.

Scenario 3

In scenario 3 we start from the original case again. For this scenario we assume that the potential market is at least 6,000 widgets. The firm is currently operating at a level of 4,992 widgets. The plant engineer makes a

Exhibit 1.13 Summary of Changes in Global Measurements (Scenario 2)

Global Measurement	First Year	Subsequent Years
T	- $118,400	- $118,400
I	+$5,000	no change
OE	no change	no change
Cash Flow (=T-I-OE)	- $123,400	- $118,400

Exhibit 1.14   Proposed Change to Widget Manufacturing Process (Scenario 3)

Workstation	Original Processing Time	Proposed Processing Time
101	15 minutes	20 minutes
102	25 minutes	23 minutes
103	10 minutes	10 minutes
104	5 minutes	5 minutes
Total Time	55 minutes	58 minutes

similar suggestion, but this time the effect is to *increase* the time required to produce the product by three minutes. In this case, as reflected in Exhibit 1.14, five minutes is added to workstation 101's processing time. The processing time at workstation 102 is decreased by two minutes. Thus, if this proposal were to be implemented, there would be a net increase in processing time of three minutes.

Scenario 3: Least Product Cost Thinking Bridge

In this scenario, the standard cost of a widget increases by $6.31. The calculations for this are shown in Exhibits 1.15 and 1.16.

The cash flows that would be estimated for this proposal, based on the increased unit cost, are shown in Exhibit 1.17. It appears that this proposal will cost the organization $36,500 in the first year and $31,500 annually thereafter. When analyzed using the least product cost method, this proposal does not appear to be a very good one.

Scenario 3: Global Measurements Thinking Bridge

Once again we ask our global measurements questions.

What prevents the firm from increasing throughput? As with scenario 2, workstation 102 restricts our ability to serve all of those potential customers who would like to purchase our widgets.

Exhibit 1.15   Revised Unit Cost after Implementing Proposal (Scenario 3)

Cost Element	Unit Cost
Raw Materials	$ 80.00
Direct Labor (58 minutes @ $0.3000)	17.40
Overhead (58 minutes @ $1.8029)	104.57
Standard Unit Cost	$201.97

Exhibit 1.16   Increase in Standard Cost (Scenario 3)

Original standard unit cost	$ 195.66
New standard unit cost	201.97
Cost increase per unit	$ 6.31

Will the total amount of throughput (T) change? The proposal, even though it increases the standard cost of the product, will increase the relative capability of workstation 102 as the time required for processing a widget at workstation 102 is reduced from 25 minutes to 23 minutes. Now 5,426 widgets per year may be processed through workstation 102 (124,800 minutes per year / 23 minutes per widget). Since the market potential is 6,000 units, the additional units can be sold. As shown in Exhibit 1.18, this is an increase of 434 widgets sold during the year. With a throughput of $320.00 per unit, the sales volume increase translates into a $138,880 increase in throughput.

Will the operational expenses (OE) of the firm change? No. Once again there is no real impact on operational expense. The firm has the same number of employees and approximately the same other costs as it had before. What has changed is that it has the ability to produce more widgets than it did previously.

Will the amount of inventory/investment (I) in the firm change? Yes, they will again spend the $5,000 for the fixture.

What is the real economic effect of this proposal? They gain $133,880 in the first year and $138,880 in future years until something else changes. The measurements for the results of scenario 3 are summarized in Exhibit 1.19.

Scenario 4

In scenario 4 we start from the original case again, but now we assume that the potential market is at least 6,000 widgets and that the firm is currently operating at a level of 4,992 widgets. The plant engineer again

Exhibit 1.17   Annual Cost Increase (Scenario 3)

Cost increase per unit	$ 6.31	
Annual volume	x 4,992	units
Annual cost increase	$ 31,500	
Cost of fixture	5,000	
First year cost increase	$ 36,500	

Exhibit 1.18   Additional Throughput (Scenario 3)

Additional Sales Volume:			
Capacity if proposal is implemented		5,426	units per year
Original Capacity		– 4,992	units per year
Increase in productive capability		434	units per year
Throughput per unit:			
Price		$400.00	per unit
Variable Expense		– 80.00	per unit
Throughput		$320.00	per unit
	(The throughput per	$320.00	per unit
Additional	unit multiplied by the	x 434	units per year
Throughput	number of units gained)	$138,880.00	per year

makes a similar suggestion. This time the effect is to *decrease* the time required to produce a widget by three minutes, as was the case in the first two scenarios. In this case, however, as reflected in Exhibit 1.20, the processing time at workstation 103 is increased by two minutes, allowing the processing time at workstation 101 to be reduced by five minutes.

Scenario 4: Least Product Cost Thinking Bridge

As with scenarios 1 and 2, which also reduced the total time required to produce a widget by three minutes, the standard cost of a widget decreases from $195.66 to $189.35. The analyses shown in Exhibits 1.5, 1.6, 1.10, and 1.11 apply equally in this case. This, again, appears to be a desirable action when evaluated by the conventional least cost analysis.

Scenario 4: Global Measurements Thinking Bridge

We ask our global measurement questions a last time.

What prevents the firm from increasing throughput? As with scenarios 2 and 3,

Exhibit 1.19   Summary of Changes in Global Measurements (Scenario 3)

Global Measurement	First Year	Subsequent Years
T	+ $138,880	+ $138,880
I	+$5,000	no change
OE	no change	no change
Cash Flow (=T-I-OE)	+ $133,880	+ $138,880

Exhibit 1.20   Proposed Change to Widget Manufacturing Process
(Scenario 4)

Workstation	Original Processing Time	Proposed Processing Time
101	15 minutes	10 minutes
102	25 minutes	25 minutes
103	10 minutes	12 minutes
104	5 minutes	5 minutes
Total Time	55 minutes	52 minutes

workstation 102 restricts our ability to serve additional customers who might like to purchase our widgets.

Will the total amount of throughput (T) change? Unlike scenarios 2 and 3, scenario 4 does not involve, or *touch*, the limiting workstation 102. Therefore, the firm will neither gain additional capacity nor lose existing overall capability because of the proposal. Sales will still be 4,992 widgets, and throughput does not change.

Will the operational expenses (OE) of the firm change? Operational expense also remains about the same.

Will the amount of inventory/investment (I) in the firm change? As with all of the other scenarios, $5,000 is spent for the fixture.

What is the real economic effect of this proposal? There is a loss of the $5,000 investment in the fixture.
   Exhibit 1.21 displays the summarized results of scenario 4.

Example Summary

The results of each analysis are summarized in Exhibit 1.22. There is also a column for you to write in *your opinion* as to which is the more correct analysis.

Exhibit 1.21   Summary of Changes in Global Measurements (Scenario 4)

Global Measurement	First Year	Subsequent Years
T	no change	no change
I	+$5,000	no change
OE	no change	no change
Cash Flow (=T-I-OE)	- $5,000	no change

Exhibit 1.22   Example Summary, First Year Dollar Gain or *(Loss)* Shown by Analyses

	Least Product Cost (LPC)	Global Measurements (T, I, & OE)	Which analytical technique do *you* believe more correctly reflects reality?
Scenario 1	$17,085	*($ 5,000)*	
Scenario 2	$ 26,500	*($ 123,400)*	
Scenario 3	*($36,500)*	$133,880	
Scenario 4	$ 26,500	*($ 5,000)*	
Range of Estimates of Bottom-line Profit Effect	$63,000	$257,280	

What we originally had thought was a nice *but minor* sort of enhancement with a cost of $5,000 and an annual benefit of about $20,000 actually embraces a range of bottom-line profitability effects of more than a quarter of a million dollars!

SUMMARY

What can we discover from the thinking bridges example? Three conclusions are evident. First, we need to think carefully about what we mean by **improvement.** Second, in each of the four scenarios, the limitations on the ability to produce or sell the product created an **Archimedes point** for the company. Finally, the **least product cost** thinking bridge appears to be flawed.

Improvement

How do we determine whether an action is an improvement? We probably can agree that an improvement to a system makes the system better. However, this question leads immediately to a second question: "better relative to what?"

In order to learn whether an action results in an improvement, we must first know what to compare it against. In the thinking bridges example, the engineer set about to reduce the amount of time required to produce a widget. The engineer's proposals in scenarios 1, 2, and 4 were successful in this effort, and—from that point of view—the proposals were improvements. But *why* did the engineer want to reduce the amount of processing time required? The intention was to increase profits by reducing the resources, and hence the cost, required to produce the product. When examined from the point of view of the global organization, however, profits did not increase.

An improvement ultimately must be defined in terms of an organization's **global goal.** An action resulting in better performance relative to the global goal is an improvement. Actions resulting in worse performance, or in no change, relative to the global goal are *not* improvements. If the primary purpose of an organization is to pursue profit, then improvement must be measured in terms of greater bottom-line profitability. In scenarios 1, 2, and 4 of the example, the intention was good—to reduce the standard cost of the item—but the result was not an increase in profits. Therefore, the action, even though successfully reducing the total time required to make a widget, was not an improvement. Improvement is evident only in scenario 3.

Archimedes Point

Some locations within an organization are particularly sensitive to changes. Something very big happens when changes touch these locations. It may be good or it may be bad, but in any event it is very big. We call such a component of an organization an Archimedes point because it marks a place to focus attention in order to get dynamic results.

It is apparent that workstation 102 plays a special role in scenarios 2 and 3. In these cases the quantity a company can sell is restricted not by the market demand but by its internal ability to produce the product. Workstation 102 represents an Archimedes point for the company in these two scenarios.

In scenario 4, workstation 102 again plays an important, though less obvious, role. It is still an Archimedes point for the company. However, since the proposed change in scenario 4 involves only workstations 101 and 103, which are not Archimedes points, nothing much happens in terms of improvement. In scenario 4 an Archimedes point was not touched; therefore, no significant system reaction occurred.

Now consider scenario 1. The company has plenty of manufacturing capacity to provide the entire quantity of widgets demanded by the market. Therefore, there is no currently active production limitation as to how much can be sold. Neither workstation 102 nor any other production workstation is an Archimedes point in the first scenario. Accordingly, there was no significant effect on the bottom line, even though the proposed change in the first scenario involved workstation 102.

Is there any Archimedes point in the first scenario at all? Every system has at least one Archimedes point. In scenario 1 it is just someplace other than in the manufacturing function. In fact, since the company has the ability to produce considerably more than it is selling in scenario 1, it appears that the Archimedes point is likely to be somewhere in either the marketing or sales function. It might be in a physical resource such as the number of sales outlets or salespeople. Or it might be a management policy. However, an apparent Archimedes point in sales or marketing also might be the result of actions taken in other areas, for example, poor delivery performance or poor quality that results in a lack of sales.

Least Product Cost

What about using reduced product cost as a guide for management actions? As we have seen in the example, least product cost provides a deceptive beacon. If the least product cost technique were to lead us in the right direction, it would seem to be just a matter of good luck.

One might suggest that if many companies are making decisions based on reducing the standard cost of products, then isn't that evidence that it works? The answer is yes, and no. Yes, many companies do this, and many of those companies are both large and have enjoyed long corporate lives. And, no, the evidence does not support the usefulness of the least product cost methodology to guide actions leading to a robust process of ongoing improvement. Four things contribute to the resolution of this apparent contradiction:

1. The intuition aspect
2. The Archimedes point effect
3. A different goal
4. The meaning of success

First, the intuition part of the least product cost thinking bridge represents what we often call management judgment. This intuition, perhaps unverbalized but based on solid experience, overrides strict adherence to the product-cost reduction tactic with sufficient frequency to mitigate the misdirection provided by the least cost model.

Second, although the more exciting aspect of an Archimedes point is dynamic results, the Archimedes point concept also has a converse attribute. When changes occur in areas of an organization that do not contain an Archimedes point, there is little bottom-line effect. Hence, even though many decisions are made in a manner that resulted in the relatively minor $5,000 loss portrayed in the thinking bridges example, occasionally powerfully correct decisions are also made.[12] Even though the data that managers receive include many misleading signals, the data are sometimes likely to touch on the critical areas. These lucky hits provide enough sense of false hope and security to last until the next lucky break happens. The company in the example would be in good shape if it made one $133,880 "right" decision for every 10 or 20 $5,000 "wrong" decisions. But controlling destiny by the roll of the dice—and knowing it—produces fear and anxiety.

Third, perhaps the effective goal of the organization is something other than increased shareholder profitability. When we discuss cost-based pricing in a later chapter, we will see that an operating strategy based on product cost can be successful under certain conditions. One of these conditions is that the managers of the firm desire only some minimum level of profits, as opposed to the open-ended goal of greater profits. In this case, the company manipulates the pressure to perform, replacing the anxiety associated with the roll of the dice with the comfort of knowing that the costs will be covered with each sale. This strategy, of course, assumes that the sales will be made.

Finally, maybe these organizations are not actually so great. We tend to perceive wealthy people and large organizations as being successful and having the ability to know the right thing to do. We then carry this reasoning one step further and feel that if they do something, it must be right, and so we attempt to imitate it. But are the operating results of these organizations really so good? Management of these organizations comes under tremendous pressure to show good results on a repetitive quarterly basis. If the roll of the dice is such that the reality of the results does not match the expectation for the quarter, there is pressure to manipulate the reported results. Many of these same companies are *downsizing* or *rightsizing*, which seems to be the flavor of today's explanations for massive layoffs, are taking extraordinary restructuring charges on their financial statements on a recurring basis, and are reducing their dividends.

Still, there is *such* a need for a thinking bridge to link actions with their bottom-line effects. If it is not to be the least-cost model, then what should it be? The global measurements T, I, and OE questions were the alternative method used to evaluate the proposals in the example. But note that the power of this method came not from the T, I, and OE metrics alone, but rather from *understanding the impact of an Archimedes point on bottom-line improvement* in each specific scenario and the ability of the T, I, and OE metrics to predict that impact. Understanding the impact of Archimedes points on the bottom line is a key to locking in a process of ongoing improvement.

NOTES

[1] H. Thomas Johnson and Robert S. Kaplan, *Relevance Lost: The Rise and Fall of Management Accounting* (Harvard Business School Press, 1987).
[2] Eliyahu M. Goldratt, *The Haystack Syndrome: Sifting Information Out of the Data Ocean* (North River Press, 1990).

[3] Eliyahu M. Goldratt and Jeff Cox, *The Goal: Excellence in Manufacturing* (North River Press, 1984).
[4] Ibid. The authors used the term *inventory*, which I have changed to *inventory/investment*.
[5] Goldratt and Cox, *The Goal*, pp. 59–60.
[6] Ibid.
[7] The nature of inventory/investment is discussed in detail in Chapter 5.
[8] Goldratt and Cox, *The Goal*, pp. 59–60.
[9] Inspired by the "engineer" example presented by Robert E. Fox in "The Constraint Theory," reprinted in James T. Mackey, Ed., *Cases from Management Accounting Practice*, Volume 8 (Institute of Management Accountants, 1992).
[10] In a broader sense, there might be two throughput effects as a result of implementing the engineer's proposal. First, if the company were following a cost-based pricing strategy, the lower unit standard cost would soon be followed by a small reduction in sales price. Since the throughput of a sale is its sales price less the truly variable cost, the price reduction would be reflected in lower throughput. The second potential effect, derived from the reduced price, is the possibility of higher sales volume resulting in increased throughput. However, as we will see in Chapter 6, the cost-based pricing strategy assumes that the customers are already willing to pay more than they are paying currently; hence, this volume effect is unlikely.
[11] The astute reader may observe that the increase in time required at workstation 102 will make it impossible to operate at the 4,992 unit level after the change is implemented. While this is true, the question would not be raised in most real-world situations. The analysis would end, and the cost savings would be recorded, when the proposal is approved.
[12] For example, we might have had a fifth scenario, similar to scenario 2, but this time with a potential market of 6,000 units and reducing the time at workstation 102 by five minutes while increasing the time at workstation 101 by two minutes. Then the analysis shown in Exhibits 1.10 and 1.11 would lead in the right direction. Never mind that the annual cash inflow would actually be $322,560 rather than $31,500 or that the rate of return is more like 6,450% rather than 630%.

2

Constraints

TWO PARADIGMS

Two paradigms of business strategy can be identified. The first, known as the **cost world,** emphasizes the reduction of existing costs as the means to bottom-line improvement. The second, called the **throughput world,** emphasizes the expansion of throughput as the means to bottom-line improvement.

Cost World Paradigm

As a practical matter, most managerial attention is devoted to those factors that managers believe they can best control or influence. Since most managers are responsible for cost centers only, they naturally perceive that their attention is best directed to cost issues. This phenomenon, along with the observation that reducing expenses increases profits, gives rise to a widely accepted business control paradigm that Goldratt and Fox have termed the cost world paradigm.[1] Cost control—and cost reduction if profits are under pressure—is paramount in the managerial mindset. The least product cost thinking bridge derives directly from this paradigm.

Expansion of throughput—even though recognized as being important—ranks second in importance in the cost world paradigm. Most employees feel they can contribute more to the bottom line through cost control than through influencing the sales variable.

Finally, the physical operating environment is accepted as a given. Most managers believe that they have little responsibility for the acquisition and disposal of assets such as buildings and machinery. In the cost world, product inventory levels are analyzed in terms of their effects on operational expense through inventory carrying charges such as interest, insurance, and property taxes. Changes to the basic investment in the organization have a tertiary priority.

Is a Paradigm Shift Needed?

Recall that the goal is greater profitability. Costs have absolute limits as to how much they can be decreased. As a practical matter, our ability to reduce operating costs and investments in fixed assets is limited. Actions such as downsizing, rightsizing—or some other term to mask the fact that employees are losing their jobs—taken to reduce costs are disruptive to operations and morale. When such actions are taken, the results though seductive, are deceptive, for they have little sustaining effect on the bottom line. Alternatively, there is no theoretical limit to an increase in sales.

The summary OE, T, and I global measurement calculations for scenarios 2 and 3 in the thinking bridges example presented in Chapter 1 are reproduced here as Exhibits 2.1 and 2.2. An Archimedes point was touched in each of these scenarios, resulting in a significant change in bottom-line profitability. What portion of the profitability change came from each of the OE, T, and I variables in these scenarios?

The change in throughput is responsible for the lion's share of the profitability change. With the product-cost reduction strategy, we act as though consideration of cost elements alone provides adequate information for decision making in cost centers. Clearly, such a cost world decision process, no matter how widespread, cannot be the key to a sustainable process of ongoing improvement.

Shift to a Throughput World Paradigm

Only by way of throughput may we expect to identify actions that will lead to exceptionally significant changes in profitability. Therefore, our decision analyses should have a heavy emphasis on throughput (T).[2] Opportunities to discover or invent actions that can have the order-of-magnitude impact representative of an Archimedes point are available only in the throughput arena.

Exhibit 2.1   Summary of Changes in Global Measurements (Scenario 2)

Global Measurement	First Year	Subsequent Years
T	- $118,400	- $118,400
I	+$5,000	no change
OE	no change	no change
Cash Flow (=T-I-OE)	- $123,400	- $118,400

Exhibit 2.2 Summary of Changes in Global Measurements (Scenario 3)

Global Measurement	First Year	Subsequent Years
T	+ $138,880	+ $138,880
I	+$5,000	no change
OE	no change	no change
Cash Flow (=T-I-OE)	+ $133,880	+ $138,880

In the late twentieth century, it became apparent that work-in-process and finished goods inventories played a larger role in ultimate profitability than conventionally had been thought.[3] Smaller work-in-process inventories imply shorter production lead times. Smaller finished goods inventories mean that we will have less old product to dispose of, leading to faster introduction of product enhancements and new products into the market. Raymond Cole and Lee Hales observed that the benefits of increased sales stemming from operational improvements far outweigh the labor cost reductions achieved.[4] Less product inventory results in a competitive advantage leading to future throughput. The positive effect of lower product inventory levels on competitive position and future throughput overshadows any cost savings associated with lower product inventories. Thus, the inventory/investment (I) metric gains importance through its influence on throughput.

At the same time, the relatively small bottom-line improvement that might result from **cost reduction** possibilities relegates the operational expense (OE) metric to a distant trailing place. In fact, selective increases in OE are likely to be necessary as sales volumes increase.

In the throughput world paradigm, throughput is the most important of the three metrics because only throughput allows order-of-magnitude improvement to the bottom line. Inventory considerations are second in importance *not* because of their effects on costs but because reducing product inventories has a strong positive effect on future throughput.

Although striving for cost reductions then holds a distant last place in the priorities of the throughput world paradigm, *future* increases in costs must be *carefully controlled.*

We believe that cognitive dissonance arises as a result of attempts to create sustainable profitability through cost reduction. When our thinking recognizes the disadvantages of a cost-oriented strategy, our paradigms are challenged. When our thinking understands the advantages, and accepts the emphasis, of the throughput world focus on revenue growth, our emphasis on the cost reduction actions of the cost world declines and we complete the paradigm shift.

CONSTRAINED ENVIRONMENTS

The thinking bridges example in Chapter 1 highlighted the significance of an Archimedes point within an organization. The Archimedes point was the factor that placed the greatest limitation, or **constraint,** on the organization's ability to increase its profitability. Consequently, the Archimedes point also presents the singular opportunity for creating significant improvement. Constrained environments are not new to financial managers. Writing in the middle of the twentieth century, the then National Association of Accountants Research director Walter B. McFarland discerned in his study of management accounting concepts that "the presence of capacity constraints is a distinguishing characteristic of short run planning."[5] He further noted that identifying the constraints of a system is a prerequisite for distinguishing relevant costs. Virtually every basic and advanced cost or management accounting textbook contains a discussion or example of maximizing contribution margin in terms of constrained resources.[6]

McFarland observed that we treat product and market segments as entities for which "fully independent" decisions may be made. He further noted that "[i]n practice, too little attention is given to interdependence of the segments."[7] Many cost and management accounting textbooks and courses have reinforced the erroneous impression of analytical independence. Managerial accounting is highlighted as focusing on parts or segments of the organization.[8] McFarland concluded that the complexity of a global approach rendered such an approach impractical (in 1966), but that he looked for substantial progress in changing from a segment to a global focus in the "near future." Presumably this progress would be the result of advances in computerized information systems.

Theory of Constraints

Goldratt and Cox originally wrote the book, *The Goal: Excellence in Manufacturing*[9] as a training manual for use with implementing OPT™ (optimized production technique) software for scheduling production.[10] The basic technique has evolved into the **drum-buffer-rope (DBR)** scheduling technique.[11] *The Goal* was loosely based on a successful implementation of a drum and rope technique. Unexpectedly, however, the implementation was followed by a number of undesirable effects resulting from the assumption that the manufacturing plant was decoupled from the rest of the organization. Goldratt and some of his colleagues then turned their attention to the process of change within organizations. The comprehensive result of their developments is known as the **theory of constraints (TOC)** and includes the **thinking processes** used to develop applications such as the drum and rope technique as well as the applications themselves.

We have seen that an Archimedes point is a fulcrum where we can apply our managerial lever to obtain order-of-magnitude bottom-line improvement. A constraint is another way of looking at the same thing; it is defined as anything that prevents an organization from achieving significant improvement. Remember that improvement is relative to the organization's global goal.

Organizations as Chains

A complex organization is similar to a chain (or, perhaps, a tangle of chains). Just as a chain has many distinct but interconnected links, an organization has numerous interdependent functions and circumstances. Just as the strength of a chain is dependent on its weakest link, so the strength of an organization's performance is dependent on relatively few critical factors.

These critical factors are the leverage points, or constraints, of the system. A constraint represents a limit to performance of the system and is analogous to the weakest link in a chain. However, recognition of the constraint also provides a dynamic opportunity—a positive point on which to focus—for *causing* improvement to occur. Furthermore, when a constraint is recognized, if supported, it provides a dynamic growth opportunity to improve the bottom line. The only way to improve the strength of a chain is to improve the strength of its weakest link. Conversely, if the strength of the weakest link is improved, then the strength of the entire chain is improved. We should focus on those factors that enhance the probability of attaining significant improvement. That is, we should focus on the constraints of the organization.

The constraint theory has modified and enhanced our understanding of the role of constraints in our organizations in at least six important ways.

1. Recognition that every system is constrained and, since every organization is a system, that every organization is constrained.
2. Recognition that very few Archimedes points are associated with any given organization.
3. Verbalization of the role of nonconstraints.
4. Recognition that constraints need not be physical in character.
5. Recognition of constraints as long-run strategic tools, as well as tactical determinants of short-run operations.
6. Recognition of the dynamic power of the concept and existence of a global constraint Archimedes point.

These six observations have immense implications for managing organizations and the practice of management accounting.

Every Organization Constrained

The realization that every organization is constrained—that is, every organization has at least one **Archimedean constraint**—leads to the conclusion that every decision directed toward improvement ought to be based on measures that relate to the system's constraint(s). In the traditional decoupled and independent organizational perception of the firm, each independent unit may or may not have a local capacity constraint. We never looked for a global constraint since the entire system was viewed as a group of unconnected analytical entities in the legacy cost world paradigm.

Very Few Archimedes Points

A chain has only one weakest link; chains are physical entities and the strength of a chain is a function of its physical composition. Our organizations are not simply physical matter, however. Rather, they are intangible entities that include plant, equipment, and people. The physical plant and equipment have varying capacities, and the people come with all of their associated emotions, relatives, relationships, prejudices, paradigms, vices, and virtues.

Statistical Fluctuations

All of these considerations ensure that there always will be unevenness, or **statistical fluctuations,** throughout the individual components of an organization.[12] As a practical matter, for statistical fluctuations to take place, substantial amounts of unused capability *must* exist throughout the organization. That is, there must be a sufficient amount of looseness in the organizational tangle of chains to accommodate the inevitable statistical fluctuations.

Recall that we define improvement in terms of performance relative to the global goal. Consider the significance of the **Pareto principle** (often known as the 80:20 rule) as it relates to the impact of actions taken for improvement. The results of actions that we take to improve our organization fall into three categories.

1. Actions resulting in significant improvement to bottom-line profitability (scenario 3 in the thinking bridge example).
2. Actions resulting in very little bottom-line effect (scenarios 1 and 4 in the thinking bridge example).
3. Actions resulting in a significant detriment to bottom-line profitability (scenario 2 in the thinking bridge example).

Applying the Pareto principle, we can expect most of the favorable impact of organizational actions to result from the 20% of the actions that fall into category 1. These category 1 actions touch on the weak links of the organizational tangle. The 80% of the actions that do not touch a weak link, those in category 2, have, at best, small favorable impacts. These category 2 actions, which are sometimes called **choopchicks,** consume a lot of time and effort—diverting management attention away from category 1 type actions—but produce little in the way of positive lasting effects. The counterproductive actions of category 3, if taken, actually have a significantly adverse impact on profitability.

Dependent Events

The 80:20 relationship tends to hold for *independent* events. However, our organizations have *interdependent* functions. The conditional linkages[13] that exist among many components of the organization result in dependent events. The combination of statistical fluctuations and dependent events ensures that very few constraints will be associated with any given system. Dependencies, such as those existing among the functions of obtaining an order, producing a product through a series of steps, shipping the product, protecting the environment, providing employee health benefits, collecting accounts receivable, and so forth, change the nature of the Pareto principle. In these dependent situations, where there is a specified correlation among the links, the Pareto principle relationship is more like a 999:1 rule.

Think about the effect of linking several tasks together. Assume that we have a project with two tasks, both of which must be completed before the project is delivered. Each task has a 50% probability of being completed on time. This simple tangle is illustrated in Exhibit 2.3.

Both individual tasks in Exhibit 2.3 must be completed on time in order for the entire project to be on time. There are four possible combinations of the individual tasks: on-time/on-time, on-time/late, late/on-time, late/late. The overall project will be on time only in the first case and late in the other three. The probability of completing the overall proj-

Exhibit 2.3 Simple Tangle of Chains

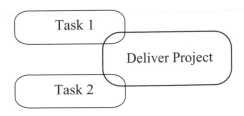

ect on time is one out of four, or 25%. This is the product of the probabilities of the individual tasks (0.5 * 0.5 = 0.25 in this case). A similar analysis with 10 tasks would have only one chance in a thousand of being completed on time.[14]

How many of our potential actions are choopchicks in the dependent situation?

Identifying the category 1 type of potential actions when there are dependent events is analogous to identifying the single weakest link in a chain. These are the Archimedean constraints of an organization. We may expect that the vast majority of our potential actions, the choopchicks of category 2, will fail to improve overall performance significantly because they do not relate directly to the requirements of the critical function.

Since only the throughput channel allows order-of-magnitude improvement to the bottom line, and since there are very few substantive constraints within an organization, the smallest organizational unit for which we are likely to identify an Archimedean constraint is a **real profit center.** Relatively few Archimedes points are found in even the largest organizations.

Recognition that any organization has, at most, a limited number of Archimedean constraints at any given time allows an information system to distinguish the global impact of actions by focusing on those few substantive constraints. Such an information system is different from the financial management legacy of concern with the "details of parts of the entity, products, departments, territories,"[15] and so forth.

Role of Nonconstraints

The importance of an Archimedean constraint is conspicuous once recognized, but what about the balance of the organization?

Since most activities take place in the 99+ percent of the organization that does not hold an Archimedean constraint, most day-to-day actions take place in unconstrained areas of activity. As a psychological matter, we have a tendency to be fascinated with the consequence of the Archimedes point, while minimalizing the importance of nonconstrained areas.

The proper behavior for unconstrained activities, which involves supporting global improvement through an appropriate relationship with constrained areas, is referred to as **subordination.** The verbalization of the role for nonconstraints implies a major paradigm shift for financial managers as well as the line managers that they support. *Every organization implementing constraint management will need to update its decision and control measurements for a large part of the organization* in order to obtain appropriate subordination.[16]

Constraints Not Necessarily Physical

Constraints are often regarded as being physical. That is certainly the case for the type of capacity constraint McFarland cites as the "distinguishing characteristic" of short-run planning. However, constraints may be categorized as being physical, policy, or paradigm. Lisa Scheinkopf observes that a relationship exists among these categories. Paradigms result in policies that, in turn, are reflected as apparent physical constraints.[17]

For example, a paradigm about the relationship between unit product cost and the bottom line may result in policies regarding efficiencies and production batch sizing. These policies, in turn, may cause a production resource to produce goods that are not needed immediately. The resource is not available for products that are required for immediate sales. Although the resource may appear to be a physical constraint, a simple change in the policy for loading the resource may be sufficient to eliminate the apparent constraint.

Constraints as Long-Run Strategic Tools

The conventional view of constraints in the financial management literature is that they are determinants of short-run tactical operations in a decoupled environment. That was McFarland's belief in 1966, and, as the following quotations reveal, it is still widely held today:[18]

"short-run decision making, as proposed by TOC . . ."[19]

"[b]ecause of its short-term focus, throughput accounting . . ."[20]

"Goldratt's world . . . takes the existing structure of the plant as given, focusing solely on short-term manufacturing solutions . . ."[21]

The assumptions of TOC "are an excellent approximation of reality for the problem TOC has been designed to solve: short-term product mix and scheduling of bottleneck resources."[22]

This short-run view of usefulness of constraints is no longer appropriate, however. The constraint theory, evolving over the last two decades, has expanded beyond a bottleneck production scheduling system into a comprehensive management philosophy.

Modern constraint management theory started with the computerized optimized production technology (OPT) scheduling software. Goldratt and Cox presented scheduling with a drum and rope in *The Goal: Excellence in Manufacturing* (1984) and also challenged the use of conventional cost accounting efficiency measures, suggesting use of the T, I, and

OE global measurements instead. Although *The Goal* gained substantial popularity, its concepts reflected the jumble of reality rather than the orderliness of a process and so they were not widely implemented.[23]

In about 1985 constraint management theory shifted from a focus on production to a broader approach. In 1986, *The Goal* was published in a revised edition with the addition of both an epilogue emphasizing ongoing improvement and a new subtitle, *A Process of Ongoing Improvement,* stressing the broader concept. Goldratt and Cox identified and verbalized a sequence of actions for establishing a process of ongoing improvement.[24] They formalized these actions as the five **focusing steps** (which we will discuss momentarily) and detailed them in a second revised edition of *The Goal* in 1992.

As the five focusing steps led implementers through tangles of chains and into constraints in areas other than production, the applications of the constraint management theory expanded into a consistent and comprehensive management philosophy. As of this writing, constraint management applications include not only DBR, buffer management, the T, I, and OE global measurements, and the five focusing steps, but also physical distribution, marketing, buy-in and sales, critical chain project management, and alignment of authority with responsibility for employee empowerment.[25]

Viewing constraints as dynamic determinants of long-run strategy has been criticized primarily by advocates of cost world allocation techniques, such as activity-based costing or activity-based management. Thomas Corbett observes that the use of TOC for the long run is not well understood. However, he also notes that "in the long-run the company will continue to be a system and, therefore, it will still have its performance limited by very few constraints."[26] With respect to long-run **cost control,** he maintains that

> *[t]he current problem is that companies do not identify and explore their constraints and this leads to unnecessary increases in overhead. One of the main reasons for the long-run variations of the overhead costs is the fact that managers do not have the company's constraints under control. In other words, the fact that managers use cost accounting [to control costs] is what causes the company's costs to increase![27]*

The strategic aspect of constraint management is implemented in two ways. First, the organization strategically determines where it wants its constraint(s) to be, and it takes actions to ensure that the constraint(s) appear where desired. That is, the question of constraint location is part of long-run strategic planning. Second, the thinking processes of the theory of constraints may be used to develop and verbalize a consistent organizationwide strategic plan. Constraint management, then, is applicable to both short-run tactical decisions and long-run strategic decisions.

Dynamic Power of the Concept and Existence of an Archimedes Point

The power of focus to achieve a goal is well known and widely accepted. Reviewing the foregoing five ways in which our understanding of constraints has been enhanced, we see that the concept and existence of Archimedean constraints within organizations lead to a dynamic opportunity to benefit from focusing on those points.

Most organizations have not implemented the management philosophy of constraint management.[28] Hence, it is safe to say that most organizations do not explicitly consider global constraints in their formal planning and control systems.[29] Is there a way to identify the constraint management characteristics that should be embodied in the information system?

There are many types of constraints. Some constraints may be tactical, some strategic. Some constraints may be physical, others in policies or even paradigms. These paradigms and policies, if globally limiting, are reflected as identifiable physical constraints. Therefore, the Archimedean constraints of an organization are identifiable either directly or indirectly through their manifestations, in every case.

Every system has at least one Archimedean constraint, and few substantive constraints are associated with any given system. Since the Archimedean constraints are recognizable by their impact on the global goal, the information system will be able to distinguish the global impact of actions by focusing on these substantive constraints. By incorporating the Archimedean constraints of the global system into planning analyses and the periodic reporting process, an organization can harness the dynamic power of constraints in a measurable way that is reflected in the bottom line.

TOC FOCUSING PROCESS

The global approach of the theory of constraints includes a systematic process for focusing management attention on the appropriate places to realize a process of ongoing improvement:

1. Identify the system's constraint(s).
2. Decide how to exploit the system's constraint(s).
3. Subordinate everything else to the exploitation decisions.
4. Elevate the system's constraint(s).
5. If, in the previous steps, a constraint has been broken, go back to step 1, but do not allow inertia to cause a system's constraint.

As seen previously, constraints may be categorized as physical, policy, or paradigm or as tactical or strategic. Physical constraints may be classified as real or apparent, and in addition, as either internal or external to the organization. Goldratt has suggested that real physical constraints may involve internal resources, raw material availability, or market demand.[30] Apparent physical constraints result from paradigms or policies.[31]

The first three steps of the focusing process operate on both the tactical and strategic level. In the short run, the organization must deal with whatever constraints actually exist. These existing constraints are identified and exploited by deciding how to make the best use of them. The balance of the organization subordinates to the exploitation decisions.

For the long run, the senior managers of the organization select, as part of their strategic planning process, what and where they want the constraints to be.[32] The long-run strategy, then, involves the set of decisions made about desired strategic constraints and their exploitation. The organization elevates tactical constraints in a manner that causes the desired strategic constraints to appear. With a robust constraint management process of ongoing improvement, then, the long run is more directed than just a series of short-run actions strung together.

The first step in the focusing process is to **identify** the system's constraint. Constraint identification in the tactical environment is typically a reactive step that involves locating an internal resource that is currently blocking improved performance. When a tactical constraint is identified, it should be dealt with immediately unless a significant additional investment is required.[33] If a significant additional investment (and/or a significant amount of time) is required to remove the constraint, then this step will be part of the elevation step. In this latter case, the organization should proceed to the second and third steps.

Identification of the constraint in the strategic environment is a proactive step. Top management selects the strategic constraints. That is, management specifies where it *wants* the constraints of the organization to be, thereby defining the desired long-run course of the organization. Selection of the strategic constraints is the way in which the organization harnesses the power of Archimedes points, controlling the nature and location of the constraints.

The second step of the focusing process is to decide how to **exploit,** or take best advantage of, the system's constraints in the pursuit of the global goal. The exploitation process reveals the significance of the Pareto principle for dependent events discussed previously in the section on constrained environments. It is not necessary to exploit nonconstraint operations. The operations of nonconstrained areas are flexible, except as they are required to support the exploitation plan for the constraint(s).

We subordinate operations, including those of the areas holding Archimedean constraints, to the set of exploitation decisions. The purpose of subordination is to protect the set of decisions made about exploiting the constraint in the day-to-day execution of the plan. Although we frequently speak loosely of the purpose of subordination as being to "support the constraint," the subordination is actually to the decisions rather than the constraint itself. This distinction is important because it means that the organization must have specifically considered the best way to utilize its constrained resources and have communicated the decisions throughout the organization. Effective subordination, and hence effective implementation, cannot take place without communication of a sound plan.

Subordination is a major area of interest because it is here that the requisite culture change is the greatest. Conventional management accounting is based on the cost world premise that cost control and efficiency efforts in local areas will be reflected in bottom-line performance. As already seen, however, significant bottom-line improvement can be achieved only when the focus is on global Archimedean constraints. Rather than "What can this area do, by itself, to increase the bottom line," the question becomes "What must this area do to protect the exploitation decisions?"

On a tactical level, the identification, exploitation, and subordination steps relate to getting the most out of the existing physical environment. These steps are often sufficient to eliminate an apparent constraint.[34] If the first three tactical steps do not eliminate a physical constraint, then no further significant improvement is possible unless the system's constraint is **elevated.** The organization's physical reality must be changed by obtaining more of the constraining factor. Elevating a constraint often involves the expenditure of additional investment funds. This strategic question is extremely important from a future cost-control point of view because it should drive the capital expenditure decisions for all other areas of the organization as well as the strategic constraint area.

Changing the organization's physical reality changes the environmental background. The changed background may lead to a different Archimedean constraint. Here the organization has a choice. It may accept whatever constraints emerge as the cyclical five-step focusing process is followed, or it can take positive actions to establish the nature and location of its constraints. Thus, by subordinating elevation to strategic exploitation decisions, a random walk through the future may be avoided.

The fifth step of the focusing process—*if, in the previous steps, a constraint has been broken, go back to step 1, but do not allow* **inertia** *to cause a system's constraint*—offers us a warning; we must protect against the inertia of our thinking. Whenever a system's constraint is elevated sufficiently to cause a different constraint to become active, the operating characteristics of the system change. In the changed environment, both the decisions about exploiting the former constraint and the policies established for subordination to the former constraint are no longer appropriate. If inertia has set in, then the process of ongoing improvement will stall. Operations may also appear to be out of control. Lisa Scheinkopf has observed that "[e]ach of these five short sentences [the five steps], when 'really' understood, represents a **paradigm shift** in every sense of the phrase 'paradigm shift.'"[35]

Finally, the constraints may not appear where expected. In spite of efforts to subordinate to the strategic and tactical decisions, an actual constraint (or apparent constraint) may appear at an unexpected location. This could be caused by a failure to subordinate properly (the most common cause) or an external force such as a natural catastrophe or change in government policy. Therefore, we must regularly check the identification of the constraints.

The five focusing steps provide an orderly process for pursuing the global goal of greater profitability. But how can we tell if the inertia of our thinking has set in?

IDENTIFYING ONGOING IMPROVEMENT

Recall that improvement is defined in terms of the open-ended global goal of an organization. For publicly held companies, as well as most closely held companies, this goal is to make more money—now and in the future. Hence, the basic report for gauging whether or not a process of ongoing improvement exists is the earnings statement. *Improvement must result in greater profit.*

The role of the internal earnings statement within constraint management is not to report periodic profits per se but rather to facilitate recognition of ongoing improvement or to identify the existence of inertia within the system. Therefore, the earnings must be viewed over time rather than as a single earnings amount for an individual period. A profit graph reflecting a robust process of ongoing improvement is shown in Exhibit 2.4.

Note that the plot in Exhibit 2.4 is not continuous but increases in jumps. A jump in profit occurs when the organization successfully deals with a constraint. For example, such a jump would have occurred as a result of the action taken in scenario 3 of the thinking bridges example presented in Chapter 1. The pattern of successive jumps results from identifying and focusing on constraints on an ongoing basis following the cyclical steps of the focusing process. Intervening periods of less dramatic profit improvement reflect periods of adjustment to the changed reality of the organization.

In order to obtain a sustainable jump in cash flow (profitability), it is necessary to deal with a constraint, resulting in significantly increased throughput. But note that it is also necessary to control costs (I and OE).

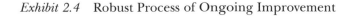

Exhibit 2.4   Robust Process of Ongoing Improvement

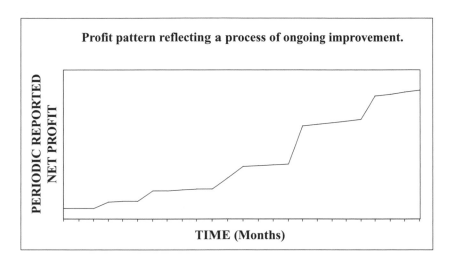

Exhibit 2.5 depicts a representative profit pattern of an organization that has dealt successfully with an Archimedean constraint, represented by a jump in profits, but that then became the victim of inertia.

The question that must be asked is, "Has an improvement process been established—and is it ongoing?" Evaluation of the pictorial presentation of comparative multiperiod net profit reports can provide the answer to this question: "Yes" in the case of Exhibit 2.4, "No" in the case of Exhibit 2.5.

Exhibit 2.5   Ongoing Improvement Stalled

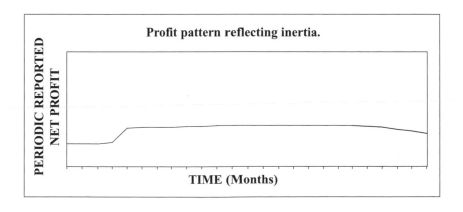

Link between Throughput and Cost

Consider the common phenomenon illustrated by the following conversation in which John and Dan were discussing the T, I, and OE metrics of the theory of constraints.

Dan reached into his briefcase, retrieved a sheaf of papers, and observed, "Here is our detailed earnings statement for last year. As I look at each of these expenses, I can see that all except materials are fixed."

"Yes," John replied, "that's why Goldratt considers only raw materials and a few other costs, such as royalties, to be variable."

"On the other hand," Dan continued, "when I look at our annual financial reports over the last 30 years, during which we grew significantly, our costs have moved right along with revenues—maintaining a fairly consistent ratio of about 95%."

Although operational expenses seem to be unrelated to sales volume changes in the short run, over a longer time frame expenses tend to parallel revenues quite closely for most organizations. In Exhibit 2.6, with costs tied to revenues, sales revenues are shown to be increasing over time. Plotted along with the sales revenue function is a cost function in which the costs are closely coupled with revenues. Profits, of course, are the difference between revenues and costs.

Exhibit 2.7 illustrates the pattern of costs that have been decoupled from a direct relationship with revenues. The uncoupled cost function of Exhibit 2.7 does increase over time as the operations expand. However, the increases are made as specific responses to elevating constraints in a systematic manner, consistent with the global strategy of the organization. The cost function that is coupled with revenues (Exhibit 2.6), however, is the result of the implicit assumption that costs are, and in fact should be, tied closely to revenues. In order to establish sustainable order-of-magnitude increases in profitability, it will be necessary to break the direct long-run linkage between throughput and operational expense.

Exhibit 2.6   Cost and Revenues Tied Together

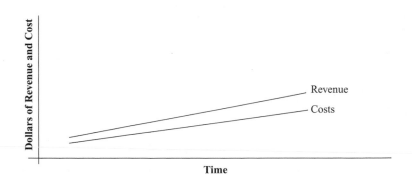

Exhibit 2.7   Costs Uncoupled from Revenues

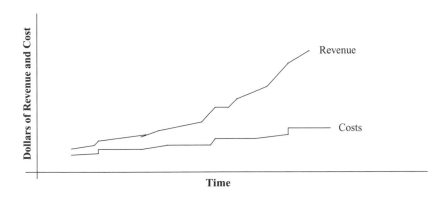

Understanding the relationship of Archimedean constraints to the financial reporting system is a key to locking in a process of ongoing improvement.

SUMMARY

We identified two paradigms of business strategy: (1) the **cost world** where cost reduction is the primary focus as a means to increasing the bottom line and (2) the **throughput world,** which emphasizes the expansion of throughput as the means to bottom-line improvement. Recognizing that cost reduction has its limits and expansion of throughput has no theoretical limits, we see that cost reduction holds a distant last place in the priorities of the throughput world paradigm, while recognition that *future* increases in costs must be *carefully controlled* becomes imperative.

Since every organization can be likened to a tangle of chains, it is understood that the strength of the organization's performance is dependent on relatively few critical factors, which become the leverage points or constraints of the system. Furthermore, recognizing that every organization has at least one Archimedean constraint shows that every decision directed toward improvement ought to be based on measures relating to the system's constraints. The modification and enhanced understanding of the constraint theory lead to a powerful recognition of the role of constraints in the organization's global goal. Constraints are identified as physical, policy, paradigm, tactical, or strategic, and the five focusing steps become a systematic process for focusing management attention on the appropriate places to achieve a process of ongoing improvement. However, most organizations have not implemented the constraint management philosophy. As a result, they neither explicitly consider global constraints in their formal planning and control system nor discover or invent actions that have an order-of-magnitude impact on a process of ongoing improvement.

Improvement is defined as the open-ended global goal of an organization. It was determined that the goal of publicly held companies, as well as most closely held companies, is to make more money—now and in the future; therefore, *improvement must result in greater profit*. The earnings statement is the basic report for gauging whether this happens in reality. Constraint management's internal earnings statement reports and facilitates recognition of ongoing improvement. Costs and revenues are decoupled, and as operations expand, the increases become systematic, specific responses to elevating constraints consistent with the organization's global strategy. Understanding the relationship of Archimedean constraints to the financial reporting system is a key to locking in a process of ongoing improvement.

NOTES

[1] Eliyahu M. Goldratt and Robert E. Fox, "The Paradigm Shift," *The Theory of Constraints Journal* 1, No. 6 (April–May 1990), pp. 7–8.

[2] Ibid., pp. 7–8.

[3] Eliyahu M. Goldratt and Robert E. Fox, *The Race* (North River Press, 1986), pp. 32–64.

[4] Raymond C. Cole and Lee H. Hales, "How Monsanto Justified Automation," *Management Accounting* (January 1992), pp. 39–43.

[5] Walter B. McFarland, *Concepts for Management Accounting* (National Association of Accountants, 1966), p. 54.

[6] But in those same textbooks, relevant costs are frequently discussed without reference to constraints.

[7] McFarland, *Concepts for Management Accounting*, p. 41.

[8] For example, Charles T. Horngren and Gary Sundem distinguished *management accounting* as "concern about details of parts of the entity, products, departments, territories, etc." and *financial accounting* as "concern with entity as a whole." *Introduction to Management Accounting*, 8th ed. (Prentice-Hall, 1990).

[9] Eliyahu M. Goldratt and Jeff Cox, *The Goal: Excellence in Manufacturing* (North River Press, 1984).

[10] As of this writing I understand that the OPT software is available from Scheduling Technology Group Limited (STG).

[11] DBR scheduling and control is discussed in Chapter 7.

[12] Examples of statistical fluctuations are the amount of time required for processing at a particular step varying with the mood, physical condition (working while having a cold, etc.), skill level, level of interest of an employee, quality of materials, employee absence due to vacation or other cause, and so forth.

[13] Conditional linkages may be thought of as the sequence in which the links of the organizational tangle of chains are hooked together.

[14] $0.5 * 0.5 * 0.5 * 0.5 * 0.5 * 0.5 * 0.5 * 0.5 * 0.5 * 0.5 = 0.5^{10} = 0.000975625 \approx 0.001$.

[15] Horngren and Sundem, *Introduction to Management Accounting*.

[16] Of course, the constraints of an organization are a matter of reality. They exist regardless of whether an organization undertakes constraint management or

implements TOC. A corollary, then, is that almost every problem dealing with planning or control—in every managerial accounting textbook—should be revised to reflect this reality.

[17] Lisa Scheinkopf, *Thinking for a Change: Putting the TOC Thinking Processes to Use* (St. Lucie Press, 1999), p. 16.

[18] The treatment of the theory of constraints (TOC) in the U.S. management accounting literature has been viewed almost entirely within TOC *versus* activity based costing (ABC—a popular cost allocation technique) or activity-based management (attempting to manage in such a way as to reduce product cost as calculated by ABC) framework. See, for example, the titles of the articles cited in the next two footnotes.

[19] J. S. Holmen, "ABC VS. TOC: It's a Matter of Time," *Management Accounting* (January 1995).

[20] J. B. MacAuthur, "From Activity-Based Costing to Throughput Accounting" *Management Accounting* (April 1996).

[21] C. J. McNair and R. Vangermeersch, *Total Capacity Management: Optimizing at the Operational, Tactical, and Strategic Levels* (St. Lucie Press, 1998), p. 63.

[22] Robert S. Kaplan and Robin Cooper, *Cost and Effect: Using Integrated Cost Systems to Drive Profitability and Performance* (Harvard Business School Press, 1997), p. 134. Anyone who wants to implement a constraints accounting system is going to need to address the ABC systems. The nature of ABC systems, and the claims of their usefulness, have evolved over the last decade. This book provides an excellent "benchmark" as to where these systems stand. The book is comprehensive relative to ABC systems and states positions clearly. The book also contains many references to TOC—most of which are out of date or reflect a very low level of understanding of TOC.

[23] Eliyahu M. Goldratt, *My Saga to Improve Production* (North River Press, 1996). (Incorporated into the current printing of Eliyahu M. Goldratt and Jeff Cox, *The Goal: A Process of Ongoing Improvement*, 2nd rev. ed., [North River Press, 1992] as an appendix.)

[24] Ibid.

[25] A developing aspect of the TOC is known as the *holistic* or *global* approach (to implementation) and is the approach recommended in this book.

[26] Thomas Corbett, *Throughput Accounting: TOC's Management Accounting System* (North River Press, 1998), p. 112.

[27] Ibid., p. 114.

[28] As of this writing, even most of those organizations that have implemented some aspects of constraint management have apparently not adopted it as an overall strategy.

[29] Even those organizations that have attempted to adapt their information systems to a TOC approach typically do not go beyond direct costing in their financial reporting. The typical internal "throughput accounting" earnings statement nowhere mentions constraints. For examples of such "much ado about nothing" statements, see Charles T. Horngren, George Foster, and Srikant M. Datar, *Cost Accounting: A Managerial Emphasis,* 9th ed. (Prentice-Hall, 1997), pp. 309, 700.

[30] Eliyahu M. Goldratt, "How Complex Are Our Systems?" in *Essays on the Theory of Constraints* (North River Press, 1990), p. 2.

[31] Rob Newbold claims "that the concept [of a real] 'external constraint' is problematic, because if it's 'external' it's easy to make an assumption that addressing it depends on someone else's actions rather than your own [particularly with respect to marketing]." He often sees "the term 'external constraint' used as an excuse . . . [he is] not sure the term is useful, or even that

there is such a thing; and it certainly has negative attributes; so for starters [he recommends] abandoning it. A 'market constraint' is better, although [he prefers] to talk about a 'marketing constraint'" (APICS CMSIG Internet discussion group, October 19 and 20, 2000). We will address this issue further in Chapter 9.

[32] Examples of factors that might influence the selection of a strategic constraint are expensive resources, a long length of time needed to elevate the resource, and the core business of the organization.

[33] Eli Schragenheim, *Management Dilemmas: The Theory of Constraints Approach to Problem Identification and Solutions* (St. Lucie Press, 1998), p. 5. Of course, the action of removing the tactical constraint should also be checked against the organization's strategy.

[34] Eliyahu M. Goldratt, *The Haystack Syndrome: Sifting Information out of the Data Ocean* (North River Press, 1990), p. 61.

[35] Lisa Scheinkopf, TOC-L/Goldratt Internet discussion group thread "Five Steps (of the TOC Focusing Process)," August 24, 1996.

3

Internal Financial Reporting

EARLY THROUGHPUT ACCOUNTING

Goldratt and Cox not only presented the T, I, and OE measurements, but also suggested a two-step product-costing method based on allocating a portion of total OE to an internally constrained area and then allocating that cost to products based on constraint time used.[1] The name **throughput accounting** was applied to the accounting procedures implied in *The Goal* early in the constraint management accounting literature.[2]

Constraint-Time-Based Costing

Assume, for purposes of illustration, that a firm produces a large number of products. About 80% of the products require the use of a particular manufacturing resource that is an Archimedean constraint. The demand for the resource's time exceeds its capacity. The resource is similar to workstation 102 in scenarios 2, 3, and 4 of the thinking bridges example presented in Chapter 1. Since this resource creates a constraint on the overall ability of the firm to deliver more of 80% of its products, it is called a **constraint resource.** It is also assumed that there are no other constraint resources in the firm. Data for illustration are summarized in Exhibit 3.1.

Exhibit 3.1 assumes that the total operational expense (OE) of the firm is $4 million. The OE incorporates all expenses, inclusive of manufacturing, selling, and general administration, except the raw materials (truly variable expenses) associated with the various products.

The first allocation step is to determine the amount of the OE that is applicable to the constraint resource. Since about 80% of the products require use of the constraint resource, 80% of the OE is considered applicable to the constraint resource.[3] Of the total OE $3,200,000, or 80%, is as-

Exhibit 3.1   Constraint-Time-Based Costing Example Data

Total OE	$4,000,000	per year
Percent of all products using constraint resource (however determined)	80%	
Amount of OE applicable to constraint resource	$3,200,000	per year
Constraint resource time available	120,000	minutes
Constraint resource OE per constraint resource minute	$ 26.6667	per minute
Standard constraint resource minutes required to produce one unit of the particular product	25	minutes per unit
OE allocated to the particular product	$666.6675	per unit
Raw material required by this product	$ 40.0000	per unit
Total constraint-based product cost of the particular product	$706.6675	per unit

signed to the constraint resource. If the constraint resource is operated at 2,000 hours per year (40 hours per week for 50 weeks), there are 120,000 minutes (2,000 hours at 60 minutes per hour) of constraint resource time available during the year. Dividing the 120,000 minutes into $3,200,000 yields a cost of $26.6667 associated with each constraint resource minute.

Many different products used the constraint resource. Taking just one particular product of the many, we find that the product uses 25 minutes of the constraint resource time for each unit produced. We then assign $26.6667 per minute multiplied by 25 minutes per unit, or a total of $666.6675 of OE, to this particular product. Adding raw materials cost, which is assumed to be $40, we arrive at a cost per unit of $706.6675. Goldratt and Cox do not specify how to cost the 20% of the products that do not use the constraint resource, but valuing them at materials cost only appears to be the most consistent approach.

Evaluating the Least Product Cost Method Using the Constraint-Time-Based Costing

Chapter 1 concluded that the power of the global measurements thinking bridge lay not in the T, I, and OE measurements, but rather in understanding the role of an Archimedes point. The constraint-time-based product costing approach represents an absorption-costing approach to product costing that *does* consider the Archimedean constraint. Perhaps, then, it will lead to a better answer if it is used to evaluate the proposed scenarios of the thinking bridges example.

Scenario 1

In scenario 1, the company can easily produce as much as the market demands. Therefore, there is no active constraint resource, and no OE is assigned to a constraint resource. The engineer's proposal, then, does not have an effect on the product cost, which is just the raw materials cost of $80. Thus, using the least-product cost thinking bridge with constraint-time-based product costing leads us to the same conclusion as the global measurements thinking bridge. The only change in cost is the $5,000 cost of the fixture.

Scenario 2

Scenario 2 is the same as scenario 1, but now there is a constraint resource at workstation 102. The cost of a widget using constraint-time-based product costing is shown in Exhibit 3.2.

Since the proposal involves increasing the time at workstation 102 by two minutes, and workstation 102 is a constraint resource, the unit cost of a widget increases by $14.423.[4] The proposal also reduces processing time at workstation 101. Since workstation 101 is not a constraint resource, the time reduction at workstation 101 would have no effect on the unit cost calculated with this method. With the unit cost increase, the proposal would not be implemented, so the method has again given the correct signal. Although the signal was correct, had we been interested in the total effect of the change, we would have extended the $14.423 by the volume of 4,992 units to arrive at a presumed additional OE of $72,000. The total OE would be unchanged except for a small effect of the $5,000 investment, but the throughput would have decreased (as in Exhibit 1.12) as a result of lowered volume had the proposal been implemented. So in this case the method leads in the right direction (do not implement the proposal) but for the wrong reason (costs would increase).

Exhibit 3.2   Thinking Bridges Example: Cost per Widget Using Constraint-Time-Based Costing

Total OE	$900,000	per year
Percent of all products using constraint resource (workstation 102)	100%	
Amount of OE applicable to workstation 102	$900,000	per year
Workstation 102 time available per year	124,800	minutes
Constraint resource OE per workstation 102 minute	$7.2115	per minute
Standard workstation 102 minutes required to produce one unit of the particular product	25	minutes per unit
OE allocated to the particular unit of product	$180.2875	per unit
Raw material required by this unit of product	$80.0000	per unit
Total constraint-based product cost of the particular unit of product	$260.2875	per unit

Scenario 3

In scenario 3 the company is again operating at capacity (4,992 units) and the constraint-time-based calculations of Exhibit 3.2 will apply again. Since the proposal in this case decreases the time required at workstation 102 by 2 minutes per unit (from 25 minutes to 23 minutes), the least-product cost thinking bridge would tell us that costs would decrease by $7.2115 a minute for 2 minutes per unit, or a total of $14.423 per unit produced. Extending the $14.423 by the current volume of 4,992 units, we would anticipate a total cost *savings* of $72,000 as a result of implementing the proposal. As in scenario 2, this information points in the right direction but for the wrong reason. There will not actually be a significant change in cost. The depreciation expense due to the $5,000 expenditure, which is probably about $40 to $80 per month, is the only cost element (out of the hundreds of cost elements that comprise OE) that has changed. The benefit will come not from a reduction in costs, but from a $138,880 increase in throughput as was shown in Exhibit 1.19.

Scenario 4

In scenario 4 time is reduced at workstation 101, which is a nonconstraint, and increased at workstation 103, which is also a nonconstraint. Hence, as with scenario 1, the proposal does not affect a constraint resource. The constraint-time-based unit cost does not change, and the method correctly indicates that the only financial effect is the $5,000 expenditure for the fixture.

Since in scenarios 2 and 3 the sources and dollar amounts of the cost assignment were significantly different from the actual effect, it must be concluded that the constraint-time-based product-costing technique is also flawed as a decision tool.[5] The constraint-based product-costing aspect of throughput accounting has now largely been discarded.[6] What remains of throughput accounting, after setting aside the constraint-time-based costing aspect, are T, I, and OE.

Throughput Accounting as Direct Costing

In view of the similarity of throughput and operational expenses to the **direct** (or **variable**) **costing** model of contribution margin and fixed expenses, throughput accounting is frequently dismissed as simply being an extreme form of direct (or variable) costing. For example, in the Institute of Management Accountants (IMA) research study of TOC, the authors state: "at the conceptual level, there is no difference between Throughput Accounting and variable costing."[7] This view of throughput accounting as direct costing is currently the predominant view.

As such, there are two effects. First, anyone working with this subject matter, especially accountants, is able to avoid addressing the accounting measurement issues by assuming that they all have been resolved in the direct costing literature. Second, it allows all of the previously existing direct costing literature to be applied. Although this literature is not necessarily erroneous, we should recognize that direct costing, as well as throughput accounting, did develop in the cost world paradigm.

The existing paradigm of throughput accounting as direct costing is therefore a legacy system that is firmly lodged in the cost world.[8] It would seem reasonable that a more appropriate paradigm of accounting would be more useful in the throughput world. Such an accounting paradigm would include both the specific recognition of the role of Archimedean constraints and the throughput effects associated with every decision.

COST CONTROL IN A THROUGHPUT WORLD

Link between Cost and Revenue

As seen in Chapter 1 (in the section on identifying ongoing improvement), it is necessary to break the proportional long-run linkage between throughput and operational expense. Long-run operational expenses tend to be tied closely to throughput for numerous reasons. Many of these reasons are tied to the product-cost concept. We have already seen that the *least product cost thinking bridge* is a widely accepted paradigm. Another example would be using the cost of a product (as calculated by a traditional absorption-costing system) to establish the asking, or target, price for a product. Product costs form the focal point of most cost accounting systems. In turn, when used for pricing, the cost accounting system ties the future revenue stream directly to the product-cost calculation. The **operating budget,** or **annual profit plan,** is also a means of linking revenues closely to costs. In most organizations, the basic means of controlling operational expense (OE) is the **budgetary process.**[9] Costs are *in control* if they are less than revenues by a comfortable amount. Budgeted costs will be considered to be *in control* if they are less than budgeted revenues by an appropriate amount. Actual costs will be in control if they do not exceed budget limitations.

The budgetary process typically starts with an estimate of sales revenue, calculated by product or product line. It then uses the estimated revenues to "drive" the budgeted costs. An appropriate balance is achieved by putting pressure on operations to bring costs in line with the sales forecast. An *appropriate balance* is generally defined as a targeted return on investment. An alternative approach to establishing the budget is to estimate the total expenses and apply pressure to sales and marketing to come up with the necessary sales estimate to achieve the targeted return on investment. In either case, the result is the same—products are the focal point, and the result of the paradigm is that revenues are closely linked with product costs.

Cost Control versus Cost Reduction

Our paradigms are powerful contributors to the inertia of our thinking. If we want to shift from the cost world paradigm to the throughput world paradigm, then a deliberate and tenacious grip on the throughput world will be needed. Distinguishing between cost reduction and cost control recognizes that constraint management leads from the cost world paradigm of cost reduction and cost recovery into the growth strategy of the throughput world.

Decision Criteria

Originally (and now mainstream thought) the constraint management thinking bridge between local decision making and bottom-line profitability results, was thought to satisfactorily measure the relationship among the expected changes in the three basic measurements of T, I, and OE. Since the goal of a publicly held profit-oriented business is to make money, many believe that the desired relationship is to increase T while at the same time reducing I and OE.

Many still view this desired relationship as axiomatic. For example, William Dettmer states, *"Obviously,* increase Throughput, while decreasing Inventory and Operating Expense."[10] In similar fashion, Mokshagundam Srikanth and Scott Robertson state: "the objective of making money *translates to* increasing throughput, reducing inventory, and reducing operating expense, all at the same time."[11] Even Thomas Corbett suggests that *"the ideal* is a decision that increases T and decreases I and OE"[12] [emphasis added in each case]. Clearly, the basic T, I, and OE measurements of the TOC have encouraged cost reduction actions.

But recall the previous discussion of the paradigm shift from the cost world to the throughput world (Chapter 2). If we are serious about this paradigm shift, then we must abandon our reliance on *cost reductions* to achieve bottom-line improvement. Rather than strive for cost reductions, we might seek **cost control** of *future* expenditures. After all, we would only need current cost reductions if our previous future spending had been out of control.

We want to put into place financial management policies and procedures that will allow us to pursue a throughput world growth strategy of increasing T while *increasing* I and OE at a decoupled and significantly slower rate, leading to an ongoing expansion in profitability. This restatement of the desired relationship recognizes that a growth strategy will ultimately require resource expansion, but not necessarily in direct proportion to the throughput expansion. This is accomplished by increasing expenditures only in response to elevating constraints or satisfying necessary conditions.

One of the most difficult constraint management paradigm shifts for accountants and financial managers to grasp is that there is *no product-cost concept* in the measurements reporting for constraint management.[13] Observant readers will contend that we have, in fact, previously discussed a constraint-time-based product costing methodology used within the constraint management framework (early throughput accounting at the beginning of this chapter). And they would be correct. But that concept, though part of the *early* constraint theory paradigm, is outside the current constraint management paradigm, which emphasizes a process of ongoing improvement.

Policies and procedures such as those shown in Exhibit 3.3 will allow us to control costs appropriately, while abandoning the product-cost concept and turning our attention to increasing throughput.

Exhibit 3.3   Cost Control Policies to Support a Process of Ongoing Improvement

	Suggested Policy or Procedure	**Purpose**
A	Costs are controlled within the budgeted amount.	The budgetary process is the basis for financial control.
B	Increases in OE are reviewed as part of the formal budgetary process.	There is an agreed upon procedure for increasing the budget when desirable.
C	Increases in budgeted OE and I are approved based on careful review of anticipated throughput effects and specification of the constraint being elevated.	All increases in budgeted OE result either in elevating a constraint (greater profits) or from a need to satisfy a necessary condition (protecting current profits).
D	The OE budget is revised immediately to reflect approved OE increases.	Warning that costs are out of control when actual expenses exceed budgeted expenses.
E	Cost reductions are neither rewarded nor specifically encouraged.	Emphasize that a focus on throughput increases, rather than cost reductions, is desired.
F	All employees are provided training in the concepts of constraint management.	Employees feel they are valued and know how they can make a difference. Employees are not frustrated when not striving for local optima.
G	It is all right to have budgetary slack.	Proposals that can be implemented without increasing costs beyond currently budgeted costs are implemented at the discretion of the responsible person.

CONSTRAINTS ACCOUNTING VERSUS THROUGHPUT ACCOUNTING

Most people who are familiar with TOC believe that throughput accounting should be used for internal financial reporting in the constraint management environment. They also believe that using the metrics of throughput (T), inventory/investment (I), and operational expense (OE) constitutes doing throughput accounting.

As noted earlier, accountants generally perceive throughput accounting as an extreme form of direct costing. As such, throughput accounting can be viewed as a product-costing technique in which only truly variable costs are assigned to product inventories or, perhaps, as a contribution income reporting technique. In the latter case, truly variable expenses are deducted from revenues to calculate *throughput* (or *throughput contribution*), which corresponds to the traditional contribution margin, and the operational expenses take the place of **fixed expenses.** That is, throughput accounting fits nicely into the existing cost world paradigm. Therefore, throughput accounting is probably not the complete answer for accounting measurement within the constraint management throughput world environment. A reporting methodology should reflect the performance of an organization *relative to the desired constraint management operating philosophy* of the organization.

Constraints Accounting Defined

It is evident that we are dealing with two different accounting techniques. First, the widely accepted throughput accounting (a form of direct costing) and second, the less well known constraints accounting (CA),[14] defined as an accounting reporting technique consistent with a process of ongoing improvement and implementation of the theory of constraints, which includes:

1. Explicit consideration of the role of constraints.
2. Specification of throughput contribution effects.
3. Decoupling of throughput (T) from operational expense (OE).

The following sections first describe an earnings statement format that is typical of the throughput accounting approach. Then an earnings statement is prepared for the same data using a constraints accounting format incorporating the three aspects of constraints accounting enumerated above.

Throughput Accounting Earnings Statement

The basic format for an earnings statement in the throughput accounting (direct costing) tradition is illustrated in Exhibit 3.4 and is populated with some hypothetical data.

Exhibit 3.4   Typical Earnings Statement in a Throughput Accounting Format

Throughput Accounting Earnings Statement
For Month Ended November 30, 20X2

	Actual	Budget	Variance	Favorable / Unfavorable
THROUGHPUT (T):				
Revenues:				
Product Atex	$ 374,400	$ 374,400	$ 0	-
Product Detron	729,025	966,625	237,600	U
Product Fonic	374,400	0	374,400	F
Product Gaton	623,119	934,679	311,560	U
Total Revenues	$2,100,944	$2,275,704	$174,760	U
Less: Commissions	105,050	113,785	8,735	F
Net Revenues	$1,995,894	$2,161,919	$166,025	U
Materials Expense	666,445	729,255	62,810	F
Throughput (T)	$1,329,449	$1,432,664	$103,215	U
OPERATIONAL EXPENSE (OE):				
Manufacturing Operations	$195,000	$ 200,000	$ 5,000	F
Sales and Marketing	170,000	180,000	10,000	F
General and Administrative	270,000	268,000	2,000	U
Total Operational Expense	$ 635,000	$ 648,000	$ 13,000	F ·
OPERATING PROFIT	$ 694,449	$ 784,664	$ 90,215	U

There are four columns—one for the actual results of operations, one for the originally budgeted amount, another for a variance, and yet another to indicate whether the variance is favorable or unfavorable. The variance is the difference between the originally budgeted amounts and the actual results. Following conventional practice, the variance is favorable if the difference tends to increase reported profitability and unfavorable if it tends to decrease reported profits. That is, it is a good thing for revenues to be more than budgeted and a bad thing for expenses to be more than budgeted.

The Throughput Accounting Earnings Statement starts with the revenues, broken down by product. For each product a variance is calculated and marked as either favorable or unfavorable. Because sales of Atex were exactly as budgeted, no variance is reported for this product. Unfavorable variances are reported for the products Detron and Gaton, drawing management's attention to the problems associated with these products. Fonic, which is apparently a new addition to the product line, has a favorable variance. Overall, revenues were $174,760 less than budgeted.

Accountants distinguish two types of budgets: **static** and **flexible.** The budget column in Exhibit 3.4 is an example of a static budget in which the results of actual operations are compared to the originally budgeted expectations. Flexible budgets are adjusted for cost control expectations at the actual activity level. For accounting in the throughput world paradigm, we recommend measuring from initial expectations because changes in throughput, not cost reductions, are the objective. A hierarchy for budgetary control with constraints accounting is discussed further in Chapter 4.

Both the sales commissions and materials expense are shown as having favorable variances. This is somewhat misleading since the sales commission is a percentage of sales revenue. The budget column shows the originally budgeted amount of sales commissions based on the originally budgeted sales revenue dollars. Since the total actual sales revenue was less than originally budgeted, the commission expense paid on sales revenues is also less than originally budgeted. Less expense is a good thing, and so the variance is reported as being favorable. In fact, the commission expense is exactly what was expected as a percentage of sales revenue. The favorable variance reported for materials expense is accounted for in similar fashion.

The operational expenses appear to be nicely under control, with favorable variances in manufacturing operations as well as in sales and marketing. The overall favorable variance of $13,000 in operational expenses offsets a portion of the unfavorable throughput variance. Thus, the operating profit is $90,215 less than had originally been budgeted.

Constrained Operating Environment

Even though the traditional Throughput Accounting Earnings Statement of Exhibit 3.4 uses the constraint management terminology of T and OE, it makes no mention of constraints.[15] The throughput accounting statement, then, may be prepared without the company even having considered its constraints. However, an understanding of the organization's constraints will be necessary for the constraints accounting report because the first aspect of constraints accounting requires specific consideration of the role played by the constraints.

The example assumes that there are three relatively independent chains within the organization. The constraints of these chains define the current capabilities, and therefore the tactics, of the company. Exhibit 3.5 shows the association of the four products with the constraints. In following the conventional direct costing paradigm, these data were not used in preparing the Throughput Accounting Earnings Statement.

The products Detron and Fonic are associated with the welding constraint because both of them require use of the welder, which is currently fully utilized. Products Atex and Gaton do not require use of the welder. The product Gaton does require a type of labor, Class D, which is in very short supply. Gaton is the only product that requires the Class D labor skills. The production of Atex is not currently restricted by any internal constraint.

Exhibit 3.5 Association of Products with Constraints

		Relevant Constraint		
		Welder	Labor Class "D"	Market (Quantity Demanded)
Product	Atex			X
	Detron	X		
	Fonic	X		
	Gaton		X	

When first preparing—or revising—the format of a financial report, the accountant must decide what data to include and how to display the data. The challenge is to summarize the data in a meaningful way. For a report to be *meaningful* it should *inform, instruct,* and ultimately *motivate* the recipient to take appropriate action. Of course, the raw data are available in detail, and specialized reports may be prepared. But the routine performance reports, such as the Constraints Accounting Earnings Statement, will provide ongoing direction to recipients of the report.

Constraints Accounting Earnings Statement

The Constraints Accounting Earnings Statement, shown in Exhibit 3.6, is built on the same financial data used to prepare the Throughput Accounting Earnings Statement (Exhibit 3.4).

Exhibit 3.6 Earnings Statement in a Constraints Accounting Format

Constraints Accounting Earnings Statement
For Month ended November 30, 20X2

	Actual	Budget	Variance	Favorable / Unfavorable
Throughput Contribution (T) Section:				
Constraints:				
Internal:				
Welder	$ 716,380	$ 632,700	$ 83,680	F Note A
Labor Class D	373,869	560,764	186,895	U Note B
External:				
Market	239,200	239,200	0	Note C
Total Throughput Contribution	$1,329,449	$1,432,664	$103,215	U Note D
Operational Expense (OE) Section:				
Greater of actual or budgeted OE	648,000	648,000		Note E
Performance Profit	$ 681,449			Note F

Note that the total actual and budgeted throughput ($1,329,449 and $1,432,664, respectively), and hence the total throughput variance ($103,215), are the same for the Constraints Accounting Earnings Statement as for the Throughput Accounting Earnings Statement. Therefore, the underlying data are the same, but the display format has been changed.

Explicit Consideration of Constraints

Placing the constraint data on the earnings statement brings constraint reporting under the auspices of the financial management function and requires its periodic reporting.[16]

The first difference between the Throughput Accounting and Constraints Accounting Earnings Statements is that *constraint* classifications replace *product* classifications. As Goldratt has observed, "constraints are the essential classification, replacing the role that products played."[17] The first aspect of constraints accounting, the explicit consideration of the role of constraints, is accommodated by enumerating the various physical constraints of the organization.

Throughput Contribution

The second aspect of constraints accounting is the specification of throughput contribution effects. The constraints accounting report highlights the impact, or lack thereof, of decisions and actions on the **throughput contribution** relative to the constraints.[18] Since all significant changes in throughput are the result of "touching" an Archimedean constraint, this presentation invites attention to the appropriate areas—the Archimedean constraints.

The top portion of the Constraints Accounting Earnings Statement (Exhibit 3.6) is designated as the *throughput contribution section*. In order to show the throughput contribution effects, we need to measure from some base point. Therefore, the Constraints Accounting Earning Statement (Exhibit 3.6) includes *budget*[19] and *variance* columns, just as does the Throughput Accounting Earnings Statement (Exhibit 3.4).

Revenue and variable expense data associated with the relevant constraints are shown in Exhibit 3.7. These data will allow the reader to reconcile the Constraints Accounting Earnings Statement throughput with that of the Throughput Accounting Earnings Statement.

Notes to the Earnings Statement

The notes to the Constraints Accounting Earnings Statement contain detail appropriate for the managerial level to which the report is directed. The notes might also take the form of "drill down" reports providing additional detail, for example, analyzing the *throughput per constraint unit* classified in various ways, for instance, by customer, product line, and so forth.

Exhibit 3.7   Throughput Data Associated with Relevant Constraints

Constraints		Actual Throughput	Budgeted Throughput
Internal:			
Welder:	Revenue	$1,103,425	$ 966,625
(Detron & Fonic)	Variable Expense*	387,045	333,925
	Throughput	$ 716,380	$ 632,700
Labor Class D:	Revenue	$ 623,119	$ 934,679
(Gaton)	Variable Expense*	249,250	373,915
	Throughput	$ 373,869	$ 560,764
External:			
Market	Revenue	$ 374,400	$ 374,400
(Atex)	Variable Expense*	135,200	135,200
	Throughput	$ 239,200	$ 239,200
Total Throughput Contribution		$1,329,449	$1,432,664
* Variable expense includes commissions and raw materials.			

The existence of an internal physical constraint, such as the welder and "Class D" labor in this example, implies that at least some customer orders have been turned away—either intentionally or unintentionally. Consequently, an analysis of the lost or rejected orders would be an appropriate addition to the notes relating to internal constraints. The availability of such evidence lends credence to the fact that the specified constraint is, in fact, an active constraint. In some cases, the "constraint" specified may turn out to be a strategically selected leverage point or focal point used for scheduling production or projects, but not a currently active constraint. In that case, the constraint should be presented as being a marketing constraint rather than a production constraint. Note A, for the welding constraint, might look something like this:

Note A: During November the sales emphasis for products using the welder was changed from Detron to Fonic. As a result of the higher throughput per constraint (welder) minute of Fonic ($8.21) versus Detron ($5.29), overall throughput increased by $83,680. The remaining unfilled market for Detron available is estimated to be 2,000 units or $360,000 of throughput.

We see, then, that there is some inherent ambiguity in the Throughput Accounting Earnings Statement (Exhibit 3.4). By treating interrelated activities (products Detron and Fonic) as independent, the Throughput Accounting Earnings Statement shows two variances: an unfavorable variance of $237,800 for product Detron and a favorable variance of $374,400 for product Fonic. There is nothing to tie the two variances together. This ambiguity is resolved in the Constraints Accounting Earnings Statement (Exhibit 3.6). By *focusing on constraints rather than products*, the net effect of interactions among parts of the organization is identified. Whereas the Throughput Accounting Earnings Statement tells the recipient about what happened to the individual parts of the organization in isolation, the Constraints Accounting Earnings Statement exposes how the individual parts of the organization interacted during the period. When people focus on isolated areas, there is a danger that the isolated area will become the whole for the individual.

Let us now turn to the second internal constraint, Class D labor. The example assumes that, at the beginning of the month, one of the organization's three employees with these skills left to accept a similar, but higher paying, position with a competitor. This saved the organization about $5,000 in wages and fringe benefits during the month (which was reflected as a favorable variance in manufacturing operations in the traditional format of Exhibit 3.4). Had a similar event occurred in any area of operations other than Class D labor or the welder, it would have been merely a statistical fluctuation in a resource level. However, because Class D labor is a constraint, the loss of this employee (whom we either were unable to, or elected not to, replace) caused us to be unable to deliver a full third of our commitment to the market. The result was a loss of one-third of the throughput of Gaton—as well as considerable customer goodwill. Note B might read as follows:

> *Note B: Reduction of the headcount of Class D labor from three to two during the month resulted in the shipment of only two-thirds of the product which uses this type of labor and a loss of $186,895 of throughput. Sales estimates that about 75% of these customers will be permanently lost, but that at least $150,000 of throughput remains available to us in this market. The marginal throughput associated with an additional Class D employee is about $900 per hour.*[20]

Note C would disclose some information about the market constraint for Atex. Probably the most significant thing about this product is that there is no variance—we sold what we expected to sell. The question is, "What are we doing to exploit, subordinate to, or elevate this constraint?" It appears that there were no effective actions in this area during the month; inertia may be playing a role here.[21]

The *Total Throughput Contribution* line in the throughput section of the Constraints Accounting Earnings Statement (Exhibit 3.6) is simply a summary of the overall throughput effects. November actions, or lack of actions, resulted in profits being $103,215 less than budgeted.

Since the total revenues and truly variable expenses are not shown on the face of the report (a major paradigm shift), note D would probably include a schedule of revenues and truly variable expenses with an appropriate amount of detail for the organizational level. The report for top management might contain the following:

Note D:		
Actual Revenue		$2,100,944
Commissions	$105,050	
Materials	666,445	771,495
Actual Throughput		$1,329,449

Finally, we emphasize that in constraints accounting the underlying financial data are arranged to allow those people implementing constraint management to have a reporting method that focuses on the Archimedean constraints of the global organization.

Operational Expenses

Our example assumes that the organization has made the paradigm shift from the cost world to the throughput world discussed in Chapter 2. The operating philosophy, then, is to focus on factors limiting the ability to generate throughput—the constraints. Operational expenses are considered to be adequately controlled if they are within the budget limitations. Adequate cost control is a **necessary condition** for the organization.

The third aspect of constraints accounting is decoupling throughput (T) from operational expense (OE). The Constraints Accounting Earnings Statement (Exhibit 3.6) is a **performance report.** We want it to *reflect the performance of the organization (and its members) relative to the desired operating philosophy of the organization.* The throughput section of the report provides the focus on increasing throughput in terms of our constraints. But since it is still necessary to check the necessary condition of adequate cost control, we add a line to the report for operational expense. The report is now a comprehensive performance report.

The operational expenses (OE) reported on the performance report require additional explanation. They are the greater of the actual or budgeted (exploitation plan) amount. If the expenses are less than budgeted on an organizationwide basis, then they are in control and no action is necessary. Whenever actual expenses are less than budget, as in our example, it is not considered to be a particularly favorable happening or important enough to report; it is simply that costs are under control. In this situation we do not want to encourage managers to lose their focus on throughput to look for cost reductions. No variance is reported. When costs are under control, there is no note E to direct additional attention to this line.

If the actual operational expense were greater than the budgeted amount, then it would be an indication that a necessary condition (costs under control) was being violated. In that event, the budgeted amount and unfavorable variance would be reported.

Actual costs may exceed budgeted costs for reasons that are currently unspecified. In that case, it would be time for some traditional cost control activity. Note E then would provide detail as to areas and amounts of variance in a manner similar to that shown in the operational expense (OE) section of the Throughput Accounting Earnings Statement (Exhibit 3.4).

Actual expenses might exceed the budgeted amounts because physical activity has been increasing and **protective capacity** has been eroded. If physical volumes have been increasing, it may be necessary to increase the budgeted amounts to provide additional protective capacity in some areas. A second reason that actual costs might exceed the budgeted amount is that the OE budget has not been revised in a timely manner. In this case there is a reasonable probability that *future costs are not being controlled effectively.* That is, the organization may not have an effective procedure for checking that future cost increases are incurred in order to elevate a constraint or satisfy a necessary condition, or that the exploitation and subordination steps have been followed.[22]

Performance Profit

Performance profit is the bottom line of the Constraints Accounting Earnings Statement and summarizes the results of operations *in a manner consistent with the organization's desired operating philosophy.* In order to emphasize the decoupling of T and OE, summary budget and variance amounts are not shown. The more interesting comparison is to previous periods in order to recognize a process of ongoing improvement or lack thereof. A graph similar to that of Exhibit 2.4 would be appropriate for this purpose.

The performance profit does not necessarily equal the operating profit shown on the traditional Throughput Accounting Earnings Statement. It also will not equal the earnings reported using generally accepted accounting principles (GAAP) for general-purpose external reporting. Therefore, senior managers, who are concerned with the external financial reports and the integrity of the fiscal reporting system, will want a reconciliation to the GAAP statements. Note F should reconcile the Constraints Accounting Earnings Statement to either the Statement of Cash Flows or to the GAAP Earnings Statement.

The Constraints Accounting Earnings Statement (Exhibit 3.6) delivers a different message than does the Throughput Accounting Earnings Statement (Exhibit 3.4). With its emphasis on revenues and expenses, the latter seems to say "sell more in order to earn more; and if you can't sell more, cut costs." The Constraints Accounting Earnings Statement, how-

ever, demands the identification of constraints and exhorts the exploitation of the constraints as well as appropriate subordination.

The traditional Throughput Accounting Earnings Statement and the
Constraints Accounting Earnings Statement are created from the same financial data. The constraints accounting report, however, also requires
that the financial data be related to the organization's constraints. Any organization that has the ability to generate direct costing information also
has the ability to prepare a Throughput Accounting Earnings Statement.
However, only an organization that has identified and understands the impact of its constraints has the ability to create a Constraints Accounting
Earnings Statement.

COMPLEXITY DIVIDE

There are two distinct forms of simplicity: one lies on the near side of
complexity and the other on the far side of complexity.[23] The separation
between the two forms of simplicity is known as a **complexity divide.** The
ability to bring focus to complexity in such a manner that acting on just a
single point can cause many interacting components to respond pre-
dictably represents the simplicity that lies on the far side of complexity.
Constraint management and its associated constraints accounting measurement are representative of the simplicity found on the far side of the
complexity divide. Consider the systems, designated as system I and system
II, illustrated in Exhibit 3.8.

Which of these systems is the more simple, and which is the more
complex? To most people it appears obvious that system I, comprised of

Exhibit 3.8   System Complexity

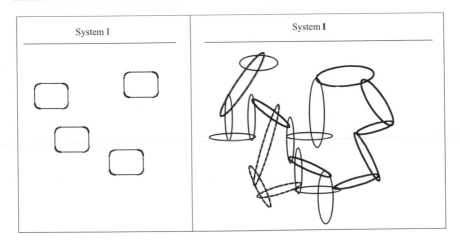

| System I | System I |

four components, is the simpler and system II, having 21 components, the more complex.

But let us look a little more closely at these systems, not in terms of the number of components but rather in terms of how many actions must be taken in order to affect the entire system. System I is defined by four apparently independent **entities.** Changing all four of these entities will require acting on all four entities. In contrast, 21 links in a tangle of chains define system II. The linkages represent physical and causal relationships existing among the individual parts of an organization. In general, the flow pattern in system II is from the bottom to the top. However, links shown as dotted lines are from the top to the bottom. In this case, acting on only the lowest link causes all of the other links to respond. From this point of view, system II is the simpler and system I is the more complex.

System I is representative of the cost world and its least product cost thinking bridge as presented in Chapter 1. The parts of the system are decoupled as independent analytical entities. The attempt is made to optimize each individual entity. Ubiquitous efficiency metrics and incentive compensation based on shares of calculated cost savings, revenue generation, or other local measurements show this to be a predominant operational strategy. Cost world measurements even become part of the social fabric of the society.[24] (In Chapter 6 we will see that cost allocation even became an expressed part of U.S. national policy in the 1930s.) A great deal of management—and good luck—is needed to coordinate all the various individual areas. Each individual area is optimized individually, placing its own demands on the remainder of the organization, and operates in a somewhat random fashion with respect to the larger organization.

System II is representative of the simplicity of constraint management and lies on the far side of complexity.[25] When actions are taken in the right place and in the right way, then the right things happen. Constraints accounting fits with the simplicity of constraint management in that when the right things are measured and reported—and when the effects of the measurements are followed through to their logical conclusions—the right things will happen. Simplicity lying on the far side of the complexity divide comes from understanding the complex relationships and having confidence in the logic that connects the measurements with unavoidable outcomes.[26] The thinking processes associated with the theory of constraints portray the logic underlying linkages within an organization.

Logic of Using Constraints Accounting to Lock in a Process of Ongoing Improvement

Chapter 1 identified two thinking bridges for assessing the impact of a projected action on the bottom line: *least product cost* and *global measure-*

ments. An example illustrating the use of the two bridges to guide operating decisions showed that in order for an action to result in an improvement, the action must take the organization closer to its goal. The example also showed that Archimedes points exist in every profit-oriented organization. When actions touch these Archimedes points, a significant and measurable change, either positive or negative, in bottom-line profitability occurs. Conversely, not much effect on organizational profitability results from actions that do not touch these points. We were forced to conclude that *a robust process of ongoing improvement (POOGI) could only stem from a focus on Archimedean constraints.*

What to Change?

Most organizations currently pursue the cost world strategy of cost recovery and reduction, spreading their efforts over all parts of the organization. Since, as shown in Chapter 2, relatively few Archimedean constraints are found in any organization, most of the organizational effort is expended in areas that do not contain an Archimedean constraint. If not much change in bottom-line profitability occurs when actions do not touch an Archimedean constraint, then *there is a need to shift the paradigm away from the cost world.*

Although most efforts do not touch an Archimedean constraint, occasionally some of the cost world efforts will touch an Archimedean constraint. In these cases, cost reduction efforts are applied to internally constrained areas. Then critical constraint capacity is reduced, and, similar to scenario 2 of the thinking bridges example in Chapter 1, there is a significant reduction in bottom-line profitability. Again we find that *there is a need to shift the paradigm away from the cost world.*

What to Change to?

If, however, significant and measurable change in bottom-line profitability occurs when an Archimedean constraint is touched and a robust POOGI can only stem from focus on Archimedean constraints, then an understanding of Archimedean constraints and the global effect of actions should guide the decision-making process. An organization currently pursuing a cost world strategy of cost recovery and reduction should *shift toward the paradigm of focus provided by the throughput world* to achieve significant bottom-line improvement.

How to Create the Change?

Since there is a need to shift the paradigm away from the cost world, and the least product cost thinking bridge is associated with the cost world, a shift away from the cost world involves a shift away from the cost thinking bridge. Also, since there is a need to shift toward the paradigm of focus provided by the throughput world, and the global measurements thinking bridge is associated with the throughput world, a shift to the throughput world involves a shift toward the global measurements thinking bridge. It is clear that *changing thinking patterns from the cost world to the throughput world also involves a change in the measurement paradigm used to evaluate actions.*

Role of Constraints Accounting

Constraints accounting fits into the logic supporting a POOGI in the following ways:

- Since a robust process of ongoing improvement (POOGI) can only stem from a focus on Archimedean constraints, the financial decision and performance measurement system should focus on Archimedean constraints.

- Since a shift to the throughput world involves a shift toward the global measurements thinking bridge, the financial decision and performance measurement system should focus on increasing bottom-line profitability.

- Since a shift away from the cost world involves a shift away from the least product cost thinking bridge, the financial decision and performance measurement system should deemphasize traditional efficiency and product cost metrics.

These three conclusions lead directly to the definition and attributes of constraints accounting offered earlier.[27]

SUMMARY

In Chapter 2 we reviewed constrained environments and saw that long-run strategy is reflected in the organization's constraints. We then looked at the cyclical five-step focusing process that constraint management uses to leverage both the current (tactical) and future (strategic) constraints in order to establish a process of ongoing improvement (POOGI).

In this chapter, an examination of throughput accounting revealed that it is a misnomer. In fact, throughput accounting is generally viewed as direct costing and is firmly rooted in the cost world. Therefore, a new earnings reporting model, the constraints accounting model, was presented. The constraints accounting financial reporting model revolved around the operating philosophy of the throughput world. It focuses on the opportunities associated with Archimedean constraints. This constraint focus *applies to both throughput generation and future cost control.* Current operational expenses are adequately controlled if they are within the budget limitations. The constraints accounting model, then, is consistent and aligned with the constraint management philosophy.

We have explored a generic and systematic view of a profit-oriented organization as being defined by its constraints in both the short run and the long run. We have also examined a cyclical process—the five focusing steps—that can provide tactical and strategic direction. There is an identified global goal and an operating philosophy to pursue that goal, and there is a means to track the organization's performance relative to the desired operating philosophy.

If the tactical constraints of an organization, which are relatively few at any given time, can be identified, exploited, and elevated, all on a recurring basis, then, knowing this, the management of an organization can embark on a process of ongoing improvement for the organization. However, a necessary condition must also be met in order for the process of ongoing improvement to be robust. The members of the organization must behave in such a way as to implement the constraint management philosophy. This behavior, which is found only on the far side of the complexity divide, is the dynamic subordination of constraint management.

Crossing the complexity divide by coordinating the internal financial reporting system with the desired management philosophy is a key to locking in a process of ongoing improvement.

NOTES

[1] Eliyahu M. Goldratt and Jeff Cox, *The Goal: Excellence in Manufacturing* (North River Press, 1984), pp. 159, 163.

[2] D. Galloway and D. Waldron, "Throughput Accounting," *Management Accounting* (U.K.) (November 1988–February 1989).

[3] Goldratt and Cox do not indicate how the 80% is to be determined. We might assume that perhaps the products using the constraint resource use 80% of the total direct labor time. Or it might be that the firm has five major product lines, and four of them (80%) require the constraint resource. At any rate, it is quite arbitrary.

[4] Time increase of 2 minutes multiplied by the OE cost of a constraint minute, $7.2115 = $14.423.

[5] Perhaps the constraint-time-based costing method will have some applicability for organizations using a cost-based pricing strategy. We will discuss this in Chapter 6 when we address pricing issues.

[6] Nevertheless, we understand that some providers of ERP (enterprise resources planning) software are basing their product-costing systems on this constraint-time costing concept and offering them as constraint management compliant.

[7] Eric Noreen, Debra Smith, and James Mackey, *The Theory of Constraints and Its Implications for Management Accounting* (North River Press, 1995). Sponsored by the Institute of Management Accountants (IMA) and Price Waterhouse, p. 13.

[8] One exception to the "throughput accounting is direct costing" paradigm is the excellent book, *Throughput Accounting: TOC's Management Accounting System*, by Thomas Corbett (North River Press, 1998). Corbett's book is consistent with the views presented herein.

[9] The *budgetary process* includes the decision making that results in the tactics of the organization *(budgetary planning)*, the *budget* (a document) that results from the plans and that has been approved by top management, and the use of the budget as a standard against which to measure actual performance *(budgetary control)*. The approved budget also performs an important internal control function by documenting management's specific approval of expenditures.

[10] H. William "Bill" Dettmer, *Goldratt's Theory of Constraints: A Systems Approach to Continuous Improvement* (ASQ Quality Press, 1998), p. 17.

[11] Mokshagundam L. Srikanth and Scott A. Robertson, *Measurements for Effective Decision Making* (Spectrum Publishing, 1995), p. 28.

[12] Corbett, *Throughput Accounting*, p. 32.

[13] For example, Noreen, Smith, and Mackey (*The Theory of Constraints*, pp. xxvii, xxix, fn. 1) say that, although Goldratt would like to "purge the term 'product cost' from our vocabulary," they have difficulty discussing [pricing] issues without referring to the product-cost concept. The proscription of product cost refers to **final costing objects** that are to be used for decision making (e.g., pricing) or performance reporting. The finance function will continue to calculate product costs where appropriate for the **GAAP** financial statements and as **intermediate cost objectives** when desired to develop some other type of data element (e.g., calculating the throughput contribution of a particular sale or order).

[14] The Institute of Management Accountants' Management Accounting Practices Committee has adopted this concept of constraints accounting. Statement on Management Accounting (Practices and Techniques) Number 4HH, *Theory of Constraints Management System Fundamentals*, paragraphs 133–136, 1999.

[15] I (inventory/investment) is not included on the earnings statement because it appears on a balance sheet as an asset classification. I is typically allocated to time periods through the accounting device of depreciation. Some I may be included on the earnings statement as the expense category, **depreciation expense.**

[16] In some cases, the constraint(s) may not be known. This could be due to the constraint having recently shifted and the emerging constraint not yet having been identified, or due to management not focusing on constraints. In both situations, the earnings statement should show that the constraint is presently unknown. This places the focus on the correct place, identifying the constraint.

[17] Eliyahu M. Goldratt, *The Haystack Syndrome: Sifting Information out of the Data Ocean* (North River Press, 1990), p. 57.

[18] *Throughput contribution* is synonymous with "throughput." I have used *throughput contribution* in order to be consistent with the existing accounting literature. McMullen refers to throughput as "throughput value added" (TVA), acquiescing to those, such as Schonberger, who would reserve the word "throughput" for production (only) cycle time. See Thomas B. McMullen, Jr., *Introduction to the Theory of Constraints (TOC) Management System* (St. Lucie Press, 1998), p. 31; Richard J. Schonberger, *World Class Manufacturing: The Next Decade* (The Free Press, 1996), p. 231.

[19] The operating budget in a constraint management environment is the result of the decisions and actions taken in the second and third steps of the five-step focusing process (exploitation and subordination). The term *budget* could be replaced by **exploitation plan.**

[20] 2,000 hours per year / 12 months = 167 hours per month; $150,000 / 167 hours = $898.20 per hour. Note that if an additional employee is hired, it is expected that Class D labor will no longer be an active constraint.

[21] This interpretation assumes that the exploitation plan was based on carrying forward the previous month's (or year's) actual results and is used to illustrate the danger of the inertia of our thinking. If Atex's budgeted sales had been based on

a plan to increase Atex's throughput, then the results would have represented excellent execution of the plan.

[22] Procedures for controlling future costs are discussed in Chapter 4.

[23] William Sloane Coffin, "Make Love Your Aim," sermon delivered at Fountain Street Church, January 19, 1997.

[24] For example, in the United States, allocated cost measurements are introduced to students in the school system at an early point. Tony Rizzo offered the following example of a mathematics problem at the elementary school level: "It cost $50 to join the soccer team," stated the worksheet. "The team played 8 games during the season. How much did each game cost?" asked the homework question (CMSIG Internet discussion group, subject: *Born with TOC knowledge*, December 18, 2001).

[25] An inevitable result of implementing an aspect of constraint management is that the managers affected recognize this simplicity on the far side of complexity. This recognition is often verbalized as being better results stemming from better planning or as having better visibility into operations.

[26] It is not enough that we have confidence in the logic; we must also have sound logic. Entities that we assume to exist must actually exist; causal relationships that we hypothesize must be valid. Constraints accounting is not the only model that lies on the far side of complexity. As we will see in Chapter 6, cost-based pricing—taken as a comprehensive management strategy—is there also, provided demand is significantly greater than supply for a firm's products or services.

[27] Constraints accounting should support a process of ongoing improvement by
- Having explicit consideration of constraints.
- Specifying throughput effects.
- Decoupling throughput from operational expenses.

4

Motivation and the Budget

MOTIVATION FOR A PROCESS
OF ONGOING IMPROVEMENT

The five focusing steps of constraint management provide a plan (an operating philosophy for the organization) but it takes people to execute the plan in accordance with the organization's philosophy. At this point we encounter the old horse and water problem.[1]

What about People?

But why should the people in the organization pursue the goal of profitability rather than some other goal?[2]

We are concerned with at least five different groups of people,[3] each group having different needs from the system. In addition, the individual members of the groups undoubtedly have diverse personal needs and objectives. Each of the groups (and each of the individuals within a group) struggles for control and attempts to pull the organizational tangle of chains in a somewhat different direction. Sometimes these tugs have little organizationwide effect, moving a local part of the organization in one direction or another but within the limits of the existing excess capacity. Other times the tugs stretch some parts of the organization to such a degree that protective capacity is eroded, allowing interactive internal physical constraints to emerge.

It is appropriate for the **owners** of the organization to establish the organization's global goal.[4] In this book we have assumed that the goal is greater bottom-line profitability and that the constraint management operating philosophy has been selected to establish a robust process of ongoing improvement leading to greater profitability. When the owners have established and clearly communicated the goal, automatic **goal congruence** of the organization with the ownership group takes place. If a group other than the owners, such as management or an external consultant, has verbalized the organization's goal, then congruence of the organizational goal with the owners is problematical.

Organizations frequently have a variety of mission statements, goals, vision declarations, and so forth, instead of a single clearly stated goal. Such statements are generally pleasant sounding, suitable for framing, may be signed by the CEO, and may actually have some influence on the perceived necessary conditions of the organization.[5] Furthermore, many organizations create mission statements for local areas of operations and then proceed to dissect, direct, and distort them to fit into the organization's overall mission statements. Such multiple-objective pronouncements lead directly to a lack of goal congruence.

The owners entrust overall administration to **top management.** This group may include some or all of the owners. By their very nature professional top managers are driven to succeed in their careers. They may have hidden agenda objectives relating more to personal career advancement than to the organization's goal. It is important for top management to demonstrate that they have the ability to make things happen and to show that they are in control. As managers move up the corporate ladder, or jump to a more attractive ladder, they need to have a resume that demonstrates their ability through specific achievements: *reduced cost 15%, increased output 8%, reduced quality defects, increased market share, improved on-time completion from 60% to 93%,* and so forth. Who do you suppose has the larger total remuneration package—the CEO of a small business that has profits equaling 50% of sales revenues of $50,000 or the CEO of a large business that has thousands of employees but that lost $100 million last year? Compensation is a means not only of acquiring wealth, but also of measuring power and career success. Sheer size is significant to this group. Multiple top management goals in a publicly held company lead automatically to ambiguity with the goal of the shareholder owners.

The desire to be in control is not unique to top management. People in the **middle management** group may be seeking promotion to top management or to a different corporate ladder. All managers want to show how vital their department and their performance are. Or they may be jockeying for control or may even just be clinging to their current positions by their fingertips. In any event, if the cost world paradigm predominates, the manager is likely to be located in a cost center that provides a relatively isolated environment similar to the independent and unconnected entities comprising system I in Exhibit 3.8. We are accustomed to measuring the performance of cost centers—and their managers—individually. After all, that is why a cost center is established. The individual manager's measurable performance, tied to the performance of the cost center, is perceived as being important to compensation and promotion decisions. It would be only a matter of luck if such local area measurements were congruent with the organizational goal when the system is viewed as an interconnected whole.

First-line supervisors find themselves between the proverbial rock and a hard place, positioned between the demands of day-to-day operations associated with producing goods or a service and pressure to satisfy the middle managers' least-cost type measurements.

Finally, there are the folks who go by a variety of names, such as **labor,** associates, worker-bees, hourly employees, and nonexempt.[6] Sometimes these employees will be unionized, further emphasizing a dichotomy with the owner and management groups.

Goal Congruence

Goal congruence occurs when personal goals are sufficiently aligned with the purpose of the organization that people enthusiastically pursue the operational philosophy. Currently, it appears that most theory of constraints implementations fail to realize anything close to their full potential.[7] An important cause of these failures is likely the lack of goal congruence.

Clearly, there are many obstacles to creating complete goal congruence between the members of the organization and the global goal of the organization. We do not claim that a single innovation will alleviate all of the conflicting pressures. However, we do believe that each member of the organization needs a *reason to actively pursue* the organization's global goal.[8]

Intuitively, we know that people want to be treated fairly. They want to know that they count for something, that they are valued, and that they are part of something bigger than themselves. They want—and need—a sense of belonging as well as a measured way of knowing that they are okay.[9]

In Chapter 3, we saw that changing thinking patterns from the cost world to the throughput world involves a change in the measurement paradigm used to evaluate actions. We observe that an employee's relationship with an organization is largely defined by what the person perceives the measurements to be as they relate to them. Most organizations reflect their cost world strategies of cost recovery and reduction in least-cost and efficiency performance measurements. Cost world strategies and their associated measurements are even reinforced by societal norms.

Deeply seated paradigms about perceived relationships between employees and the organization must be changed in order to establish a robust process of ongoing improvement in the bottom-line measurement of the throughput world. Since an employee's relationship with the organization is largely defined by performance measurements, the perception of performance measurement must be changed. But *to what* should the performance measurement be changed? Can there be a way to align the individual goals of each group with a single global goal, given the diversity of groups and individuals within the organization?

Common Denominator Factor

A company that wants to achieve goal congruence must initiate an action that affects both owners and all employee groups. Is there such a common denominator factor among the various groups? One common theme—*MONEY*—touches every one of the groups. As the budgetary process permeates the organization, some aspect of money touches each of the groups vying for control.

We are not the first to attempt to use money, either real or promised, to align goals. Bonuses, profit-sharing, gain-sharing, and stock options are all common terms in remuneration plans today, and all involve attempting to use money to create an extraordinary level of motivation. General profit sharing bonuses are commonly offered as inducements to obtain or retain employees. A dilemma exists when bonuses are offered for performance improvement, but the employees do not know how they can improve performance beyond what they are currently doing. Such nonspecific performance bonuses tend to become viewed as entitlements.

In order to achieve goal congruence, we propose a fair incentive compensation plan, which we call a POOGI Bonus, to act as a dynamic motivator for driving the pursuit of the global goal through a process of ongoing improvement.

The POOGI Bonus does not rely on intermediate goals or objectives. Rather, the POOGI Bonus provides real recognition of the success achieved by the organization members when they work together to create a process of ongoing improvement consistent with the constraint management philosophy. The POOGI Bonus is a decisive test of sincerity, providing a significant bonus that is tied directly to bottom-line improvement. Of course, if the process of ongoing improvement has become stalled, there is no bonus—for anyone.

Logic of a POOGI Bonus

One might argue that it is not necessary for *everyone* in the organization to be involved in implementing the process of ongoing improvement and, hence, to participate in a POOGI Bonus plan. After all, significant improvement—in terms of the global goal—can occur only at an Archimedean constraint. Therefore, one might state, only those people who are directly associated with the current constraint need to participate actively in the improvement process. But to take this point of view is to disregard the importance of the interdependencies that exist between constrained and nonconstrained areas. The POOGI Bonus communicates how employees' actions can and do make a difference. Therefore, all members of the organization should participate in the POOGI Bonus plan.

The POOGI Bonus is based on the monetary value of the amount of bottom-line improvement and, as we know, *major improvement can come only through the throughput channel.* Employees, knowing that their contributions are valued, are motivated to struggle with the concept of subordination and at least give the constraint management philosophy a try by working toward the common global goal of bottom-line improvement through elevating global constraints. When an Archimedean constraint is actually elevated because of these efforts, the employees see that the POOGI Bonus is real and is tied to the elevation. A significant and substantial bonus is earned. Employees are again confirmed in their belief that they are an integral and valued part of the organization; motivation to work toward the common global goal is strongly reinforced.

Significant Bonus

A *significant* bonus means that a *large percentage* of the bottom-line improvement is paid; this is a relative measure. A typical bonus percentage for this purpose is 50% of the bottom-line improvement over the previous period.[10] Anything less as a percentage would probably not pass the decisive "sincerity test" and hence would be insufficient to provide real recognition of achievement. If a significant bonus is paid, then those employees receiving the bonus will be confirmed, in a tangible and measurable way, in their feelings that their contributions are valued.

Substantial Bonus

When an Archimedean constraint is elevated, substantial improvement is realized. Substantial improvement means that the improvement is a large monetary amount; this is an absolute measure. Since the POOGI Bonus is a significant percentage of the large monetary improvement, the *elevation of an Archimedean constraint is always accompanied by a substantial bonus.* The bonus is large in terms of the absolute monetary amount.[11] Note that the POOGI Bonus does not automatically continue, but rather must be earned anew in each period. The POOGI Bonus is an *extraordinary bonus paid for extraordinary performance.*

The POOGI Bonus is not a general profit-sharing bonus, but rather a specific gain-sharing bonus paid for executing the cyclical constraint management philosophy. If the inertia warned about in the fifth step of the focusing process sets in, then the process of ongoing improvement is interrupted, and no further bonus is earned. This sends a strong signal that the POOGI has become stalled and that the global goal of the organization is in jeopardy. It also provides a strong motivation to get the process back on track.

Mechanics of a POOGI Bonus

Performance profit is the bottom line of the Constraints Accounting Earnings Statement presented in Chapter 3. Performance profit summarizes the results of operations *in a manner consistent with the desired constraint management operating philosophy*. Since improvement resulting from operations is measured by an increase in the performance profit from a previous period, such an increase can be used as the basis for the POOGI Bonus. The POOGI Bonus is paid as a *percentage of the increase* in performance profit relative to a comparison period.[12]

Education and Training

Education and training will be required to establish a robust process of ongoing improvement. For the POOGI Bonus to be effective, employees must understand how they can influence profitability significantly by adopting the desired constraint management operating philosophy. Many changes, some involving very basic beliefs and the organizational culture, will be necessary for most organizations implementing the constraint management philosophy. Such paradigm shifts do not come easily. So, we will assume that everyone in the organization has completed an appropriate training course.[13] The POOGI Bonus Orientation Course will provide the employees with an understanding of how they can influence profitability. Employees will know where and how to focus their efforts.

Since the objective of having a POOGI Bonus is goal congruence, the plan applies equally to everyone in the organization. That is, *everyone participates in the same way*, receiving an equal percentage of base pay as a bonus. There must be no competing incentive plan to pull a subset of the organization in a different direction. Having completed the orientation course, employees not only perceive, but also understand, that there is fairness of treatment.

At this point, employees have the confidence derived from concrete knowledge of where and how to focus efforts for participation in the POOGI Bonus plan. When empowered by management, employees—who now have achieved an incentive status by participating in the bonus plan—feel a sense of ownership and personal commitment. They understand that an important purpose of the bonus plan is for them to be an integral part of the global organization, and they believe that they have the tools to make a difference. Now the organization is beginning to satisfy the employees' needs for belonging and acceptance. Trust between the diverse groups within the organization is built. At the same time, the individual employees are embracing the constraint management approach to improvement.

The way in which constraint management treats cost control further reinforces the sense of belonging and acceptance. Instead of being an element of variable expense, people are viewed as valued assets because the POOGI Bonus plan provides no incentive for reducing the current workforce. *Beware the betrayal of trust.*

POOGI Bonus Characteristics and Calculations

A POOGI Bonus plan has characteristics similar to the following:

1. The POOGI Bonus is an exceptional bonus for exceptional performance.
2. Everyone in the organization is covered by the plan.
3. The POOGI Bonus is the organization's only incentive compensation plan.
4. 50% of the increase in performance profit from a previous period (as calculated using constraints accounting) is added to a POOGI Bonus pool each month.
5. One-twelfth of the POOGI Bonus pool balance is paid out each month.[14]
6. Every participant in the POOGI Bonus plan receives a percentage of the monthly payout equal to the individual's gross pay over the previous 12 months divided by everyone's gross pay for the same period of time.
7. In the event the POOGI Bonus Pool becomes negative there is no recoupment, but negative amounts are carried forward and must be recovered before additional bonus payments are made.
8. Base pay amounts are competitive within the current employment market without the promise of a bonus payment.

The POOGI Bonus calculation is added to the face of the Constraints Accounting Earnings Statement as a continuation. This reporting treatment is illustrated in Exhibit 4.1.

Increased profits are the representation of a *process of ongoing improvement.* Exhibit 4.1 starts with the bottom line, performance profit, of the Constraints Accounting Earnings Statement shown in Exhibit 3.6. The performance profit for November 2002 is $681,449.

We assume that the organization has selected an annual basis for measuring improvement for the POOGI Bonus. The bonus calculation is

Exhibit 4.1   Bonus Calculation

Performance Profit (Nov 20X2)	$ 681,449
Comparison Performance Profit (Nov 20X1)	500,000
Increased Performance Profit	$ 181,449
Add to Bonus Pool (50% of increase)	$ 90,725

compared to the performance profit of the same fiscal month in the previous year. For purposes of our example, we assume that the process has been going on for at least a year and that the bonus is paid monthly, if appropriate.[15]

The performance profit for the comparison period, November 20X1, was $500,000 (assumed for the example). Deducting the $500,000 from the November 20X2 performance profit of $681,449, we arrive at an increase in performance profit of $181,449. This increase is split (before taxes) between all POOGI Bonus participants and the shareholders (owners) by adding 50% of the increase to a **bonus pool.**

The bonus pool is spread over the wage and salary base, as illustrated in Exhibit 4.2.

We assume that the month of November 20X2 started with a balance of $1,801,275 in the bonus pool representing the unpaid bonuses that have accumulated between December 20X1 and October 20X2. The unpaid bonus pool relates to wage and salary earnings of $3,666,667 at the beginning of November. These are the total wages and salaries that were paid over the 11-month period from December 20X1 through October 20X2.

During November, the employees earned total wages and salaries of $333,333. This includes everyone's salaries and wages: owners who are also managers, professional top and middle managers, first-line supervisors, hourly employees—everybody.[16] The November 20X2 salaries and wages are added to the beginning balance to arrive at an updated base of $4 million at the end of November. The November 20X2 bonus pool portion of the performance profit ($90,750, as calculated in Exhibit 4.1) is added to

Exhibit 4.2   POOGI Bonus Payout Percentage Calculation

Calculation Element	Previous Balance	+	Current Month	=	Total Amount	Payout
POOGI Bonus Pool	$1,801,275	+	$90,725	=	$ 1,892,000	
divided by						= 47.3%
Wage and Salary Base	$3,666,667	+	$ 333,333	=	$4,000,000	

the bonus pool to bring the total in the bonus pool to $1,892,000. Dividing the bonus pool ($1,892,000) by the wage and salary base ($4,000,000) gives a payout percentage of 47.3%. This means that the bonus pool is equal to 47.3% of the last 12 months' wages and salaries.

Exhibit 4.3 reflects the addition of the current value of the POOGI Bonus pool to the Constraints Accounting Earnings Statement.[17]

We add three additional lines to the performance report. The balance of the bonus pool at the end of October is added to the November addition to the bonus pool, which results in the balance of the pool at the end of November 20X2.[18] Then we boldly show the POOGI Bonus pool as a percentage of the wage and salary base. This is of primary *personal* interest to the recipients of the report. When the bonus is paid on about December 15, each employee receives a portion of the bonus pool corresponding to his or her portion of the wage and salary base.

For example, assume that the bonus is being paid at the rate of one-twelfth of the bonus pool each month. An individual employee, Bob Smith, who had earned $27,720 in the previous 11 months and $2,904 in November, would have total earnings of $30,624 ($27,720 + $2,904) included in the total $4 million wage and salary base. The total amount of bonus to be paid in December is $157,667 (one-twelfth of the POOGI Bonus pool balance of $1,892,000). Bob Smith's portion of the wage and salary base is 0.7656% ($30,624 / $4,000,000 = 0.007656). Multiplying the total December payout of $157,667 by 0.007656, we find that Bob Smith's bonus payment is $1,207.10 in December.[19] In similar fashion, a participant who had gross earnings of $77,000 in the previous 11 months before November and $7,000 in November would receive $3,311.01 in December ($84,000 / $4,000,000 * $157,667). A new participant who just started in November and who has earned only $2,000 at this company would receive $78.84 (2,000 / 4,000,000 * $157,667).

Exhibit 4.3   Displaying the Value of the POOGI Bonus Pool

Performance Profit (Nov 20X2)	$ 681,449
Comparison Performance Profit (Nov 20X1)	500,000
Increased Performance Profits	$ 181,449
Add to Bonus Pool (50% of increase)	90,725
Bonus Pool Balance October 31, 20X2	1,801,275
Bonus Pool Balance November 30, 20X2	$1,892,000
Current Value of POOGI Bonus Pool (as percentage of wages and salaries) November 30, 20X2	**47.3%**

Reporting the POOGI Bonus

The display of the bonus data in Exhibit 4.4 is appropriate for those who receive a copy of the earnings statement, but most employees probably do not receive this detailed data. Then the question arises: how should the POOGI Bonus results be communicated to the broader group of employees? Of course, the real communication arrives in the paycheck. Nevertheless, supplemental reporting by posting the essential information on office and plant bulletin boards and by e-mail to individuals in remote locations is desirable. A reporting format appropriate for bulletin board display on a standard size (8 1/2″ x 11″ or A4) sheet of paper is illustrated in Exhibit 4.4.

POOGI Bonus Summary

A significant POOGI Bonus can provide the motivating dynamic to establish goal congruence. The POOGI Bonus gives individuals at all organizational levels a reason to vigorously pursue the global goal through a robust process of ongoing improvement using the constraint management philosophy. If the process is successful, the amount of the bonus will be substantial relative to each individual's base pay.

Paradigms are powerful contributors to the inertia of thinking. We know that our paradigm ought to be in the throughput world, but our current paradigm (reinforced by years—even generations—of rules, training, and measurements) is in the cost world. A powerful incentive to break through the inertia of the cost world paradigm is a key to locking in a process of ongoing improvement. The POOGI Bonus can provide that incentive.

Exhibit 4.4   Reporting the POOGI Bonus

The value of the

POOGI Bonus

is

47.3%

as of November 30, 20X2

ROLE OF THE FINANCIAL MANAGER

Constraint management provides an organizationwide, or holistic, approach to management. Financial management, as the single function permeating the organization, has an important role to play.

Financial Managers' Dilemma

When making the paradigm shift from the cost world to the throughput world, financial managers, trained to manage by the numbers, often find themselves in a dilemma as illustrated in Exhibit 4.5. This exhibit uses one of the TOC thinking processes, an **evaporating cloud,** to state the dilemma.[20]

In order to (A) assist operational management to establish a process of ongoing improvement, financial managers must (B) provide information appropriate for exercise of sound budgetary control. This means that their (D) recommended actions must be based on well-established cost world measurements. An example of such a recommended action is the assertion that the minimum price of each product sold must be high enough to recover the full absorption cost of the product, plus a target gross profit.

In order to (A) assist operational management to establish a process of ongoing improvement, financial managers must (C) let experience and intuitions guide their decisions. Financial managers must therefore (E) recommend actions be taken that are not based on well-established cost world measurements. An example of this would be a financial manager's support of a line manager's contention that the minimum price of a prod-

Exhibit 4.5   Financial Managers' Dilemma

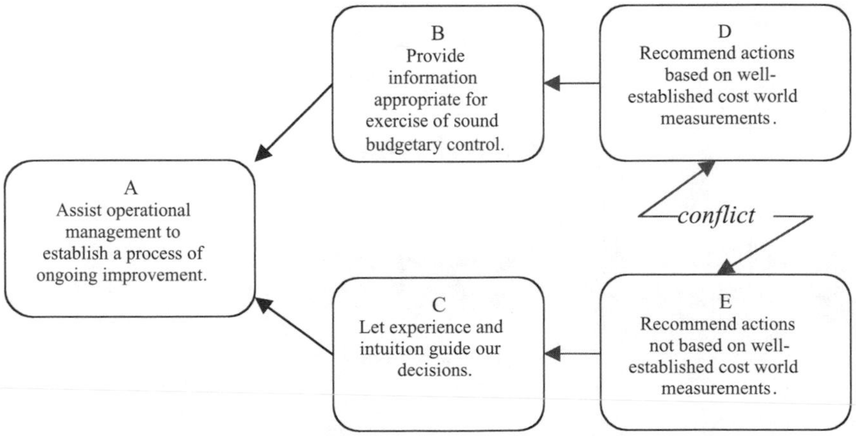

uct needs to be only high enough to recover the marginal (variable) cost of the product.

Financial managers, as prudent conservatives, find themselves caught in a dilemma. They feel pressure to maintain a hard and fast adherence to well-established procedures based on traditional cost world measurements, and at the same time they feel pressure to break the cost world rules in many situations. Their experience tells them that simple movement along the conflict arrow results in trading one set of undesirable effects for another. For example, insisting that each product or sale recover its fully allocated cost leads to missing out on some sales that would provide a positive throughput contribution and a nice bottom-line impact. However, if financial managers pursue a marginal cost pricing strategy, they run the risk of starting a price war from which the industry does not recover. The competitive response to marginal cost pricing initiatives is a historical concern for financial managers, and the concern applies in a constraint management environment as well.[21]

As a result of the conflicting pressures, managers attempt to use information provided by the accounting system for planning and control, but override the accounting measurements based on intuition—the least product cost thinking bridge described in Chapter 1. On some days the accounting controls take precedence, and on other days intuition wins out. The result is an oscillation between intuitive bold steps toward expansion and contraction dictated by cost accounting measurements.

This type of conflict is familiar to financial managers. They often think of themselves as serving two masters—the integrity of the fiscal reporting system and the support of entrepreneurial management.[22] One manager, who served as both controller and director of marketing, described his typical workday as "sitting at his desk and choking himself." However, we must set jokes aside because this is a very serious matter. *Failure to break out of the dilemma portrayed in Exhibit 4.5 is enough to prevent the formation of a robust process of ongoing improvement.* Therefore, we will examine the cloud closely to determine whether something can be done to break at least some of the linkages.[23]

Since the financial manager's dilemma shown in Exhibit 4.5 represents a deep, longstanding, and widespread conflict, we may assume that the needs expressed in B and C are legitimate and valid. We should find our solution, then, in the linkages between these desirable requirements and the prerequisite conditions of recommending actions D based on, and E contrary to, well-established cost world measurements.

Underlying Assumptions

Underlying every arrow in the thinking processes of the theory of constraints are assumptions that provide the rationale for the perceived logical linkage. The simple process of reading the relationship adding the word "because" and then filling in the remainder of the phrase to complete the sentence may surface many assumptions.

Some assumptions surface in the following manner. The first linkage (arrow) examined is between B and D as reflected in Exhibit 4.6.

In order to provide information appropriate to the exercise of sound budgetary control, financial managers must recommend actions based on well-established cost world measurements *because:*

- Well-established cost world measurements are reliable.
- Reductions in the standard cost of products flow through to the bottom line.
- Each product sold must recover its **full cost** and provide a contribution to profit.[24]
- Well-established cost world measurements have been reliable in the past.
- The accounting system makes sense of all the small items that need to be considered.
- It is too expensive to operate a second comprehensive information system.
- Budgetary control means reducing existing cost levels.[25]

In similar fashion, the C and E linkage is repeated in Exhibit 4.7, and assumptions underlying the C–E arrow are surfaced.

In order to let experience and intuition guide decisions, financial managers must recommend actions that are not based on well-established cost world measurements *because:*

- The data provided by the accounting system are generally too late for operational decision making.
- The data provided by the accounting system are generally too aggregated for operational decision making.

Exhibit 4.6   Financial Managers' Dilemma: B–D Linkage

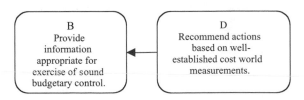

Exhibit 4.7   Financial Managers' Dilemma: C–E Linkage

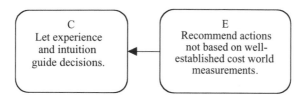

- Most aspects of the business have not been precisely defined and quantified by accounting measurements.
- Data in the accounting system have been created to satisfy legal and external reporting requirements but are inappropriate for planning and control.
- The accounting measurements do not capture much of our employees' intuition.
- Accounting measurements are not intuitively reliable.

Finally, assumptions that underlie the D–E arrow shown in Exhibit 4.8 are surfaced.

Recommending actions based on well-established cost world measurements is in conflict with recommending actions not based on well-established cost world measurements *because:*

Exhibit 4.8   Financial Managers' Dilemma: D–E Linkage

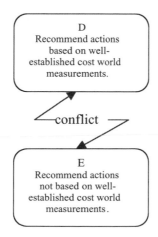

- The accounting system measures all facets of the organization.
- The cost world measurements are not consistent with our intuition.
- The cost world measurements do not guide us correctly.
- The cost behavior implicit in the cost world measurements is not realistic.

Invalidating Assumptions

Surfacing assumptions provides us with a better understanding of why we feel that the entity at the tail of the arrow is necessary in order to obtain the entity at the head of the arrow. But a better understanding does not get us out of the dilemma. In fact, the simple method that we used to surface the assumptions did not require a check to determine whether there was any validity to the assumptions that surfaced.

We will need to evaluate the assumptions to see whether they are both true and relevant. If we recognize that an assumption is clearly false—or otherwise not actually relevant for a linkage—then that linkage is broken in our mind. If an assumption appears to be true, then perhaps we can take an action to introduce something new into the environment that will allow us to have the head of the arrow without the tail.[26] That is, the injection will allow us to break out of the conflict.

Exhibit 4.9 lists the assumptions surfaced, asks whether each is true, and suggests some injections that could invalidate the assumption.

With respect to the first assumption, that *well-established cost world measurements are reliable*, in the last several decades accountancy and financial reporting have become increasingly complex.[27] Accountancy has been repositioned from its status as practical art to its role as an oracle. The fact is that we do not know whether the legacy cost world accounting measurements are reliable.

We examined the second assumption extensively in the thinking bridges example in Chapter 1 and concluded that "least product cost provides a deceptive beacon in almost every case." This assumption is clearly false.

If all products produced are sold and if each individual unit of product is sold at a price greater than its full cost, the firm will indeed make a profit. However, nowhere is it written that all products produced will be sold for more than their full cost. If the combination of products sold were such that the combined revenues exceeded the total expenses of the organization, the third assumption would be invalidated. But that does not provide the same degree of specific guidance as the original assumption. Therefore, we look for another injection: the measurements provided for decision making are reliable for supporting a process of ongoing improvement.

Exhibit 4.9 Financial Managers' Dilemma: Assumptions and Injections

Arrow	Assumption	True or False	Possible Injection
1 B–D	Well-established cost world measurements are reliable.	?	The bottom-line effect of actions based on decision measurements is clearly visible.
2 B–D	Reductions in the standard cost of products flow through to the bottom line.	False	
3 B–D	Each product sold must recover its full cost and provide a contribution to profit.	?	The measurements provided for decision making are reliable for supporting a process of ongoing improvement.
4 B–D	Well-established cost world measurements have been reliable in the past.	True	There is a reliable alternative to cost world measurements to guide future decisions.
5 B–D	The accounting system makes sense out of all the small items that need to be considered.	True	We have a data processing system that reliably, comprehensively, and inexpensively collects and processes comprehensive financial data and allows reporting in a flexible manner.
6 B–D	It is too expensive to operate a second comprehensive information system.	?	The bottom-line benefit of operating a second comprehensive system clearly exceeds its cost. The same data collection and processing system provides information for both external financial reporting and internal financial control consistent with the throughput world.
7 B–D	Budgetary control means reducing existing cost levels.	False	Cost reductions are neither rewarded nor specifically encouraged.
8 C–E	The data provided by the accounting system are generally too late for operational decision making.	?	Timely decision information is available.
9 C–E	The data provided by the accounting system is generally too aggregated for operational decision making.	?	Data provided by the accounting system for operational decision making clearly reveal the global incremental effects of decisions.
10 C–E	Most aspects of the business have not been precisely defined and quantified by accounting measurements.		
11 C–E	Data in the accounting system have been created to satisfy legal and external reporting requirements, but are inappropriate for planning and control.		

continued

Exhibit 4.9 Financial Managers' Dilemma: Assumptions and Injections
(continued)

12 C–E	Much of our employees' intuition is not captured by the accounting measurements.		
13 C–E	Accounting measurements are not intuitively reliable.		
14 D–E	All facets of the organization are measured by the accounting system.		
15 D–E	The cost world measurements are not consistent with our intuition.		
16 D–E	The cost world measurements do not guide us correctly.		
17 D–E	The cost behavior implicit in the cost world measurements is not realistic.		

With respect to the fifth assumption, from a control point of view the journal and ledger structure of a modern double-entry accounting system relying on a journal and ledge structure is rightfully highly regarded for the one function it performs really well—it reliably, comprehensively, and inexpensively collects, processes, and summarizes many small pieces of financial data into predefined reports.

In our discussion of cost control in a throughput world (see Chapter 3), we saw that budgeted costs are in control if they bear a desired relationship to revenues, whereas actual costs are in control if they do not exceed budget limitations. If we accept this reasoning, then the assumption that budgetary control means reducing existing cost levels is false. However, since declaring this assumption false required us to have a different understanding of the term *budgetary control*, we might want to look for an injection also. A policy that *cost reductions are neither rewarded nor specifically encouraged* was previously suggested as an injection for this purpose (see Exhibit 3.3). The reader is encouraged to consider the remainder of the potential injections.

Accounting, often called the *language of business*, forms the backbone of the formal communication system within a profit-oriented organization. The decisions and culture of an organization will be reflected in the way it accounts for its operations.[28] As the culture of an organization moves from a cost world to a throughput world orientation on the far side of the complexity divide, the financial manager will need to be proactively involved in rethinking and restructuring the financial reporting system. The financial manager plays a critically important role in this respect.

ESTABLISHING A BUDGETARY REVISION AND REPORTING PROCESS

Significant improvement can be achieved only by dealing with Archimedean constraints. At the same time, sometimes it is necessary to increase spending, either as an increase in operational expenses or as a capital expenditure, in order to elevate a constraint. The budget must be revised in a timely manner to take advantage of such desirable opportunities.

Constraints and Necessary Conditions

Some capital and operational expenditures may be proposed that, even though they do not have the promise of an Archimedean constraint, are required to satisfy a perceived *necessary condition* for the organization. Failure to satisfy some necessary conditions may lead to significantly increased costs without associated throughput effects (e.g., damages resulting from a lawsuit). In other cases, failure to satisfy necessary conditions may jeopardize the organization's operating strategy, as in the case of unmet environmental standards resulting in the complete shutdown of the organization. The physical operating environment, governmental action (laws and regulations), power groups (such as labor unions or special interest groups), market forces and competitive pressures, and management (through organizational policies)—all have the ability to impose necessary conditions.

A constraint is anything that prevents an organization from achieving better performance relative to its global goal of greater profitability. Necessary conditions certainly fit this definition of a constraint. Necessary conditions may be either satisfied or unsatisfied. A satisfied necessary condition is simply a special type of constraint that does not have associated *positive* throughput effects. Our planning techniques, tied to the organization's constraints, must include the constraints that appear as necessary conditions.

The profit effects of our actions are determined by the relationships between revenues and costs. At best, efforts targeted at cost reduction are likely to be choopchicks; at worst, they can have devastating side effects regarding the erosion of trust, creating unanticipated constraints by destroying protective capacity[29] and luring management into the easy thought that cost cutting can lead to continuing long-run profit improvement. Our planning techniques, then, should emphasize revenue enhancement as opposed to cost reduction. Sometimes, however, revenue enhancement also involves spending.

Expenditures made specifically for elevating identified constraints are likely to have short payback periods, implying high rates of return. Expenditures made for purposes other than elevating constraints or satisfying necessary conditions, even though they may be desirable from the point of view of individual members of the organization or customers, do not support the global goal of the organization. Therefore, as was suggested in Chapter 3, the planning techniques used by an organization should *justify any increases in operational expense and inventory/investment based on projected throughput effects and specification of the constraint being elevated or necessary condition being satisfied.*

Since neglecting control of future expenditures can easily derail a POOGI, we discuss how future cost control in the constraints accounting environment is obtained through the budgetary process. The decision process resulting in budget revisions is vitally important in controlling future expenditures in a constraints accounting environment.

POOGI Budget Committee

If a POOGI Bonus plan, as described in the first part of this chapter, is in effect, then all members of the organization will have a proprietary interest in the POOGI. Therefore, it is recommended that a POOGI Budget Committee having wide representation of the various personnel constituencies be established. The POOGI Budget Committee has two purposes: (1) to recommend budget increases to management when appropriate; (2) to allow committee members to serve as the primary validating communication contact between the OE budget and the employees.

When examining proposals to increase the budgeted expenditures, the committee should review and verify the following five items to ensure that the organization is following the steps of a POOGI.[30]

1. The proposal should be written and contain cash flow estimates of amount and timing.
2. Every proposal should address a specified active tactical or strategic constraint or a necessary condition.[31]
3. Conscious exploitation decisions have been made.
4. Appropriate subordination to the exploitation decisions takes place in the area requesting the budget increase. Obviously, appropriate subordination cannot occur if exploitation decisions have not been made and communicated.
5. Potential erosion of protective capacity has been considered in the proposal.

The purpose of the POOGI Budget Committee is neither to create the original budget nor to ensure that the budget is "balanced." Rather, its purpose is to ensure that operational decisions having new financial consequences are made in a manner that is consistent with the process of ongoing improvement. The POOGI Budget Committee is advisory to management and is part of a larger budgetary process. The committee recommendations are approved—or not—at the appropriate managerial level, and that approval becomes the actual authority for the financial management function to modify the budget. The financial management function may also be involved in preparing or reviewing the cash flow analyses for the proposals before the POOGI Budget Committee reviews them.

Somewhere in the organization it is necessary to assign responsibility for declaring current constraints. Since the first task of the POOGI Budget Committee is to see whether proposals address constraints, this committee is also a reasonable place to assign the tactical identification confirmation function. A department requesting a budget increase to elevate a constraint is making two very important claims—that it holds an Archimedean constraint and that it knows how to elevate it in a manner consistent with the strategic plan. This is where decoupling of operational expense from throughput becomes applicable. We do not make expenditures because the revenues are there; rather, we only increase expenditures with a specified bottom-line effect.

The communication purpose of the POOGI Budget Committee cannot be overemphasized. As stated, the purpose of the POOGI Bonus is to obtain congruence between global organization goals and individual employee goals. This congruence is realized in the following way:

- Individual employees are given an extraordinary reward, which recognizes their participation as an integral part of the organization, when measurable improvement is made in movement toward the goal of the organization's owners.

- The extraordinary reward is large enough to attract and maintain the employees' attention.

- The amount of extraordinary reward is significantly influenced in a positive way by elevating Archimedean constraints and in a negative way by failing to control future expenditures.

Employees participating in the POOGI Bonus plan are vitally interested in seeing the effects of their subordination efforts reflected in their bonuses. They are also very interested in the negative effect of increased expenditures in reducing the amount of the bonus. By having a broad personnel base represented on the POOGI Budget Committee, information about the identity of current tactical and strategic constraints, actions being taken to address (exploit, subordinate, and elevate) the constraints, and credible explanation of cost increases can be transmitted to the remainder of the workforce. All employees should have real representation on, and access to, the committee. In an organization that has responded to the need for goal congruence, the POOGI Budget Committee becomes the tangible evidence of empowerment.

Empowerment Conflict

Employee empowerment may create conflicts similar to those illustrated by the evaporating cloud shown in Exhibit 4.10. The objective is to create and, once created, maintain a process of ongoing improvement (POOGI).

In order to create and maintain a POOGI, employees must see the empowerment as genuine. All employees need to feel that their efforts are valued. If the announced empowerment is just a sham, employees will feel a betrayal of trust rather than fair treatment. Remember: motivation comes from the perception of fair treatment and an entrepreneurial spirit associated with the relative amount of the bonus rather than from the absolute monetary amount of the bonus.

Employees at all organizational levels look for signs that goal congruence exists among the four employee groups.[32] Since employees want to believe that the next management level is taking their input seriously, the POOGI Bonus Committee's recommendations must be respected. After all, empowerment implies authority. Overriding the committee decision would indicate that the empowerment is a sham. Some employees are closer to the working situation, and their intuition about real capacity usage is often correct. They have the best feel for shopfloor operations.

In order to maintain a POOGI, however, management's authority must be preserved. Things will tend to fall apart without a clear chain of command. Not all employees want decision-making authority, but there is a need to assign responsibilities. A successful organization must maintain its focus. There simply comes a time when it is necessary to proclaim that the "buck stops here."

In order to preserve management's authority, managers must often override the POOGI Budget Committee. Many assumptions underlie this relationship. Managers want to demonstrate that they are in charge. Some

Exhibit 4.10   Empowerment Cloud

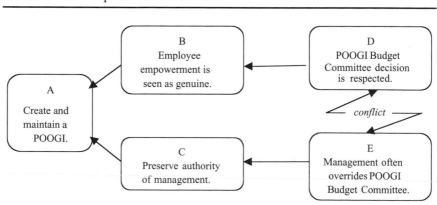

managers may have individual goals that are not congruent with the global goal of greater bottom-line profitability. For example, recognizing the typical relationship that base pay increases with the number of people supervised, some managers might be interested in empire building. Managers who have not yet made the paradigm shift to the throughput world are likely to believe that existing expenditure levels must be rigorously controlled through cost reduction efforts or full cost recovery through each sale. It may be believed that management has better intuition than the POOGI Budget Committee, but note that the Committee will include both line and financial management representation also. Finally, not all managers believe in empowering other employees, and some may think that the POOGI Budget Committee will not act responsibly.

Clearly, the potential for conflict exists. On one hand, management wants to respect the POOGI Budget Committee's decisions, but on the other hand, management often wants to override the Committee's recommendations. The assumptions underlying the arrows must be examined, and one of the assumptions invalidated when this situation arises.

Reporting Budget Revisions

The budget is the physical centerpiece of a budgetary process for planning and control. It is a detailed, written plan showing the firm's plans for the period covered and the probable effects this plan will have on the firm.[33] We use the term *budget* in a general sense, referring collectively to an annual profit plan, projected (or pro forma) cash flow statement, operating budget, or other similar document. However, readers should fit the discussion into their specific environments. In relatively simple organizations, the budget, as we describe it, is probably the primary planning and control document. However, if the focus of the constraint management implementation is a single profit center of a more complex organization, then the budget as described herein will be internal to the profit center and some sort of interfacing document with the larger organization will be necessary. In this latter case the terminology *corporate requirements* may be substituted where we refer to generally accepted accounting principles (GAAP).

The budget revision process within constraints accounting is different from the more familiar annual budgeting cycle. In the conventional annual cycle, the setting is one of waiting for a window of time to come around before requests for budget increases may be made. Major changes to the budget and operating plans are made only once a year. The managerial objective, vis-à-vis the conventional budget, is to have the year end with actual earnings as close as possible to initial expectations.

The operating environment of constraint management, however, exhibits a sense of urgency. In the constraint management environment new expenditures are authorized, and the budget is revised, as quickly as possible when opportunities to elevate Archimedean constraints are identified. Since elevation of an Archimedean constraint is always accompanied by a substantial increase in bottom-line profits, the anticipated earnings change significantly as often as constraints are elevated. The changing earnings expectations can make it difficult for people reviewing the actual earnings reports to interpret whether the operating performance is good. Therefore, it is necessary to have a reporting model that will sort out where the actual operations stand vis-à-vis the budget on any given day.

Prospective Budget

A hierarchy for analyzing the continually changing perspective of prospective (future expected) earnings during the year is provided in Exhibit 4.11.

Exhibit 4.11   Hierarchy for Prospective Earnings Analysis

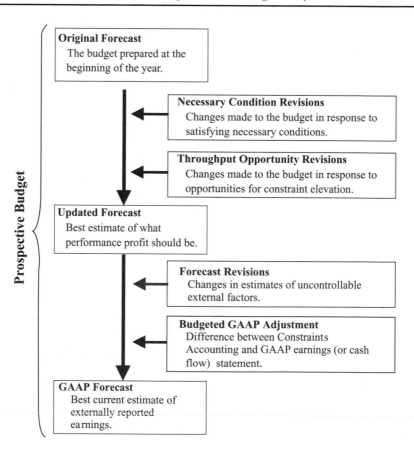

Original Forecast
The budget prepared at the beginning of the year.

Necessary Condition Revisions
Changes made to the budget in response to satisfying necessary conditions.

Throughput Opportunity Revisions
Changes made to the budget in response to opportunities for constraint elevation.

Updated Forecast
Best estimate of what performance profit should be.

Forecast Revisions
Changes in estimates of uncontrollable external factors.

Budgeted GAAP Adjustment
Difference between Constraints Accounting and GAAP earnings (or cash flow) statement.

GAAP Forecast
Best current estimate of externally reported earnings.

Prospective Budget

Most organizations prepare an operating budget on an annual basis. When this operating budget has been approved at the appropriate level (president, chief executive officer, board of directors), it serves as specific instructions to middle-level managers and gives spending authorization for those items approved in the budget. The budget also sets the initial expectations for the operating performance for the year. This is the best estimate of what will happen during the year and its effect on the bottom line of the organization. This will also be the basis for providing forward-looking information to security analysts and other interested external parties. This budget is termed the *original forecast* in Exhibit 4.11.

As the year progresses, the actual operations will turn out to be different from the budgeted operations.[34] Exhibit 4.11 highlights four general types of variation that may occur during the year.

First are the *necessary condition revisions.* These revisions are made to the budget in order to accommodate newly identified necessary conditions. Since the organization has already adapted to its necessary conditions,[35] revisions of this type should occur relatively infrequently and probably indicate a fundamental change in the operating environment of the organization. Thus, the identification of an emerging necessary condition should also be accompanied by managerial appraisal of the potential consequences of the new necessary condition.

Second are the *throughput opportunity revisions*—the changes made to the operating budget in response to opportunities for constraint elevation. Each of these budget revisions represents a specific improvement opportunity. That is, each is expected to result in an identifiable increase in profitability for the organization. Throughput opportunity revisions are not the only actions taken for improvement in the organization, just those that require additional funds. Many improvements can routinely be made that do not require additional funds. Such routine improvements take place throughout the organization within the existing budget limitations. They do not require additional funds and will appear as part of the operating results for the period.

When the original forecast has been adjusted for the necessary condition and throughput opportunity revisions, the result is an *updated forecast.* The updated forecast is the best current estimate of what the performance profit should be for the budget or **scheduling period.** The updated forecast is the amount shown in the budget column of the Constraints Accounting Earnings Statement illustrated in Exhibit 3.6 and reproduced here as Exhibit 4.12.

The updated forecast is the base point for internal reference. The expenditure portion of the updated forecast provides the responsibility budget to which the organization's managers adhere. For internal purposes, differences between the updated forecast and actual operations are accounted for as variances and explained in the *retrospective budget* (discussed below).

Exhibit 4.12   Earnings Statement in a Constraints Accounting Format

				Favorable /
Constraints Accounting Earnings Statement For Month ended November 30, 20X2				
	Actual	Budge t	Variance	Unfavorable
Throughput Contribution (T) Section:				
Constraints:				
Internal:				
Welder	$ 716,380	$ 632,700	$ 83,680	F Note A
Labor Class D	373,869	560,764	186,895	U Note B
External:				
Market	239,200	239,200	0	Note C
Total Throughput Contribution	$1,329,449	$1,432,664	$103,215	U Note D
Operational Expense (OE) Section:				
Greater of actual or budgeted OE	648,000	648,000		Note E
Performance Profit	$ 681,449			Note F

In some cases, the organization may provide forward-looking information to external parties. Third, *forecast revisions* may be made for some budget items. These revisions represent changes in expectations due to changes in the external macroeconomic environment within which the organization operates. Fourth, the constraints accounting principles used in calculating the performance profit are somewhat at variance with GAAP. Therefore, it will be necessary to adjust the earnings by the reconciling amount when providing forward-looking estimates for external parties such as security analysts. The reconciled earnings are the *GAAP Forecast,* the best estimate of forward-looking externally reported earnings.

Retrospective Budget

The prospective budget relates to *expectations* only and does not tell us about what actually happened. To see how actual operations compared to the expectations, a retrospective budget is needed. A retrospective hierarchy for earnings analysis is portrayed in Exhibit 4.13.

The retrospective analysis starts with the updated forecast shown in the prospective analysis of Exhibit 4.11. This is the original expectation adjusted for responses to newly emerging necessary conditions and new throughput opportunities. The updated forecast is the best estimate of what the performance profit should be and is adjusted for *recurring operating variances*. Recurring operating variances appear in the variance column of Exhibit 4.12.

The recurring operating variances differ from variances reported in traditional accounting systems in two ways. First, since changes in antici-

Exhibit 4.13   Hierarchy for Retrospective Earnings Analysis

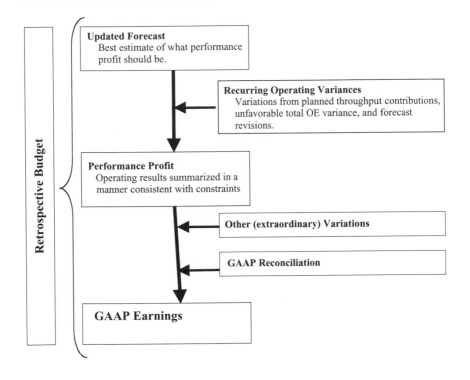

pated costs have already been incorporated into the updated forecast, no variable expense adjustment is made as is done when using a conventional flexible budget. The updated forecast replaces the flexible budget in legacy budgeting systems. Second, if operational expenses are less than the updated forecast, then we do not want to emphasize cost performance and no variance is reported. In this case, any variance would be favorable and would appear as a reconciling item in the reconciliation to the GAAP statement. Finally, since the retrospective budget does not formally include the forecast revisions, they are also included in recurring operating variances. The result of adjusting the updated forecast for the recurring operating variances is the *performance profit*. This is the same performance profit as shown in Exhibit 4.12.

Exhibit 4.11 then shows an adjustment for *other (extraordinary) variations*. This is just a place to put anything that has not been accounted for previously. Note that items included here bypass the performance profit used for calculating the POOGI bonus. Nonoperations-related investment income is an example of an item that might be classified as an *other variation*. If a POOGI Bonus plan is in effect, then the bonus amount added to the POOGI Bonus pool are also included in this other category. Expenditures that bypass the POOGI Budget Committee (discussed in footnote 31) would appropriately be included in this *other variations* category.

Finally, including the reconciling items to adjust the performance profit to a GAAP basis brings the retrospective earnings analysis to the *GAAP earnings.*

Properly implemented, the budget revision and reporting processes ensure that opportunities to elevate Archimedean constraints are swiftly implemented while maintaining visibility into the process of ongoing improvement and rigorously controlling increases in future expenditures. The budget revision process in a constraint management setting is a key to locking in a process of ongoing improvement.

SUMMARY

The **owners** of the organization must establish the global goal for the organization, and when the goal is clearly communicated automatic **goal congruence** of the organization with the ownership group takes place. However it takes people to execute the plan in accordance with their philosophy. It is therefore paramount to align the individual goals of each group and individuals, regardless of their diversity within the organization, with a single global goal, established by the owners. Since all people should be treated ethically and fairly, a POOGI Bonus is proposed, based on the monetary value of the amount of bottom-line improvement, to act as a dynamic motivator for driving the pursuit of the global goal through a process of ongoing improvement.

The budget is the physical, detailed, written plan showing the organization's plans for the period covered and the probable effects it will have on the organization. The budget is the centerpiece of a budgetary process for planning and control. The financial manager will be proactively involved in rethinking and restructuring the financial reporting system. And a key to locking in a process of ongoing improvement is establishing a Budgetary Revision and Reporting Process in a constraint management setting.

NOTES

[1] "A man may well bring a horse to the water, But he cannot make him drinke without he will." John Heywood as quoted in *Bartlett's Familiar Quotations* (Little, Brown and Company, 1937).
[2] Discussion within theory of constraints circles suggests that there are three interrelated elements (profitability, employee satisfaction, and customer satisfaction), any one of which may be made the goal and the other two necessary conditions. The hypothesis is that the result will be the same in any case. We specifically reject that view. The organizational goal is to be open-ended; that is,

we always want more of it. Necessary conditions are satisfied at some specified level; we want enough of them. More than enough of a necessary condition is not necessarily a bad thing, but given the choice between movement toward the goal and extra amounts of a necessary condition, movement toward the goal is strongly preferred. See Goldratt Satellite Program (GSP) Tape 8, *Strategy.*

[3] Owners, top management, middle management, first-line supervision, and labor.

[4] Goldratt has observed, "If a company has even one share traded on Wall Street, the goal has been loudly and clearly stated. . . . to make more money now as well as in the future." See Eliyahu M. Goldratt, *The Haystack Syndrome: Sifting Information out of the Data Ocean* (North River Press, 1990), p. 12.

[5] See, for example, Chapter 3, *More than Profits,* in James C. Collins and Jerry I Porras, *Built to Last: Successful Habits of Visionary Companies* (HarperBusiness, 1994).

[6] Exempt or nonexempt is from the Fair Labor Standards Act (FLSA) in the United States. Information on the FLSA is available at http://www.paychex.com/library/exempt.html#FLSA.

[7] For example, according to a posting on the CMSIG Internet discussion list, Goldratt has stated that "Out of nine successful implementations only about one has spread to other sections or functions and about five no longer exist." Mike Holland, quoting *POOGI Forum Letter # 6,* January 11, 2001.

[8] *A reason for people to subordinate appropriately* is a *net concept* and includes not having a preponderance of reasons not to subordinate appropriately. The net reason may be addressed in two ways: (1) provide greater reason for people to subordinate properly, and/or (2) reduce the reasons for people not to subordinate properly.

[9] At the time of this writing, a succinct summary of motivational literature is available at http://www.accel-team.com, a site dedicated to improving organizational productivity through a team-building approach.

[10] The very highest level of management of the profit center selects the bonus percentage.

[11] A desirable (and reasonable) amount for a POOGI Bonus plan might be in the range of 50 to 100% of base pay over a year. *Management must not succumb to the temptation to reduce the percentage amount of the bonus if the bonus should happen to exceed expectations.* Just as there is no particular objective amount for the POOGI Bonus to reach, there is no maximum limit that can be paid. Each time a substantial bonus is paid, a substantial amount more than was previously earned is also left with the owners.

[12] For example, a comparison period might be the same fiscal month in the previous year, a rolling (monthly) annual amount, or a year-to-date amount.

[13] We call this a POOGI Bonus Orientation Course. Such a course requires about 16 hours (spread out) at a minimum. The following topics would be covered: essential constraint management terminology, global goal and constraints, an overview of how all parts of the organization are affected by the constraint management innovation, specific details of the expected impact on the individual's particular area of operations, revised work rules, empowerment limits, communicating within the TOC thinking process framework, expectations, damage to the organization resulting from the betrayal of trust, sources of company-sponsored education, independent resources for individual growth, and, of course, the mechanics of how the POOGI Bonus works.

[14] There are many options for paying the POOGI Bonus. One-quarter of the bonus pool could be paid quarterly. All of the bonus pool might be paid when payments are made. Each option has advantages and disadvantages. Our personal preference is for the bonus to be paid regularly and reliably. By paying the bonus

out at the rate of one-twelfth each month, the month-to-month fluctuations in the amount of bonus paid will tend to be damped. This will also allow the recipients to plan their personal expenditures. Others prefer to have the bonus paid quarterly in order to make a greater impression. The payment of one-twelfth each month also protects against premature payments.

[15] A newly formed organization can use an annual profit plan (budget) presented on a constraints accounting basis for the comparison period.

[16] Even individual consultants might be included in this group if they have completed an appropriate POOGI Bonus Orientation Course.

[17] For the accountants, who must do the bookkeeping for the bonus, sample journal entries are illustrated in the Appendix.

[18] The division of the POOGI Bonus pool by the wage and salary base ($1,892,000 / $4,000,000) might also be shown. While such a disclosure has no real information content, it may give certain recipients of the statement a comfortable feeling as to the source of the percentage quoted.

[19] To check that the bonus is being paid at 47.3% of the base wages and salaries, we may multiply the payout by 12 months and divide by the individual's wage or salary base. In this case, $1,207.10 \times 12 / $30,624 = 0.473$ or 47.3%.

[20] The evaporating cloud is one of the TOC thinking process structures. It describes a conflict in terms of perceived necessary conditions for obtaining the objective of the cloud in box A. In the case of each straight arrow, the cloud may be read as, "In order to have (the head of the arrow), (I, we, or someone) must have (the tail of the arrow)." For example, the relationship between A and B may be read as, "In order to assist operational management to manage well, financial managers must provide information appropriate for exercise of sound budgetary control." The relationship between the D and E boxes is one of conflict and may be read as, "(the D box) is in conflict with (the E box)."

[21] See for example, Eric Noreen, Debra Smith, and James Mackey, *The Theory of Constraints and Its Implications for Management Accounting* (North River Press, 1995). Sponsored by the Institute of Management Accountants (IMA) and Price Waterhouse, pp. 70–71.

[22] An example appears in Chapter 33 of Eliyahu M. Goldratt and Jeff Cox, *The Goal: A Process of Ongoing Improvement,* 2nd rev. ed. (North River Press, 1992, pp. 272–273), where the plant manager and the plant controller conspire to cook the books in order to present a more accurate picture of operations.

[23] Breaking any linkage in the diagram means that at least one of the apparently conflicting entities (D and E) is not actually required in order to have the objective. Breaking a linkage is referred to as *evaporating the cloud.*

[24] *Full cost* means that all of the organization costs are associated with individual units of product.

[25] Here the reader is encouraged to surface additional assumptions.

[26] The *something new* is known as an injection in TOC terminology—something that does not exist in the environment at the present time, but that is to be injected into the environment in the future. The thing injected could be a physical resource, but it also could be a policy change or even knowledge resulting in a changed perception of the environment.

[27] The American Institute of Certified Public Accountants now recommends a minimum of 150 hours (five years) of college work as preparation for a professional accountant. Cost accounting techniques have been developed to take full advantage of the power of modern computers, running costs through multiple allocations using hundreds of allocation bases (cost drivers) and resulting in a product-cost assignment that is then proclaimed to be the *truth.* Probably nowhere has the accounting report become more mystical than the U.S.

tax form 1040 on which the income tax is labeled as "Add lines 40 and 41." As this page is being written (January 14, 2002), the (U. S.) Financial Accounting Standards Board—citing standards overload and concerns about the quantity, complexity, and lack of retrievability—has announced simplification projects for their future standards.

[28] For example, as this is being written, the bankruptcy of Enron Corporation dominates the financial—and much of the general—press. It appears that there was a failure to communicate the existence of some $27 billion in liabilities. Although it is not clear at this point that the Enron Corporation's reporting was in conflict with the applicable accounting rules, it does appear that the accounting procedures followed the culture of the organization and that the management initiatives were structured to take advantage of the accounting procedures.

[29] All necessary functions not containing an active constraint must have some amount of capacity available to accommodate statistical fluctuations in operations. Even an internal physical constraint must have enough protective capacity to accommodate its own statistical fluctuations.

[30] A form for assembling this information is illustrated in Chapter 10.

[31] Management may sometimes want to increase expenditures beyond the budgeted amount, but may not want to submit or justify the proposal to the POOGI Bonus Committee. We would not want to have the POOGI Budget Committee trump management's judgment and prerogative. After all, making such decisions is a primary management function. Therefore, a secondary channel should be established to accommodate these **out of POOGI expenditures.** Attributes of this secondary channel should include two provisions: (1) increased expenditures for I or OE are not included in performance profit, and (2) revenues are included in performance profit unless clearly directly associated with the specific expenditure.

[32] Top management, middle management, first-line supervision, and labor.

[33] Wilber C. Haseman, *Management Uses of Accounting* (Allyn and Bacon, 1963), p. 673.

[34] Some managers pride themselves on the ability to have operations actually occur exactly as estimated or budgeted over extended periods. This probably indicates a great deal of excess capacity throughout the organization.

[35] If the organization is viable, it must have adapted to its necessary conditions. That is the meaning of necessary condition.

5

Constraints Accounting Terminology and Technique

BASIC FINANCIAL CONTROL METRICS

The preceding chapters have concentrated on the organization-wide application of constraint management using constraints accounting as a catalyst to create a process of ongoing improvement. If an organization elects to implement constraints accounting for internal reporting, or uses constraints accounting concepts in its planning and control decision processes, then the members of the organization will face the novelty of the constraints accounting terminology and a wealth of alternative meanings. To the extent that constraint management and its associated accounting represent a paradigm shift, they lead into new and unexplored domains. We must recognize that our existing language does not contain words with commonly understood definitions suitable for the constraint management paradigm.

Although the rules of these new domains are relatively few, they are different from those for which our education, previous training, experience, and language have prepared us. Therefore, we should approach constraints accounting measurements with diligence, examining each element to ensure that we know what it means in the constraint management context and in what ways it differs from more traditional measurements. Therefore, we will review the constraints accounting global measurements of throughput, inventory/investment, and operational expense in detail. Then we will explore a proposal for allocating inventory/investment (I) to operational expense (OE) when calculating performance profit. Finally, we will explore the ways in which operating decisions are affected as we use the global T, I, and OE measurements within a constraints accounting framework to guide decision making as our analysis changes from the cost world to the throughput world.

What Is Throughput?

In addition to the common meaning as the physical amount passing through a system, the term *throughput* is used as a technical term in at least nine different ways within the constraint management community:

1. As in the conceptual expression, *throughput world.*
2. The rate at which a system generates money through sales.
3. The rate at which money is generated by the sale of specific units or services.
4. The cash generated by a specific sale.
5. The net cash flow.
6. The net profit.
7. The return on investment (ROI).
8. The objective of an organization.
9. The measurement unit for the purpose of an organization.

First is *throughput* in the role of the expression, *throughput world,* as contrasted with the *cost world* in Chapter 2. In the throughput world, *throughput*'s emphasis is on the revenue portion of the rote throughput calculation. It is only through this revenue channel that order-of-magnitude[1] improvement can be achieved.[2] Here the use of *throughput* is more as a concept than as an actual metric. Throughput is what we want to emphasize.

The second through fourth measurements above are the numerical sense in which the term *throughput* (T) is used in constraints accounting. These three measurements are similar in that each represents the difference between revenue and variable expense. The differences are that (2) relates to a period of time, such as a month or a year, (3) relates to a costing object other than a time period, such as a product line or a customer, and (4) is expressed on a per unit or order basis.[3] All three variations of throughput (T) are just the financial manager's old friend *contribution margin*: sales revenue less the variable expenses associated with the sales revenue.

By the mid-1990s, many managers of not-for-profit organizations (NFPO) had read *The Goal: A Process of Ongoing Improvement* and wanted to use the constraint management principles in their organizations. A frequent initial action by these managers was to redefine the T, I, and OE metrics to fit the specific characteristics of their unique organizations. Goldratt addressed the not-for-profit issue in 1995, observing that throughput is not always measured best in financial terms.[4] He suggested that the best measure of *throughput* is one that tells the organization if it is making progress toward its stated purpose. This was a use of the term in its conceptual sense, but conferred a status of equality between the purpose of an organization and throughput.

A Role for "Conventional" T, I, and OE in NFPOs

Even though profit per se is not a purpose of not-for-profit organizations (NFPOs), a sufficient—perhaps even increasing—cash flow is generally a necessary condition for the continued existence of these organizations. Cash flows also frequently determine what services the NFPO can offer. The NFPO is just as susceptible to being misled by traditional absorption cost accounting rules, training, and measurements as the profit-oriented organization is when it evaluates some of their programs based on an economic analysis. The conventional T, I, and OE—with T being the contribution factor—metrics can be used for these analyses much as they are used in a profit-oriented organization. The difference is that, for the NFPO, the impact on breakeven—rather than improvement relative to the purpose—is being measured. That is, the NFPO is using the T, I, and OE metrics to check the attainment of a necessary condition rather than to measure progress toward the organizational purpose.

In redefining throughput in a manner that would allow the throughput world concept and terminology to be applied to not-for-profit organizations, multiple meanings of throughput have evolved. These include net cash flow (5 above), the objective of an organization (8 above), and the measurement unit for the purpose of an organization (9 above).

Proliferation of Meanings

When the new definition of throughput provided by Goldratt for NFPOs was applied to profit-oriented organizations, net cash flow (5), net profit (6), and return on investment (7) were added to the list of meanings of throughput for profit-oriented organizations.

Net operating cash flow and net profit (earnings) are similar concepts when viewed from an accounting perspective; both are bottom-line earnings measurements. The difference is that conventional (GAAP) net profit is typically calculated using the *accrual basis* of accounting, while *net operating cash flow* is the profit calculated using the *cash basis* of accounting. Both earnings and cash flows are presented as part of the periodic GAAP financial statements.

Although ROI, as calculated in a discounted cash flow analysis, is useful for evaluating future investments, the use of ROI as a bottom-line measurement generated by the accounting system is dubious because the investment base is not reliable. Capital expenditure analysis is discussed in Chapter 10.

The purpose of a profit-oriented organization is not the throughput metric, however, and the throughput in itself does not measure the attainment of the organizational purpose. All three constraints accounting measurements (T, I, and OE) must be considered in order to assess an impact on profitability.

With so many different meanings for the term *throughput,* some authors have introduced their own terminology in an effort to clarify the situation. Two alternative expressions for throughput that have garnered substantial support in the literature are **throughput contribution**[5] and **TOC throughput value added (TVA).**[6] In the remainder of this book we will use the terms *throughput* or *throughput contribution* (T or t) to refer to the difference between revenues and the truly variable expenses associated directly with the revenues. *Throughput* may be associated with any desired period or cost object.

Despite their apparent simplicity, interpretation of the T, I, and OE measurements in various environments (manufacturing, service, not-for-profit, etc.) has brought into focus a difficulty with the T, I, and OE metrics. When we push them to their limits as accounting measurements, they do not form a consistent set. The definitional (and accounting) problem lies in the matching of costs and revenues or, in constraints accounting terminology, operational expenses, and inventory with throughput. This matching process is inherently arbitrary. Operational expenses are matched in the current period (Net Profit = T − OE). Inventory/investment is assigned to operational expense a little at a time over a number of periods.[7] Ultimately, all inventory/investment will be reclassified as operational expense and will be matched with throughput.

Revenue

The revenue side of the T calculation is straightforward but with a cash flow orientation. Goldratt and Fox observe that throughput "must be interpreted as money entering from outside the system being measured . . . and cannot possibly be associated with a reallocation of money within the system."[8] That is, there are no profits until firm sales have been made—no money; no sale. This means that pseudo (or nominal) profit centers, as mentioned in Chapter 1, are not used with constraints accounting.

Two common situations may require a different treatment for sales revenue recognition using constraints accounting. First is the circumstance in which an organization sells a product with a "money back" guarantee of which many customers take advantage. Second is a manufacturer that "sells" its product to dealers but carries the financing itself with the product as collateral. These manufacturers may be compelled to offer incentives such as price concessions, to either the dealers or the final customer, in order to effect the ultimate sale of the products. Each case calls for the deferral of revenue recognition until a firm final sale to a consumer is made at a firm price.[9] Of course, money generated by the system could come from sources other than sales (e.g., interest).[10]

Some organizations deduct sales commissions from gross sales in the calculation of the revenue. This is a questionable practice for two reasons. First, it really doesn't matter whether the sales commissions are treated as negative revenue amounts or as expenses—the effect on T is the same in either case. The desire to treat the variable expenses differently for selling expenses as opposed to manufacturing expenses probably harks back to a legacy financial management control system in which cost centers played an important role. Second, a sales commission that would be appropriate for inclusion in T encourages the sales force to generate greater sales dollars by selling more. In our discussion of tactical exploitation, we will see that the product mix may have a greater impact on the bottom line than previously believed. Sales commissions and goal congruence are discussed under the heading of tactical subordination in sales.

Costs

All costs, other than those truly variable costs assigned as a part of throughput, are classified as either OE or I. The basis for this classification and the subsequent reclassification of I as OE depend on the purpose for which the cost is being classified.

The three types of costs included in the global measurements are:

1. Truly variable expenses.
2. Operational expenses (OE)—regularly recurring expenses for providing short-term capacities and applying those capacities of the organization in generating throughput. **Short-term capacity** is capacity, which if not used during the current fiscal period, must be purchased anew to be used in a future period (e.g., personnel services or rent on a month-to-month lease).[11]
3. Inventory/investment (I)—significant costs incurred on a sporadic basis that provide elements of **long-term capacity**. Capacity is simply the ability to do or create something. *Long-term capacity* is expected to benefit a number of fiscal periods (equipment that we purchase today and can use in future years as well as in the current period).

Truly Variable Expense

The truly variable expenses are incurred as a direct result of generating revenue and vary directly and proportionately with sales volume; these costs, if significant, are included as a part of the throughput (T) calculation. Truly variable expenses would not be incurred in the absence of the specific sales; hence, these may also be called *throughput expenses*. Although truly variable expenses are sometimes defined as purchased materials cost, the variable expense concept is somewhat broader.[12] In addition to raw materials, deductions include all variable amounts that are paid to external entities. Obvious examples of truly variable expenses, beyond raw materials, are purchased parts and royalties.

Constraints accounting uses the method of **account classification** to categorize expenses as variable or not variable.[13] The appropriate constraints accounting model for financial analysis of routine tactical decisions starts with materials as the only obvious variable expense. Other costs would be considered to be variable, or incremental, only after extremely careful analysis identifying quite specifically (e.g., people by name rather than as statistics) the costs that are expected to change.[14] The constraints accounting rule is to classify costs as fixed *when in doubt*.

Other Views of Variable Expense

The question of whether a cost is variable has to do with how the cost increases or decreases in response to volume changes. This response, in turn, is a function of a combination of structural factors (e.g., the unit used for measuring activity and the amount of time allowed for adjusting costs to a new activity level) and behavioral factors (such as decisions made by management and the direction of change in the activity level).

The variable expense concept has become somewhat confused in both practice and in the literature. Thus, one article might state that an organization that includes only variable material, labor, and variable overhead "would be using a pure variable cost construction," while four paragraphs later noting that the direct labor component of manufacturing costs has become "less significant, and what exists is fixed."[15] The "pure variable cost construction" is an example of the direct costing method discussed in Chapter 3. Like constraints accounting, the accounting implementation of direct costing typically relies on the method of account classification for separating costs into fixed and variable categories. The schemes used for assigning individual accounts to a fixed or variable category traditionally with direct costing have classified costs as variable *when in doubt*.[16]

Many managers believe that product costs, when calculated using the absorption-costing technique, provide an estimate of the long-run variability of costs. They find the absorption product-cost model particularly useful with respect to pricing decisions. The absorption-costing valuation of product costs is also required for external reporting in accordance with GAAP and often for tax computations. If we abandon the absorption-costing model for pricing, it will be necessary to replace it with something else. The pricing problem is discussed in detail in Chapter 6.

The traditional output-volume absorption-costing model is now challenged as inappropriate for strategic analyses because it considers only the manufacturing cost of a product and relates the costs to output volumes rather than the activities that cause the costs' existence. Transaction, or activity-based costing (ABC), systems[17] have been suggested as an alternative to the traditional model for strategic cost analyses.[18] The TOC perceives the detailed nature of activity-based costing and activity-based management as being potentially devastating choopchicks, having the ability to derail a process of ongoing improvement. These activity-based systems fail to consider the impact of constraints and divert attention from core causes. Instead of focusing on the details of individual activities, constraint management emphasizes the holistic view through its emphasis on Archimedean constraints.

Operational Expense

Operational expense (OE) was originally defined as all the money the system spends on turning inventory/investment into throughput. OE comprises those costs that are not deducted from revenues in the calculation of T (e.g., materials, royalties, and, perhaps, sales commissions) or categorized as a part of I.[19]

   Local operating expense draws distinctions among responsibility centers for decision purposes. For control, it is still necessary to trace expenditures to their point of incurrence responsibility. Budgeted OE should be broken down to the level of the responsible manager. Control reports showing current actual and projected spending should be given to the individual managers. No allocations of cost, no matter how seductive, should be included in this category.

Inventory/Investment

Inventory/investment (I) has been defined as all the money the system invests in purchasing things the system intends to sell. As originally described, the symbol I, for inventory, included all of the organization's assets. As the application of the TOC has been expanded into the service and not-for-profit sectors, the definition of I has become somewhat confused in practice. As with throughput, it appears that the term *inventory/investment* is now used in several ways within the TOC community:

- *Total assets,* the traditional TOC accounting definition.[20]
- *Capital,* the "owner's current value of the investment in the organization to keep it going."[21]
- *Incremental inventory,* a change in cash investment that is made. This may result from a capital expenditure or a change in work-in-process and other current position levels.

- A notion of *what's in the pipe*, which represents the work (including finished goods) that is currently being done to create throughput.[22] This may or may not have a cost measurement associated with it.

- *Raw materials cost* (or *truly variable* production cost[23]), which is the monetary valuation assigned to stocks of raw materials and product inventories.

The term *inventory/investment (I)* refers collectively to these possible meanings.

From the traditional throughput accounting point of view, I includes all the assets of the organization. Resources in progress and finished goods inventories are valued as materials (and any other truly variable manufacturing) cost only—that is, no "value added" costs are recognized as part of I.[24] The objective here is to eliminate the generation, or smoothing, of apparent profits through a cost allocation process. Note that this is just another instance of the traditional direct costing versus absorption-costing controversy that has existed in the accounting literature since the 1930s. Nevertheless, it is still an important point for organizations when first implementing the flow concepts of constraint management. When first implementing constraint management techniques such as drum-buffer-rope scheduling, work-in-process and finished goods inventory levels are frequently reduced significantly in a short period. Managers should be aware that the income reported under GAAP might fluctuate unfavorably for a short time as inventory is drained from the system.[25]

Nature of Investment

What expenditures should be treated as investments and charged to I when the paradigm changes from throughput accounting to constraints accounting?

Both traditional GAAP and throughput accounting **capitalize** the cost of tangible long-term assets such as land, property, plant, and equipment. The costs of internally developed intangibles typically are expensed in the period incurred. Intangibles include items such as patents, research and development, training, computer software, and goodwill acquired in a business combination. A portion of capitalized cost (except for land and goodwill) is periodically transferred to expense through depreciation or amortization.[26]

An investment is an expenditure that is made in the expectation of identifiable future benefits—the *return on investment.* A pattern of future increase in net profit provides the future benefits for a profit-seeking organization. For constraints accounting purposes, the tangibility of the investment is not significant; but the ability to specify the expected future improvement, at least up to the projected payback point, is significant. For example, consider an expenditure of $200,000 made to pave and illuminate an employee parking lot. This may be good for general morale, but it is not tied to specific future increases in T or decreases in OE. Such an expenditure, though properly capitalized under GAAP, would be treated as OE in the constraints accounting model. However, an expenditure of $200,000 for in-house training on the theory of constraints may be made with the specific expectation that resultant profit increases will more than recover the $200,000 expenditure in months 3 through 6. This latter expenditure, though appropriately expensed immediately under GAAP, might be capitalized in the constraints accounting model and $50,000 charged to OE in each of months 3, 4, 5, and 6.

It is necessary to capitalize only material (in the accounting or legal sense of *substantial*) amounts. For the constraints accounting purpose of identifying an improvement pattern, an investment, or group of investments, is material if the failure to capitalize the investment will change the reported profit pattern to the extent that it no longer reflected the reality of improvement. Therefore, an organization should have a threshold for capitalization. The appropriate threshold is situationally specific and dependent on the current level of net profit. The existence of a POOGI Bonus plan, such as discussed in Chapter 4, may also influence the determination of **materiality.**

Length of Reporting Period

The basic reporting period for financial (external) accounting is one year. GAAP distinguishes between current assets, which are expected to be used within a year, and long-term assets, which have been capitalized. Although interim reports may be prepared, the primary concern is the proper matching of revenues and expenses for the annual period. Neither throughput accounting nor constraints accounting distinguishes between current and noncurrent assets.

Internal management reports are typically prepared based on a monthly reporting period. An organization that has successfully established a pattern of ongoing improvement should find that its environment changes quite rapidly; on the other hand, inertia could also set in very quickly. Hence, to fulfill its purpose, the accounting system must also report quite rapidly.

Cost Flow Assumption

An allocation question regarding the materials and product inventory cost flow assumption has not been addressed meaningfully within the constraint management literature and remains an open question.[27] Eli Schragenheim suggests taking advantage of the simplicity of a moving average value of materials.[28] He presents this as a compromise between meeting the requirements of historically based cost accounting (GAAP) and economic reality suggestive of a replacement cost metric.

After removing value added elements (direct labor and manufacturing overhead) from product valuation and generally reducing product and production lead times as well as product inventory levels, this issue is probably not very important. Nevertheless, TOC is not a "zero inventory" philosophy of production management. If an organization requires significant raw materials inventories and is faced with an economic environment of high inflation, for example, the cost flow assumption might become important for income reporting.

The financial reporting (GAAP) question relating to inventory valuation involves the division of costs between the earnings statement and the balance sheet. A company that has relatively high product inventories—say two turns per year—holds six months of production costs in product inventories. In this case, a 10% error in inventory valuation would represent two to three weeks of product costs and could possibly result in a material misstatement of net earnings. However, a company with relatively low inventories—say, 52 turns per year—holds only about one week of product costs in inventories. In the latter case, the same 10% valuation error translates into only a few hours of production costs and is unlikely to be material. Therefore, as a company moves from a high to a low inventory environment, the inventory valuations question has decreasing importance.

Depreciation

An allocation question exists within TOC pertaining to the association of noncurrent asset costs to time periods (that is, depreciation, depletion, and amortization). The throughput accounting approach contemplates the transfer of these costs from I to the OE category through the depreciation mechanism as it is handled for financial reporting purposes. Thus far, the TOC literature has not addressed the issue of various established depreciation methods (straight-line, accelerated, etc.).

Constraint theory emerges as being somewhat inconsistent with respect to cost allocations. On the one hand, cost allocations are unequivocally considered inappropriate,[29] and, on the other hand, they are recommended as a convenient mechanism for handling wasting assets. A second inconsistency arises in that some inventory/investment costs are written off as a reduction in throughput (e.g., materials) and others are treated as increases in operating expense (e.g., depreciation). When addressing inventory cost flow and capital asset write-off methods appropriate for use with constraint management, the financial manager should bear in mind the relevance of the choopchick concept and the cash flow orientation of the TOC as well as the three attributes of constraints accounting.

A **payback allocation method** for charging capital investment costs to OE is consistent with the constraints accounting approach. This method uses the anticipated cash flows up to the payback point, as specified in the capital expenditure analysis, for the write-off schedule.

CAPITAL WRITE-OFF METHODS

The constraints accounting measures of T (throughput) and OE (operational expense) are generally satisfactory for computing reported performance profit as it relates to routine operations. However, the way that costs are assigned to I (inventory/investment), and the subsequent transfer of I to OE, may cause reported performance profit to depart from the reality of improvement. Such departure could nullify the ability to use the pattern of profits over time to identify ongoing improvement or the existence of inertia as suggested at the end of Chapter 2. If a POOGI Bonus plan is in effect, the distortion might prevent elevating constraints when the elevation requires a major capital expenditure.

Most capital write-off methods are accrual accounting techniques used to allocate portions of a large cost among several time periods. That is, cost is reclassified (or transferred) from being an asset to being an expense (I to OE).[30] Three methods for handling this transfer are depreciation, direct write-off, and the payback allocation method.

Depreciation

The throughput accounting literature suggests that depreciation should be recognized in the same way that it is for GAAP purposes.[31] Depreciation refers to the systematic allocation of the acquisition cost of plant and equipment to several fiscal periods. Amortization and depletion are similar to depreciation but apply to intangible assets and natural resources.[32]

There are several well-known and accepted capital write-off methods, including straight-line, declining balance, and sum-of-the-years' digits depreciation methods. The objective of these depreciation methods is to appropriately match costs with revenues in the periods in which the revenues are ultimately earned and received. Thus, an asset such as a machine that is expected to last ten years might have 10% of its cost transferred to expense each year for 10 years. These depreciation methods share three characteristics. Each allocates the acquisition cost of an asset. Each allocates the cost over a number of periods representing the estimated economic life of the asset. Each rests on the **going concern assumption.**

Direct Write-Off

In a constraint management environment, a viable alternative to the means of depreciation for the write-off of large cost amounts is to treat them as expense

(OE) at the time of the expenditure. The justification underlying this treatment is that large expenditures are incurred only to elevate Archimedean constraints. When an Archimedean constraint is elevated, a substantial increase in performance occurs. Therefore, such costs may be expected to have net cash inflows sufficient to recover both their acquisition cost and added recurring costs so quickly that allocation to time periods is not necessary.

Payback Allocation Method

The payback allocation method is specifically designed for a constraint management environment. The objective of the payback allocation method is twofold:

1. To permit identification of the point at which inertia has stalled a process of ongoing improvement.
2. To be neutral, with respect to earnings reporting, for investments that have not yet proven that they are improvements.

In the payback allocation method, the periodic charge to income is set by the anticipated pattern of cash flows specified in the capital expenditure analysis for the investment.[33] As a result, performance profit does not reflect improvement until the cash inflows (throughput contribution effects) exceed the investment costs. This is expected to occur at the end of the payback period—hence the name, *payback allocation method*. This technique assumes that real improvement does not occur until after the investment costs have been recovered.

Periodic Reported Performance Profit

If performance profit is to be used to judge whether an organization has established a process of ongoing improvement, then the profit measure (periodic reported performance profit) must present a picture that is consistent with the underlying reality of improvement. Two profit concepts concern us: the intuitive notion of **economic profit** and the concept of **periodic reported profit.** Economic profits represent reality; periodic reported profits reflect accounting measurement. To be an effective surrogate for economic profits in gauging a process of ongoing improvement, periodic reported profits must satisfy three requirements.

1. Periodic reported profit should increase when economic profits increase during a period.
2. Periodic reported profit should decrease when economic profits decrease during a period.

3. Periodic reported profit should not change when there is no change in economic profits during a period.

Example

Assume that an organization has embarked on a process of ongoing improvement and has had good success, increasing monthly profits from $100,000 at the base point to about $300,000 at the end of nine months. These results, reflecting a process of ongoing improvement, are illustrated in Exhibit 5.1 (monetary amounts in the example are in thousands of dollars).

All of this has been accomplished through the identify–exploit–subordinate steps of the theory of constraints focusing process without additional investment. Now the organization has identified an action to elevate the constraint that requires an additional investment. A capital expenditure (I) of $450,000 is required for each of two months, or $900,000 of investment in total. When the expenditure has been made, it is expected that an additional net cash inflow (T) of $100,000 per month will be realized for a period of five years.

This is a very nice proposal. It addresses a constraint; payback is less than a year; and the discounted rate of return is greater than 125%. The addition of $100,000 to profits is significant at the current profit level, so this investment should appear as an identifiable sustained improvement in profit.

The following cases show the effect of using (1) conventional depreciation as recommended in the throughput accounting literature, (2) direct write-off to OE, and (3) the payback allocation method. Actions other than the proposed investment are not reflected in order to isolate the effect of the write-off technique used.

Depreciation

Consider the throughput accounting technique of using depreciation to effect the transfer of I to OE. Any one of several depreciation methods

Exhibit 5.1 Comparative Reported Profit: Nine Months of Successful Improvement

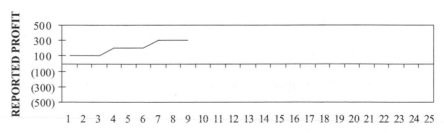

might be used; most of them are *time-based methods*.[34] The straight-line method assigns an equal amount of expense to each period. Accelerated methods (sum-of-the-year's-digits and declining-balance), which assign greater amounts of investment cost to earlier periods, may also be used. For our purposes it will be sufficient to scrutinize only the straight-line method. The accelerated methods would add nonimprovement-related distortion, or noise, to the profit pattern.

Straight-line depreciation in our example would be $15,000 per month ($900,000/60 months). Exhibit 5.2 reflects no effect on net profits in periods 10 and 11 when the investment is put into place. Following that, an $85,000 increase in profit would be shown for 60 periods ($100,000 − $15,000). An unambiguous pattern of improvement is represented.

The role of profit reporting for constraint management is to identify a POOGI. The use of conventional depreciation as illustrated in Exhibit 5.2 appears to be consistent with this understanding of the role of profit reporting. By spreading the investment cost over a protracted length of time, the amount of I allocated to a particular interim period becomes immaterial to the interim period. The income statement emphasizes T and cash OE. The I that has not been transferred to OE through depreciation remains on the balance sheet to be recognized as small amounts of OE in many future periods. Ultimately (60 months later), the entire amount of I has been transferred to OE.

Direct Write-Off

The direct write-off technique avoids the problem of multiperiod allocation entirely and is completely consistent with the cash flow approach emphasized by TOC elsewhere (e.g., in the calculation of T). Exhibit 5.3 reveals the profit pattern resulting from this approach.

Does Exhibit 5.3 show a process of ongoing improvement? From the perspective of periods 10 and 11, it appears that a catastrophe has occurred. After period 12 things improve, but how long will it take to over-

Exhibit 5.2   Reported Profits Using Straight-Line Depreciation

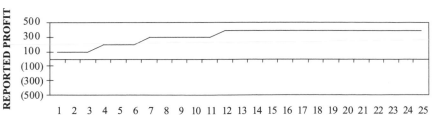

Exhibit 5.3   Reported Profits with Project Cost Write-Off Directly to OE

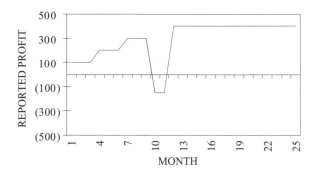

come the two periods of loss? We know that the expenditure results in improvement. However, the profit pattern depicted using a direct write-off to OE reflects either a weakening situation or, at best, an ambiguous situation. The direct write-off method does not result in reported profit amounts that consistently reflect the underlying reality. The direct write-off method fails to unambiguously answer the question, "Is this investment an improvement?"

Payback Allocation

Column (2) of Exhibit 5.4 shows the cash flows used for the capital expenditure analysis of the investment. The cash flows are reclassified from column (2) into investment amounts and cash inflow amounts in columns (3) and (4). The cash inflows in column (4) also represent the expected change in throughput during the estimated economic life of the proposal.[35] Column (5) contains the amounts of the periodic charges to income for transferring I to OE calculated using the payback allocation method. Column (6) shows the amount of unrecovered investment.[36] The amounts shown in column (5) are obtained from column (4) up until the point that the investment has been completely recovered (i.e., until the end of the payback period). This occurs at the end of period 20 in the case of Exhibit 5.4. At that point the write-off is complete. Finally, the change in reported profit—that is, the bottom-line effect of using the payback allocation method—is shown in column (7). The amounts in column (7) show that the bottom-line effect of the investment proposal is expected to be neutral until it has returned its initial investment amount at the end of period 20. Cash inflows received after period 20 represent the return on investment, or improvement, resulting from the investment.

Using the anticipated pattern of cash flows specified in the capital expenditure analysis as the basis for allocating I to OE is consistent with a

Exhibit 5.4   Estimated Payback Allocation Cash Flows ($000)

(1)	(2)	(3)	(4)	(5)	(6)	(7)
Period	Cash Flow	Investment Amount (I)	Cash Inflow	Payback Allocation	Unrecovered Investment Remaining	Change in Reported Profit
			Throughput (T)	Operational Expense (OE)	Inventory/ Investment (I)	
10	-450	450	0	0	450	0
11	-450	450	0	0	900	0
12	100	0	100	100	800	0
13	100	0	100	100	700	0
14	100	0	100	100	600	0
15	100	0	100	100	500	0
16	100	0	100	100	400	0
17	100	0	100	100	300	0
18	100	0	100	100	200	0
19	100	0	100	100	100	0
20	100	0	100	100	0	0
21	100	0	100	0	0	100
•	•	•	•	•	•	•
•	•	•	•	•	•	•
71	100	0	100	0	0	100
72	0	0	0	0	0	0

constraints accounting approach.[37] This profit pattern resulting from the payback allocation method is displayed in Exhibit 5.5.

Observe that the profit pattern shown in Exhibit 5.5 using the payback allocation method is similar to that of Exhibit 5.2 using straight-line depreciation. The major distinction is that when using the payback allocation method the *improvement* is not recognized until period 21, when the

Exhibit 5.5   Reported Profits Using Payback Allocation Method

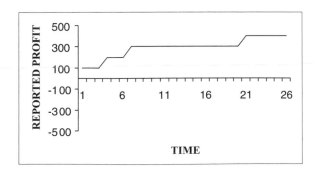

entire investment amount has been recovered. With depreciation, the *improvement* is shown to occur in period 12, as soon as the investment has been made. A less obvious distinction is that the payback allocation method reflects the entire amount of the improved cash flow as improvement ($100,000 per month), while the depreciation method reflects the improved cash flow less the periodic depreciation ($85,000 per month).

The use of estimated payback cash flows to allocate I to OE, like the use of conventional depreciation, appears to be consistent with our understanding of the role of profit reporting within a constraints accounting framework. However, there is a difference in timing as to when the improvement appears. When the payback allocation method is used, no improvement is recognized until the initial investment is fully recovered.

Murphy Strikes

The bottom-line profit patterns shown for the foregoing cases (Exhibits 5.2, 5.3, and 5.5) assume that the future reality matches the initial expectations—that is, that the cash flows resulting from the investment are exactly as were estimated in the capital expenditure analysis. Let us modify the example. Assume that **Murphy** strikes.[38] Actual experience is as projected for nine months (the payback period), but then no further cash flows are forthcoming. In this case, the undertaking is neither an improvement nor a detriment. The investment is fully recovered, but the real profit effect is nil. The reported profit patterns, reflecting the Murphy effect, are shown in Exhibits 5.6, 5.7, and 5.8.

The use of conventional depreciation (illustrated in Exhibit 5.6), which previously appeared to furnish the appropriate answer to the question asked, now reflects an improvement in periods 9 through 20 and a great failure in period 21. This introduces the same sort of ambiguity into the profit pattern that exists with the direct write-off method.[39] It does not correspond to the reality that the project is neither an improvement nor a detriment.

Exhibit 5.6   Reported Profits Using Straight-Line Depreciation: Neither Improvement nor Detriment

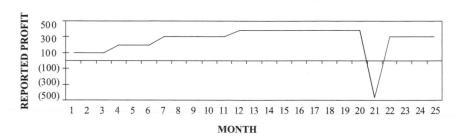

Exhibit 5.7   Reported Profits with Project Cost Write-Off Directly to OE: Neither Improvement nor Detriment

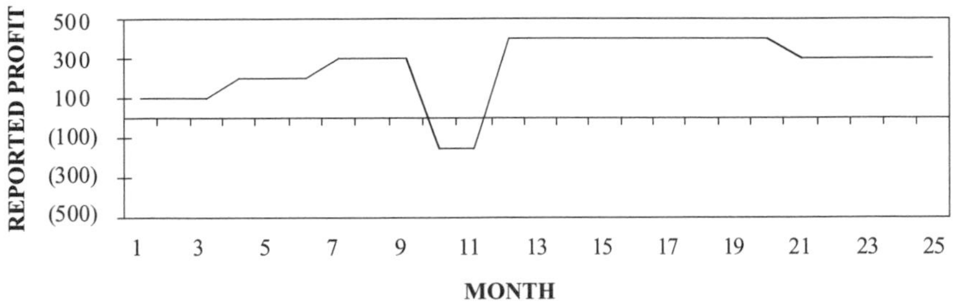

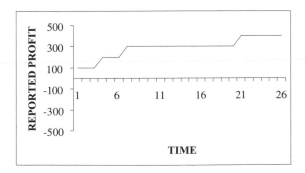

The reported profit pattern shown in Exhibit 5.7, using a direct write-off to OE, continues to bounce about.

Again the direct write-off method does not allow us to identify a process of ongoing improvement or the lack thereof.

Finally, Exhibit 5.8 shows the reported profit pattern using the payback allocation method when Murphy strikes.

Only the payback allocation method reflects the reality of the project's lack of net improvement impact, either favorable or unfavorable. Neither the direct write-off method nor the use of conventional depreciation allows the performance profit metric to be used reliably to identify a process of ongoing improvement. The payback allocation method provides the answer to the question as to whether the investment is an improvement both when the future occurs as originally projected and when the future is at variance with the initial projections.

Exhibit 5.8   Reported Profits Using Payback Allocation Method: Neither Improvement nor Detriment

Example Miscellany

The fact that the payback allocation method is based on the net cash flow projections employed in the initial analysis of the desirability of the project has two implications.

First, periodic cash flow estimates must be incorporated into the formal decision process. These cash flows are estimates—an expectation, or a best guess calculation. Protection against manipulation must be incorporated into the decision process itself. The POOGI Bonus Committee recommended in Chapter 4 is an example of a control to provide this protection. Projects addressing Archimedean constraints, and thus expected to result in real improvement, typically have short payback periods and thereby are relatively immune from serious manipulation.

Second, actual results are unlikely to match exactly the initial projections. Substantive differences result either from the project being much better than projected or from the project's failure to provide the anticipated improvement. The payback allocation model reflects these deviations as either improvement or detriment when they occur. Therefore, the reported performance profit, calculated using the suggested payback allocation method, reveals actual improvement, including throughput deviations from specifically stated future expectations.

Alternative Reporting Formats

When a proposal involving a capital expenditure is approved for implementation, the budget should be revised immediately to reflect the approval. This budgeted amount becomes a detail line item in the OE budget. For example, let us assume that the investment proposal examined related to the operational expense (OE) section of a Constraints Accounting Earnings Statement as shown in Exhibit 5.9[40] and that the current month is the one identified as period 14 in Exhibit 5.4.

The budget would have been revised to increase the budgeted OE by $100,000, the amount shown in column (5), row period 14 of Exhibit 5.4. The actual OE is also increased by $100,000, the amount of the write-off of

Exhibit 5.9 Original Operational Expense (OE) Section of Earnings Statement

	Actual	Budget	Variance	Favorable/ Unfavorable
Operational Expense (OE) Section:				
Greater of actual or budgeted OE	648,000	648,000		Note E

I to OE. This amount was fixed at the time the budget increase was approved and will never be the cause of a variance. The revised operational expense (OE) section is shown in Exhibit 5.10.

We expect that throughput (T) will also increase by $100,000, so there is no anticipated change in performance profit.

Sources of Future Improvement

Consider for a moment the nature of the inventory/investment (I) transfer to operational expense (OE) when the payback allocation method is used. If the *budget revision process* recommended in Chapter 4 has been adopted, then the only undertakings that will be reflected in these capital write-off transfers are those that meet the following criteria.

1. The undertaking addresses an active tactical or strategic constraint.
2. The undertaking has quantifiable anticipated throughput effects.
3. The undertaking has the support of a broad-based budget committee.

These undertakings are the **sources of future improvement** for the organization—the initiatives that will propel the process of ongoing improvement to the next levels. The very existence of these substantial initiatives is evidence that the POOGI is robust. To the extent that the T flows are relatively stable, the magnitude of the I transfers reflects the amount of improvement that may be expected when the payback periods have been reached. Conversely, the lack of such initiatives may provide an early warning of a stalled POOGI.

Since the sources of future improvement have significant information value, they may be disclosed separately on the earnings report as illustrated in Exhibit 5.11.

Note G would provide detail about the sources of future improvement. If the list is short enough, the individual initiatives might be listed as shown in Exhibit 5.12.

When the payback period is reached, the budgeted and actual I charges against earnings stop, but other factors remain the same. At that

Exhibit 5.10   Revised Operational Expense (OE) Section of Earnings Statement

	Actual	Budget	Variance	Favorable/ Unfavorable
Operational Expense (OE) Section:				
Greater of actual or budgeted OE	748,000	748,000		Note E

Exhibit 5.11   OE Section of Earnings Statement Reflecting Sources of Future Improvement

	Actual	Budget	Variance	Favorable/ Unfavorable
Operational Expense (OE) Section:				
Greater of actual or budgeted cash OE	648,000	648,000		Note E
Sources of future improvement	100,000	100,000		Note G
Greater of actual or budgeted OE	748,000	$748,000		

time, the bottom-line measure of performance profit will increase by the amount of the previous monthly write-off of I to OE.

If the list of initiatives is long, then note G could be presented in general terms, such as:

> **Note G:** *The total sources of future improvement average $33,333 per month and have an average of 6.3 months before improvement is reflected in performance profit. Initiative # 2 will result in a $50,000 increase in performance profit in June 20X3.*

The note should specifically identify the more significant elements if the list is unbalanced as to either magnitude of improvement or timing of improvement.

Once an expenditure for improvement has been made, the reality of the setting is changed and the resources acquired by the expenditure become, simply, part of the new overall environment. It is neither necessary nor desirable to attempt to match the expenditures and revenues of a particular improvement action.

Use of the payback allocation method for the write-off of investment to operational expense allows the financial reporting system to reliably distinguish whether an organization has become the victim of inertia or has established a robust process of ongoing improvement.

Exhibit 5.12   Specific Identification of Sources of Future Improvement

	Note G: Sources of Future Improvement November 30, 20X2			
	Initiative	Current Write-Off to OE	Date Improvement Reflected in Performance Profit	Cumulative Total Future Improvement
1	Short description of initiative # 1	$ 20,000	February 20X3	$ 20,000
2	Short description of initiative # 2	50,000	June 20X3	70,000
3	Short description of initiative # 3	30,000	August 20X3	100,000
	Total sources of future improvement	$ 100,000		

EXPLOITATION DECISIONS

In this section we explore the ways in which the global T, I, and OE measurements affect exploitation decisions as we use the measurements to guide decision making within a constraints accounting framework. Exploitation decisions that are supported by cost analysis, such as production batch sizing, throughput (or sales) mix, and pricing, are influenced by constraints accounting measurement in similar ways. The setup cost component of the production batch-sizing model and throughput mix are considered in this chapter, and the pricing question is considered in the next.

Exploitation has to do with getting the most throughput out of the existing environment. The significant constraints accounting attribute in the financial analyses for exploitation is the explicit recognition of the throughput effect of **opportunity costs.** The major financial impact will always be in terms of potentially expanded or lost throughput. If the analysis does not reveal a significant throughput effect, then it points to a choopchick.[41]

Setup Cost

Consider the case of setup cost, which is a component of the traditional batch-sizing model. The traditional model is illustrated in Exhibit 5.13.

The cost of setting up equipment consists of the labor and materials costs, with the labor cost portion likely comprising the major portion. As the quantity of units produced with each setup (which is the production batch size) increases, the total annual setup cost and average setup cost per unit decrease. Larger batch sizes imply fewer batches and less cost.

Exhibit 5.13   Traditional Batch Size Model

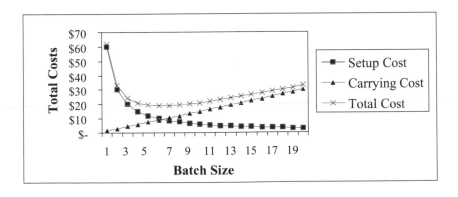

The traditional perspective of setup cost is shown in Exhibit 5.13 and subsequent exhibits by the "square" line.

Consider an example with the following characteristics:

- Annual carrying cost: $ 3 per unit
- Annual sales: $ 10,000,000
- Annual raw materials usage: $ 6,000,000
- Setup time for a resource: 2 hours
- Materials consumed in setup: $ 0
- Labor and labor-related costs: $ 30 per hour
- Annual resource time available: 2,000 hours

The traditional calculation of the setup cost for this resource would be calculated as shown in Exhibit 5.14.

The $60 per setup is the amount represented by the "square" line for the traditional analysis in Exhibit 5.13.

Reexamine the model of Exhibit 5.13 with reference to constraints accounting. If the resource being set up is not a capacity-constrained resource and labor is essentially fixed, then reducing the number of setups or time required for an individual setup on the resource will have no effect on labor costs. Only when the setup involves destruction of expensive materials would the costs behave as the traditional model assumes. The constraints accounting analysis of the setup cost for a nonconstraint resource is shown in Exhibit 5.15.

The nonconstraint resource setup cost would actually plot as the horizontal line traced by the "diamonds" in Exhibit 5.16. Thus, setup time reductions on nonconstraint resources will be, at best, choopchicks.

If the resource is an internal physical constraint, however, then setup time is actually production time lost to the entire chain of events. Here the opportunity cost of the lost throughput to the entire chain provides the appropriate relationship to profitability. The opportunity cost may include current sales that are turned away because of lack of capacity or future sales that are not made when current customers who do not receive timely deliveries seek out alternate suppliers. In the case of a constraint resource, the traditional model considerably understates the impact of re-

Exhibit 5.14   Cost of Setup: Traditional Analysis

(setup time	x	labor rate)	+	materials used	=	Setup cost
(2 hr / setup	x	$30 / hr)	+	$0	=	$60 / setup

Exhibit 5.15   Cost of Setup: Constraints Accounting Analysis—
Nonconstraint Resource

Change in total labor and materials cost due to setup	=	Setup cost
$0	=	$ 0 / setup

ducing the setup time or number of setups. A constraints accounting analysis of setup cost for the constrained resource based on current sales turned away is shown in Exhibit 5.17.

The constrained resource curve is shown in Exhibit 5.18. The constrained resource curve is dramatically steeper and starts at a radically higher point than the traditional analysis. The traditional analysis curve shown in Exhibits 5.13 and 5.16 is repeated in Exhibit 5.18 for purposes of comparison. It will be found at the bottom of the graph, very close to the horizontal axis. Recognition that the throughput effect, as reflected in opportunity cost, defines the nature of relevant costs for a constrained resource leads to a different perception of the situation.

When viewed through the lens of constraints accounting, *the traditional analysis of setup costs is faulty in every case.* For unconstrained areas, the cost is slightly overstated, and the effect is similar to that previously observed in scenarios 1 and 4 of the thinking bridges example (Chapter 1) and summarized in Exhibit 1.22, which is repeated here as Exhibit 5.19.

For activities holding an internal physical constraint, the financial impact of the traditional analysis, which relies on historical cost, is significantly understated in a manner similar to scenarios 2 and 3 of Exhibit

Exhibit 5.16   Setup Costs: Traditional and Nonconstraint Analyses

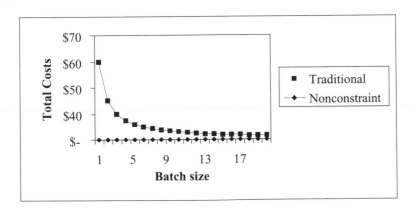

Exhibit 5.17   Cost of Setup: Constraints Accounting Analysis, Constrained Resource

Annual sales		$10,000,000
Annual raw materials usage		6,000,000
Annual throughput (T)		$ 4,000,000
T/Constraint time available	=	Opportunity cost of constraint hour
($4,000,000/yr) / (2,000 hours/yr)	=	$2,000 / hour
(setup time) x (opportunity cost)	=	Setup cost
2 hours / setup x $2,000 / hour	=	$4,000 / setup

5.19. Similar limitations apply to the financial analyses supporting other operating decisions.

Throughput Mix

An organization may sell a variety of products and services comprising several product lines in an assortment of geographical market areas. The organization may have multiple methods of distribution and various classes of customer. The relative contributions of these individual elements to the total throughput of the organization is referred to collectively as the **throughput mix.**

Exhibit 5.18   Setup Costs: Traditional and Constrained Resource Analysis

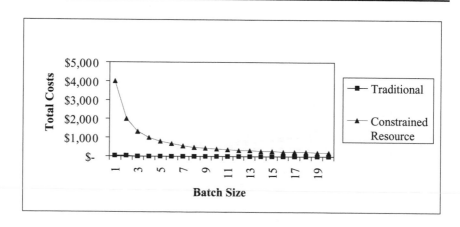

Exhibit 5.19   Example Summary: First Year Dollar Gain or (*Loss*) Shown by Analyses

	Least Product Cost (LPC)	T, I, & OE (TIOE)	Which analytical technique do *you* believe more correctly reflects reality?
Scenario 1	$17,085	($ 5,000)	
Scenario 2	$ 26,500	($ 123,400)	
Scenario 3	($36,500)	$133,880	
Scenario 4	$ 26,500	($ 5,000)	
Range of Estimates of Bottom-line Profit Effect	$63,000	$257,280	

Throughput Mix with Production Constraint

When there is an internal physical constraint in the production area, the company does not have sufficient internal capacity to satisfy all of the demand for its products or services. In this case, decisions must be made about what products to sell in which markets and to which customers.

Let us use an example to study the decision process for this case. Some production data for the Example Company are presented in Exhibit 5.20.[42]

The Example Company currently has the capability to produce three products—Atex, Detron, and Fonic. As shown in Exhibit 5.20, the market potential (i.e., the maximum amount that could be sold with the current pricing and market conditions) is 2,080 units of Atex, 4,160 units of Detron, and 2,080 units of Fonic per year. Atex requires raw materials costing $65 for each unit produced and comprised of material ARM, which has a standard cost of $30, and raw material CRM, which costs $35. In similar fashion, Detron's raw materials cost $95 and Fonic's are $65.

The raw materials are processed through a number of operations involving welding, cutting, polishing, grinding, and assembly. Atex does not require the welding operation, and Fonic does not go through assembly. The process and setup times required for each product are shown in Exhibit 5.20. From this data it is apparent that the welder is an internal phys-

Exhibit 5.20   Example Company: Production Data

	Atex	Detron	Fonic		
Market potential (units)	2,080	4,160	2,080		
Raw materials used and cost					
ARM	$ 30.00	$ 30.00			
CRM	35.00	35.00			
ERM		30.00			
FRM			$ 65.00		
Materials cost per unit	$ 65.00	$ 95.00	$ 65.00		

| **Direct labor and process time** (minutes): | | | | Annual resource minutes | |
				Total available	Needed to meet potential
* Welder	0	34.000	14.000	124,800	*170,560
Cutter	24.000	9.000	15.000	249,600	118,560
Polisher	33.000	14.000	22.000	249,600	172,640
Grinder	20.000	18.000	27.000	249,600	172,640
Assembler	8.000	17.000	0	124,800	87,360
Direct labor minutes per unit	85.000	92.000	78.000		
* Internal constraint					

Setup time required per production batch (minutes):			
Welder	0	30.000	15.000
Cutter	360.000	240.000	120.000
Polisher	120.000	120.000	120.000
Grinder	30.000	30.000	60.000
Assembler	0	0	0
Setup time per batch	510.000	420.000	315.000
Setup minutes per unit			
(batch size = 20 units)	25.500	21.000	15.750

Direct labor: 8 employees earning $10.00 per hour and working 2,080 hours per year.

ical constraint. A total of 170,560 minutes of process time in the welding operation would be required to satisfy the entire market potential for the three products. However, only 124,800 minutes of welding time are available for the year.[43] Not all of the potential quantities demanded can be satisfied, and it will be necessary to decide what products to sell.

Sales and operational expense data for the Example Company are provided in Exhibit 5.21.

The average unit sales prices for Atex and Detron are $175 and $275, respectively. The budgeted operational expense, inclusive of manufacturing overhead, direct labor, sales and marketing, and general admin-

Exhibit 5.21   Example Company: Sales and Operational Expense (OE) Data

	Atex	Detron	Fonic
Current sales mix (units)	2,080	3,515	0
Unit sales price (current)	$ 175.00	$ 275.00	$ 180.00
Sales commissions	5% of sales	5% of sales	5% of sales
Budgeted annual operational expense (OE):			
Manufacturing overhead		$ 332,800	
Direct labor		166,400	
Sales and marketing		72,000	
General and administrative		100,000	
Total budgeted operational expense (OE)		$ 671,200	

Production overhead rate: $332,800 / $166,400 = 200% of direct labor cost

istrative expense, is $671,200 per year. The company uses a production overhead rate of 200% of direct labor cost, calculated by dividing the budgeted manufacturing overhead of $332,800 by $166,400 of budgeted direct labor cost.

Budgeted sales are 2,080 units of Atex, 3,515 units of Detron, and no Fonic. Both Detron and Fonic require use of the constrained welding resource. In making the decision to emphasize Detron over Fonic, the company first calculated the product cost using absorption costing as shown in Exhibit 5.22.

Exhibit 5.22   Product Unit Cost Summary (Absorption Costing)

Traditional Unit Cost Summary			
	Atex	Detron	Fonic
Materials cost	$ 65.000	$ 95.000	$ 65.000
Setup labor @ $10.00 per hour	4.250	3.500	2.625
Factory overhead @ 200% of setup labor	8.500	7.000	5.250
Direct labor @ $10.00 per hour	14.167	15.333	13.000
Factory overhead @ 200% of direct labor	28.333	30.667	26.000
Total unit cost	$120.250	$151.500	$111.875

Exhibit 5.23   Gross Margin Analysis

	Atex	Detron	Fonic
Unit selling price	$ 175.00	$ 275.00	$ 180.00
Unit cost	120.25	151.50	111.87
Gross margin per unit	$ 54.75	$ 123.50	$ 68.13
Gross margin as % of sales	31%	45%	38%
Rank in terms of profitability	3	1	2

The unit costs were then used to rank the products in terms of their **gross margin.** This ranking is reflected in Exhibit 5.23.

Detron was ranked first, with the largest gross margin at 45%, followed by Fonic at 38%, and Atex at 31%.

Being aware of the limitations of traditional absorption costing for decision making, the company also checked the contribution margins. As shown in Exhibit 5.24, the ranking remained the same.

The company used the gross margin ranking, as confirmed by the contribution margin analysis, to guide it in its decision to use the welding capacity to produce as much Detron as possible and turn any remaining welding capacity to the production of Fonic. Since each unit of Detron required 34 minutes of welding process time plus 1.5 minutes of setup time,[44] or a total 35.5 minutes, the company can produce 3,515 units of Detron.[45] Because the potential market is 4,160 units, the Detron consumes the entire welding capacity and no Fonic is produced. This results

Exhibit 5.24   Contribution Margin Analysis

	Atex	Detron	Fonic
Unit selling price	$ 175.00	$ 275.00	$ 180.00
Variable expense:			
Materials	$ 65.00	$ 95.00	$ 65.00
Sales commissions at 5%	8.75	13.75	9.00
Total variable expense	$ 73.75	$ 108.75	$ 74.00
Contribution margin per unit (t)	$ 101.25	$ 166.25	$ 106.00
Contribution margin as percent of sales	58%	61%	59%
Rank in terms of profitability	3	1	2

Exhibit 5.25   Budgeted Profit Emphasizing Detron over Fonic

Budgeted Earnings Statement
Original Forecast—Emphasizing Detron over Fonic

Throughput (unit contribution margins (t) from Exhibit 5.23)		
Detron (3,515 units @ $166.25)	$ 584,369	
Atex (2,080 units @ $101.25)	210,600	$ 794,969
Operational expense		
Direct labor	$ 166,400	
Manufacturing overhead	332,800	
Sales and marketing	72,000	
General and administrative	100,000	671,200
Net Profit		$ 123,769

in a budgeted profit of $123,769 as shown in Exhibit 5.25. In general, management is pleased with this outcome.

The foregoing analysis is flawed from a constraints accounting point of view. It fails to correctly incorporate into the decision the first two attributes of constraints accounting—explicit consideration of the role of constraints and specification of throughput contribution effects. Let us look closely at the decision process steps that were followed:

- It was determined that the market potential was greater than the company's ability to supply it; that is, there is an internal constraint in the system.
- The potential products were ranked in terms of profitability using the unit gross margin and/or throughput contribution margin (either in dollars or percentages).
- The rankings were used to determine how much of each product would be offered to the market while remaining within the physical capabilities of the company.

That is, preference decision (ranking the products by profitability) was *made without explicit consideration of the constraint and failed to consider the impact of the constraint on throughput.* Only the question of how much to produce, given a previous preference decision, addressed the constraint.

The constraints accounting analysis illustrated in Exhibit 5.26 incorporates the explicit recognition of the throughput contribution effects of the constraint.

Exhibit 5.26 Constraints Accounting Analysis

	Atex	Detron	Fonic
Unit selling price	$ 175.00	$ 275.00	$ 180.00
Variable expense:			
Materials	$ 65.00	$ 95.00	$ 65.00
Sales commissions at 5.00%	8.75	13.75	9.00
Total variable expense	$ 73.75	$ 108.75	$ 74.00
Throughput contribution (t) per unit	$ 101.25	$ 166.25	$ 106.00
Physical constraint minutes per unit	0	34	14
Throughput value of product in terms of constraint minute (t/cu)	infinite	4.89	$ 7.57
Rank in terms of profitability	1	3	2

The constraints accounting analysis ranks the products in the opposite order. Atex appears to be the most profitable in terms of the welding constraint. Since Atex does not require use of the welder, its return is infinite in terms of welder time. Fonic returns half again as much throughput for each welder minute used as does Detron. The constraints accounting preference decision, then, is to make all 2,080 units of Atex and as much Fonic as is possible and can be sold, turning any remaining welder capacity to the production of Detron. Since each unit of Fonic requires about 14 minutes for processing and an average of 45 seconds for setup, the Example Company can produce all 2,080 units of the market potential for Fonic in 30,680 minutes (14.75 minutes per unit * 2,080 units). That will leave 94,120 minutes on the welder for Detron, during which 2,651 units of Detron may be produced (94,120 minutes divided by 35.5 minutes per unit). The budgeted result of this revised throughput mix is shown in Exhibit 5.27.

The updated forecast of Exhibit 5.27 reveals an increase in budgeted net profit of $76,840 from $123,769 to $200,609, or an increase of 62% resulting from the revised throughput mix.

Beyond Product Throughput

The throughput per constraint unit, when calculated for each product, does not tell the entire story. For example, the sales to individual customers might be as shown in Exhibit 5.28.

Inspection of Exhibit 5.28 shows that the Example Company would prefer to sell Detron to customer 02, with a throughput per constraint unit (t/cu) of $6.36, than Fonic to customer 05, which has a t/cu of $5.85. The company would also want to consider that customer 05 accounts for

Exhibit 5.27   Budgeted Profit Emphasizing Fonic over Detron

Budgeted Earnings Statement
Updated Forecast—Emphasizing Fonic over Detron

Throughput (unit contribution margins (t) from Exhibit 5.25)		
Atex (2,080 units @ $101.25)	$ 210,600	
Detron (2,651 units @ $166.25)	440,729	
Fonic (2,080 units @ $106.00)	220,480	$ 871,809
Operational expense		
Direct labor	$ 166,400	
Factory overhead	332,800	
Sales and marketing	72,000	
General and administrative	100,000	671,200
Net Profit		$ 200,609

almost half of the total throughput. They should also estimate the effect that reducing sales of Fonic to customer 05 might have on other sales to customer 05.

Finally, the Example Company would ensure that its tactical exploitation decisions were consistent with the strategic exploitation decisions embodied in the organization's strategic plan.[46] For example, assume that the

Exhibit 5.28   Sales by Customer

Customer	Product	Quantity	Price	Throughput	Throughput per constraint unit (t/cu*)	Customer t/cu*
Cust 01	Atex	416	$ 180.00	$ 44,096		
	Detron	530	$ 322.86	112,210	$5.96	
	Fonic	416	$ 180.71	44,377	$ 7.23	$8.04
Cust 02	Atex	270	$ 189.05	30,941		
	Detron	162	$ 337.65	36,574	$6.36	
	Fonic	241	$ 211.00	32,643	$9.18	$10.76
Cust 03	Atex	369	$ 180.96	39,451		
	Detron	48	$ 256.14	7,120	$4.18	
	Fonic	109	$ 208.07	14,461	$8.99	$18.43
Cust 04	Atex	145	$ 194.16	17,321		
	Detron	80	$ 209.57	8,327	$ 2.93	
	Fonic	599	$ 186.67	67,290	$ 7.62	$7.96
Cust 05	Atex	880	$ 162.67	78,792		
	Detron	1,831	$ 258.96	276,497	$4.25	
	Fonic	715	$ 159.27	61,710	$5.85	$5.52
Total				$871,810		
* Constraint unit (cu) is welder minutes.						

Example Company had determined, for whatever reasons, that it desired to have the cutter become the constraint. That is, the cutter has been designated as the *strategic constraint*. Detron makes better use of the cutter, in terms of throughput per cutter minute,[47] than does either Fonic or Atex. The calculations are shown in Exhibit 5.29.

Management will need to assess the potential damage that would result from shifting production from Detron to Fonic. In the short run, $76,840 is to be gained from throughput opportunity revisions (the difference between the budgeted net profits shown in Exhibits 5.25 and 5.27). The conflict may be set out in the form of an evaporating cloud as shown in Exhibit 5.30.

The objective of the cloud (A) is to increase the value of the company.[48] In order to increase the company's present value, we must (B) exploit the current tactical constraint, which is the welder. In order to exploit the current tactical constraint, we must (D) use the constraint to produce the higher t/cu product (emphasize Fonic over Detron). However, in order to (A) increase the value of the company, we must (C) subordinate to the exploitation decisions for the strategic plan, which is to have the cutter become the constraint. In order to subordinate to the exploitation decisions for the strategic plan, we must (E) produce products that will make the best use of the strategic constraint (emphasize Detron over Fonic). Emphasizing Fonic over Detron is in conflict with emphasizing Detron over Fonic.

The assumptions that underlie each of the arrows should be checked. For example, the D to E conflict arrow assumes that the production capability is limited to the existing internal capacity. If outsourcing some of the welding for either Fonic or Detron were a possibility, this assumption would be invalid and the conflict would not exist. In similar fashion, an assumption underlying the linkage between C and E is that the company will lose the future market for Detron if the current market for Detron is not also served. This may or may not be a valid assumption.

Exhibit 5.29   Throughput per Cutter Minute

	Atex	Detron	Fonic
Average throughput per unit (Exhibit 5.26)	$101.25	$166.25	$106.00
Cutter time required for processing and setup for one unit	42 minutes	21 minutes	21 minutes
Throughput (t) per cutter minute	$2.41	$7.92	$5.05
Rank if cutter were to become a constraint	3	1	2

Exhibit 5.30   Evaporating Cloud: Tactical versus Strategic Constraint

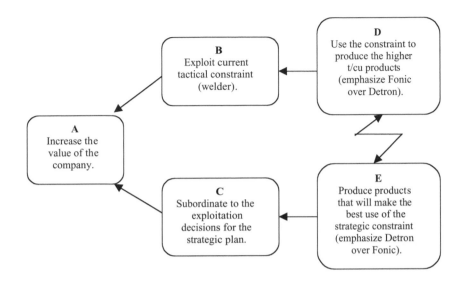

Throughput Mix with Marketing Constraint

As important as it is to consider throughput stated in terms of an internal physical constraint, we must also know when a measurement of throughput per constraint time is not appropriate.

Let us again use the Example Company data from Exhibit 5.17. However, now assume that the market potential for Detron is only 1,500 units. In this case, the Example Company has sufficient production capacity to provide all of the products demanded. As shown in Exhibit 5.31, the most heavily loaded resources are budgeted at only about two-thirds of their capacity. Here the throughput *mix* is not so important; the company's primary concern is to get more of any throughput.

If a company's only constraining factor can be categorized as a marketing constraint and the company has identified a desired constraint as part of its strategic plan, or if it expects a currently external constraint to become internal at a particular resource, then it has identified a **pseudo-constraint.**[49] We will illustrate the effects of using a pseudo-constraint for decision making in Chapter 6 where we discuss a constraints accounting approach to pricing.

SUMMARY

We determined that constraint management and its associated accounting represent a paradigm shift, and our existing language does not contain

Exhibit 5.31   Budgeted Load on Production Resources

Resource	Annual minutes available	Minutes required for market potential (without setup)	Minutes required for market potential (with setup)	Time utilized for production	Time utilized including setup
Welder	124,800	80,120	83,930	64.2%	67.3%
Cutter	249,600	94,620	162,540	37.9%	65.1%
Polisher	249,600	135,400	169,360	54.2%	67.9%
Grinder	249,600	124,760	136,370	50.0%	54.6%
Assembler	124,800	42,140	42,140	33.8%	33.8%

words with commonly understood definitions suitable for the constraint management paradigm. Although there are many different definitions of *throughput,* for the remainder of the book we use the terms *throughput* or *throughput contribution* (T or t) to refer to the difference between revenues and the truly variable expenses associated directly with the revenues and with any desired period or cost object.

The interpretation of the T, I, and OE measurements in various environments brings into focus a difficulty with the T, I, and OE metrics. The definitional (and accounting) problem lies in matching costs and revenues. Ultimately in constraints accounting terminology, all inventory/investment will be reclassified as operational expense and be matched with throughput. Constraints accounting does not take into consideration pseudo (or nominal) profit centers when calculating the revenue side of the (t) calculation. However, when firms sell products with a money back guarantee or the manufacturer "sells" products to its dealers, while carrying the financing itself, using the product as collateral, in constraints accounting each case calls for a deferral of sales recognition until a firm final sale is made at a firm price. Regarding sales commissions, in constraints accounting it is treated as negative revenue amounts or as expenses since the effect on T is the same.

In global measurements there are three types of costs: truly variable expenses, operational expenses (OE), and inventory/investment (I). When categorizing expenses as variable, constraints accounting uses the method of **account classification.** The constraints accounting model for financial analysis of routine tactical decisions starts with materials as the only obvious variable expense. Costs that are not deducted from revenues in the calculation of T comprises the operation expenses (OE). For control, budgeted OE and all expenditures must be able to be traced, to the point of incurrence responsibility. No allocation of costs should be included in reports showing current, actual and projected spending. All three constraints accounting measurements (T, I, and OE) must be considered in order to assess an impact on profitability.

The constraints accounting framework, specific consideration of the role of constraints, specification of throughput contribution effects, and decoupling of throughput (T) from operational expense (OE), guides decision-making, as our analysis changes from the cost world to the throughput world.

The provision of transparent internal reporting techniques that support exploitation analysis, in a manner consistent with an organization's desired management philosophy, is a key to locking in a process of ongoing improvement.

NOTES

[1] Order of magnitude = 10 times as large.

[2] While cost elements are limited in the amount by which they can be decreased, there is essentially no limit as to how much the revenue, and hence throughput, can increase. Even decreases in variable costs cannot be turned into spectacular improvement without a significant increase in sales volume.

[3] Sometimes a lower case 't' is used to represent the unit throughput metric.

[4] See the discussion of Not-for Profit Measurements, and particularly the comments of James Holt and Tony Rizzo (John A. Caspari, "Not-for-Profit Measurements," last revised July 26, 2000, archived at http://casparija.home.comcast.net/aweb/RJ1.HTM as of February 25, 2004). A detailed discussion of constraints accounting in a NFPO environment is beyond the scope of this book.

[5] Charles T. Horngren, George Foster, and Srikant M. Datar, *Cost Accounting: A Managerial Emphasis, 9th Edition* (Prentice-Hall, Inc., 1997), p. 698.

[6] Thomas B. McMullen, Jr., *Introduction to the Theory of Constraints (TOC) Management System* (St. Lucie Press, 1998), p. 31. This is also known simply as *throughput value added.*

[7] Raw materials cost is reassigned as an asset to work-in-process, which in turn is reassigned to the asset finished goods and thence to cost of goods sold (an expense appearing on the earnings statement). Costs that have been capitalized as assets are reassigned to expense through depreciation or amortization.

[8] "The Fundamental Measurements," *Theory of Constraints Journal* 1, No. 3 (August–September 1988), p. 5.

[9] If the monetary value of the returns or incentives can be estimated reliably, this may be accomplished with a "reverse accrual" of questionable amounts into a valuation account.

[10] "The Fundamental Measurements," p. 6.

[11] OE includes recurring payroll costs. But an interesting question is whether personnel costs *ought* to be included in this OE category. In Chapter 10 we will discuss personnel costs as inventory/investment (I).

[12] "The Fundamental Measurements," p. 6, and Robert S. Kaplan and Anthony A. Atkinson, *Advanced Management Accounting,* 2nd ed. (Prentice-Hall, 1989), p. 419.

[13] The *method of account classification,* in which the general ledger expense accounts are categorized as containing fixed or variable expenses, is sometimes known as the *accounting method.*

[14] This is an example of behavioral factors determining the way in which the cost changes. Experience shows that costs tend to be somewhat sticky at previous levels of incurrence when activity levels decrease. Also, rather than view employees as factors of production, TOC managers view employees as an integral part of the continuing organization.

[15] Robert A. Howell and Stephen R. Soucy, "Cost Accounting in the New Manufacturing Environment," *Management Accounting* (August 1987), pp. 47–48. Emphasis added.

[16] *Separating and Using Costs as Fixed and Variable: A Summary of Practice,* Accounting Practice Report No. 10 (Institute of Management Accountants, 1960), p. 14.

[17] The activity-based costing system is also a form of absorption costing, but it attempts to identify input volume measures rather than output volumes.

[18] John K. Shank and Vijay Govindarajan, *Strategic Cost Analysis: The Evolution from Managerial to Strategic Accounting* (Richard D. Irwin, 1989).

[19] Since the original definition specified that OE costs contribute to the conversion of I to T, the TOC contemplates a category of cost that does not fit the T, I, or OE categories: *waste.* As a practical matter, this *waste* classification is not used. From a constraints accounting point of view, classifying costs into such a waste category would be inappropriate as a choopchick.

[20] Eric Noreen, Debra Smith, and James Mackey, *Theory of Constraints and Its Implications for Management Accounting* (North River Press, 1995). Sponsored by the Institute of Management Accountants (IMA) and Price Waterhouse. p. 57, footnote 3.

[21] Eli Schragenheim, TOC-L Internet discussion, 95-11-24. Note that this capital amount is from the point of view of the organization, not a purchaser of stock in the organization on a stock exchange.

[22] Ibid.

[23] Note that the costs referred to here as being variable vary with production rather than with sales.

[24] The notion of capitalizing payroll costs is discussed in Chapter 10. If that were to be done, the capitalized cost would be classified as I.

[25] This phenomenon is illustrated in most conventional managerial and cost accounting textbooks and will not be belabored here. The point is that managers must be aware of this short-term effect and take appropriate actions to trim any potential negative effects.

[26] Externally purchased intangibles have been treated as assets and written-off over what is generally an arbitrarily long time frame under GAAP. However, the accounting for goodwill has been the subject of recent regulatory activity by the Financial Accounting Standards Board and SFASB 142 Goodwill and Other Intangible Assets changed the GAAP treatment of goodwill considerably in August 2001. See also SFASB 121 for the treatment of impairment of other assets. As this is being written (March 2002), AOL Time Warner Inc. is writing off $54 billion of goodwill in the current quarter!

[27] Cost flow assumptions include: first-in, first-out (FIFO), last-in, first-out (LIFO), next-in, first-out (NIFO), or replacement cost, average cost, and standard costs.

[28] Eli Schragenheim, "T, I, OE—Simple?" Internet TOC discussion November 27, 1995 archived at the Constraint Accounting Measurements web site as of December 11, 2003.

[29] "Laying the Foundation," *The Theory of Constraints Journal* 1, No. 2 (April–May 1988), p. 16.

[30] Recall that for financial reporting purposes all costs are classified either as an asset or an expense. Assets appear on the balance sheet, and expenses are deducted from revenues on the earnings statement.

[31] Eliyahu M. Goldratt and Robert E. Fox, "The Fundamental Measurements," *The Theory of Constraints Journal* 1, No. 6 (April–May 1990), p. 13.

[32] The payback allocation method presented in these notes applies equally to "intangible" factors (amortization) as to tangible factors. See also the previous discussion of the nature of investment. Depletion is beyond the scope of this discussion but is similar to the usage-based depreciation methods.

[33] This cash flow analysis should exist as part of the budget revision process described in Chapter 4. If the analysis does not exist, then the expenditure should be treated as an expense (OE) in the period in which the expenditure becomes irrevocable.

[34] Some depreciation methods are based on usage rather than time (e.g., units of production, hours operated, or miles driven). These methods create the appearance of the write-off being a variable cost rather than a fixed cost. This may accurately reflect the underlying reality, as in the case of a heavily scheduled aircraft or a die that can be used for only a predictable number of stampings and that must then be replaced. In such cases it may make sense to transfer the I cost to the T calculation, as is done for raw materials, rather than to OE.

[35] If the proposal involved an increase in cash OE, then column (4) would include both the T and cash OE effects. This would not affect the payback allocation.

[36] This unrecovered investment is also the balance of inventory/investment (I) that would appear on a constraints accounting balance sheet, were one to be prepared. However, a constraints accounting balance sheet typically is neither presented nor prepared. As we shall see, the interesting data bears a one-to-one relationship with the Constraints Accounting Earnings Statement.

[37] The three attributes of constraints accounting are satisfied as follows. Specific consideration of the role of constraints and specification of throughput contribution effects are part of the budgetary revision process discussed in Chapter 4. Throughput is related to new inventory/investment rather than operational expense.

[38] Murphy's Law: If anything can go wrong, it will.

[39] Exhibit 5.6 assumes that the remaining balance of I is written off when the impairment is recognized. In practice, the unrecovered asset amount would probably continue to be shown as an asset, reducing future reported profits by $15,000 per month for the next 51 months.

[40] Exhibit 5.9 is repeated from the OE section of the Constraints Accounting Earnings Statement presented in Chapter 3.

[41] Even when satisfying a necessary condition, there should be a significant throughput effect. The effect of not satisfying a necessary condition is an opportunity cost; if it does not exist, then it calls into question the authenticity of the necessary condition.

[42] This data is similar to data used in the Executive Decision-Making Seminar (EDM) of the Avraham V. Goldratt Institute (SIM10) but with a higher price for Detron. A similar presentation is also available in Emerson O. Henke and Charlene W. Spoede, *Cost Accounting, Managerial Uses of Accounting Data* (PWS-Kent Publishing Co., 1991), pp. 822–829. Users who are licensed to use the Goldratt or TOC Center Simulators are invited to contact the authors at constraint-dynamics@comcast.net to arrange to obtain a parameter file (PARAMS.900) for the simulation of the Example Company data.

[43] One welder unit for 2,080 hours per year * 60 minutes per hour.

[44] 30 minutes per setup divided by 20 units per setup = 1.5 minutes per unit (data from Exhibit 5.17).

[45] 124,800 minutes available divided by 35.5 minutes required per unit = 3,515 units.

[46] The existence of such strategic exploitation decisions implies that the organization has appraised its long-run strategy within the framework of constraints management as suggested in Chapter 2. If this is the case, then it is likely that the TOC thinking processes (TP) have been employed and that a map of the strategy for executing a robust process of ongoing improvement exists in the form of a **future reality tree** showing the expected results and supporting **prerequisite trees** (or **IO maps**) and **transition trees.** See Appendix D, pp. 247–280 in H. William Dettmer, *Breaking the Constraints to World-Class Performance* (ASQ Quality Press, 1998) for a comprehensive TP example.

[47] The terminology, *throughput per constraint unit,* is intentionally avoided in this case. At the present time, the cutter has plenty of capacity and is not an active tactical constraint.

[48] Since the present value of the company is the present value of the future earnings of the company, this objective is equivalent to *making more money now and in the future.* The objective, A, could also be expressed as an increase in the POOGI Bonus, reflecting the congruence of goals.

[49] *Pseudo-constraint* is a term we have coined to refer to a local and internal resource treated as a constraint and used for scheduling or other decision purposes when the real constraint is not perceived as being under the control of the local area of operations. A pseudo-constraint may be called a scheduling point, leverage point, bottleneck, or drum. All of these terms are legitimate, but if they do not represent a real constraint, then actions, other than scheduling, taken based on them are destined to be choopchicks.

6

Pricing

COST-BASED PRICING

Pricing decisions are another aspect of tactical exploitation. The pricing decision is important because it represents an Archimedean constraint in many organizations; therefore, addressing it appropriately will result in large changes of profitability. Despite its importance, the pricing decision remains neglected in the constraint management literature.[1] In this chapter we examine the traditional cost-based pricing mechanism used by many organizations. We conclude that cost-based pricing can be a viable pricing technique in certain circumstances.[2] We also find that the traditional cost-based pricing technique is inconsistent with constraints accounting in that it fails to incorporate the constraint into the decision process. Then we address a constraint-based pricing technique, examining the use of an internal physical constraint as the foundation for cost-based pricing. But this technique maintains a close linkage between throughput (T) and operational expense (OE). Therefore, we conclude the chapter by developing a constraints accounting approach to pricing that considers all three attributes of constraints accounting.

It has been suggested that absorption-costing methods, such as activity-based costing, rather than throughput methods, should be used for pricing decisions.[3] Archie Lockamy and James Cox studied six firms implementing TOC and noted that five of the firms considered price as resulting from costs a strategic objective.[4] They also considered controlling product cost as important.[5] Most of the firms they studied "used traditional product costing and variances from budget from their accounting systems to assist in establishing a product price," even though they recognized the problems associated with traditional product costing for decision making.[6] None of the firms they studied had developed an alternative mechanism for establishing prices.[7] Thomas McMullen, through his alter ego, Detective Columbo, observes that some allocations are required for external reporting, but he questions why we allocate labor and overhead costs to products for internal purposes—when there is no volume linkage between the costs and the product. The best answer his group can come up with is, "Because we always do."[8]

Using Product Costs to Set Prices

Because the cost basis for pricing appears to be pervasive, we will first look at the cost-based pricing model. Although market forces ultimately establish prices, costs impact the pricing decision by providing relevant information for establishing minimum prices, for establishing target prices, and for evaluating the profit effect of proposed prices and price changes.

How are these costs used in pricing decisions? There are four basic situations:

1. In some cases the prices are regulated. One simply follows the regulations (which are frequently based on some measure of full cost).

2. The market is purely (or quite) competitive, and a market price exists. The competitive price is the sales price. The product cost is compared to the competitive price, and the decision revolves around whether to sell the product in that market. Small price differences may be expected to result in substantial differences in quantities sold.

3. The market has a "price leader" or some other mechanism to indicate an appropriate price. Managers use the information available to establish a price. Product cost itself might be such a mechanism. For example, Robert Kaplan and Anthony Atkinson suggest, "If all companies in an oligopoly use cost plus pricing formulas, then the pricing structure will be stable even during periods of declining demand. At a time when all firms in the industry face similar cost increases due to industry-wide labor contracts or materials price increases, firms will implement similar price increases even with no communication or collusion."[9]

4. Finally, when we have relatively little information about market prices, we may presume that there is a maximum price that the market will tolerate. If we price above that amount, we will not be able to sell our products, or we will sell inadequate quantities. Once we set the price for a particular market segment, it may be difficult to raise. The remainder of this pricing chapter explores this fourth situation.

Cost-Based Pricing and the Product-Cost Concept

Chapter 3 showed that there is no product-cost concept in the theory of constraints. The IMA research report on TOC observes: "product costs are much lower under TOC accounting than conventional absorption costing."[10] If we actually eliminated the product-cost concept, then we would not be able to make such a comparison, and we would be forced to look for a new paradigm. Since the concept is so widely accepted, however, there must be a good reason to know product costs. Hence, we will explore product-cost accounting and its legitimate use in pricing.

In Chapter 5 we discussed using the payback allocation method to allocate costs for associating investment costs with time periods. Since it is an accounting technique, discussions of cost allocation almost always seem to revolve around the financial reporting question of "which costs and revenues should be recognized as related to current period profits on the earnings statement and which costs and revenues should be deferred to a future time period on the balance sheet."[11] Costs, then, are allocated between the earnings statement (as expenses) and the balance sheet (as assets). Product cost is used as a device to effect this allocation with respect to physical product inventories (or partially completed services). First, costs are allocated to units of product; second, the costs associated with the individual units of product are allocated to the earnings statement or balance sheet, depending on whether the units have been sold.

Constraint management discussions of cost allocation usually focus on differences in reported income. When physical sales volumes are greater than production volumes, then the level of product inventories will be reduced. In this case, the use of traditional absorption-costing techniques will result in less reported net profit than would direct costing or throughput accounting. Conversely, for periods in which production exceeds sales, inventories increase and absorption-costing methods report a greater profit, so-called **inventory profits.** This distinction has proved to be important in constraint management implementations because inventory levels are frequently reduced in the initial stages of implementation. If the performance-reporting measurement is based on absorption costing, then the intended result of the implementation (reduced inventory level) is reflected as poor performance, with attendant consequences for the managers implementing constraint management.

We might also use product-cost calculations for decision making using the least-cost thinking bridge discussed in Chapter 1. Again, the use of product cost as a decision tool was found to be defective. Goldratt has suggested that product-costing procedures were built on two assumptions: that labor cost was essentially linearly variable with physical output volume and that overhead was only a small part of total costs.[12] He further suggests that the allocated product cost provided a powerful analytical tool when it was developed in the late nineteenth and early twentieth centuries because it allowed products to be analyzed independently. Goldratt then observes that the basic assumptions no longer hold. As a result, he declares product costing to be obsolete. It appears to have generally been accepted, within constraint management circles, that there is no legitimate use for the product-cost concept.

At a basic level, the argument made is that since overhead costs were small relative to the direct labor application base, the distortion introduced was insignificant. The problem with this argument is that if the overhead costs are insignificant, then the allocation is not needed to begin with. It seems that the problem was not to judge the profitability of the products independently, but rather to *set prices* in such a way to ensure that each product contributed to profits in a manner that, when taken in combination with all of the other sales of the organization, the overall organization would produce a profit. However, we have not tested the absorption-costing model as a basis for setting prices.

Cost Allocation

We will first examine the cost allocation process and then its use in pricing. Each allocation follows a simple four- or five-step process:

1. Determine the total cost to be allocated: for example, $100 of overhead.

2. Determine the allocation base: for example, 6 direct labor hours (DLH) for product A and 4 DLH for product B equals 10 total DLH.

3. Make the unit cost calculation: divide the total cost by the base ($10/DLH).

4. Put the unit cost with the elements of the base: $60 for product A and $40 for product B.

5. Put the allocation to use (optional step): Make a journal entry reflecting the allocation or make a decision based on the allocation.

The first four steps of the allocation process are summarized and illustrated in Exhibit 6.1.

At this point we have a notion of product cost ($60 for product A and $40 for product B).

Using Product Costs

The allocated product cost can be used in several different ways. Exhibit 6.2 shows the fifth step of the allocation process and employs two variations of the allocated product cost for illustration.

Exhibit 6.1   Cost Allocation Example

Step	Action	Result
1	Determine the total cost to be allocated.	$100 of manufacturing costs
2	Determine the allocation base.	6 labor hours for product A 4 labor hours for product B = 10 total labor hours
3	Make the unit calculation (divide the total cost by the base).	$100 / 10 labor hours = $10 per labor hour
4	Put the unit cost with the elements of the base.	Cost of product A: 6 hr x $10/hr = $60 Cost of product B: 4 hr x $10/hr = $40

In case 1, as shown in Exhibit 6.2, the allocated product cost is used to assign cost to time periods based on the location of the product at the end of the time period. If we sold product A for $115 but did not sell product B, then at the end of the time period product A would have been shipped to the customer and product B would be in the warehouse waiting to be sold. Using generally accepted accounting principles or GAAP, we could say that we had a gross profit of $55 (= $115 − $60) and still have an asset (product B), which cost $40.

Using allocated product cost for a pricing decision is a different issue. A markup is applied to the calculated product cost in order to arrive at a targeted selling price. In this example, it is assumed that the markup is equal to 100% of product cost, or that the price is equal to 200% of cost. Hence, the asking price for product A will be $120 (200% of $60), and the price for product B will be $80 (200% of $40).

Exhibit 6.2   Using Allocated Costs

Step	Action	Result
5 (Optional step)	Make a journal entry or decision reflecting the allocation.	Case 1: Assign costs to time periods. Product A is sold; $60 is assigned to the current period and appears on the *Income Statement* as the cost of sales. Product B is not sold; $40 appears on the *Balance Sheet* as Finished Goods Inventory.
		Case 2: Set a price for a product. Price = 200 % of cost Price for product A: 200% of $60 = $120.00 Price for product B: 200% of $40 = $80.00

A cost-based approach to pricing provides a simple and convenient way to establish prices for individual products. Robert Anthony has observed that the "empirical evidence supports the premise that prices tend to be based on full costs."[13] The pricing technique of adding a markup to allocated costs, which was widely accepted by the 1950s, is built on a foundation originating in World War I with respect to government cost reimbursable contracts, experimented with during the 1920s, cast into American national policy in the 1930s by the National Industrial Recovery Act, and ratified by government price controls in the 1970s.[14]

At this point it may appear that the products are being treated independently, but let us take an example a little further and examine how this cost-based pricing scheme works with respect to the overall organization. Exhibit 6.3 provides some basic data useful for the example.

Exhibit 6.4 shows the calculation of overhead rates and the assignment of overhead to units of product using the five-step allocation process. The two columns for calculations in Exhibit 6.4 represent the traditional **GAAP** "manufacturing cost only" model and the full cost model advocated by the more rigorous versions of activity-based costing (ABC).

The unit overhead data are combined with labor and materials in Exhibit 6.5 in order to arrive at a complete unit product cost as would be computed using GAAP.

Exhibit 6.6 shows the same thing for activity-based costing using the full cost concept.

The data from Exhibits 6.5 and 6.6 are used to set target prices as shown in Exhibit 6.7. In Exhibit 6.7, an arbitrarily selected markup on manufacturing cost of 54% is used to set the traditionally calculated (GAAP) target price. The ABC product-cost markup of 10% was selected

Exhibit 6.3   Data for Cost-Based Pricing Example

Product	A	B	C	D
Annual market potential	200 units	200 units	300 units	400 units
Materials unit cost	$200	$150	$100	$50
Labor per unit	10 hours	20 hours	20 hours	10 hours
Manufacturing overhead				$320,000
Selling, general, and administrative expenses				$240,000
There are 8 direct labor employees who each work 2,000 hours per year and earn $10.00 per hour, for a total annual direct labor cost of $160,000				

Exhibit 6.4   Allocation of Overhead Costs to Units of Product

Step	GAAP	ABC
Determine the total cost to be allocated.	MfgOH = $320,000	MfgOH = $320,000 SG&A = 240,000 Total = $560,000
Determine the allocation base.	8 employees x 2,000 DLH per employee = 16,000 direct labor hours (Note that this is the same in either case—the cost accounting method does not change reality.)	
Make the unit cost calculation.	$320,000 / 16,000 DLH = $20 / DLH	$560,000 / 16,000 DLH = $35 / DLH
Put the unit costs with the elements of the base.	A: 10 DLH @ $20 = $200 B: 20 DLH @ $20 = $400 C: 20 DLH @ $20 = $400 D: 10 DLH @ $20 = $200	A: 10 DLH @ $35 = $350 B: 20 DLH @ $35 = $700 C: 20 DLH @ $35 = $700 D: 10 DLH @ $35 = $350
Make a journal entry or decision reflecting the allocation.	We will use this data for a pricing decision.	

in order to yield the same overall profit as would the traditional GAAP method if all products were sold. (This equal profit will be proven in Exhibits 6.8 and 6.9.)

Observe that the pricing process results in different prices for each product depending on which price base (traditional GAAP or ABC) is used. For instance, product A has a target price of $770 when based on traditional GAAP product cost. However, when based on ABC cost, the price is $55 less or $715, a 7% difference. Nevertheless, both pricing schemes will arrive at the same overall budgeted profit.

In Exhibit 6.8 the target prices calculated in Exhibit 6.7 are extended by the quantities that have been budgeted for sale (the full market potential in this example).

Even though the individual target prices for the products are different when using the two costing methods, the total revenue generated is

Exhibit 6.5   Traditional GAAP Product Cost

	Product	A	B	C	D
Raw Material		$200	$150	$100	$ 50
Direct labor 10, 20, 20, 10 hours @ $10		100	200	200	100
Manufacturing overhead 10, 20, 20, 10 hours @ $20		200	400	400	200
Traditional GAAP product cost		$500	$750	$700	$350

Exhibit 6.6   Activity-Based Costing (ABC) Product Cost

	Product	A	B	C	D
Raw material		$200	$150	$100	$ 50
Direct labor 10, 20, 20, 10 hours @ $1 0		100	200	200	100
Manufacturing overhead 10, 20, 20, 10 hours @ $35		350	700	700	350
Activity-based costing (ABC) product cost		$650	$1,050	$1,000	$500

the same under each method.[15] This is not a coincidence; rather, it occurs because the markups were deliberately selected to generate the same amount of profit.

Exhibit 6.8 proves that the total budgeted sales dollars will be the same, regardless of which cost base is used, as long as the full market potential of units sold is reached. Since the physical volumes are the same, the total variable cost of materials is also the same. Hence, the total profits are the same. The total budgeted profit, as shown in Exhibit 6.9, is $84,000. This is the case regardless of which costing method is used.

The foregoing discussion shows the mechanics of setting a *target* price, but we do not know if the customers will buy the products at these prices. Therefore, we need to add the customer to the model. Let us assume that the utilities of our products for our customers, in conjunction with competitive pressures, are such that the maximum unit amounts that our customers would be willing to pay are as shown in Exhibit 6.10.

In comparing our asking prices to the prices our customers are willing to pay, we find that our $770 asking price for product A calculated using GAAP costing, and the $725 target price calculated using activity-based costing, are higher than the $600 that our customers are willing to pay. Therefore, we will not sell product A. The target prices for products B, C,

Exhibit 6.7   Setting the Target Price

	Product	A	B	C	D
Traditional GAAP product cost (from Exhibit 6.5)		$500	$ 750	$ 700	$350
Markup (arbitrarily selected) on cost		54%	54%	54%	54%
Target price per unit based on traditional GAAP cost (154% of cost)		$770	$1,155	$1,078	$539
ABC product cost (from Exhibit 6.6)		$650	$1,050	1,000	$500
Markup (to yield same *overall* profit as above) on cost		10%	10%	10%	10%
Target price per unit based on full ABC product cost (110% of cost)		$715	$1,155	$1,100	$550

Exhibit 6.8   Total Budgeted Sales Revenue

Product	A	B	C	D	Total
Target price based on traditional GAAP cost (from Exhibit 6.7)	770	$ 1,155	$ 1,078	$ 539	
Quantity budgeted to be sold (from Exhibit 6.3)	200	200	300	400	
Total budgeted sales	$154,000	$231,000	$323,400	$215,600	$924,000
Target price based on full ABC product cost (from Exhibit 6.7)	$ 715	$ 1,155	$ 1,100	$ 550	
Quantity budgeted to be sold (from Exhibit 6.3)	200	200	300	400	
Total budgeted sales	$143,000	$231,000	$330,000	$220,000	$924,000

and D are less than the amounts that our potential customers are willing to pay, so we will sell those three products.

At this point, we will assume that the company is using the traditional GAAP costing approach to pricing. If we do not sell product A, then we will lose the $114,000 throughput of product A ($770 price less $200 materials = throughput of $570 per unit; 200 units @ $570 = $114,000), resulting in an overall loss of $30,000.[16] However, this need not be a problem; we simply re-price our remaining products. We use the same five-step allocation procedure shown in Exhibit 6.4, but now we remove the 2,000 labor hours associated with product A from the base so as to have a base of 14,000 labor hours. This results in a higher overhead rate of $22.85714[17] per labor hour and product costs as shown in Exhibit 6.11. The revised prices and resultant sales dollars are also shown in Exhibit 6.11. The 63.7% markup used in Exhibit 6.11 was again selected to result in the desired profit of $84,000. The profit generated by the three remaining prod-

Exhibit 6.9   Profit If All Products Are Sold

Sales		$924,000
Materials[a]		120,000
Throughput contribution margin		$804,000
Operational expenses (from Exhibit 6.3)		
Labor	$160,000	
Manufacturing overhead	320,000	
Selling, general, and administrative	240,000	720,000
Profit		$ 84,000

[a] The materials data are shown in Exhibit 6.3. The total materials cost is (A: 200 units @ $200 = $40,000 + B: 200 units @ $150 = $30,000 + C: 300 @ $100 = $30,000 + D: 400 @ $50 = $20,000) a total of $120,000.

Exhibit 6.10   Which Products Will Be Sold?

Product	A	B	C	D
Cost-based target price (GAAP cost from Exhibit 6.7)	$770	$1,155	$1,078	$539
Cost-based target price (ABC cost from Exhibit 6.7)	$715	$1,155	$1,100	$550
Price customer is willing to pay	$600	$2,000	$1,700	$2,000
Will customer purchase?	No	Yes	Yes	Yes

ucts, as shown in Exhibit 6.11, is just a rounding error away from the originally budgeted profit of $84,000.

Opportunity Gap

Note that, with our now downsized product offerings, the prices of all remaining products still are well below the amounts that the customers are willing to pay. The original target price and the revised target price are shown in Exhibit 6.12. The last line of Exhibit 6.12 reflects the difference between the revised target price and the price that the customers are willing to pay. The term **opportunity gap** indicates the difference between what a customer would be willing to pay and the target price.

Having an opportunity gap means that the company is able to raise its prices, if desired, to maintain its margins. It will then be able to have those nice, predictable earnings financial analysts so love. Of course, if the opportunity gap no longer exists for a company that is following a cost-based pricing strategy, then the company will not be able to maintain its earnings level. The cost-based pricing strategy will work as long as there is

Exhibit 6.11   Revised Budgeted Cost, Price, and Profit

Product	B	C	D	Total
Material	$150	$100	$ 50	
Labor	200	200	100	
Overhead @ $22.85714	457	457	229	
Total product cost per unit	$807	$757	$379	
Markup @ 63.7%	514	482	241	
Target price	$1,321	$1,239	$620	
Quantity	200	300	400	
Sale	264,200	$371,700	$248,000	$883,900
Materials				80,000
Labor				160,000
Manufacturing overhead				320,000
Selling, general, and administrative				240,000
Profit				$ 83,900

Exhibit 6.12   Effect of Re-Pricing Products

Product	B	C	D
Cost-based target price (GAAP cost from Exhibit 6.7)	$1,155	$1,078	$539
Target price after removing product A from allocation base (Exhibit 6.11)	$1,321	$1,239	$620
Price customer is willing to pay	$2,000	$1,700	$2,000
Will customer purchase?	Yes	Yes	Yes
Opportunity gap	$679	$461	$1,380

a substantial opportunity gap and there are no serious competitors who do not "play the game." It worked in the United States from the 1930s until the 1970s and beyond.

The opportunity gap between the cost-based price and the price customers are willing to pay *must* exist for a cost-based pricing scheme to work. James Hangstefer observes that the ability "to raise prices without losing volume or incurring customer anger is a key qualitative indicator" of market-position strength.[18] The ability to raise prices, as noted by Hangstefer, is both evidence of the opportunity gap and an indicator of an environment in which the cost-based pricing strategy might work well.

If an overall opportunity gap does not exist for an organization that is pursuing a cost-based pricing strategy, then the organization must (1) introduce new products that do have an opportunity gap, (2) reduce costs sufficiently to create an opportunity gap for existing products, (3) change its strategy to one more suitable for the market environment that it faces, or (4) go out of business.

The cost-based pricing methodology provides a useful mechanical process for setting prices—that is, a pricing strategy. The cost-based pricing strategy is a means of ensuring a "satisfactory" profit rather than a maximum profit. There is no attempt to earn as much as possible when using the cost-based pricing strategy. On the positive side, it might result in a price so low that potential competitors would receive no signals as to the desirability of the market.

The entire cost-based pricing discussion was conducted without reference to specific identification of the organization's constraints. If an unrecognized internal physical constraint exists in the organization using cost-based pricing, then the organization will either expand its capacity, rolling the additional expenditures into its cost-based prices, or base its cost-based prices on the actual volume level achieved. Even though constraints are not specifically documented, they do limit the organization's performance. Since the traditional cost-based pricing method does not incorporate the constraint into the pricing process, it fails as a constraints accounting decision technique. This same phenomenon operates with respect to the throughput mix decision (see Chapter 5).

Comparison of GAAP to ABC Cost-Based Pricing

Before we leave this discussion of the traditional cost-based pricing technique, we need to explore the ramifications of the different prices that result from using a GAAP-based cost as opposed to an activity-based cost for pricing. We might assume that for any product or service for which we wish to establish a cost-based target price the market can be depicted as shown in Exhibit 6.13.

The horizontal axis of Exhibit 6.13, which represents the perceived value of the offering for the customer ranging from a low perceived value on the left side to a high perceived value on the right, is divided into three sections representing the inclination of potential customers to buy the product or service. The dark vertical line represents the target price. At the far left of the range is a group of customers for whom the price is too high. These customers do not purchase the product. In the middle are customers who purchase the product or service, but who complain about the price; these customers are readily open to price-based offers from competitors. At the far right is a group of customers who are delighted with the price and who would be willing to pay even more for the product or service.

The problem is that we don't know what the distribution looks like. Three potential distributions, labeled A, B, and C, are shown in Exhibit 6.13. Any one of the three could represent reality. As a result, when we set

Exhibit 6.13   Perceived Value to Customer

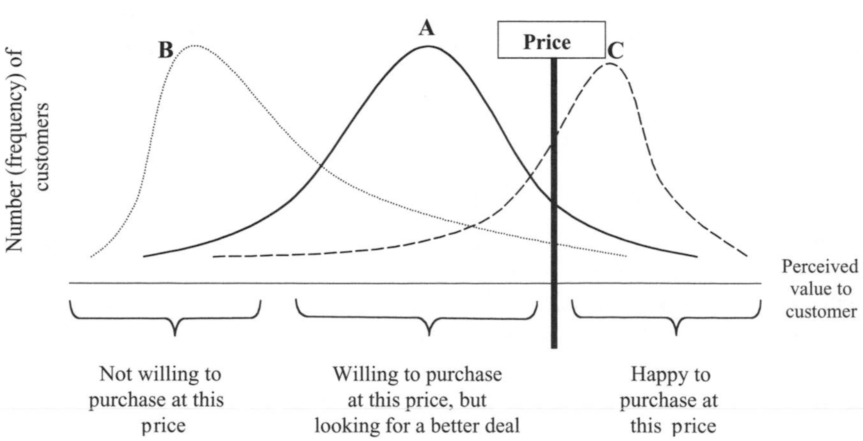

a target price, we cast it into a relatively uncertain distribution of customer-perceived value. Since the price that customers are willing to pay is a function of the product's utility for the customers, and the target price that is charged by the company is entirely determined by the company's costs, it would be only unlikely coincidence if the price represented the most advantageous for the company.

In order to explore the dynamics of pricing in an uncertain environment, we created a simple **Monte Carlo simulation.** This simulation assumed a company selling nine products. A market potential was randomly generated for each product in terms of units that could be sold—provided that the asking price was not more than customers were willing to pay. Other input variables such as ABC allocation base data, raw materials price, and labor hours required per unit were also randomly generated. The result was nine products with widely differing characteristics from a financial point of view. For example, the characteristics of three of the products are summarized in Exhibit 6.14.

These structural input data (the elements illustrated in Exhibit 6.14) were then held constant during the individual iterations of the simulation run. Asking, or target, prices were calculated based on both traditional direct labor manufacturing cost and on full activity-based costs using the allocation techniques discussed earlier in this section. The calculated product-cost amounts were increased by markup percentages to arrive at simulated asking prices. The markup percentages were selected to yield equal net profits if all products were sold in a manner similar to that shown in Exhibit 6.7. That is, budgeted profit was the same for both traditional and ABC product costing.

In each individual iteration of the simulation run, the uncertainty regarding the customers' perception of value implicit in Exhibit 6.13 was incorporated into the simulation model by randomly and independently generating a maximum price that customers would be willing to pay for each product. This maximum price was then compared to the asking price

Exhibit 6.14   Sample Simulation Data

Product	G	H	J
Market potential	25 units	30 units	150 units
ABC allocation bases:			
Base 1	1,021	311	657
Base 2	14	14	29
Base 3	18	2	9
Raw materials cost per unit	$486.00	$385.00	$119.00
Labor hours per unit	4.6	2.0	4.1

that had been calculated for the product. If the maximum price that the customer was willing to pay was greater than the asking price, then the simulation considered the product to be sold at the asking price. This situation is illustrated by distribution A in Exhibit 6.15. However, if the asking price was more than the customer was willing to pay, illustrated by distribution B in Exhibit 6.15, the product was not sold for that iteration.

The simulation allowed comparison of the dynamics of the traditional GAAP pricing scheme to that of activity-based costing in an uncertain market. The results of the simulation after 5,000 iterations are summarized in Exhibit 6.16.

The average profit generated using the traditional cost-based pricing method was $288,231. Keeping all elements of the simulation the same, except using activity-based costing for the pricing model, average profits were $155,636, which is 46% less than the traditional cost-based pricing method. The traditional pricing method resulted in greater profit than the ABC method in 61% of the iterations.

These results are interesting because the provision of more accurate product costs for pricing purposes is often cited as an advantage of activity-based costing techniques over traditional pricing techniques.[19] In particular, the greater the amount of indirect cost (manufacturing overhead and Selling, General, Administrative (SGA)) and the greater the diversity in "products, customers and processes," the more important to use a full cost model with multiple allocation bases **(cost drivers)**.[20] If we were to use less than full cost or only a single allocation base, then we would assign too much cost to "low overhead" products, resulting in their not being competitively priced. At the same time, we would assign too little cost to "high

Exhibit 6.15   Simulated Sales Distributions

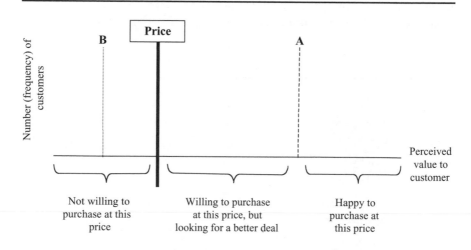

Exhibit 6.16   GAAP versus ABC Cost-Based Pricing: Simulation Results

Cost technique	Traditional (GAAP)	Activity based
Average (mean) profit	$288,231	$155,635
Iterations showing profits rather than losses	68%	67%
Average capacity utilization	62%	71%
Iterations for which GAAP profit is more than ABC profit	61%	

overhead" products, resulting in a price too low to recover the overhead they caused.

This leads us to question, Why? Why does the simulation result in greater profitability when prices are based on traditional GAAP costing with a single allocation base than with the presumably more sophisticated activity-based costing method?

Two forces were at work here. First, if we assume that the activity-based costing model provides a more accurate view of a product cost, then the pricing model based on traditional direct labor actually was doing some "marginal" (less than full cost) pricing. This had the effect of making better use of available, but otherwise unused, resources. Traditional full cost pricing turns out to be just a *politically correct* way to do marginal pricing. Second, the magnitude of difference between the lowest priced product and highest priced product is greater using the ABC cost as opposed to the traditional cost (18.3 times greater versus 4.6 times greater in the simulation). The higher priced products were sold significantly less frequently or not at all. We should recognize that when the proponents of activity-based costing claim that other models apply *too little* or *too much* cost to products, their reference point for measuring is a preconceived notion of how much the cost *should* be, not the market value for the product.

Cost-Based Pricing Summary

The pricing strategy of setting prices based on the calculated cost of a product is widely employed. This is a viable strategy *provided that an opportunity gap exists*. The traditional cost-based pricing method results in a systematic method of marginal pricing that results in greater profitability when used for pricing than does the activity-based costing method. Both the traditional and activity-based cost-based pricing strategies may be undertaken without reference to constraints.

CONSTRAINT-BASED PRICING

In the previous section we explored cost-based pricing without reference to constraints; in this section we explore two additional pricing possibili-

ties. First, we look at using an internal physical constraint as the foundation for cost-based pricing, as some enterprise resource planning vendors
recommend as a way to incorporate constraints into the pricing decision.
Such a technique would implement the first attribute of constraints accounting—explicit consideration of the role of constraints. This technique considers constraints but does not consider throughput effects, nor
does it decouple throughput (T) from operational expenses (OE). Second, we use the pricing simulator discussed in the previous section to in-
vestigate the use of randomly selected prices. Such a random pricing
mechanism would implement the third attribute of constraints accounting—decoupling of throughput from operational expense.

Cost-Based Pricing with Constraint-Time-Based Costing

In Chapter 3 we explored a constraint-time-based costing method. Perhaps we could use this technique to establish prices for our products,
thereby overcoming the objection that the constraint has not been considered in the pricing decision. Continuing with the cost-based pricing example presented, Exhibit 6.17 repeats the basic data from Exhibit 6.3 along
with additional data about the amount of time required at each of two resources (designated #1 and #2). Each of these resources is available for
2,000 hours each year.

 The first step is to determine whether a physical constraint exists. We
can check for an internal physical constraint in this case by calculating the
total hours required of the resources to meet the market potential. These
calculations are shown in Exhibit 6.18.

Exhibit 6.17 Example Data for Cost-Based Pricing Using a Constraint-
Time Base

Product	A	B	C	D
Production resource #1 time required per unit	2 hours	4 hours	2 hours	1 hours
Production resource #2 time required per unit	1 hour	1.5 hours	2 hours	3 hours
Annual market potential	200 units	200 units	300 units	400 units
Materials unit cost	$200	$150	$100	$50
Labor per unit	10 hours	20 hours	20 hours	10 hours
Manufacturing overhead				320,000
Selling, general, & administrative expenses				240,000
There are 8 direct labor employees earning $10.00 per hour and working 2,000 hours per year, for a total annual direct labor cost of $160,000. Production resources #1 and #2 are each available 2,000 hours per year.				

Exhibit 6.18   Resource Hours Required for Market Potential

Product	A	B	C	D	Total
Resource #1 hours per unit	2	4	2	1	
Resource #2 hours per unit	1	1.5	2	3	
Market potential (units)	200	200	300	400	
Total hours required of resource #1	400	800	600	400	2,200
Total hours required of resource #2	200	300	600	1,200	2,300

Resource #1 is required for 2,200 hours to produce the full market potential, and 2,300 hours of resource #2 are needed. Since only 2,000 hours are available on each of the resources, each is potentially an internal constraint. Let us start by assuming that resource #2 is the constraint. After all, resource #2 requires more total hours to meet the market potential (2,300 hours) than does resource #1 (2,200 hours). The allocation of operational expense (OE) to individual products is shown in Exhibit 6.19.

Step 1 of the allocation process is to determine the total cost to be allocated. In this case, we are using the constraint management concept of OE; therefore, so the cost to be allocated consists of all non-truly variable costs, including direct labor, manufacturing overhead, and selling and general administrative expense—for a total of $720,000. The only cost not included in this allocation is that for the raw materials for each product. The constraint-time-based allocation is similar to the activity-based costing allocation in that it is a full cost model. The allocation base is the amount of constraint time available over the time period represented by the OE.

Exhibit 6.19   Constraint-Time-Based Allocation of OE to Products: Resource #2

Determine the total cost to be allocated.	Direct Labor = Mfg Overhead = SG&A = Total Operational Expense (OE)=	$160,000 320,000 240,000 $720,000
Determine the allocation base.	Annual hours of resource #2 available	2,000 constraint hours
Make the unit cost calculation.	$720,000 / 2,000 constraint hours	$360.00 per constraint hour
Put the unit cost with the elements of the base.	Product Allocation A: 1.0 hour @ $360 B: 1.5 hours @ $360 C: 2.0 hours @ $360 D: 3.0 hours @ $360	OE per unit $ 360.00 $ 540.00 $ 720.00 $1,080.00

The constraint selected is resource #2 and has 2,000 hours available for the year. Dividing $720,000 of OE by 2,000 constraint hours available, we arrive at $360 per constraint hour. Finally, the allocated cost is associated with individual units of product, charging $360 of OE for each hour of constraint time required by a product. Product A, which requires one hour of resource #2 in its production, is assigned $360 of OE. In similar fashion, costs are allocated to products B, C, and D.

In Exhibit 6.20, the full constraint-time-based unit cost of each of the products is calculated by adding the allocated portion of OE to the cost of raw materials. A markup of 10.19% was added to arrive at initial target prices.

In selecting the 10.19% markup on total cost, two factors were considered. First, it was necessary to establish an assumed physical sales volume. Since the market potential exceeds the available capacity, it was necessary to decide what products will not be sold. The accepted constraint management way of making such a decision is to rank the products in terms of their throughput per constraint unit (t/cu). However, this technique is not useful in this case because throughput cannot be calculated until a price is known, and our task here is to set the prices initially. Even if the prices had already been set using a constraint-time-based pricing technique, the effect of the technique would have been to price products in such a way that they all had approximately equal throughputs per constraint unit.[21] Therefore, the assumed volume levels were arbitrarily set at about 87% of the market potential (2,000 resource #2 hours available divided by 2,300 resource #2 hours required for market potential), resulting in assumed sales of 173, 174, 261, and 348 units of products A, B, C, and D, respectively.

Having established the assumed volumes, we could then select a markup percentage that would yield approximately the same $84,000 overall profit as was the result of the traditional GAAP and activity-based examples in the previous section. The proof of this profit is shown in Exhibit 6.21.

Exhibit 6.20   Constraint-Time-Based Price: Resource #2

Product	A	B	C	D
Raw materials	$200.00	$150.00	$ 100.00	$ 50.00
Allocated OE (from Exhibit 6.19)	360.00	540.00	720.00	1,080.00
Total constraint-time-based cost	$560.00	$690.00	$820.00	$1,130.00
Markup (selected to yield same $84,000 profit as Exhibits 6.9 and 6.11)	10.19%	10.19%	10.19%	10.19%
Target price per unit based on constraint-time based product cost (110.19% of cost)	$617.06	$760.31	$903.56	$1,245.15

Exhibit 6.21   Proof of Profit If All Products Sold (Constraint Is Resource #2)

Product	A	B	C	D	Total
Price per unit	$617.06	$760.31	$903.56	$1,245.15	
Raw materials	200.00	150.00	100.00	50.00	
Unit throughput	$417.06	$610.31	$803.56	$1,195.15	
Sales quantity (units)	173	174	261	348	
Throughput	$72,151	$106,194	$209,729	$415,912	$803,986
Operational expense					720,000
Profit					$ 83,986

But, what if we used the "wrong" constraint for pricing our products? Exhibit 6.22 again calculates the OE allocation but this time using resource #1 as the constraint.

The first three steps in Exhibit 6.22 are almost the same as were calculated for resource #2 (Exhibit 6.19). The allocation method chosen does not change the reality of operational expense incurred (at least not in the short run), so OE still totals $720.000. Since there are 2,000 hours available for resource #1, the quantity of the allocation base (2,000 hours) remains the same. Of course, these are hours of resource #1 rather than resource #2. Once again, the allocated OE cost of a constraint hour is $360. However, the allocation of OE to individual units based on resource #1 is notably different. These OE allocations to individual products using resource #1 hours as the base are shown in Exhibit 6.22.

The different allocation to products results in a significantly different set of prices. Constraint-time-based prices for the four products are shown in Exhibit 6.23.

Exhibit 6.22   Constraint-Time-Based Allocation of OE to Products: Resource #1

Determine the total cost to be allocated.	Direct Labor = Mfg Overhead = SG&A = Total Operational Expense =	$160,000 320,000 240,000 $720,000
Determine the allocation base.	Annual hours of resource #2 available	2,000 constraint hours
Make the unit cost calculation.	$720,000 / 2,000 constraint hours	$360.00 per constraint hour
Put the unit cost with the elements of the base.	Product Allocation A: 2.0 hour @ $360 B: 4.0 hours @ $360 C: 2.0 hours @ $360 D: 1.0 hours @ $360	OE per unit $ 720.00 $ 1,440.00 $ 720.00 $ 360.00

Exhibit 6.23   Constraint-Time-Based Price: Resource #1

Product	A	B	C	D
Raw materials	$200.00	$ 150.00	$ 100.00	$ 50.00
Allocated OE (from Exhibit 6.19)	720.00	1,440.00	720.00	360.00
Total constraint-time-based cost	$920.00	$1,590.00	$820.00	$410.00
Markup (selected to yield same $84,000 profit as Exhibits 6.9 and 6.11)	10.13%	10.13%	10.13%	10.13%
Target price per unit based on constraint-time based product cost (110.13% of cost)	$1,013.20	$ 1,751.07	$903.07	$451.53

The prices that were established using resource #1 as the constraint will also allow a profit of about $84,000 to be earned if all budgeted products are sold (see Exhibit 6.24). The sales volumes reflected in Exhibit 6.24 are set at approximately 91% (2,000/2,200) of the full market potential.

The target prices calculated using constraint-time bases are compared in Exhibit 6.25 along with the more traditional GAAP cost and activity-based costing prices.

When constraint resource usage is not uniform across products as is the case in this example, the constraint-time-based target price varies significantly. This effect magnifies an often cited criticism of product costing based on traditional labor—as direct labor becomes a smaller portion of total cost, a small distortion (inaccuracy in computation or assumption) is overstated in the product cost.[22] But this avoids the question. If the objective is to determine the **true cost** of a product, then the search will prove to be fruitless. However, if the purpose is to establish prices for products such that a target profit may be achieved, then all three of the cost-based methods (GAAP, activity-based, and constraint-time-based), if applied consistently, work.

Exhibit 6.24   Proof of Profit If All Products Sold (Constraint Is Resource #1)

Product	A	B	C	D	Total
Price per unit	$1,013.20	$ 1,751.07	$903.07	$451.53	
Raw materials	200.00	150.00	100.00	50.00	
Unit throughput	$ 813.20	$ 1,601.07	$803.07	$401.53	
Sales quantity (units)	181	182	273	364	
Throughput	$ 147,189	$ 291,395	$219,238	$146,157	$803,979
Operational expense					720,000
Profit					$ 83,979

Exhibit 6.25   Summary of GAAP, Activity-Based, and Constraint-Time-Based Target Prices

Price based on:	A	B	C	D
Traditional GAAP	$770.00	$1,155.00	$1,078.00	$539.00
Activity-based costing	$715.00	$1,155.00	$1,100.00	$550.00
Constraint resource #2	$617.06	$760.31	$903.56	$1,245.15
Constraint resource # 1	$1,013.20	$1,751.07	$903.07	$451.53
Price customer is willing to pay	$600.00	$2,000.00	$1,700.00	$2,000.00

If the organization were to elevate its internal physical constraint sufficiently, or if demand fell sufficiently, the constraint would shift to the market. In that case, the constraint-based price would be based on materials cost only since there would be no internal constraint on which to base the price.[23] When we consider the use of these data, we realize that the constraint-time-based cost may not be so different from the more traditional product-costing methods. Recall that our purpose of establishing a cost-based price is to set a price that will allow a target profit level to be achieved. Comparing the prices in Exhibit 6.25 to the prices that customers are willing to pay, we see that, in this example, the same effect—that customers do not purchase product A—exists regardless of the pricing method used. But note that the magnitudes of the opportunity gaps are different.

Constraints Accounting Evaluation of Constraint-Time-Based Pricing

The constraint-time-based pricing technique could not be useful unless either price stability were of no consequence in the market or an internal constraint were firmly and strategically positioned. Beyond that, this technique shares all the characteristics of other cost-based pricing techniques. The constraint-time-based pricing technique meets the first attribute of constraints accounting but does not satisfy the second and third characteristics. By basing the price on constraint time required for the product, there is explicit consideration of the role of constraints. However, throughput contribution effects of alternative prices are not measured. Instead, the pricing scheme largely equalizes the throughput contributions of the various products. Finally, rather than decouple throughput from operational expense, pricing based on constraint time closely links the two. In fact, this linkage is the objective of cost-based pricing schemes.

DECOUPLING THROUGHPUT
FROM OPERATIONAL EXPENSE

Constraint-time-based pricing, as well as the other cost-based target pricing methods discussed, result in T that is closely linked to OE. If we are to implement the third aspect of constraints accounting, decoupling T from OE, in the pricing function, then it will be necessary to find a different mechanism—perhaps even in a different paradigm—for pricing.

Previously, we presented the results of a Monte Carlo simulation of the bottom-line effects of basing prices on a full cost measurement such as activity-based costing. These simulation effects were contrasted with traditional GAAP product cost, which includes manufacturing costs only. The results, summarized in Exhibit 6.16, showed that the traditional GAAP model produced greater average (mean) profits than the activity-based model. The GAAP model also produced profits more frequently. The simulation model had two-thirds of the operational expense in manufacturing costs and one-third as SGA expense. If using only two-thirds of the operational expense as the basis for costing were better than using all of it, perhaps using even less operational expense would be better yet. The simulator was modified to create a target price by adding a randomly generated target throughput amount to the variable cost (raw materials) of the products. No operational expense was included as an element of the target throughput. The results of this revised simulation run, as well as the previous runs are shown in Exhibit 6.26.

The random pricing resulted in average simulated profits of $363,184. This was 46% greater than the average profit when prices were based on traditional GAAP costing and 133% greater than the average profit using activity-based-costing. Exhibit 6.26 also shows that the random target pricing technique incurred losses more frequently than either the GAAP or the activity-based methods. The implication of the greater average profitability combined with the more frequent losses is that the totally random method resulted in significantly greater variability in profitability

Exhibit 6.26   Simulation Results: Random Pricing

Cost Technique	Traditional (GAAP)	Activity Based	Random
Average (mean) profit	$288,231	$155,635	$363,184
Iterations showing profits rather than losses	68%	67%	60%
Average capacity utilization	62%	71%	56%
Iterations for which GAAP profit is more than ABC profit	61%		
Iterations for which random profit is more than ABC profit			54%

than the other methods.[24] The simulation also showed that the random pricing method resulted in using less capacity of the organization than did the other methods.

Using a randomly generated markup can break the linkage between operational expense and throughput. Breaking the linkage produces significant benefits through a combination of increased margins for some products and filling otherwise unused capacity for others.

CONSTRAINTS ACCOUNTING APPROACH TO PRICING

The first part of this chapter dealt with historical cost pricing models appropriate for use when the overall organizational objective is to have stable and satisfactory profits. For historical cost pricing models to be successful in achieving stable and satisfactory profits, it is also necessary that there be a large opportunity gap. Then the constraints accounting concepts of explicit consideration of constraints and decoupling T from OE were added to the pricing model. Specifying throughput contribution effects adds the final attribute of constraints accounting.

The constraints accounting target pricing analysis has two components:

1. Determination of a **springboard base.**
2. Selection of a target amount of **throughput premium** above any throughput provided by the springboard base.

The ultimate target price is the sum of these two components. For instance, if the springboard base were $2 and the target throughput premium $3, then the target price would be $5.

Let us continue the Example Company case, presented in Chapter 5, to compute some target prices. We will pick up at the updated forecast (Exhibit 5.27) based on selling all three products (Atex, 2,080 units; Detron, 2,651 units; and Fonic, 2,080 units). Assume that a new product, Haton, is being considered. Each unit of Haton will need 2 units of material CRM at $35 per unit and will require 23 minutes of time on the welder. Recall that the welder is an internal physical constraint and that products Detron and Fonic use the welder. The required times on the other production resources are: Assembler, 10 minutes; Cutter, 12 minutes; Grinder, 15 minutes; and Polisher, 16 minutes.

Determination of the Springboard Base

A mechanical calculation determines the springboard base. The question answered by this portion of the pricing analysis is, "What is the lowest price that would allow the product to be sold without reducing the overall profitability of the organization?"

In the constraint management environment, analyses differ depending on the relationship to the constraint. Therefore, the starting point in a constraints accounting pricing analysis always is to determine the relationship of the product (or order) being priced to the constraint. Two possibilities exist:

1. The product or order requires use of an internal physical constraint resource,

2. The product or order does not require use of an internal physical constraint resource.

Springboard Base with Internal Physical Constraint

When the product under consideration requires use of an internal physical constraint resource, the objective of the pricing analysis is to decide how to make the best use of the constraint (i.e., decide how to exploit it). A new product (or variant of an existing product for sale in a segmented market) will necessarily supplant, or reduce, the sales of an existing product. In this case, the objective of the springboard base portion of the target price is to ensure that the throughput of the new product is at least sufficient to replace the lost throughput (an opportunity cost) of the products or orders being replaced.

The method of estimating lost throughput opportunity cost depends on whether the replacement is made in an incremental or step-type market. In the **incremental market,** the assumption is one of many customers, each being asked the same price and each having a relatively small share of the overall throughput mix (Detron and Haton) using the constraint. In this case we do the analysis on a unit of product basis. A **step-type market** is characterized by changes that take place in lump-sum amounts relating to a relatively broad range of activity and typically occur when a relatively few customers account for the major portion of our business.

Incremental Market. We will look at the springboard base for the incremental market first. The minimum costs that must be recovered by Haton may be divided into two types: unit-coupled costs and value-coupled costs. Unit-coupled costs are truly variable costs that vary in total with the number of units that are sold (or produced). Value-coupled costs are costs that are expressed and calculated as a percentage of sales value.

Since the welder is an active constraint, producing Haton will necessitate the reduction in output of either Detron or Fonic.[25] In Exhibit 5.26 we have seen that Fonic has a higher throughput per constraint minute than Detron ($7.57 per welder minute versus $4.89 per welder minute); the organization should therefore maintain its production of Fonic and reduce output of Detron in order to produce Haton. The relevant opportunity cost for the springboard base is the *lost throughput of Detron that would not be sold* to make way for the Haton. The springboard base for Haton would be calculated as shown in Exhibit 6.27.

The unit-coupled costs associated with the introduction of Haton are raw materials (2 CRM for each unit of Haton) and the *opportunity cost* of the Detron that will not be sold if Haton were to be introduced. Each unit of Haton requires two units of raw material CRM at $35, or a total of $70 per unit of Haton. Each unit of Haton produced will require 23 minutes on the welder, which is an internal physical constraint. The decision has been made to reduce production of Detron as necessary if Haton is introduced. Therefore, 23 minutes of Detron production will be lost for each unit of Haton produced. Existing throughput is reduced by $4.89 for each minute of welder time used to produce Haton. Twenty-three minutes @ $4.89 is $112.47 of lost throughput from reduced sales of Detron for each unit of Haton produced. The total unit-coupled costs of producing Haton, then, are $182.47.

The only value-coupled cost in this case is the sales commission of 5% of the selling price. The value-coupled cost presents us with a bit of a problem in that we have not yet calculated a price. However, if we divide the price-coupled cost rate by 1 minus the rate, we will arrive at an equivalent rate that we can apply to the unit-coupled costs to arrive at the total value-coupled costs. For this example the calculation is [0.05/(1.00 − 0.05) * $182.47 = $9.60]. Adding the unit-coupled and value-coupled costs, we arrive at the springboard base of $192.07.

This springboard base is a breakeven amount that leaves the organization equally well off, other things being the same, whether the new product is sold at a price equal to the springboard base or existing prod-

Exhibit 6.27 Springboard Base for Haton with Internal Constraint and Incremental Market

Unit-coupled costs to be recovered in the springboard base:	
Raw material CRM (2 CRM @ $35.00)	$ 70.00
Lost throughput of Detron (23 minutes of constraint time (welder) used for each unit of Haton @ $4.89, the throughput rate of Detron as calculated in Exhibit 5.26)	112.47
Total unit-coupled costs	$182.47
Value-coupled costs to be recovered in the springboard base:	
Sales commission @ 5.00% [(commission rate) / (1 - (commission rate)] * (unit-coupled costs)	9.60
Springboard base per unit for Haton (total costs to be recovered)	$192.07

ucts are retained. The composition of the springboard base is shown in a graphical format in Exhibit 6.28.

This $192.07 springboard base for Haton will recoup the out-of-pocket and opportunity costs of selling Haton but will not change the overall throughput of the organization. The springboard base sets a *lower bound on the target price*. The actual target price selected will be higher than the springboard base; how much higher is the question of the throughput premium. If the market for Haton will not support a price greater than $192.07, then Haton should not be introduced. However, any price above $192.07 may be expected to enhance the throughput mix and increase the profits of the Example Company.

In calculating the anticipated throughput effects of alternative target prices, the unit-coupled costs will remain the same per unit, but the value-coupled costs will change for each different price examined. If the projected volume of Haton required more time on the constraint than is currently used for production of Detron, then the analysis must be expanded to include the effect on the other products using the constraint (Fonic).

Step-Type Market

Let us change our assumption about our customers to that of a step-type market rather than an incremental market. The step-type market calls for a somewhat different approach to the calculation of the throughput effect. We will continue with the assumption that the current throughput mix is as previously shown in Exhibit 5.28 and repeated here as Exhibit 6.29.

Customer 03, a relatively new customer that the Example Company has been cultivating, has asked the Example Company to bid on supplying

Exhibit 6.28   Composition of Springboard Base ($)

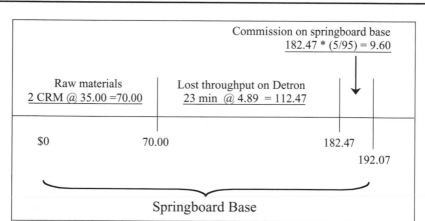

Exhibit 6.29   Sales by Customer

Customer	Product	Quantity	Price	Throughput	Throughput per Constraint Unit (t/cu [a])	Customer t/cu [a]
Cust 01	Atex	416	$ 180.00	$ 44,096		
	Detron	530	$ 322.86	112,210	$5.96	
	Fonic	416	$ 180.71	44,377	$7.23	$8.04
Cust 02	Atex	270	$ 189.05	30,941		
	Detron	162	$ 337.65	36,574	$6.36	
	Fonic	241	$ 211.00	32,643	$9.18	$10.76
Cust 03	Atex	369	$ 180.96	39,451		
	Detron	48	$ 256.14	7,120	$4.18	
	Fonic	109	$ 208.07	14,461	$8.99	$18.43
Cust 04	Atex	145	$ 194.16	17,321		
	Detron	80	$ 209.57	8,327	$2.93	
	Fonic	599	$ 186.67	67,290	$7.62	$7.96
Cust 05	Atex	880	$ 162.67	78,792		
	Detron	1,831	$ 258.96	276,497	$4.25	
	Fonic	715	$ 159.27	61,710	$5.85	$5.52
Total				$871,810		

[a] Constraint unit (cu) is welder minutes.

their ongoing need of about 550 units of Haton as well as their current volumes of Atex, Detron, and Fonic.

The welder is an active constraint, and each unit of Haton requires the use of 23 welder minutes. Therefore, if Haton is supplied to customer 03, it will be necessary to cut back on orders of Detron or Fonic somewhere else. The customers want the entire quantities of their orders, or none of that product at all, from the Example Company. Management has made the policy decisions that such cuts will come neither from customer 03, who is viewed as a growth customer consistent with the strategic plan, nor from customer 05, who receives special consideration by virtue of being the largest customer. After eliminating the orders for customers 03 and 05 and for Atex, which does not conflict with production of Haton, six orders remain from which the volume reduction must come if Haton is to be produced for customer 03. These six orders are shown in Exhibit 6.30.

In order to produce 550 units of Haton, each requiring 23 minutes on the welder, it will be necessary to free up at least 12,650 minutes of welding time (550 units * 23 minutes per unit = 12,650 minutes). This time could be obtained in a number of ways. For example, eliminating order number 1, Detron for customer 01, would release 18,020 minutes and would reduce throughput by $112,210. Other combinations of orders that would provide the necessary time are shown in Exhibit 6.31.

Exhibit 6.30   Orders Potentially Displaced by Haton

Order	Customer	Product	Quantity	Welder Minutes	Total Minutes	Throughput
1	Cust 01	Detron	530	34	18,020	$112,210
2	Cust 01	Fonic	416	14	5,824	$ 44,377
3	Cust 02	Detron	162	34	5,508	$ 36,574
4	Cust 02	Fonic	241	14	3,374	$ 32,643
5	Cust 04	Detron	80	34	2,720	$ 8,327
6	Cust 04	Fonic	599	14	8,386	$ 67,290

As shown in Exhibit 6.31, eliminating the combination of orders 2, 3, and 5 would have the smallest total throughput opportunity cost. Now that the business to be turned away is known (orders 2, 3, and 5), the springboard base is computed in a manner similar to the incremental case presented in Exhibit 6.27, replacing the lost throughput *per unit* with lost throughput *per order* in the analysis. The springboard base calculation is shown in Exhibit 6.32.

Since the analysis deals with complete orders, rather than incremental units, the calculations reflect the entire amount of 550 units of Haton. No attempt is made to express the opportunity costs on a unit basis because the selection of orders to be eliminated is dependent on the entire 550 unit volume level. Had the Haton bid been for a significantly different volume than 550 units, a different set of orders might have been eliminated.

The total cost that must be recovered for this bid to be a breakeven proposition for the company is $134,503. If desired, a minimum desired unit price may be calculated by dividing the total minimum desired price of $134,503 by 550 units to arrive at $245 per unit.

Exhibit 6.31   Throughput Effect of Eliminating Orders

Order Numbers Eliminated	Total Welder Minutes Recovered	Total Throughput Reduction as a Result of Eliminating These Orders: Opportunity Cost
1	18,020	$112,210
2, 3, and 4	14,706	$113,594
2, 3, and 5	14,052	$ 89,278
2, 3, and 6	19,718	$148,240
3, 4, and 6	17,268	$136,507
4, 5, and 6	14,480	$108,260

Exhibit 6.32   Springboard Base for 550 Units of Haton for Customer 03

				Order (550 units)
Order-coupled costs:				
Raw materials (2 CRM @ $35.00 * 550 units)				$ 38,500
Opportunity cost of lost throughput on existing orders:				
Order	Customer	Product	Throughput	
2	01	Fonic	$44,377	
3	02	Detron	36,574	
5	04	Detron	8,327	89,278
Total order-coupled cost to be recovered				$127,778
Average t/unit = $89,278 / 550 units = $162.32				
Average t/cu = $162.32 / 23 minutes = $7.0574				
Value-coupled costs:				
Commission @ 5.00% (.05/.95 * $127,778)				6,725
Springboard base for 550 units of Haton (total costs to be recovered)				$134,503
Springboard base per unit (total price / 550 units)				$245

Note that the selection of orders to be eliminated did not strictly follow the sequence of throughput per constraint unit (t/cu). Comparing Exhibit 6.28 with Exhibit 6.32, we see that Fonic for customer 01, which was eliminated, had throughput of $7.23 for each welder minute, while Detron for customer 01, which had throughput of only $5.96 per welder minute, was retained. The springboard base of $245 per unit for the step-type market is about 27% greater than the springboard base of $192.07 calculated for the incremental market (Exhibit 6.27). One reason for the difference is the different t/cus of the orders eliminated. A second reason is that by eliminating orders as blocks of units, it was necessary to eliminate orders until the capacity needed for Haton was exceeded. The three orders eliminated released 14,052 minutes on the welder, but only 12,650 minutes were needed for the production of Haton. This means that 1,402 unused minutes are available on the welder. The opportunity cost of this time was also included in the springboard base for Haton.

One might ask whether the welder is still a constraint in this case. Since we can identify the business that we will be turning away, the answer is yes. In some cases this unused capacity resulting from **step-type changes** in volume can be quite significant. For example, suppliers to original equipment manufacturers (OEM) often have a few contracts for large volumes. A company having 6,000 hours available on its strategic constraint resource annually might have contracts and opportunities as shown in Exhibit 6.33.

Exhibit 6.33   Existing and Potential Contracts

Contract	Status	Annual Constraint Hours Required	Constraint Capacity Required	Constraint Capacity Used (cumulative for existing contracts)
1	Existing	1,500	25%	25%
2	Existing	1,200	20%	45%
3	Existing	1,300	22%	67%
Opportunity				
4	Available	3,000	50%	*117%*
5	Available	2,500	42%	*109%*

The firm is operating at only 67% of capacity. Nevertheless, it is turning away business (contracts 4 and 5). Thus, it appears that the firm has substantial excess capacity and at the same time has an internal physical constraint. This situation appears to call for two things. First, treat the resource as a tactical constraint for exploitation decisions and subordination.[26] Often these two steps are sufficient to release additional capacity, which might allow contract 4 or 5 to be accepted within the existing resource limitations. Second, search for **temporary free products** to fill the currently unused capacity.

Before we turn our attention to the throughput premium component of a target price, we will complete our discussion of the springboard base by addressing free products.

Springboard Base for Free Products

Products not requiring time on a capacity-constrained resource, whether because the product routing does not include an internal physical constraint or because the system does not have an active constraint resource, are known as **free products.** Temporary free products sold in a competitive market, properly segmented from the company's other business, are advantageous for filling unused productive capacity on a short-term basis. A competitive market is desirable because the organization may enter and leave this type of market conveniently and change its prices at will.[27] The effective segmentation of the market is necessary to prevent price changes for temporary free products from affecting pricing of the core business of the organization.

Assume that the Example Company's market potential for Detron is only 1,500 units rather than 4,160 units and that there is no internal physical constraint. Once again, the truly variable cost of the product establishes the springboard base. Any amounts received above the springboard base will flow directly into the bottom line.

The springboard base of $73.69 for Haton as a free product is calculated in Exhibit 6.34. It still includes both unit-coupled costs and value-coupled costs. However, no opportunity cost is associated with lost throughput of other products not sold due to production of Haton since no tradeoff at a constraint is necessary.

The springboard bases that we have calculated in this section satisfy the constraints accounting attributes of specific identification of the role of constraints and specification of throughput contribution effects. However, the springboard bases calculated are very much directly tied to costs.[28] We now direct our attention to the last aspect of constraints accounting, decoupling throughput (T) from operational expense (OE).

Target Throughput Premium

We have seen how to establish a springboard base, but, of course, we would not be willing to sell the product at that price. Selection of a target amount of throughput premium *above any throughput provided for by the springboard base* is the second aspect of setting a target price.

The springboard base simply establishes a lower bound for the price. But how much above that lower bound should we ask for the product? A constraints accounting algorithm for setting the target throughput premium above the springboard base should:

- Be consistent with a process of ongoing improvement (POOGI). That is, it should establish a *process* to systematically change the throughput mix in such a way that the bottom line is improved.

- Include a provision for encouraging decoupling throughput from operational expense.

The throughput premium decision involves a great deal of management judgment. Recall that we are dealing with the group of pricing situa-

Exhibit 6.34   Springboard Base for Haton as a Free Product

Unit-coupled costs to be recovered in the springboard base:	
Raw material CRM (2 @ $35.00)	$70.00
Lost throughput of other products not sold due to production of Haton (No other products affected.)	0.00
Total unit-coupled costs	$70.00
Value-coupled costs to be recovered in the springboard base:	
Sales commission @ 5.00%	
[(commission rate) / (1 - (commission rate)] * (unit-coupled costs)	3.69
Springboard base per unit for Haton (total costs to be recovered)	73.69

tions in which we do not know with confidence how much customers are willing to pay for our products. This group includes existing products for which we have used cost-based pricing to establish target prices.

Our technique for selecting the appropriate target throughput premium will be to first establish a reasonable range of potential target throughput amounts and then to select a specific amount from within that range. We will discuss the target throughput premium separately for products using an internal physical constraint and for free products because the data available for the pricing decision are different for those cases.

Throughput Premium with Internal Constraint

Continuing with the Example Company and the incremental market situation, Exhibit 6.35 illustrates the selection of a target price. There are a lot of data to comprehend, so we will examine them thoroughly. Exhibit 6.35 shows the calculation of the throughput premium and target price for Haton.

The springboard base of $192.07 that we calculated for Haton (in Exhibit 6.27) is shown on line A in Exhibit 6.35. We call this a *springboard base* because we want the actual throughput provided by Haton to spring above this amount. But what reasonable premium could we expect to receive above this springboard base?

When an active internal physical constraint exists, it is possible to calculate a throughput per constraint unit (t/cu). We know that we have cus-

Exhibit 6.35 Throughput Premium and Target Price for Haton: Internal Constraint and Incremental Market

A	Springboard base of Haton per unit (from Exhibit 6.27)	$192.07
B	Throughput per constraint unit (t/cu) at springboard base (t/cu at lower bound for target price) (from Exhibit 6.27)	$4.89
C	Highest throughput per constraint unit (t/cu) of products currently being sold (from Exhibit 5.26)	$7.57
D	Scope of existing t/cu above Springboard base t/cu (C - B)	$2.68
E	Adjusted throughput premium scope (arbitrary premium of 20% applied to allow for price expansion) [D * (1 + 0.20)]	$3.22
F	Arbitrarily selected target throughput premium percentage for Haton (from Pricing Selector in Exhibit 6.36)	35%
G	Target throughput premium per constraint unit (E * F)	$1.13
H	Total target throughput premium per unit of Haton (23 minutes * G)	$25.99
I	Sales commission on target throughput premium (H * 5/95)	$1.37
J	Target price for Haton (A + H + I)	$219.43

tomers who are willing to pay the prices that resulted in the existing t/cu. Therefore, the existing t/cus are reasonable amounts to expect. When there is an internal physical constraint, we can use the existing t/cu as a basis for estimating a reasonable range of target prices for a new product (Haton).

The t/cu at the springboard base, shown on line B, represents a starting place; the company would not want to sell the new product, Haton, for an amount less than $192.07. The lost throughput on Detron included in the springboard base is $4.89 per welder minute, or a total of $112.47 for the 23 minutes required to produce a unit of Haton. Line C shows the greatest t/cu that we are currently receiving, $7.57. This is the throughput per constraint minute of Fonic as calculated in Exhibit 5.16. Subtracting the springboard base t/cu ($4.89) from the greatest t/cu being received ($7.57) yields $2.68, which is the scope of the existing t/cu above the springboard base t/cu and is shown on line D. The existing scope of throughput above the springboard base for the 23 minutes required to produce a unit of Haton would be $61.64 (23 minutes @ 2.68).

If the upper bound on the target price were to be limited to the existing range of throughputs per constraint unit, then there would also be a limit to this portion of the process of ongoing improvement. Such a limitation can be avoided by extending the upper bound on the target price beyond the scope. In Exhibit 6.35 this is done on line E by expanding the existing scope by an arbitrarily chosen amount of 20%.[29] This is the first of two arbitrary values that we use in this pricing technique. The purpose of each is to help establish a target throughput amount that has been decoupled from operational expenses. The price expansion premium is $0.536 per constraint unit (20% of $2.68), or $12.33 per unit of Haton (see Exhibit 6.37). This results in a total adjusted throughput premium scope of $3.22 ($2.68 + $0.536 = $3.22) per constraint unit.[30] The target throughput premium should fall within this $3.22 scope.

On line F of Exhibit 6.35, we see the second selection of an arbitrary value. In this case the *Pricing Selector* shown in Exhibit 6.36 was used to select a percentage to apply to the adjusted scope. This spin resulted in 35%. Any random selection method, such as selecting the next number in sequence from a table of random numbers or the *RAND()* function in an electronic spreadsheet, would serve the same purpose.

The target throughput premium for Haton is calculated on line G. The randomly selected percentage on line F is applied to the adjusted scope of $3.22 on line E to arrive at $1.13 as the target throughput premium per constraint unit.

On line H the throughput premium per constraint unit is converted to a throughput premium per unit of Haton. Multiplying $1.13 by the 23 minutes required to produce a unit of Haton results in $25.99 of target throughput premium per unit.

Exhibit 6.36   Pricing Selector

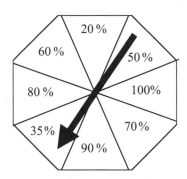

Pricing Selector: Multiply adjusted throughput premium scope by percentage selected by spinner to obtain target throughput premium for product.

It will be necessary to pay the 5% sales commission on the throughput premium as well as the springboard base. Therefore, the additional commission is calculated on line I by multiplying the target throughput premium of $25.99 by 5/95 for an additional commission of $1.37.

Finally, the target price of $219.43 is calculated by adding together the springboard base (line A), the target throughput premium above the springboard base (line H), and the commission on the target throughput premium (line I).

Exhibit 6.37 shows the range of potential target prices for Haton. The potential range of target prices builds on the springboard base. The diagram of the springboard base in Exhibit 6.13 is repeated in the shaded area of Exhibit 6.37 to illustrate the total composition of the potential target prices.

Target Throughput for Free Product

When the product or order being priced is a free product, data concerning current t/cu amounts are not available with respect to an active constraint. Therefore, some other means must be found to set the lower and upper bounds of the scope of the target throughput.

If a strategic pseudo-constraint has been identified and the product in question requires use of the strategic pseudo-constraint, then the *throughput per pseudo-constraint unit (t/pcu)* might be used as a base point for establishing an upper bound on the potential target price.

One reason, among a number of possible reasons, that the strategic constraint is not also the active tactical constraint might be that the target

Exhibit 6.37   Composition of Unit Target Price Range for Haton ($ per Unit)

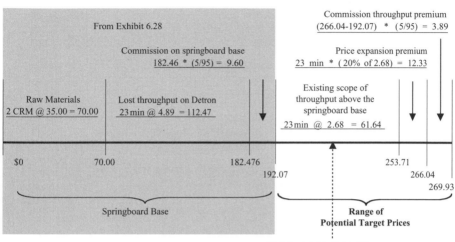

From Exhibit 6.28		Commission throughput premium (266.04-192.07) * (5/95) = 3.89

Commission on springboard base
182.46 * (5/95) = 9.60

Price expansion premium
23 min * (20% of 2.68) = 12.33

| Raw Materials
2 CRM @ 35.00 = 70.00 | Lost throughput on Detron
23 min @ 4.89 = 112.47 | Existing scope of
throughput above the
springboard base
23 min @ 2.68 = 61.64 |

$0   70.00   182.476   253.71
                                                    192.07   266.04
                                                                                        269.93

Springboard Base   Range of
                          Potential Target Prices

Target price selected *in this case*
(192.07 + 25.99 + 1.37) = 219.43

prices set in the past have been too high. Therefore, the lower bound on the target price for a free product should be less than that which would be represented by the lowest existing throughput per pseudo-constraint unit. Experimentation with the pricing simulator previously mentioned showed that expected profitability was increased for free products when the scope of the target throughput range started at a point somewhat greater than zero. An arbitrary mechanical means of calculating such a point might be to take the midpoint between the lowest of the existing t/pcu and zero.[31] This will result in some products being priced at relatively lower prices than are currently being charged. Such lower prices may lead to increased unit sales volumes. The throughput contributions of these increased volumes flow through to the bottom line.

When sales volumes increase sufficiently, the constraint shifts to an internal location. At this time, the *pricing technique also shifts* from the free product to the internally constrained model, and the throughput mix is *systematically improved as part of the process of ongoing improvement*. A pseudo-constraint pricing example for a free product is shown in Exhibit 6.38, which assumes that the welder is the strategic pseudo-constraint.

The target throughput analysis for Haton as a free product starts with the springboard base of $73.69 as was calculated in Exhibit 6.34. The lower bound on the target throughput, shown on line C, is arbitrarily established at one-half the existing throughputs per strategic pseudo-constraint unit (line B). The difference between the highest throughput

Exhibit 6.38   Target Throughput and Price for Haton as a Free Product:
Price Based on Pseudo-Constraint (Welder)

		Per unit
A	Springboard price of Haton per unit (from Exhibit 6.34)	$73.69
B	Lowest throughput per pseudo-constraint unit (t/pcu) of products currently being sold (from Exhibit 5.26)	$4.89
C	Lower bound on target throughput (arbitrarily selected as the midpoint between zero and B)	$2.45
D	Highest throughput per pseudo-constraint unit (t/pcu) of products currently being sold (from Exhibit 5.26)	$7.57
E	Scope of existing t/pcu above lower bound (D – C)	$5.12
F	Adjusted throughput scope (arbitrary premium of 20% applied to allow for price expansion) [E * (1 + 0.20)]	$6.14
G	Target throughput percentage for Haton (from Price Selector in Exhibit 6.39)	80%
H	Target throughput per pseudo-constraint unit (F * G)	$4.91
I	Total target throughput per unit of Haton (23 minutes * H)	$112.93
J	Sales commission on target throughput (I * 5/95)	$5.94
K	Target price for Haton (A + I + J)	$192.65

per pseudo-constraint unit currently being received (line D) and the
lower bound on target throughput is the existing throughput scope (line
E). On line F the scope is expanded by the previously arbitrarily selected
amount of 20% to permit the possibility of improved margins. At line G
the *Pricing Selector* is spun again, this time landing on 80% (Exhibit 6.39).

By multiplying the adjusted throughput scope by the 80% target
throughput percentage selected by the spinner, a target throughput of

Exhibit 6.39   Pricing Selector

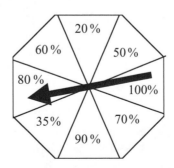

Pricing Selector: Multiply adjusted
throughput scope by percentage selected by
spinner to obtain target throughput premium for product.

$4.91 per pseudo-constraint unit is obtained (line H). Changing the focus of the analysis from the pseudo-constraint to the product, Haton, the target throughput per pseudo-constraint unit (welder minute) is multiplied by 23 minutes of welder time required for each minute of Haton produced to arrive at a target throughput of $112.93 for Haton (line I).

Finally, a provision is made for the sales commission or other value-coupled costs on line J. Adding together the springboard base, target throughput, and sales commission, we calculate the target price of $192.65 on line K.

If no strategic constraint has been identified, there is no basis for establishing a starting point for the pricing decision. In this case, the decision appears to be entirely a managerial judgment call. Management might set upper and lower bounds on the target price and use a pricing selector within that range.

Other Pricing Observations

This final pricing segment contains further observations relative to the pricing decision.

Future Analyses

The target prices calculated will be a price for planning. If Haton is actually introduced at this price, it will be part of the new reality of the organization. At that time, the various detailed elements comprising the target pricing analysis are no longer relevant as associated with Haton. Once the price has been established, the relevant factors for future analyses are just the price, truly variable costs, and constraint usage. For instance, the relevant data for future analyses of Haton are shown in Exhibit 6.40.

Exhibit 6.40 Data for Future Analyses Relating to Haton: Incremental Market

| Situation | Target Price Selected | Variable Costs | | Throughput | Tactical Constraint Units | Strategic Constraint Units |
		Materials	Commission			
With internal constraint	$219.43	$70.00	$10.97	$138.46	23 minutes	23 minutes
Data source	Exhibit 6.35	Exhibit 6.27	Exhibit 6.27 Exhibit 6.35			
As a free product	$192.65	$70.00	$9.63	$113.02	Not applicable	23 minutes
Data source	Exhibit 6.38	Exhibit 6.27	Exhibit 6.34 Exhibit 6.38			

Tactical and Strategic Constraints Different

If the internal tactical constraint is not the same as the strategic constraint, then the pricing analysis of Haton using the internal physical constraint should also be accompanied by a complimentary analysis of the new product as a free product with respect to the strategic constraint. The target price would then be selected from the intersection of the target price ranges of both analyses, if possible, thus satisfying the requirements of both the strategic and tactical constraints.

Ongoing Improvement

The pricing techniques explored in this section involve a significant amount of arbitrary estimates. This uncertainty is introduced intentionally in order to test penetration of the opportunity gap in pricing. Intentional arbitrariness was introduced in three areas:

1. The amount of expansion percentage applied to the throughput scope to test higher prices. This is a management judgment call.
2. Selection of the throughput premium percentage that was used to determine exactly where, within the overall range of potential target prices, the target price would be set. This was selected by using some type of random number generator in order to enforce randomness.
3. In the case of a free product, the value used for the lower bound on target price was calculated by a formula, but the formula was chosen arbitrarily.

Track the percentages used and the success rates in obtaining sales or winning bids to assist in adjusting the formulas and arbitrary values in the future. The techniques that have been described should be scrutinized closely for potential negative branches prior to implementation.

Crossing a Free Product Boundary

Actions taken with respect to free products should result in an increase in volume sold of those products. At some point, the reduction in the protective capacity of nonconstraint resources will cause an emerging constraint. *A new constraint changes everything and should be treated as a strategic, rather than tactical, decision moment.*

Incremental OE and I

In some cases, introducing a new product or crossing a free product boundary will require an actual increase of operational expense or inventory/investment—as contrasted with reassignment of resources from other organizational areas. Such increased OE or I expenditures should be handled in accordance with the established budgetary revision process (previously discussed in Chapter 4). The increased expenditures, even though occurring in lump-sum amounts rather than as incrementally variable per unit amounts, represent a true variation in costs and should be treated as unit-coupled costs in a pricing analysis. The springboard base analysis for such a situation would be similar to the example for a step-type market presented in Exhibit 6.32. Additional capacity purchased (I) and additional operational expense (OE) incurred become fixed as part of a new reality for future analyses.

Protective Capacity

Increases in sales of temporary free products should typically take place in an incremental fashion. Protective capacity levels need to be monitored carefully so as to not impede the production of the organization's core products.

SUMMARY

This chapter explored conventional cost-based pricing, constraint-time-based pricing, and a constraints accounting approach to pricing. The cost-based and constraint-time-based techniques were not responsive to the attributes of constraints accounting and therefore were not appropriate for use with constraint management.

A springboard base answers the traditional accounting question, "What is the minimum price that can be charged without reducing profits?" Of course, the minimum price is not our objective. We want to set a target price above the minimum price. Traditional accounting analysis does not answer the question, "How much above the minimum price should our price be?" However, some simulation research has suggested that greater profitability may be achieved with lower capacity utilization by avoiding cost-based pricing models. If there is an active internal constraint, then some business is intentionally turned away, and it is possible to know exactly what business is turned away. This means that there is the ability to experiment with prices in an orderly manner and without significant danger of downside risk. Constraints accounting extends the scope of financial analysis by providing a dynamic means for improving exploitation decisions and hence bottom-line profitability.

The establishment of a constraints accounting approach to setting target prices addresses an Archimedean constraint that exists in almost every profit-oriented organization and is a key to locking in a process of ongoing improvement.

NOTES

[1] For example, in their review of the TOC literature incorporating 396 citations, Mabin and Balderstone do not include any aspect of pricing in the index. Victoria J. Mabin and Steven J. Balderstone, *The World of the Theory of Constraints: A Review of the International Literature* (St. Lucie Press, 2000). Robert J. Campbell discusses cost-based pricing with TOC in his book *Competitive Cost-Based Pricing Systems for Modern Manufacturing* (Quorum Books, 1992), Chapters 5, 6, and 9. Thomas Corbett's *Throughput Accounting* (North River Press Corp., 1998) summarizes TOC pricing on pages 119–130.

[2] The conditions required for a traditional cost-based pricing technique to be effective are that both (1) customers are willing to pay a greater amount than the cost-based price and (2) the firm desires only satisfactory, as opposed to greater, profits.

[3] D. Waldron, interview cited by David Dugdale and T. Colwyn Jones, *Accounting for Throughput* (The Chartered Institute of Management Accountants, CIMA, 1996), p. 18.

[4] Archie Lockamy III and James F. Cox III, *Reengineering Performance Measurement: How to Align Systems to Improve Processes, Products, and Profits* (Richard D. Irwin, 1994), p. 98.

[5] Ibid.

[6] Ibid.

[7] Ibid.

[8] Thomas B. McMullen, Jr., *Introduction to the Theory of Constraints (TOC) Management System* (St. Lucie Press, 1998), pp. 217–224.

[9] Robert S. Kaplan and Anthony A. Atkinson, *Advanced Managerial Accounting* (Prentice-Hall, 1989), p. 187.

[10] Eric Noreen, Debra Smith and James Mackey, *The Theory of Constraints and Its Implications for Management Accounting* (North River Press, 1995), sponsored by the Institute for Management Accountants (IMA) and Price Waterhouse, pp. xxvii, xxix.

[11] Recall that the *earnings statement* (or income or P&L statement) is represented by the formula: Sales minus Expenses = Net Profit. The *balance sheet* (or statement of financial position) is represented by the formula: Assets = Liabilities plus Owners Equity.

[12] Eliyahu M. Goldratt, *Haystack Syndrome: Sifting Information Out of the Ocean Data* (North River Press, 1991), pp. 38–39.

[13] Robert N. Anthony, *Tell It Like It Was: A Conceptual Framework for Financial Accounting* (Richard D. Irwin, 1983), pp. 37–38.

[14] C. J. McNair and Richard Vangermeersch, *Total Capacity Management: Optimizing at the Operational, Tactical, and Strategic Levels* (The IMA Foundation for Applied Research, 1998), Chapter 9.

[15] The different target prices are emphasized because one of the authors has often heard it stated that the base selected does not make a difference to the prices, and it is simply a matter of selecting the appropriate markup percentage.

[16] $84,000 budgeted profit less $114,000 throughput lost from Product A = −$30,000.

[17] $320,000 of manufacturing overhead divided by 14,000 labor hours = $22.85714 per labor hour.

[18] James B. Hangstefer, "Revenue Margin: A Better Way to Measure Company Growth," *Strategic Finance* (July 2000), p. 43.

[19] For example, see Robert S. Kaplan and Robin Cooper, *Cost and Effect: Using*

Integrated Cost Systems to Drive Profitability and Performance (Harvard Business School Press, 1998), pp. 166–170.

[20] Ibid., p. 164.

[21] The throughput per constraint unit (t/cu) will be equal for each product if the markup is made on OE costs only. If the markup is made on total unit costs (that is, including materials and other truly variable costs), as is done in this example, the t/cu will vary somewhat from product to product because of different ratios of variable costs to constraint time required.

[22] Robert S. Kaplan and Robin Cooper, *Cost and Effect, Using Integrated Cost Systems to Drive Profitability and Performance* (Harvard Business School Press, 1998), pp. 2–3.

[23] It has been suggested, "In retail, the market is always the constraint" (Tony Rizzo, CMSIG Internet discussion list May 11, 2001 Subject: Pricing). If this is so, then a retailer that routinely establishes prices by marking up the wholesale price by some percentage is an instance of this pricing technique.

[24] Experimentation with the simulator revealed that, by introducing a relatively small constant (k) addition to the price, such that the price became (raw materials cost + k + random markup), a large (threefold) increase in profitability combined with a higher probability of profitability than either the GAAP or activity-based methods resulted.

[25] If such a reduction is not required, either because the welder is not really a constraint (that is, it is a pseudo-constraint) or because the organization is expanding capacity on the welder, then the analysis should be for a free product rather than an internal physical constraint.

[26] This might be called a **secondary constraint,** a resource having some of the characteristics of a physical constraint, but which also has characteristics of a pseudo-constraint. Exploitation decisions and subordination actions for the secondary constraint should be consistent with the subordination to the primary constraint—the market in this case.

[27] One way to communicate with customers is through the price. Set a price high enough in a competitive market, and the customer does not purchase from you. Set the price low enough, and the customer does purchase from you. The customer feels in control, and there is no ill will when the company turns business away in this manner.

[28] The costs may be either historical costs or opportunity costs. Both are cost-based measurements.

[29] A different amount, such as 10%, 40%, or 150%, might have been chosen. Twenty percent was chosen simply as being not too far apart from the existing amounts—this is strictly a management judgment call.

[30] ($2.68 + $0.54) or (120% of $2.68) or (1.2 * $2.68).

[31] This, as well as the other arbitrarily selected values in this section, is just that— arbitrarily selected. A different value with the same purpose would do as well.

7

Tactical Subordination in Manufacturing

TACTICAL SUBORDINATION

Tactical subordination refers to subordinating actions taken by members of the organization to the exploitation decisions for tactical, or currently active, constraints. Most day-to-day operating activities fall into this category. In this chapter we look at constraints accounting support for tactical subordination in manufacturing. The following two chapters examine examples for project management and sales. Because subordination is unique to the particular situation, at the beginning of each example we devote some attention to the specific operating environment.

Our first example, taken from the functional area of manufacturing, illustrates subordination control within a drum-buffer-rope production-scheduling environment. Constraints accounting supports buffer management by providing information that can be used to identify emerging constraints.

DRUM-BUFFER-ROPE SCHEDULING

The first TOC application, popularized in *The Goal: Excellence in Manufacturing*, is known as a drum-buffer-rope (DBR) scheduling system. The principles of DBR are well documented and will not be repeated here.[1] DBR will be explored just enough to gain a sense of what type of buffer management reporting is associated with DBR so that correct subordination actions can be taken. The essential parts of a DBR production scheduling system are illustrated in Exhibit 7.1.

The **drum** in a DBR scheduling system sets the pace for the flow of products started into process. The drum may be at the market (shipping),

174

Exhibit 7.1   Essential Components of a DBR Scheduling System

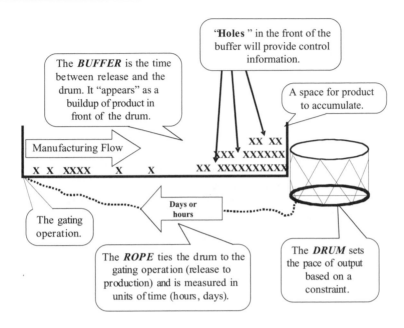

at an internal constraint, or both. When the drum is at shipping, it is equivalent to a **master production schedule (MPS)** in a MRP II system. A **rope,** which is measured in units of time, ties the drum to the **gating operation,** where material is released to initiate the production or other process. The product is started into process at the gate a rope length of time before it is due at the drum. The rope length is longer than we actually expect the process to take. Therefore, the product will tend to pile up in front of the drum. The *buffer* in DBR may be described as a **time buffer** and consists of the entire time from material release to the estimated time of processing by a constraint resource or scheduled shipment. The pile of inventory in front of the drum is the physical manifestation of the time buffer. Of course, it will be necessary to have a place to store this pile of work. Such physical space is called a **space buffer.** Some things that we expect to be in the pile may have been delayed at some point in the manufacturing process. These delayed items, which we expect to be there but which are not, create holes in the buffer.

The rope length (which is measured in time units such as minutes, hours, or days) also defines the size of the time buffer. The rope length represents the amount of time before the product is due at the drum that the process is started. The rope must be long enough to allow for:

- Processing times at all of the individual operations to be performed.
- Normal statistical fluctuations in processing times.
- Delays due to unscheduled or unexpected events (sometimes referred to as Murphy).
- Queue (waiting) times due to **noninstant availability** of resources.

Buffer holes provide clues as to the proper buffer size. The blend of available, but currently unused, capacity and time available to recover from delays serves to protect the flow of product through the manufacturing process. The buffer size—that is, the rope length or amount of time allowed for an order to be completed—should be large enough to allow most orders to be completed without expediting.

The general pattern of the length of delays illustrated by the skewed frequency distribution shown in Exhibit 7.2 applies in most cases. The provision of time buffers large enough to accommodate the right-hand *tail* of the distribution for every unit that is produced would imply very large work-in-process inventories and correspondingly long production lead times. If enough time is allowed to complete all orders routinely, the buffers will be very large.

A hypothetical time buffer is illustrated in Exhibit 7.3. In this example the rope is 15 days long. The drum is either the shipping schedule, a tactical internal physical constraint, or a strategic pseudo-constraint.[2] The average time for our product to flow through this system is about seven to eight days, or one-half of the rope length.

At any given time, the buffer can be expected to be about one-half full. Some items will arrive at the drum sooner, some later. An **expedite**

Exhibit 7.2 Protecting against Statistical Fluctuation

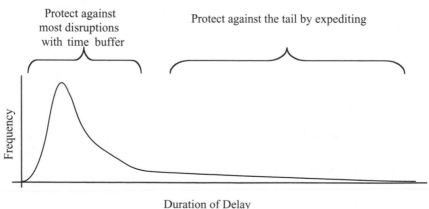

Exhibit 7.3   Buffer, Buffer Holes, and Expedite Zone

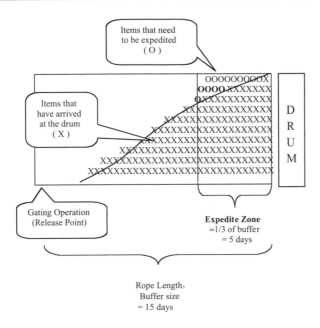

zone, consisting of approximately one-third of the buffer length, is established. In Exhibit 7.3, the Xs represent orders that have been completely processed and are sitting on the shipping dock waiting to be shipped. The Os represent items that have been in process for ten days but that have not yet reached the drum (i.e., are not ready to be shipped). Most of these O items will be finished on time without heroic effort. However, some are destined to be completed in the tail of the delay distribution (Exhibit 7.2) unless they are expedited to prevent them from missing their shipping dates.

Organizations implementing constraints accounting should have purged legacy control measures that focus on the efficiency of individual areas of operation (such as those provided by standard cost variance reporting) from both their data collection and data reporting systems. Buffer management reporting is the subordination control mechanism that replaces legacy efficiency reporting. Buffer management reporting is a replacement, not an add-on, control mechanism.

BUFFER MANAGEMENT REPORTING

Buffer management, which relies on analysis of buffers, is a central subordination control mechanism associated with constraint management. In the manufacturing environment, buffer holes give us the data to answer these four subordination questions:

1. How do we know whether the buffer size is too large or too small?

2. When is protective capacity being eroded?

3. What priority should an individual job have relative to other jobs?

4. Where should local enhancement initiatives be focused?

Three reports will give us the answers to these questions:

1. Buffer Hole Percentage Trend

2. Buffer Hole Report

3. Buffer Hole Pareto Analysis

Detecting Buffer Holes

The common element of these reports is the detection of buffer holes. An item is considered to be a buffer hole if it has not reached the drum by an expedite zone length of time before it is scheduled to be there. Detecting buffer holes requires little new data. All we need to know to determine whether a particular item is a hole in the buffer is the time at which the item is *due at the drum (DAD),* the length of the rope, the length of the expedite zone, and whether the item has *arrived at the drum (AAD).* The organization's database system[3] should have the date that the item is due at the drum (DAD) because that data is used to calculate the order release date to the gating operation. It is necessary to collect data about when an item arrives at the drum (AAD). This is a new piece of data. We need only to know *if* the item has arrived at the drum, a *yes/no* question, in order to identify a buffer hole. Nevertheless, we will document the time of arrival in order to have the ability do additional analysis.

Assume that the current date is June 16, that the organization is using a rope length of 15 days, and that the expedite zone is set at one-third of the rope. The set of orders for which the release date (= DAD – rope) is before the current date, the start of the expedite zone (= DAD – length of expedite zone) is before the current date, and for which there is no AAD (i.e., the item has not yet arrived at the drum) is the set of buffer holes. Let us examine the detection of buffer holes in more detail. (Examples of detecting buffer holes are shown in Exhibit 7.4.)

- Order 101 is due at the drum on June 17, subtracting the rope of 15 days yields a release date of June 2, and a five-day expedite zone started on June 12. Since this order has not yet arrived at the drum, it is a buffer hole.

Exhibit 7.4   Detecting Buffer Holes

			Start of		
Order Number	Due at Drum (DAD)	Release Date	Expedite Zone	Arrival at Drum (AAD)	Buffer Hole ?
Current Date: 06/16/20X1					
Rope Length: 15 Days					
Expedite Zone Length: 1/3 of rope = 5 days					
101	06/17/20X1	06/02/20X1	06/12/20X1	No	Yes
102	06/23/20X1	06/08/20X1	06/18/20X1	06/14/20Xl	No
103	06/23/20X1	06/08/20X1	06/18/20X1	No	No
104	07/17/20X1	07/02/20X1	07/12/20X1	No	No
105	08/24/20X1	08/09/20X1	08/19/20X1	06/15/20X1	Pile

- Order 102 is due at the drum on June 23, subtracting the rope of 15 days yields a release date of June 8, a five-day expedite zone starts on June 18, and the order arrived at the drum on June 14. Since today is June 16 and the item is already at the drum, order 102 is not a buffer hole.

- Order 103 also is due at the drum (DAD) on June 23 and has order release and expedite dates of June 8 and June 18. Since it is only June 16, this order is not yet a buffer hole.

- Order 104 is due at the drum on July 17. The order release date is July 2, and the start of the expedite zone will be July 12. This order has not caused a buffer hole because it has not yet reached the expedite date.

- Order 105 is not due to be released until August 9.

Order 105 is an interesting case because it is already sitting in front of the drum. Either there has been an error in the paperwork somewhere or order 105 was started early. If the latter is the case, then order 105 was not yet expected in the buffer. Although this is not a hole in the buffer, it is an undesirable situation. Completing work on this order early may have led to an increased incidence of noninstant availability of resources or reduced protective capacity. Either of these possibilities would require the buffer to be larger than necessary, extending production lead time and increasing inventory/investment. For want of a better term, we call this situation a **buffer pile** because such early (or unordered) items will tend to pile up in front of the drum.

Buffer Hole Percentage Trend

The items that enter the expedite zone of a buffer as holes will reveal whether the buffer is too large or too small.[4] If there are never holes in a buffer expedite zone, then the buffer is much larger than it needs to be. This results in longer than necessary production lead times and in the need to carry large inventories. However, buffers that often have many holes in the expedite zone are too small. The frequency of occurrence of buffer holes, then, may be used to determine the proper buffer size in a particular situation. The general rule is that too many holes mean the buffer is too small and too few holes indicate that the buffer is too large.

We can protect against the right-hand *tail* of the delay distribution (total manufacturing time beyond about two standard deviations longer than the average; see Exhibit 7.2) either by increasing the size of the buffer or by expediting things that are late. It is desirable to have a few buffer holes appear in the expedite zone. Reducing the number of buffer holes by increasing buffer size means holding more work-in-process inventory, which, in turn, implies longer production lead time.

Buffer Hole Percentage Trend Report

The buffer size (rope length) is flexible and should be adjusted as appropriate to accommodate changing conditions.[5] This is a management judgment decision regarding the tradeoff between production lead time and expediting to protect against the tail of the delay duration distribution. For example, let us assume that management has decided that a buffer size that results in about 4% of the jobs entering the expedite zone is appropriate and comfortable for the organization.[6] This decision is part of the exploitation plan for the constraint. A Buffer Hole Percentage Trend report is illustrated in Exhibit 7.5 and is used to validate the size of a buffer.

The raw data on which the Buffer Hole Percentage Trend report is based are just the percentage of items shipped each day that had created a hole in the expedite zone of the buffer.[7] The report shows an upper control limit at 5.5% of items expedited (the top horizontal line) and a lower control limit at 2.5% expedited (the lower horizontal line). The small gray circles represent the individual data points, one for each day. For example, if 150 orders were shipped on one day and 7 of those orders had created buffer holes in the expedite zone, the observation for that day would have been 4.7% (7 divided by 150). The wavy line running through the center of the data is a 15-day moving average of the percentage of expedited orders. This line shows the trend of the data.

The purpose of the Buffer Hole Percentage Trend report is *only* to confirm the suitability of the buffer size. If the buffer is of appropriate

Exhibit 7.5   Buffer Hole Percentage Report

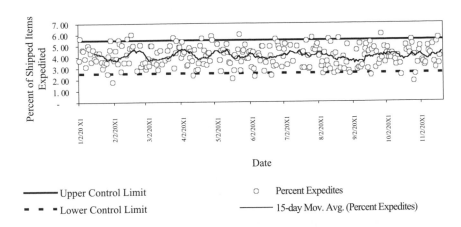

size, the percentage of orders expedited on any given day should generally fall within the upper and lower control limits.[8] The buffer represented in Exhibit 7.5 appears to be about the right size; no change in rope length is needed.

The buffer represented in Exhibit 7.6 illustrates a different situation. In this exhibit the buffer size appears to be appropriate until about the middle of May. At that point the moving average closes the upper control limit. The moving average then remains close to the upper limit until the end of July, at which point it breaks through the upper control limit indicating that some managerial action in needed.

Exhibit 7.6   Buffer Hole Percentage Trend

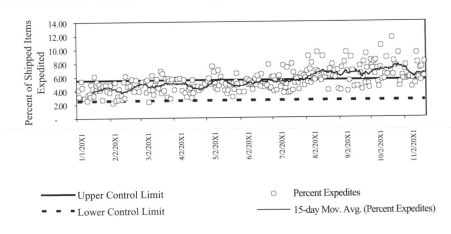

But exactly what management action is needed? Since the 4% average of expedited orders to total orders established by management is part of the exploitation decisions, this question may be phrased more accurately as: *What action should be taken in order to subordinate to the exploitation decision?*

The fact that more buffer holes are appearing points toward erosion of protective capacity available in the system. The flow of work through a system is protected by the combination of unused time in a time buffer (time available to recover from a disruption) and unused capacity at physical resources.[9] Potential causes of the erosion of protective capacity shown in Exhibit 7.6 include greater demands placed on the system (selling more), shifting demands placed on the system (change in product mix), reduction in physical capacity (new employees replacing experienced operators, increase in equipment breakdowns, employee absenteeism, electric service interruptions, more instances of noninstant availability), or failure of some people to subordinate properly. In all of these cases, time is the dependent variable. The product makes its journey through the organization more slowly, resulting in more orders entering the expedite zone of the buffer. The *subordination action* that should be taken is to expand the size of the buffer (length of the rope) to compensate for the reduced protective capacity. The 15-day rope might be expanded to a 17- or 18-day rope.[10]

Had the moving average broken through the lower control limit, it would have been a sign that the system had more protective capacity than needed. That is, the time buffer was larger than necessary. Again, the question is: *What action should be taken in order to subordinate to the exploitation decision?* In this case the rope, and corresponding production lead time, would be shortened incrementally until the average was again within the control limits. In this manner, the enhancements to the operating environment are incorporated into the overall process, ultimately allowing shorter, but very reliable, quoted lead times and the associated competitive advantage.[11]

The only purpose of the Buffer Hole Percentage Trend report is to provide an indication of appropriate rope length overall. Other reports will provide more specific information relating to the subordination for individual orders or areas.

Buffer Hole Report

In addition to providing indications relative to buffer size and level of protective capacity, hole data from the buffers provide clear priorities as to task importance. Everything in process has the same importance; all are jobs that the organization has agreed to deliver or that it otherwise desires to have in process. If the delivery performance of one of these jobs is in jeopardy, then that is the job that should have priority. Therefore, first priority goes to jobs or orders that have caused holes in the expedite zone of the buffer.[12] There is a need to identify those specific orders that have created holes in the expedite zone of the buffer. The Buffer Hole Report shown in Exhibit 7.7 satisfies this need.

The Buffer Hole Report shows a list of orders that have not made it to the drum area (shipping, in this case) within 10 days after being released to production on a 15-day rope. That is, the expedite zone is 5 days. These orders are holes in the expedite zone of the shipping buffer.

The purpose of the report is to identify those orders that may need special attention in order to be shipped on time. The items that appear on this report are the items that have a higher priority than the other work in progress. All areas should give priority to these orders. Since these orders are in danger of missing their shipping dates, they are also candidates for overtime assignment. Other orders (those that are not in the expedite zone) should not receive specific overtime because there is no reason to believe that their due dates are in danger.

The Buffer Hole Report illustrates four entries representing typical situations. These entries and the nature of subordination actions appropriate for each situation are shown in the following paragraphs.

Job #10 has been on the report for a long time.[13] It has already missed its shipping date. This job is waiting for outside parts. The purchasing agent had the data necessary for the comment at the time the part order was placed with ABC Supply and entered it at that time. Therefore, when the item entered the expedite zone and the Buffer Hole Report was prepared, the comment was already included.[14] We might assume that the

Exhibit 7.7   Buffer Hole Report

				Buffer Hole Report				
				Shipping Buffer				
				August 18, 20X0				
				Expedite Zone Days = 5				
Hole Identification	Customer	Release Date	Last Operation	Last Operation Date	Next Operation	Expedite Date	Scheduled Shipping Date	Scheduling Comments
Job #10	Acme - St. Charles	04/05/X0	Repair	04/12/X0	Welding	04/15/X0	04/20/X0	Part on order from ABC Supply. Due 11-03-X0. Acme notified.
Job #20	Chas Charles Co	08/07/X0	Opn 5	08/15/X0	Grinding	08/17/X0	08/22/X0	In grinding queue 8/17, should be finished on 8/19
Job #30	Peterson Mfg	08/07/X0	Cutting	08/07/X0	Welding	08/17/X0	08/22/X0	Awaiting drawing approval by Rob Davis. Rob is on vacation until Sept 1
Job #40	Star Manufacturing	08/08/X0	Polisher	08/15/X0		08/18/X0	08/23/X0	*EXPEDITE*

purchasing agent has taken all of the appropriate subordination actions such as checking with other suppliers, checking that the customer really is happy to wait seven months to have its order filled, and so forth. By having the order appear on the report, others, beyond the purchasing function, are challenged to ask the question: Is there *something that I can do* to protect the exploitation plan to ship the order by 4/20/20X0?

Job #20 represents what will be the majority of entries on this report. This job is progressing satisfactorily and is expected to ship on time without further assistance. Even though the order has created a hole in the expedite zone of the buffer, there is no need to take additional actions at this time. Consider the 5-day expedite zone of the 15-day rope as illustrated in Exhibit 7.8.

The length of the 15-day rope was established and adjusted until about 4% of the orders entered the 5-day expedite zone. That means that about 96% of the orders are completed within 10 days and never enter the expedite zone. Of the 4% that do enter the expedite zone, most (probably more than three-fourths) will be completed before the 15-day rope ends. Having about 4% of the orders enter the expedite zone is part of the exploitation plan. Missing shipping dates is not part of the exploitation plan; shipping on time is part of the exploitation plan.[15] The appropriate subordination actions with respect to this type of buffer hole, then, are fourfold:

1. Since it is not known whether this order is one of the 3% that may be expected to ship on time as is or the 1% that must be expedited, locate the item and determine its status.

Exhibit 7.8   **Expedite Zone**

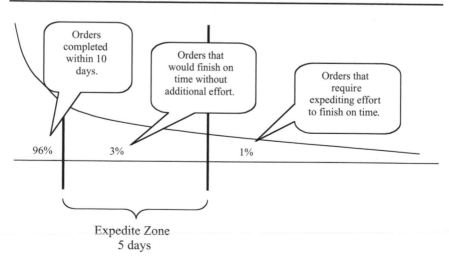

Expedite Zone
5 days

2. If the order appears to be in the 3% group, annotate the Buffer Hole Report to reflect the status and next action date if appropriate. Job #20 will be checked again on August 19 to be certain that it is still on track for on-time shipment.

3. If the order appears to be in the 3% group, but a specific next check time is not known, monitor the item on a regular basis to ensure its on-time shipment.

4. If the order appears to be in the 1% group or is too close to call (err on the side of paranoia here), take appropriate actions to expedite the item.

Job #30 has a promise to ship to Peterson Manufacturing by August 22. However, it appears that the vacation schedule of one of our employees, Rob Davis, is about to become a problem for our customer, Peterson Manufacturing. This report will have widespread distribution, and the general culture of the organization will probably determine whether this happens. If the culture is such that the members of the organization understand what needs to be done, and there is a motivating reason for them to do it, then there is a good chance that somebody will take the initiative to see whether the approval can come from elsewhere.

Job #40 makes its first appearance on the report today. The comment, *EXPEDITE*, is generated by the computer software in the absence of other comments. Its purpose is to alert all report recipients that this item is in danger of missing its shipping date and that no corrective action has yet been identified.

The **buffer manager,** a new position for organizations undertaking constraint management, will follow up on this item. When its status is determined more fully, the appropriate comments will be added to the report. If the item appears to be a 1% type of item, the buffer manager will also immediately initiate appropriate expediting actions.

The DBR system subordinates the production flow to the schedule of the constraints. Buffers accommodate the statistical fluctuations inherent in the system. When the statistical fluctuation exceeds the safety provided by the buffer, buffer management identifies the relatively few specific orders that need to have special attention.

Buffer Hole Pareto Analysis

A final aspect of buffer management involves focusing attention on the areas where the greatest difference for improvement can be made. As illustrated in Exhibit 7.9, orders that cause buffer holes in the expedite zone are likely to have become stuck at some point in the system.

Product will tend to become "stuck" at areas that either are not subordinating properly (the most frequent case) or that do not have adequate protective capacity. A Pareto analysis of where in the process the orders that have created buffer holes are located can identify the areas that are not subordinating well or have inadequate protective capacity. Although the product may be anywhere in the process at any given time, it will most frequently be found in the problem area. A **tracking zone** is established for this purpose.[16] When a buffer hole appears in the tracking zone of the buffer, we do not take extraordinary actions but rather simply determine the source (current product location) of the hole. The location should be recorded by time period and resource. These data may be summarized as a histogram for individual resources, as illustrated in Exhibit 7.10. The same data are shown in a statistical format in Exhibit 7.11, and Exhibit 7.12 portrays similar data over time.

These data will help establish priorities for nonconstraint enhancement. Exhibits 7.10 through 7.12 show that the welder is the primary source of schedule disruptions. Exhibit 7.12, which shows a comparison of resource areas over time, also illustrates that we would not expect the data to be static. In fact, the Exhibit 7.12 data indicate that in week 3 the grinder was a greater source of schedule disruption than the welder. The grinder data for week 3 may have been due to a machine malfunction, employee absenteeism, or some other cause. Weeks 4 and 5 still show the grinder at above-average amounts, but it is probably under control again, with the decreasing higher levels representing catching-up.

Problems in Support Areas

Buffer management will also detect many problems in support areas. Support areas are not directly reflected in buffer hole reporting because buffer holes are traced only to areas that actually work on the product.

Exhibit 7.9   Tracking Source of Buffer Holes

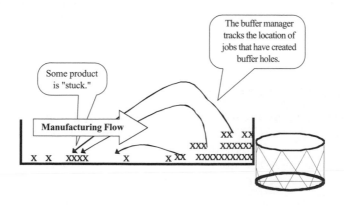

Exhibit 7.10   Histogram Summarizing Buffer Hole Source

```
XXX
XXX
XXX
XXX
XXX
XXX
XXX
XXX                          XXX
XXX                          XXX      XXX
XXX      XXX                 XXX      XXX
XXX      XXX      XXX        XXX      XXX

Welder   Cutter   Polisher   Grinder   Assembler
```

However, the initial tracing is only a starting point. Is the area an emerging or near constraint? Is the area waiting for an approval or some other administrative procedure? Tracing and recording the next level of cause will result in detecting support areas in need of attention.

SUMMARY

Recall that tactical subordination refers to subordinating to the exploitation decisions for tactical, or currently active, constraints and that most day-to-day operating activities fall into this category. Buffer management as defined in constraint management completely replaces conventional management reporting systems. Constraints accounting supports buffer management by providing information that can be used to identify emerg-

Exhibit 7.11   Statistical Presentation Summarizing Buffer Hole Source

Resource	Frequency	Percent
Welder	11	52
Cutter	2	10
Polisher	1	5
Grinder	4	9
Assembler	3	14

Exhibit 7.12   Source of Shipping Buffer Holes by Week

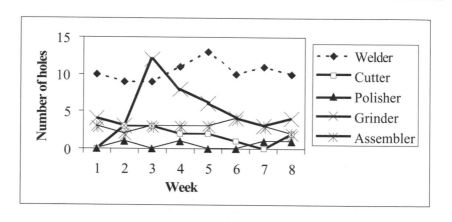

ing constraints. Constraints accounting replaces legacy accounting efficiency reporting systems. When this happens, the two systems constraint management and constraints accounting merge into one. Buffer management gives all members of the organization the security of knowing that they are taking appropriate action, since the information provided by the buffers allows knowledgeable employees at all levels to respond appropriately to statistical fluctuations and changing demands on the system. The replacement of legacy control systems with buffer management incorporating buffer reporting is a key to locking in a process of ongoing improvement.

NOTES

[1] Eliyahua M. Goldratt and Robert E. Fox, *The Race* (North River Press, 1986); Eliyahua M. Goldblatt, *The Haystack Syndrome: Sifting Information Out of the Data Ocean* (North River Press, 1991); Eli Schragenheim and H. William Dettmer, *Manufacturing at Warp Speed: Optimizing Supply Chain Financial Performance* (CRC Press, 2000); and Mark J. Woeppel, *Manufacturers Guide to Implementing the Theory of Constraints* (St. Lucie Press, 2001).

[2] A strategic pseudo-constraint would be used as a drum resource in order to prevent the standard operating procedures for manufacturing from changing when the tactical constraint oscillates back between the market and a strategic internal constraint.

[3] We assume that the organization has at least a relatively inexpensive computer system appropriate for the size and nature of the business. For example, the Microsoft Office software suite or its equivalent could provide the basic software. We assume the availability of a web browser, spreadsheet, and relational database for our discussions.

[4] Recall that the buffer is a time buffer. The buffer size is the same thing as the rope length.

5 Since the buffer size (rope length) is established in a heuristic manner, based on actual operations, the rope length is the amount of time required to reliably ship a product on time. Therefore, in a make-to-order environment the **quoted lead time** must be at least as long as the rope.

6 Goldratt has recommended 5% as a starting place (*Goldratt Satellite Program* Tape 1, 1999). The organization's actual experience will provide some guidance as to how to adjust these parameters on an ongoing basis.

7 The data shown in Exhibit 7.5 assume that the organization ships an average of 100 orders each day, with a maximum of 200 orders and a minimum of zero orders on any particular day. The average of orders that create a hole in the expedite zone of the buffer on any particular day is 4% +/-1.5% of total orders shipped that day but is rounded to the nearest whole number. Within those ranges, the data are generated as a uniform random number. Data are not shown for days on which fewer than 40 items were shipped because the control limits would be measuring in greater detail than the interval of the data justify. For example, if 10 orders were shipped, 4% expedites would be 0.04 * 10 = 0.4 expedites. Since we only deal with whole orders, we would expect either zero expedites (0%) or one expedite (10%), each of which lies outside the control limits.

8 Realistic data are likely to have a much greater variance than the data used in the illustrations. Therefore, it will not be unusual for observations to fall outside the control limits. This is not a cause for concern, and corrective action is not needed based on *this* chart (Exhibit 7.6). Other measurements will indicate specific areas of concern.

9 We often think of protective capacity as being a function of individual resources only. However, Schragenheim and Dettmer have shown through simulation studies that it is also a function of the overall protective capacity in the system. Information on their simulation offerings may be obtained at http://www.mbe-simulations.com/ as of February 25, 2004.

10 Note that if the new rope length, for example, 18 days, is still less than the quoted lead time, this action will have no immediate effect beyond the production function. However, if the rope were now longer than the quoted lead time, then it would also be necessary to coordinate with sales and marketing.

11 For example, at the Electronic Division of the Ford Motor Company the average (for all sites and all products) time required from material release to shipping was 10.6 days. After two years of just-in-time (JIT) implementation, the average time had been reduced to 8.5 days. This was further reduced during one year of TOC implementation to 2.2 days and subsequently to less than two shifts. (*Source:* Avraham Y. Goldratt Institute web site, www.goldratt.com request article, ford.htm, August 1, 2001).

12 If giving that job priority creates a fatal conflict (a fatal conflict in this case is one that results in a shipping date being missed) with another job that has also caused a hole in the expedite zone, then *a responsible manager needs to make a decision* as to which customer's order will be shipped on time and which customer is to be offended.

13 Having the item remain on the report ensures that someone looks at it on a regular basis. If there are so many of these long-overdue items on a buffer hole report that they are routinely ignored or they obscure the more recent data, then these might be moved to a separate report. Sometimes a separate field for a revised shipping date is added to the database.

14 The Buffer Hole Report might be a hard copy report or a virtual report available electronically on demand.

[15] We are continually amazed at the number of people who believe that their customers prefer the quote of a short promised delivery date (say 7 days) which is missed 20 to 40% of the time (and with a large variance) to a reliable promise (say 15 days) that ships on time over 99.7% of the time.

[16] The tracking zone may be the same as the expedite zone. However, it may prove useful to start the tracking earlier in order to deepen the statistic. About one-half of the rope length or checking about 40% of the orders has been suggested. See Goldratt, *The Haystack Syndrome*, pp. 139–140.

8

Tactical Subordination in Project Management

Our second example of constraints accounting support for tactical subordination relates to a project management environment. In this environment the constraint management application is known as the **critical chain**.[1] Even though the critical chain is a relatively new constraint management application, it is already reported as being extremely powerful with respect to project management.[2] As with the drum-buffer-rope application in manufacturing, the constraints accounting focus will again be on time buffers. In critical chain project management, the buffers are associated with individual projects as well as a drum resource.

Two aspects of critical chain project management differ from conventional project management. First, is the notion of a critical chain, which is the longest set of dependent activities from the start to the completion of a project explicitly, considering the availability of resources? The second, and more significant, difference from conventional project management lies in the way projects are scheduled and managed. We start our discussion of the critical chain environment by examining how people use common sense to protect their promises.

COMMON-SENSE SCHEDULING

In order to schedule the various parts of a project, an estimate of the duration—or time required—for each individual component (activity or task) is needed. How long will it take to complete an individual activity or task? The estimate of the time required for a given task, when accepted by those charged with responsibility for the task, also becomes a promise of delivery date to the next activity in the project.

Let us assume that 10 days is an accurate estimate of the average

Exhibit 8.1   Median Time Required for Resource and Task

Resource and Task	Median Time Required
A–Y	10 days

time required for a resource, A, to complete a task, Y.[3] We might represent this task A–Y as shown in Exhibit 8.1.

Put five tasks, each similar to the A–Y task together as a simple project. How long does it take to complete the project? If each of the five tasks requires 10 days, the project should progress as shown in Exhibit 8.2. The overall project should take 50 days (5 tasks * 10 days per task) to complete.

Given the normal statistical fluctuations of day-to-day operations, task A–Y could be completed in less than 10 days one-half of the time. However, one-half of the time task A–Y will require more than 10 days. Will this have an effect on our project? That is, will sensible people really schedule the project as though each task will be completed in its median time?

Not completing task A–Y on time one-half (50%) of the time may be expected to have a significant adverse effect on the next resource in the project, which will be unable to schedule its work reliably.[4] Since people like to deliver what they promised, such an unreliable situation is objectionable to everyone. Supervisors will not be able to schedule efficiently. Those performing the work will be under pressure to deliver work that is not completed by the scheduled time (and half of the work will fall into this category). Sensible people who want to keep their promises prevent this situation by adding some safety time to the estimate.

Enough safety is added to the time estimate for the task to allow it to be completed within the estimated duration about 90% of the time. Most people seem to feel that this 90% estimate is reasonable. If it appears that

Exhibit 8.2   Project Progress

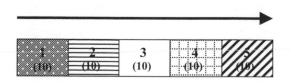

a particular activity will fall into the 10% tail of the distribution, then expediting actions will be taken to meet the 90% estimate. These relationships are shown in Exhibit 8.3.

In order for task A–Y to be completed (without expediting) within its estimated duration 90% of the time, it will be necessary to allow 18 days for the task. That is, 8 days of safety will be added to the estimate as reflected in Exhibit 8.4.

Our previous simple project, linking five similar tasks together, did not consider the need for safety in the scheduling. Adding safety to each task, we arrive at the sequence shown in Exhibit 8.5. This becomes the schedule for the project. Now each of the five tasks is allowed 18 days—10 days for the median time required plus 8 days of safety. The overall project should take 90 days (5 tasks * 18 days per task) to complete.

When the project is actually undertaken, it may or may not be completed within the scheduled amount of time. A typical portrayal of actual operations as compared to the schedule is reflected in Exhibit 8.6.

The first task is completed earlier than expected (8 days as opposed to the 10-day average). However, the people involved in this first task do not report its completion until the entire time allowed (18 days) has passed. The second activity is also completed in less than the average time (6 days), but true to **Parkinson's Law**[5] the person doing this second task manages to stretch it out to the full 18 days scheduled. The third task is fin-

Exhibit 8.3   Distribution of Actual Time Required for Task A–Y

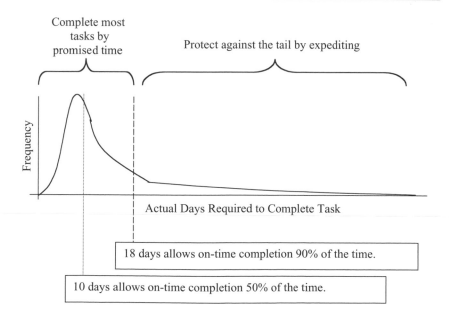

Complete most tasks by promised time

Protect against the tail by expediting

Frequency

Actual Days Required to Complete Task

18 days allows on-time completion 90% of the time.

10 days allows on-time completion 50% of the time.

Exhibit 8.4   10-Day Task with Safety Time

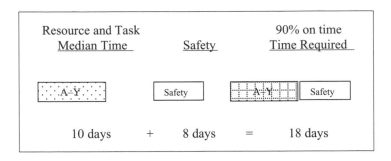

ished in slightly more than the average time (12 days actual as opposed to 10 days average) but well within the safety allowed for the task. Nevertheless, the fourth task is not started until its scheduled time. The fourth task encounters difficulty and takes longer than even its safety time, delaying the starting time for the fifth task. The fifth task is completed in 16 days and within its allotted time of 18 days, but the entire project is nonetheless late. There were—or could have been—early finishes for three of the five tasks. Three factors, (1) delayed reporting, (2) Parkinson's Law, and (3) scheduling wait squander the safety. The overall project does not get the advantage of the safety built into each task. We must conclude that adding safety time to each individual task, though improving the probability of each individual resource meeting its internal delivery date, fails as a safety mechanism when viewed from the perspective of the project as a whole.

Each of the first three types of delay observed in Exhibit 8.6 is related to the existence of a schedule for the individual tasks in the project. Only the fourth type of delay, in which the task was actually completed late, was an attribute of the task itself. Although the first task was completed in only 8 days, the completion was not reported until all 18 days allowed had passed. But note that the very concept of an early completion carries the connotation of a promised completion date. *Some aspect of the organization's culture must discourage the reporting of early completion.* In the second task, the operator could have completed the task early but instead chose to drag it out to fully consume the 18 days allowed. This instance of

Exhibit 8.5   Adding Safety to Each Task

1 (10)	Safety (8)	2 (10)	Safety (8)	3 (10)	Safety (8)	4 (10)	Safety (8)	5 (10)	Safety (8)

Exhibit 8.6   Actual Operations Compared to Schedule

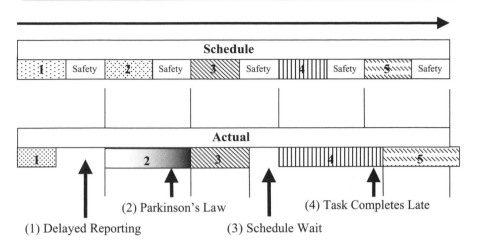

(1) Delayed Reporting

(2) Parkinson's Law

(3) Schedule Wait

(4) Task Completes Late

Parkinson's Law is dependent on the concept of the time allowed, which in turn depends on the promised completion date reflected in the schedule. Again, something in the culture must discourage early task completion. The third type of delay, waiting for the scheduled start time before starting the task, is also dependent on having a scheduled time. Finally, note that none of the three delays related to scheduling caused a task to extend beyond its promised completion.[6]

The major part of the delay in the project is caused by the combination of having a schedule for each task and the promises of individuals in the organization with respect to the schedule. Eliminating the schedule could perhaps eliminate this type of delay. Experience has shown that a chain of activities can be protected to about the 90% level, with approximately one-half as much safety as is necessary to protect each individual activity to 90%.[7] It is also useful to set no specific interim delivery dates for an individual chain of activities.

What would happen if the individual tasks of the project were simply sequenced, rather than scheduled, and if the organizational culture changed so much that the implied promise was for all members of the organization to do their best rather than to meet a schedule for individual tasks?[8]

The questions just posed do not eliminate the need for safety time in the estimates, but it adjusts the positioning of the safety from being associated with individual tasks to being associated with the project as a whole. The sequence estimate (based on the median time), associated safety, and actual results for our project would then appear as reflected in Exhibit 8.7.

Again, the first task is completed in 8 days. Because there is no scheduled completion date and the culture is different, there is no pres-

Exhibit 8.7   Sequence Estimates, Associated Safety, and Actual Results

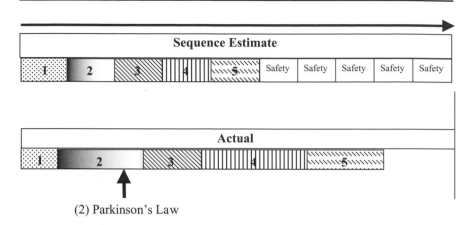

(2) Parkinson's Law

sure to delay reporting completion of the task. The second task, which could have been completed in 6 days, is again stretched out to 18 days. Even though the culture of the organization is changing, there will likely be a residual memory because cultural change does not take place instantaneously. The person working on the second task may not trust the managers who have told him that it is "OK" to complete the task as quickly as possible (and, as a consequence, display considerable amount of idle time).[9] So the second task is shown as lasting 18 days. The third, fourth, and fifth tasks are completed in the same amounts of time as in the previous example: 12, 22, and 16 days, respectively. As a result, the entire project is completed well within the time allowed for the entire project.

We must conclude that it is more effective to have safety time associated with the project as a whole rather than with individual tasks within the project. Less total safety is needed to protect a chain of activities than is needed to protect each activity individually. We will now turn our attention to the concept of a critical chain, and then we will combine the critical chain with our new understanding of common-sense sequencing as opposed to scheduling.

CRITICAL PATH VERSUS CRITICAL CHAIN

Consider the project network shown in Exhibit 8.8.[10] This project network, consisting of five tasks, has an upper and a lower leg. On the upper leg, task V must be completed before task W, and on the lower leg task X must be completed before task Y. Both tasks W and Y must be completed before work can begin on task Z. The distinction between a critical path and the critical chain is illustrated in Exhibits 8.9 and 8.10. The time esti-

Exhibit 8.8   Project Network

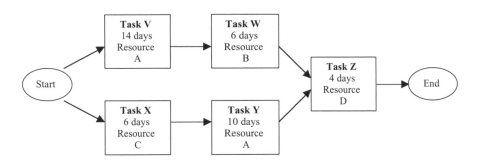

mates shown in Exhibit 8.8 are typical 90% estimates (i.e., they include safety time for each task). The time estimates shown in Exhibit 8.8 are typical 90% estimates—that is, safety is included for each task. Exhibit 8.9 shows a conventionally computed critical path.[11]

Going along the top path, task V is expected to require 14 days to complete; task W to require 6 days; and task Z 4 days. Therefore, the top path requires 24 days to complete (14 + 6 + 4 = 24). On the lower path, task X is expected to require 6 days, task Y 10 days, and task Z 4 days. The lower path is expected to require only a total of 20 days to complete. The conventionally computed critical path is the top path *(start—task 1—task 2—task 5—end)*, requiring 24 days, and is highlighted by the dotted arrows. This path appears to be critical because any delay on this path will cause a delay for the entire project.

Resource A, however, is used for both task V and task Y. Since a given resource can do only one thing at a time, resource A cannot start on task Y until it has first completed task V. Therefore, the longest sequence of activities through the network will actually be *start—task V—task Y—task Z—end* as highlighted by the dashed arrows in Exhibit 8.10.[12]

The longest sequence of tasks requires 28 days for completion of the project (14 + 10 + 4 = 28). This sequence, which incorporates the dependency relationships that exist among the various resources comprising the organizational tangle of chains, is known as the critical chain. The critical chain may, or may not, be the same as the critical path.

We will complete our discussion of the critical chain environment by combining the critical chain concept with our observations about common-sense sequencing for single- and multiproject settings.

PROJECT MANAGEMENT CONSTRAINTS

We have not mentioned *constraints* thus far in our project management discussion. Since the critical chain of activities controls the duration of a proj-

Exhibit 8.9   Conventional Critical Path

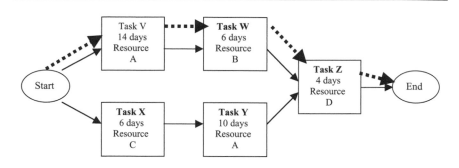

ect, the critical chain is frequently regarded as analogous to a constraint.[13] From the constraints accounting point of view, this analogy is inaccurate. We will not consider the critical chain to be identical to a constraint. Critical chain project management cannot have a powerful bottom-line impact if applied only in a local, nonconstrained area of operations. It must be associated with a global constraint to have a significant bottom-line impact. In fact, the constraint of an organization may not even lie on the critical chain of a given project. We will refer to a critical chain as a *critical chain,* and we will reserve the word *constraint* for bottom-line limiting factors. In similar fashion, we will restrict the term *exploit* to decisions relating to constraints and the term *subordination* to the exploitation decisions. If we do not use these terms carefully, we may seduce ourselves into thinking that we are doing constraint management when, in fact, we are only optimizing locally.

Critical Chain

Even though the critical chain may not be a *constraint* within our meaning of the word, viewing the critical chain as a leverage point and applying the

Exhibit 8.10   Critical Chain

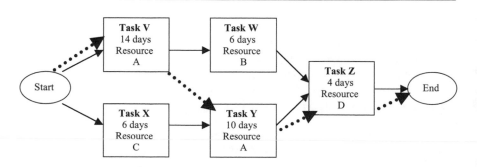

subordination rule to it have allowed the combination of common-sense sequencing with the critical chain concept to produce the critical chain project management technique. Traditionally, a project is considered successful if it is completed on time and within budget while maintaining the desired scope. Most projects suffer from the types of delays observed in Exhibit 8.6 (delayed reporting, Parkinson's Law, waits for scheduled start times, late completions). As a result, most projects fail one or more of the traditional criteria for success.

Single-Project Sequencing

We will examine sequencing for a single project first. The critical chain project sequencing technique concentrates safety at the end of chains of activities. This safety time, provided at the end of a sequence of activities, is another type of time buffer. The buffer represents time that is not in general expected to be used but that must be provided for, if projects are to be completed on time reliably. Exhibit 8.11 shows the same project as illustrated in Exhibit 8.10 rescheduled, with estimated task durations cut in half and project and feeding time buffers inserted.

The changes made when inserting the safety time buffers into the project are as follows.

- Estimated task times have been cut in half to remove safety from the task estimate and have a 50% chance of completing task in scheduled time. That is, the median time is used rather than the 90% estimate.[14]

Exhibit 8.11 Critical Chain with Buffers

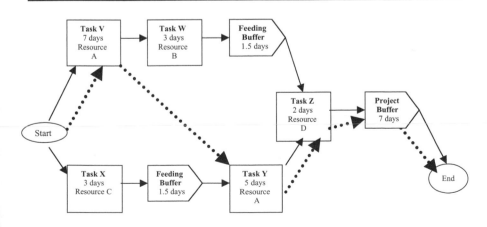

- One-half of the safety time removed from the individual task estimates, reflecting the statistical phenomenon that an entire chain of
  events can be protected with less total safety than protecting each of
  the individual tasks, is added back in the form of time buffers:
  - A **project buffer** equal to one-half of the restated critical chain
    task times is placed at the end of the chain.
  - **Feeding buffers** equal to one-half of the task time on the feed-
    ing chains are placed where noncritical chain tasks integrate
    with the critical chain.[15]

The critical chain after insertion of the buffers is *start—task V—task
Y—task Z—project buffer—end*. This chain requires 21 days (7 + 5 + 2 + 7 =
21). The result is that the estimated overall length of time expected to
complete the project schedule is reduced from 28 days (Exhibit 8.10) to
21 days (Exhibit 8.11). The same project is shown as a Gantt chart highlighting relative times in Exhibit 8.12.

In Exhibit 8.12 the three critical chain activities and project buffer
have been placed on the same line within the bold outlined box. The project buffer is one-half the length of the sum of the activities on the critical
chain.[16] The noncritical chain activities are shown as feeding into the critical chain at the appropriate points. Feeding buffers protect the critical
chain from disruptions on the feeding paths. Safety included in the feeding buffers does not increase the estimated completion date of a project,
but safety included in the project buffer does extend the estimated completion date.

Sequencing and buffering a single project plan is useful for organizations that do projects only occasionally. Many organizations operate in a

Exhibit 8.12   Gantt Chart Showing Relative Times

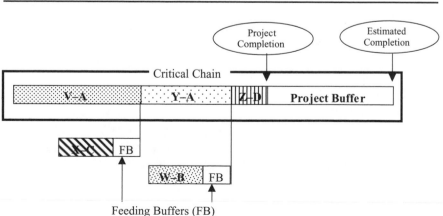

multiproject environment, either as the nature of their products (e.g., construction) or as specific areas within the organization (e.g., engineering). In the latter case, resource contention among the several projects must be resolved.

Multiple-Project Sequencing

We saw that the specific resolution of resource competition within the project network is the distinguishing feature for the critical chain of a project, as contrasted with a critical path. In a multiproject environment, several projects may contend for the same resource. Consider the three projects represented in Exhibit 8.13.

The three projects individually have been sequenced as buffered critical chains. Nevertheless, inspection of the three projects *taken together* reveals a great deal of resource contention. At the outset, projects 1 and 2 each require use of the yellow resource. In similar fashion, the feeding chains of projects 1 and 3 compete for the blue resource. Shortly into the sequenced execution of the projects, all three projects are competing for both the red and brown resources. Toward the end of the project task sequences, both projects 1 and 2 need the green resource.

The practice of assigning two or more comparably sized tasks to one individual with the understanding that those tasks are to be performed

Exhibit 8.13   Buffered Projects Highlighting Critical Chains

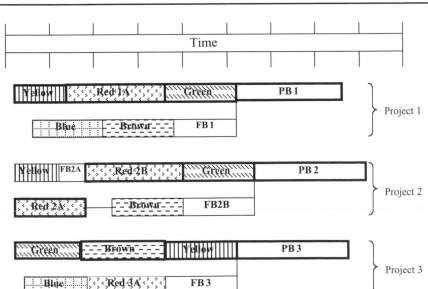

during the same calendar period is known as **multitasking.**[17] The sequence shown in Exhibit 8.13 is an invitation for the people to whom the tasks are assigned to attempt to work on several tasks at the same time, switching back and forth from one to another. Pressure to do such switching is encouraged by the matrix organizational structure of many project-type organizations.

In the matrix organization structure one manager, a project manager, is responsible for an individual project. The resources used to complete the tasks of the project are organized into functional departments and are under the control of a different set of managers, the department heads. The environment portrayed in Exhibit 8.13 is deceptively simple. The project networks actually imply interrelationships among at least eight managers—five department heads and three project managers—that are likely to have conflicting agendas.[18]

The project managers spend a great deal of their time encouraging the department heads to work on their individual projects. The department heads attempt to satisfy the project managers by showing progress on all of the projects at the same time. This compromise solution is accomplished by switching their resources back and forth among the projects before individual tasks are completed. This switching back and forth has two consequences. First, each time a switch is made some time is lost for the changeover. More significantly, however, the projects have been coupled at each step. If a difficulty is encountered on a task for one project, that delay is also transferred to the other tasks that the resource is working on. The crux of the matter is that *the sequence of Exhibit 8.13 is not feasible* within the scheduled time frame.[19]

The constraint management approach to multiproject sequencing starts with reducing the opportunity for multitasking. The most heavily used resource—and hence the resource most likely to be in contention—is used as a *drum for starting projects*. This has two effects. First, it ensures that the projects started are within the capacity of the organization. Second, fewer projects are in process (than would be if all projects were started immediately), thus providing less opportunity for resource contention for all of the resources, not just the most heavily used resource.

The red resource, being the most heavily loaded resource in Exhibit 8.13, is used as the drum resource. That is, the red resource is scheduled so that only one project at a time is assigned to it. Using the red resource as a drum, the projects are staggered, as is shown in Exhibit 8.14.

There is a significant difference between the two sequences. At first brush, it may seem that the sequence in Exhibit 8.14 will take longer to complete than the one portrayed in Exhibit 8.13. The staggered sequence of Exhibit 8.14, however, has a much higher probability of being completed on time because the resource contention has been significantly reduced.[20]

Exhibit 8.14   Projects Staggered on Drum (Red) Resource

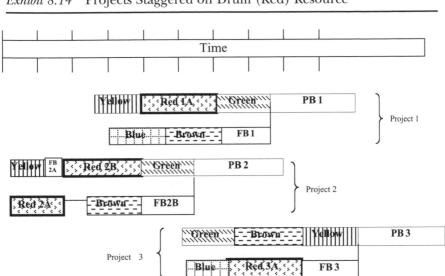

We have buffered the critical chains of the three projects, but we have not done anything to protect the schedule of the drum resource. If the drum is off schedule, we may expect that all of the projects tied to the drum resource will also be off schedule. Therefore, we will add another set of buffers to the projects' network. This buffer, which we will call a **drum-feeding buffer,**[21] recognizes that the drum resource schedule used to establish the starting times of projects needs to be protected in addition to the critical chains of the projects.

For example, in Exhibit 8.14, for project 1 the yellow resource feeds the red drum resource. In similar fashion in project 3, the blue resource feeds the red drum resource. Therefore, drum-feeding buffers are placed following the yellow resource in project 1 and the blue resource in project 3. The red resource activity 2B in project 2 is on the critical chain and is already protected from disturbances from the yellow resource by a feeding buffer (FB2A). In summary, buffers are added whenever there is an entry to a critical chain or to a drum resource. The additional buffers are reflected in Exhibit 8.15.

SUBORDINATION REPORTING IN PROJECTS

Decisions about how to exploit the organization's constraints determine the projects that should be undertaken. These projects, which are selected because they address either an Archimedean constraint or a necessary condition, are part of the tactical or strategic exploitation plans. Subordi-

Exhibit 8.15   Projects Network Including Drum-Feeding Buffers

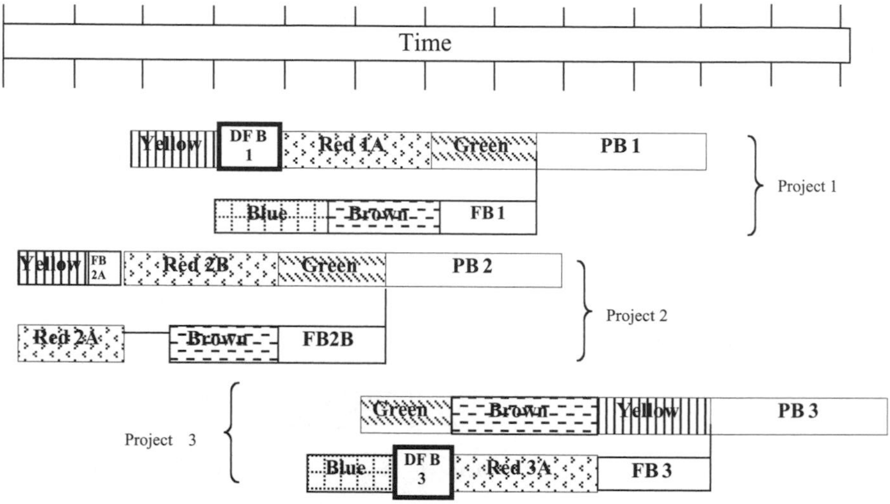

nation efforts are directed toward delivering the projects by their promised due dates and within their original scope. We no longer speak of bringing a project in "on budget." Rather, the legacy project cost reporting is replaced in the constraints accounting environment by the cost control considerations previously discussed in Chapter 4.[22]

Because safety time has been concentrated in the time buffers and every task is connected to a buffer, buffer data disclose the likelihood of successful completion of a project.

Determining Buffer Penetration

Two notably different approaches may be used to deal with buffers in critical chain project management. The first approach, which is incremental to traditional project management and the most frequently used today, relies on periodically updated estimates of times to complete each of the remaining tasks on a chain. A second approach, which is discussed at the end of this chapter, lies on the far side of the complexity divide and does not routinely require time estimates for individual tasks. The first approach is illustrated by Exhibit 8.16.

The project schedule consists of two tasks, A and B, and a project buffer. Each of the tasks has been estimated to take 10 days. The project buffer has been established at one-half of the chained task times, or 10 days. This schedule is illustrated in the upper portion of Exhibit 8.16. After 5 days the project schedule is updated. Departments currently working

Exhibit 8.16   Buffer Penetration

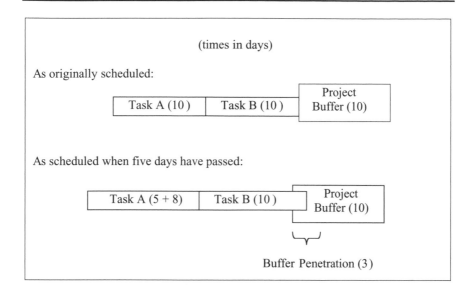

on tasks report estimated times required to complete their tasks. In this case, it is estimated that task A has 8 days remaining before completion. Since task A is linked directly to task B, the effect is to push task B to the right and into the project buffer as illustrated in the lower portion of the figure. We might say that there is 30% buffer consumption or penetration (3 days of penetration/10 days of buffer). The estimated completion time of the project remains at 30 days as the buffer absorbs the variation in required task time.

This estimate of buffer penetration is only as good as the estimates of the time remaining to complete the current task and the originally estimated time required to complete each of the remaining critical chain tasks of the project. In this way, each of the remaining task time estimates becomes both necessary and important to the buffer consumption reporting process. Visually, the project is *pushed* into, or penetrates, the project buffer. As shown in Exhibit 8.17, the amount of the buffer penetration is the sum of the individual variations from estimated task durations up to the reporting point.

Determining Task Priorities

The buffer penetration data are used to prioritize activities and direct expediting actions. The general rules for prioritizing project tasks when a resource has more than one task that might be started are to work first on

Exhibit 8.17   Buffer Penetration Calculation

		Time Elapsed 5 days	Originally Estimated Duration	Currently Estimated Duration	Current Estimated Buffer Penetration
(1)	Task A		10 days	13 days	+3 days
(2)	Task B		10 days	10 days	0 days
(3)	Totals		20 days	23 days	+3 days
(4)	Project Buffer		10 days	Project Buffer Consumption (3 days/10 days)	30%
(5)	Estimated Delivery		30 days	30 days	

the task with the most depleted buffer and, if no buffers have been affected, to work first on critical chain tasks.

When more than one buffer is involved, project buffers have priority over the feeding buffers. Critical-chain-feeding buffers and drum-feeding buffers have equal priority—except that a drum-feeding buffer has greater priority if, and only if, the drum area is a real internal physical constraint[23] and there is not sufficient work waiting in front of the drum area. In the latter case—the drum constraint—the tasks feeding the drum-feeding buffer take precedence because of the potential permanent loss of throughput due to starving a constraint.

CRITICAL CHAIN BUFFER REPORTS

Formal project reporting needs to be done on three levels. Senior management will be concerned with projects that have strategic importance. Each project manager needs to know the status of his or her projects. Each resource or department manager needs to know the relative importance of tasks currently being, or about to be, worked on, as well as what additional work may be expected in the near future.

Reporting for senior management should focus on overall strategy. Strategic projects are approved specifically (or according to a defined set of rules) as part of the strategic plan. These reports for senior management are highly summarized. Typically, such a report may be expected to contain data relating to identification of the strategic project,[24] degree of completion, buffer consumption, and prognosis. A frequently adopted rule of thumb is to consider a project to be entirely on schedule if less than one-third of the project buffer has been consumed. If between one-third and two-thirds of the project buffer has been consumed, then the project is reviewed and, if appropriate, plans are made to take action when and if necessary. Projects that have penetrated into the last one-third of the project buffer are in danger of missing their projected delivery dates and are expedited. The report for senior management should always contain comments as to the prognosis for projects that have penetrated into the last third of the project buffer and may contain comments for projects in the middle third. Exhibit 8.18 is an example of such a report that illustrates each of the three buffer situations.[25]

Project managers receive (or have on-line access to) prioritized lists of all penetrations into buffers for their projects. These reports typically list first the project buffers in sequence of the amount of buffer consumption as a percent of the project buffer. In similar fashion, a prioritized list of critical-chain-feeding and drum-feeding buffers showing consumption follows. The amount of consumption as well as the amount of buffer remaining, the particular task that is currently active on the chain causing the consumption, and the resource area in which the task is located are shown for each buffer.

Each resource or department manager needs to know the relative importance of tasks currently being worked on. Therefore, department managers receive (or have on-line access to) a list of the tasks for their departments that show all of the tasks currently being worked on and the status of the buffers to which those tasks are connected. This report is sequenced in the same manner as the project manager's report. In addition, a department manager needs to know what work is coming to the department in the near future and what the relative priorities of that work are. To accommodate this need, the department manager receives a second report containing similar information that shows tasks that are coming to the department within a time frame specified by the department manager.

Exhibit 8.18   Strategic Project Status

As of September 30, 20X1				
		Completion		
Project I D	Percent	Scheduled Date	Project Buffer	Prognosis
Broadway Plant	37%	Jul 31, 20X2	12%	
Hope Product	20%	Dec 31, 20X1	81%	Lead engineer on leave of absence until 12/1/20X0.
Project 3	80%	Oct 30, 20X1	50%	OK

Automated Buffer Management Reporting

Look again at the three projects network shown in Exhibit 8.15. Even though the projects network illustrated is simple, it nevertheless has nine separate buffers. Clearly, an organization that has dozens of projects, with each project using scores of resources and having hundreds of tasks, would find specifying and updating the interrelationships among the projects cumbersome at best and perhaps even intractable.[26] Therefore, most organizations implementing the critical chain concept take advantage of computer application programs that are readily available to handle these complexities. These organizations use the buffer reporting routines and formats available in the specific application program used.

CURRENT STATUS OF CRITICAL CHAIN

At the time of this writing, critical chain is a relatively recent development (*Critical Chain* was first published in 1997)[27] and how to best interpret buffer penetration remains controversial.[28] It is already abundantly clear, however, that critical chain offers a powerful tool for project management.

As a new management paradigm, implementation of critical chain requires that everyone associated with the projects have at least some familiarity with its concepts. And in order to implement critical chain as described, it is necessary to define the project networks and resolve resource contentions within each project.

The major effects of critical chain include the following:

- Individual projects are completed with significantly shorter durations.
- The total time needed to complete several projects is significantly reduced.
- Promised delivery dates are met with must greater reliability.
- Capacity is freed up.

We expect the effects of critical chain to be derived from five sources:

1. Better initial planning, particularly with respect to resource contention.
2. Staggered starting of projects based on drum resource schedules.
3. Taking advantage of compensating statistical fluctuations by moving the provision for safety time from individual tasks to the ends of chains of tasks.

4. Taking advantage of early finishes of individual tasks.

5. Use of buffer management reports to guide tactical management actions.

Anecdotal evidence indicates that, at the present time, the benefits of critical chain are in large part being derived only from the first two sources.

Implementing the critical chain application apparently requires a significantly greater level of planning than is typically being done.[29] As projects are staggered on a drum resource, the opportunity for multitasking among projects is significantly reduced. These two factors—better planning (leading to better communication) and **task focusing**—account for the reported successes with critical chain.[30]

Culture Change

In addition to better planning and reduced multitasking, organizations reporting success in implementing the critical chain invariably mention the need for change in the organizational culture. Such successes are typically reported in terms of quicker and more reliable project completion as opposed to sustained bottom-line effect. The only cultural change that has been accepted widely in practice is awareness by those managers involved in the initial critical chain implementation of the damage that multitasking does to schedule reliability. Managers no longer ask to see simultaneous progress on several projects requiring the same resource and accept the project schedules as dictated by the drum resource. Task focusing becomes the norm for all employees.

The critical chain techniques described thus far require that a great deal of attention be paid to the schedule for individual tasks. The individual task times for the project are initially estimated and planned carefully. As the project plan is executed, data about the anticipated completion time for each task are collected on a continuing basis. Even the notion of taking advantage of an *early finish* implies that there is some measure of a *correct* or *right* duration for each task. Since each task has an implied correct duration and sequence, a de facto schedule exists. And with the existence of a schedule, Parkinson's Law comes into play as well.

The implication is that current implementations of critical chain are being undertaken as local initiatives rather than as components of a larger *process of ongoing improvement.* We must conclude that culture changes are not widespread and that relatively little of the quicker and more reliable project execution effects associated with the statistical characteristics of project execution are being obtained in practice.

SIMPLIFIED CRITICAL CHAIN

In order to eliminate the undesirable effects of scheduling, such as Parkinson's Law, it will be necessary to eliminate the schedule. In this section, we present a simplified view of critical chain that does not rely on detailed project schedules.[31] This alternative is available only to organizations that have made the cultural journey across the complexity divide, satisfying the three necessary conditions discussed in Chapter 3. Instead of having an implied duration for each task, only dates relating to the overall project duration and project buffer are scheduled. The data needed for this are:

- Estimated length, or duration, of the project.
- Either the start date for the first task of the project or the promised delivery date for the completed project.
- Length of the project buffer.

The relationships of these data are shown in Exhibit 8.19.[32]

Project Length

The total scheduled length, or duration, of the project is established by using a parametric method. In the simplest case, an organization undertaking many similar projects might simply estimate the same duration for all of the projects. For example, all projects might be estimated at 270 calendar days (about nine months).[33]

Project Start Date

The start date for the project may be established in three ways, depending on the circumstances:

Exhibit 8.19   Simplified Critical Chain View of Project Structure

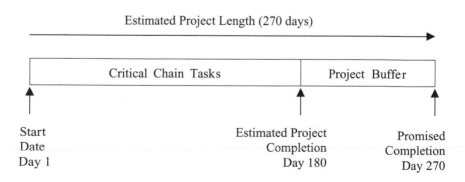

1. Management may just set the date directly. In this case, the promised delivery date (or completion date) is calculated by adding the project length to the start date.

2. If a drum resource is being used to stagger the starting times of projects, then the start date will be determined by the first available time slot on a drum resource. The calculated promised delivery date is an *as-soon-as-possible* type of date.

3. Finally, the start date may be set by working backwards from the desired delivery or completion date and deducting the project duration. In this latter case, if a drum resource were being used, time for the project would be reserved on the drum resource as appropriate. The desired delivery date would be adjusted as necessary before being offered as a *promised* date.

Project Buffer

The length of the project buffer is established as a portion of the overall estimated duration. For example, the project buffer might be set at one-third of the overall duration. Continuing the example, if the overall duration were estimated to be 270 days, then the project buffer would be 90 days long and would start at day 181.

Critical Chain Tasks

The time allowed for completion of the critical chain tasks, is arrived at by deducting the project buffer from the estimated project length. The project tasks are still *sequenced* in the level of detail that is proving to be useful in planning now. However, the critical chains of the projects would be identified somewhat arbitrarily. The hypothesis here is that either identification of the correct chain segment to place on the critical chain will be obvious or, alternatively, competing chain segments will be so close to the same length that the segment that actually lies on the critical chain will be a matter of statistical fluctuation. Only project buffers are used to consolidate safety time to allow for normal statistical fluctuations.

Combining the data above, we arrive at the simplified critical chain view of the project. Rather than attempt to track each temporary buffer penetration caused by individual tasks, with simplified critical chain the project is considered to be progressing satisfactorily up until the time at which the beginning of the project buffer is reached.[34] Neither estimated nor actual times are recorded for individual tasks. The objective of estimating the task chain length is to have the actual project completion occur in less than the estimated duration one-half of the time.

Reporting for Simplified Critical Chain

Buffer management may provide answers for subordination questions in simplified critical chain in a manner similar to reporting in the drum-buffer-rope scheduling environment in Chapter 7. Data are needed to answer the following questions:

- How long should the project buffer be?
- When is protective capacity being eroded?
- Where should local enhancement initiatives be focused?
- What priority should an individual task have relative to other tasks?

With respect to the project buffer size, we need to measure where to begin and where to end the buffer. We would like the estimated time for critical chain tasks—that is, the point at which the project buffer begins—to be such that projects are completed without using any of the buffer approximately one-half of the time.[35] The importance of where the buffer starts is twofold. First, it marks the earliest point at which data are obtained for buffer management purposes. Second, the beginning of the project buffer represents the first point at which management considers whether to attempt to influence the timing of the project completion. Exhibit 8.20 shows a graph of a moving average (consisting of the last 20 projects) of the percentage of projects penetrating into the project buffer.

If the moving average were to break through the upper (or lower) control limit, then the time estimated between the project start date and the promised delivery date would be increased (or decreased) for new projects.

The end of the project buffer, of course, is the promised delivery date. We want our projects to be reliably delivered on time. We also want to promise our projects as early as possible to develop the competitive advantage associated with speed. Managerial expediting may be used to protect against a long tail on the distribution of completion times (see Exhibit 7.2). When the duration of a project extends into the project buffer, management should evaluate the risk of the project not being completed on time and take expediting actions as appropriate.[36]

Expediting may take two forms. In the first form, resources use buffer penetration to prioritize tasks among projects when more than one task is available for the resource to work on. This type of expediting is routine and is part of normal operating procedures. A second type of expediting involves managerial intervention and revision of plans. We will call this type of expediting **intervention expediting.** Common examples of intervention expediting are reassigning resources and interrupting a task on

Exhibit 8.20   Probability of Buffer Penetration

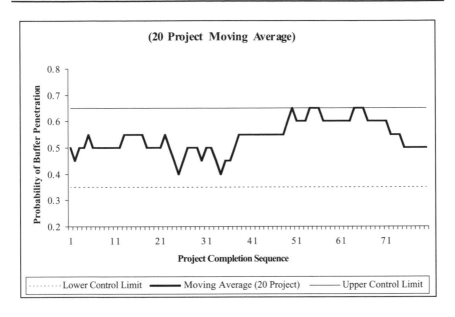

one project in order to work on a task for a different project (multitasking).

Most projects[37] should be completed by the promised date without intervention expediting. However, if all projects are completed when promised without intervention expediting, then the project buffer is probably longer than it needs to be. Some intervention expediting is desirable to permit shorter project buffers and the associated shorter promised delivery dates. If the extent of intervention expediting is such that it becomes difficult to complete projects by their promised delivery dates, then either subordination efforts are inappropriate or the project buffers are too short.

Sometimes, as when an organization has dozens or hundreds of projects requiring a few months to complete, the project management environment shares characteristics of the drum-buffer-rope environment where orders are somewhat similar. The rope length (production lead time) is typically measured in hours or days. Many separate orders are produced, with no single order dominating the process. The individual orders share substantial similarities in terms of processes used. In these cases, reports similar to those illustrated in Chapter 7 for DBR reporting may be used for the questions of when protective capacity is being eroded and where local enhancement initiatives should be focused. In contrast, long durations—often extending over several years—significant resource usage, structural individuality, and strategic importance exemplify many project management environments. These differences mean that project time-buffer data cannot be used to answer subordination questions in the same manner as it is in a drum-buffer-rope situation.

Although project management may be seen to have global implications within an organization, it is often separated out as a special case. That is, it becomes a local implementation of what is claimed to be a constraint management application. Without doubt, project management manifests some very significant apparent potential effects. The causes of these beneficial effects include (1) reductions in multitasking, (2) better communication, (3) culture change, (4) better visibility into project status, and (5) taking advantage of statistical characteristics of the system to obtain bottom-line improvement.

SUMMARY

Since culture change refers to a global organization, and the claimed critical chain implementations are often of a local nature, it is clear that the requisite level of organizationwide culture change has not been obtained. In fact, the local critical chain implementation is likely to be adding to the load on the global constraint. Second, the adaptations made to accommodate the local implementation—such as redefining the term *constraint*—were flying in the face of everything that we had written before. We therefore found that we needed to identify not only the problems with conventional critical path analysis, but also the problems with most existing critical chain implementations. Extending the logic, this led in turn to our statement of simplified critical chain (SCC). Simplified critical chain includes the nonconstraint-related aspects of multitasking, communication, and network sequence development and visibility. SCC also incorporates global culture change and taking advantage of statistical fluctuations, and it is entirely consistent with the constraint management philosophy.

When applying the sets of constraint management and constraints accounting rules to the critical chain application, its dynamic potential bottom-line effects are unleashed—and its inclusion within the global goal framework of the total organization becomes a key to locking in a process of ongoing improvement.

NOTES

[1] The critical chain concepts were first exposed in Eliyahu M. Goldratt, *Critical Chain* (North River Press, 1997). Another book of interest is Robert C. Newbold, *Project Management in the Fast Lane: Applying the Theory of Constraints* (St. Lucie Press, 1998). Lawrence P. Leach claims that he coined the term *critical chain* project management (CCPM) to refer to a combination of critical chain and conventional project management concepts as expressed by the Project

Management Institute. Frank Patrick has an informative web site at www.FocusedPerformance.com.

[2] For example, Lucent Technologies' Outside Plant Fiber Optic Cable Business Unit was an early adopter of critical chain in 1999. The reported results (1999 versus 1998) were that they were able to complete three times the number of projects, with the average lead time cut in half and 97% on time completion as opposed to 40% on-time before introducing critical chain. Nevertheless, it is not clear how much of the reported effects are due to a full critical chain implementation and how much are due to greater discipline in planning with respect to resolving resource contention.

[3] There are three types of *averages*. The *median* is the middle observation of a set of numbers (half are above and half are below this amount), the *mean* is the arithmetic average of a set of numbers, and the *mode* is an amount that occurs more frequently than others.

[4] This situation is the internal counterpart to the situation involving unreliable deliveries to external customers noted previously (Chapter 7, note 7). Consider the effect of unreliable deliveries on the customer. In order for a customer to tolerate unreliable deliveries, the customer must maintain additional inventories or protective capacity. This customer will wisely switch to a more reliable supplier as soon as one becomes available.

[5] "Work expands so as to fill the time available for its completion." See C. N. Parkinson, *Parkinson's Law* (Riverside Press, 1957).

[6] The Parkinson's Law type of delay may have an adverse effect on the promised completion time if Murphy strikes in the latter part of the task.

[7] Newbold, *Project Management in the Fast Lane*, pp. 93–94.

[8] This implied promise of *doing one's best* is sometimes called the **roadrunner** or **relay race** work ethic. This work ethic suggests that the person operating a resource work as quickly as possible, while maintaining high quality, when she or he has work to do. When the resource does not have work to do, the person blatantly displays his or her availability and waits patiently until work arrives.

[9] The culture change associated with implementing constraint management techniques should not be underestimated. This is particularly problematic for organizations that have undergone cost-cutting layoffs during periods of profitability. This is known as the **green curve** effect in TOC. The threat of being penalized for displaying idle time hangs like the sword of Damocles.

[10] This is a traditional diagram of a project network. One tool of the TOC thinking processes, the evaporating cloud, is used in this book. When used with the TOC thinking processes, arrows indicate either necessary or sufficient conditions for cause-and-effect relationships. No such cause and effect is implied in this project network diagram; the arrows here simply represent precedent relationships.

[11] For the example, the path shown is that calculated by the popular project management program, Microsoft Project98, for this network.

[12] Actually, there is no required sequence between task V and task Y. Thus, task Y could be done before task V. An undesirable situation, known as **multitasking,** could easily occur in this situation. If both task V and task X were started at the same time, then we would expect task X to be completed while task V was still in process. At that point there may be pressure for resource A to demonstrate progress on both task V and task Y. That would require resource A to switch back and forth between the two tasks. Each switch causes delays by the amount of time required for the changeovers and the duration of each task. Even more detrimentally, the duration of each task is extended by the amount of time that the resource is working on the other task.

[13] For example, in his definition for critical chain, Newbold says "It is typically regarded as the constraint . . . of a project" (Newbold, *Project Management in the Fast Lane,* p. 264), and Leach says as a part of his definition for *constraint,* "In a project, the generic term for factors that effect the possible start and finish dates of an activity" (Goldratt, *Critical Chain,* p. 302).

[14] This is a huge culture change for most organizations. We are asking the people responsible for the individual tasks to give up the safety that has been built into the tasks. For this to happen, managers must understand that activities will rarely take their estimated time and that projects will take longer than the estimated time about half the time. Similarly, those doing the activities must trust management, and have a reason to be willing to risk giving up the safety time in their estimates *that experience has shown to be necessary.*

[15] In this example, both of the feeding paths have only one activity. Therefore, the activity and the chain for the path are the same thing, and there actually would be no safety savings on the feeding paths due to a chain of activities requiring less safety than that required for protecting each of several individual activities.

[16] One-half, or 50%, of the median times of the activities has been confirmed to work well and safely in practice. However, this is not a hard and fast rule, and there has been considerable discussion suggesting rather more painstaking mathematical algorithms. The 50% recommendation is based on human behavior considerations rather than statistical precision. Our recommendation is to treat great precision in buffer sizing as a choopchick at first and search for more precise measurement only when your implementation experience guides you in that direction.

[17] Anthony R. Rizzo, in the discussion of multitasking, CMSIG . cmsig@lists.apics.orgList April 2, 1997.

[18] Of course, the conflicting agendas are a symptom of a lack of goal congruence, as discussed in Chapter 4

[19] The schedule in Exhibit 8.13 would be feasible if the estimated task duration times had been inflated to include the entire task processing times of all competing tasks or if each project had dedicated resources. The effect of including the entire task processing times is to schedule the total duration of each project for the time estimated to complete all three projects. The effect of each project having dedicated resources is to require two or three times as many resources to do the projects. Both of these appear to be frequent occurrences in project management.

[20] In the sequence shown in Exhibit 8.14, some resource contention relating to the green resource remains. We should avoid the temptation to refine the sequence further, even if easily done by our computers. Since there is a great deal of uncertainty in the estimated durations, the *noise* in the system probably overwhelms the benefit of further sequencing efforts.

[21] The drum-feeding buffer also has been called a constraint resource buffer, a strategic resource buffer, and a constraint buffer.

[22] Some **cost reimbursable contracts** for projects, or contracts having provisions for **progress payments,** may require special budgetary consideration.

[23] Recall that the test of whether a real internal constraint exists is that desirable business is being turned away.

[24] Organizations in which essentially all work is project-oriented and performed on a contract basis may provide a comprehensive picture of all projects for senior management.

[25] Entries on the buffer reports are frequently highlighted in the color green when less than one-third consumed, yellow when buffers have been penetrated to the middle third, and red when penetration extends into the last third of the buffer.

[26] Two additional types of buffers that have not been mentioned are a **capacity buffer** and a **resource buffer.** The capacity buffer is included on the schedule for the drum resource to prevent starting projects more frequently than the system can handle. The resource buffer does not take up time but is an early warning device to notify resources in advance of when they will be needed for critical chain tasks. This is useful since the start dates for individual tasks are not scheduled in critical chain project management.

[27] Goldratt, *Critical Chain.*

[28] See the discussion of "Buffer Management" on the CMSIG Internet discussion list, August 2000. cmsig@lists.apics.org

[29] Recognizing this difference, the Product Development Institute recommends specific insertion into the critical chain network, at the beginning of each project, a task representing detailed planning and an associated buffer. They call this buffer a **planning buffer.** (Tony Rizzo, *Implementing the TOC Multi-Project System: A Workshop For New-Product Development Enterprises,* The Product Development Institute (973) 581–1885, September 2001).

[30] Multitasking is the practice of assigning more than one task to an individual; multitasking is a *management* attribute. *Task focusing* refers to the actions of an individual employee; task focusing is the practice of working on only one task until it is completed and then switching to work on the next task.

[31] What is referred to here as simplified critical chain is similar to the notion of simplified drum-buffer-rope (S-DBR) introduced and discussed by Eli Schragenheim and H. William Dettmer in Section III of their book, *Manufacturing at Warp Speed: Optimizing Supply Chain Performance* (St. Lucie Press, 2000).

[32] The view of the project shown in Exhibit 8.11 contrasts with the more detailed task view illustrated by the projects represented in Exhibit 8.15.

[33] In more complex situations, the project length would be established using characteristics of the project such as the number of individual tasks included in the project or other parameters, but not the summation of estimated times to complete the individual tasks on a critical chain.

[34] Remember that employees both know what the appropriate actions are and have solid reasons to take the action. If significant *and unusual* difficulty is encountered in completing a task, the employee should notify the appropriate manager, and corrective action can be taken.

[35] The one-half point is an arbitrary selection. For example, we might have well have started the project buffer at the point where only 10% of the projects were completed. In that case, buffer penetration would be interpreted somewhat differently, and the associated action signals would be different.

[36] It may be possible to quickly eliminate many projects from consideration as immediate expediting candidates by making a mechanical risk assessment of comparing the percentage of tasks completed to the percentage of estimated project duration elapsed. For example, consider a project consisting of 300 tasks. If the project buffer represents one-third of the time allowed for completing the project and 290 tasks have been completed when the project enters the project buffer, the ratio of task completion (290 tasks/300 tasks = 0.97) to elapsed time (180 days/270 days = 0.67) is 1.4, and there is a high probability of completing the project on time. However, if only 100 of the 300 tasks had been completed, then the ratio would be 0.5 and managerial expediting might be needed.

[37] By *most* we mean more than 90%.

9

Tactical Subordination
in Sales

Our final example of constraints accounting support for tactical subordination relates to the selling environment. In addition to potential internal constraints, sales—or the **market** as it is frequently known in constraint management circles—is always a constraint. We will want to decide how to exploit the market and subordinate the sales function to the full set of exploitation decisions. In this chapter we first examine the role of **sales funnels** in a process of ongoing improvement. We also discuss the impact of revenue-based sales commissions on subordination. Finally, we move from constraint management within an individual entity into the supply chain through a discussion of leveraging constraints to create compelling sales offers.

SALES FUNNELS

If the organization has internal tactical or strategic constraints, then the sales function may be viewed as relating to production through a sales funnel. A sales funnel defines the flow of sales orders into the organization, with the objective of achieving harmony in the sales inputs and production outputs. From the undefined **cacophony** of potential business, some individual *notes*, or identified potential sales opportunities, make their way into the sales funnel where they flow through to create the *score* to which the production or project drum beats.

We will examine the calculations for each part of the sales funnels illustrated in Exhibit 9.1. Our scenario uses the same data for the Example Company used for illustration in Exhibit 5.19. However, now we will assume that the company has *strategically selected* the polisher as the desired internal constraint. The scenario portrayed also assumes that the welder is the current tactical constraint.

218

Exhibit 9.1   Sales Funnels

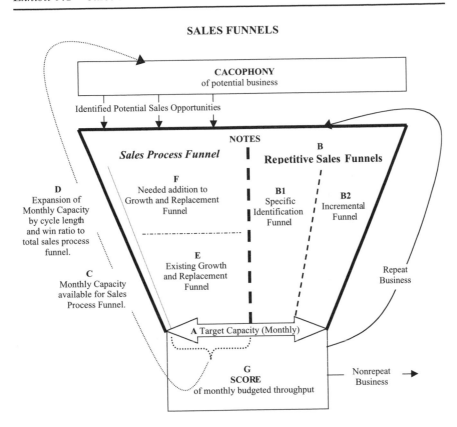

SALES FUNNELS

Section A: Target Capacity Available

At the base of the funnel (Exhibit 9.1) and designated by the letter, *A,* is the target capacity available for the organization. Calculation of the target capacity available is shown in section *A* of the sales funnel report (Exhibit 9.2). This is the narrow, or limiting, end of the funnel and represents the capacity constraint. Because this is the capacity that we want to utilize, we call it the *target capacity.*[1]

The number of hours that the resources might be available during a month is calculated. The company is working only one shift.[2] Up to one hour of overtime could be scheduled, on the average, each day. That gives a maximum availability of an average of 45 hours per week. Dividing 52 weeks by 12 months, we arrive at an average of 4.3 weeks, or 195 hours per month.[3] The monthly amount is extended by the quantity of the resources on hand in order to determine the resource hours available. Only the few locations that are constraints or **near-constraints** need to be considered.[4]

Exhibit 9.2   Target Capacity Available

Example Company
Sales Funnel (months)

November 30, 20X2

Working hours available:	4.33 weeks @ 45 hours = 195 hours maximum per month	
Number of resources	2	1
Resource	Polisher	Welder
Maximum hours available	390	195 hours
Protective capacity percent	11%	11%
Protective capacity	43	21 hours
Estimated hours available for production	347	173 hours
Estimated capacity minutes	20,810	10,405 minutes
Estimated setup minutes	6,547	468 minutes
Target capacity available (for the SCORE)	14,263	9,937 minutes

Thus, in Exhibit 9.2 only the welder (tactical constraint) and polisher (strategic constraint) are shown.

All resources, even constraint resources, need to have some amount of protective capacity. Any unused capability of the system is available for the role of protective capacity, regardless of whether specifically identified as such. Nevertheless, when estimating the capacity of the system, it is necessary to specifically set aside the desired amount of protective capacity. In the example, 11% of the maximum time available is set aside as protective capacity, with the balance available for production.[5]

Since the individual production operations of the Example Company are stated in terms of resource minutes needed, the hours are converted to minutes. An additional amount of time is set aside for setups, maintenance, and so forth. We are left with the amount of capacity available to be filled through sales.

Section B: Repetitive Sales Funnels

Two basic types of sales may be used to fill this target capacity: repetitive sales of the same products to the same customers and new offerings to either the same or different customers. The repetitive sales funnels are shown in Exhibit 9.3. Repetitive sales may be either specifically identified or statistically estimated as an incremental funnel.[6]

The specific identification funnel (**B1**) consists of those orders that recur because of an ongoing relationship with the customer. Each of these orders is identified along with its estimated resource consumption. The throughput of each recurring order is shown in order to allow the ultimate calculation of budgeted throughput as shown on a Constraints Accounting Earnings Statement (illustrated in Chapter 3).

The specific identification funnel comprises the recurring monthly sales to the company's larger and more stable customers. Even so, this business is not guaranteed to continue. Specific customers or orders may be lost due to competitive pressures, poor quality of products or services, or changing customer needs. Change in these orders is likely to have a significant effect on the organization. Therefore, the orders shown in the specific identification funnel must be regularly reviewed and considered to prevent loss of this business or to plan new offerings as appropriate.

In this scenario, there is no statistically estimated incremental funnel ($B2$) because the specific identification funnel fills the available capacity. If there were an incremental funnel, it would be included on the report with

Exhibit 9.3 Existing Repetitive Sales Funnels (Monthly)

Example Company
Sales Funnel (months)

November 30, 20X2

	Customer	Product	Quantity	Price	Estimated Minutes		Throughput
B1	**Specific Identification Funnel**				Polisher	Welder	
1	Cust 01	Atex	35	$ 180.00	1,155	0	$ 3,710
2	Cust 02	Atex	23	$ 189.05	759	0	2,636
3	Cust 03	Atex	31	$ 180.96	1,023	0	3,314
4	Cust 04	Atex	12	$ 194.16	396	0	1,433
5	Cust 05	Atex	73	$ 162.67	2,409	0	6,536
6	Cust 01	Detron	44	$ 322.86	660	1,496	9,316
7	Cust 02	Detron	14	$ 337.65	210	476	3,161
8	Cust 03	Detron	4	$ 256.14	60	136	593
9	Cust 04	Detron	7	$ 209.57	105	238	729
10	Cust 05	Detron	153	$ 258.96	2,295	5,202	23,105
11	Cust 01	Fonic	35	$ 180.71	770	490	3,734
12	Cust 02	Fonic	20	$ 211.00	440	280	2,709
13	Cust 03	Fonic	9	$ 208.07	198	126	1,194
14	Cust 04	Fonic	50	$ 186.67	1,100	700	5,617
15	Cust 05	Fonic	60	$ 159.27	1,320	840	5,178
B2	**Incremental Funnel** (statistically estimated)						
	There is no incremental funnel in this case. If there were, it would be added here in a format similar to the specific identification funnel.				0	0	0
B	**Total Monthly Repetitive Sales Funnel**				12,900	9,984	$ 72,965
	Divide by Target Capacity Available (**A**)				14,263	9,937	
	Capacity utilization by Repetitive Funnel				90.4%	100.5%	

the specific identification funnel. The minimum data requirements for the repetitive incremental funnel section would include identification of the source of the repetitive business, the estimated constraint capacity required to support these sales and, if integrated with the budget, estimated throughput.[7]

The percentage of the target capacity of the constraint and near-constraint resources consumed by the repetitive sales funnels is shown at the end of Exhibit 9.3. The existing specific identification funnel, which was developed in order to exploit the tactical constraint (the welder), is expected to consume the welder's entire capacity. The welder has an expected usage of 100.5% (the total repetitive sales funnel, 9,984 minutes, divided by the target capacity available, 9,937 minutes).[8]

Since the existing specific identification funnel fills the target capacity, we will modify the scenario to break the constraint at the welder before discussing the sales process funnel (E and F). Acquisition of an additional welding resource unit will break the welding constraint. The existing repetitive sales funnels no longer fill the capacity target capacity available. The revised target capacity available is shown in Exhibit 9.4.

Exhibit 9.4 shows two differences when compared to Exhibit 9.2. First, the welder column is shown in *small italics* because it would no longer be shown on the report at all. The welder is no longer a constraint or near-constraint. Second, the cutter has been added to the report because it is the next most heavily scheduled resource after the polisher. The repetitive sales funnels now appear as shown in Exhibit 9.5.

This figure is similar to Exhibit 9.3. The welder column is no longer shown because only 50% of the welder capacity is used and the welder is no longer a constraint. The total throughputs of the individual orders re-

Exhibit 9.4   Target Capacity Available (after Addition of Second Welder)

Example Company
Sales Funnel (months)

November 30, 20X2

Working hours available:	4.33 weeks @ 45 hours = 195 hours maximum per month			
Number of resources	2	2	*2*	
Resource	Cutter	Polisher	*Welder*	
Maximum hours available	389.7	390	*390*	hours
Protective capacity percent	11%	11%	*11%*	
Protective capacity	43	43	*43*	hours
Estimated hours available for production	347	347	*347*	hours
Estimated capacity minutes	20,810	20,810	*20,810*	minutes
Estimated setup minutes	9,353	6,547	*935*	minutes
Target capacity available (for the SCORE)	11,457	14,263	*19,875*	minutes

Exhibit 9.5   Existing Repetitive Sales Funnels (Monthly, after Addition of Second Welder)

Example Company
Sales Funnel (months)   November 30, 20X2

	Customer	Product	Quantity	Price	Estimated Minutes		Throughput
					Polisher	Cutter	
B1	**Specific Identification Funnel**						
1	Cust 01	Atex	35	$ 180.00	1,155	840	$ 3,710
2	Cust 02	Atex	23	$ 189.05	759	552	2,636
3	Cust 03	Atex	31	$ 180.96	1,023	744	3,314
4	Cust 04	Atex	12	$ 194.16	396	288	1,433
5	Cust 05	Atex	73	$ 162.67	2,409	1,752	6,536
6	Cust 01	Detron	44	$ 322.86	660	396	9,316
7	Cust 02	Detron	14	$ 337.65	210	126	3,161
8	Cust 03	Detron	4	$ 256.14	60	36	593
9	Cust 04	Detron	7	$ 209.57	105	63	729
10	Cust 05	Detron	153	$ 258.96	2,295	1,377	23,105
11	Cust 01	Fonic	35	$ 180.71	770	525	3,734
12	Cust 02	Fonic	20	$ 211.00	440	300	2,709
13	Cust 03	Fonic	9	$ 208.07	198	135	1,194
14	Cust 04	Fonic	50	$ 186.67	1,100	750	5,617
15	Cust 05	Fonic	60	$ 159.27	1,320	900	5,178
B2	**Incremental Funnel** (statistically estimated)						
	There is no incremental funnel in this case. If there were, it would be added here in a format similar to the specific identification funnel.				0	0	0
B	**Total Monthly Repetitive Sales Funnel**				12,900	8,784	$ 72,965
	Divide by Target Capacity Available (*A*)				14,263	11,457	
	Capacity utilization by Repetitive Funnel				90.4%	76.7%	

main the same (after all, the existing orders have not changed). Since all of the resources now have unused capacity, the tactical constraint has shifted from the welder to the market. The strategic constraint selected by management is still the polisher, which is at 90.4% of capacity.

Recall that in Chapter 5 we carefully determined the relative profitability (throughput per constraint unit) of each product with respect to the active internal constraint—the welder. This led to a sales preference ranking for the products in the order of (1) Atex, (2) Fonic, and (3) Detron. Whenever a constraint shifts, it is appropriate to reconsider previous exploitation and subordination decisions.[9] Exhibit 9.6 repeats the data and information regarding relative profitability by product from Chapter 5 and also includes the recalculation of the sales preferences if the polisher becomes the tactical constraint.

Exhibit 9.6   Relative Profitability by Product

	Atex	Detron	Fonic
Unit selling price	$ 175.00	$ 275.00	$ 180.00
Variable expense:			
Materials	$ 65.00	$ 95.00	$ 65.00
Sales commissions at 5.00%	8.75	13.75	9.00
Total variable expense	$ 73.75	$ 108.75	$ 74.00
Throughput contribution (t) per unit	$ 101.25	$ 166.25	$ 106.00
If Welder is tactical constraint:			
Welder minutes per unit	0	34	14
Throughput value of product in terms of welder minute (t/cu)	infinite	$ 4.8897	$7.574
Rank in terms of profitability	*1*	*3*	*2*
If Polisher is tactical constraint:			
Polisher minutes per unit	33	14	22
Throughput value of product in terms of polisher minute (t/cu)	$ 3.0682	$ 11.875	$ 4.8181
Rank in terms of profitability	*3*	*1*	*2*

Comparison of the throughputs per minute for each product in the existing sales funnel reveals the importance of subordinating to *strategic* exploitation decisions as well as exploitation decisions for the current *tactical* constraint.[10] When stated in terms of the polisher minutes, the preference ranking—(1) Detron, (2) Fonic, and (3) Atex—is exactly the opposite from the ranking when the welder is the constraint. If the company is able to switch back and forth between products for emphasis, that is well and good. However, in subordinating to tactical exploitation decisions emphasizing Atex and Fonic, strategically desirable sales of Detron might be permanently lost.

At any rate, the tactical constraint is now in the market. To say that the tactical constraint is in the market is to say that it is desirable to obtain additional sales.

Sections C and D: Expansion to Sales Process Funnel

New sales are desirable to replace existing repetitive sales that have been lost and for growth. The process of obtaining additional sales is captured in the **sales process funnel,** which consists of identified potential sales opportunities that are being pursued by the company's sales force. Since not all sales prospects are converted into firm sales, the sales process funnel must be larger than the target capacity to be filled. The first question is, "How large should the sales process funnel be?" The answer to this question is provided by the information in Exhibit 9.7.

Exhibit 9.7   C and D Expansion of Monthly Capacity to Sales Process Funnel

Example Company
Sales Funnel (months)

November 30, 20X2

			Estimated Minutes		
C	**Monthly Capacity Available for Sales Process Funnel**		Polisher	Cutter	
	Target capacity available (*A*)		14,263	11,457	minutes
	Monthly Repetitive Sales Funnel (B)		12,900	8,784	
	Monthly capacity available for Sales Process Funnel		1,363	2,673	minutes
D	**Total Sales Process Funnel needed** (to fill target capacity)				
	Funnel Expansion				
	Multiply C by sales cycle length:	6 months	8,178	16,038	minutes
	Divide by win ratio:	30.0%	27,260	53,464	minutes
	Total Sales Process Funnel needed (to fill target capacity)		27,260	53,464	minutes

We want to pursue enough identified potential sales opportunities to create and sustain an internal constraint, but not so many that we cannot deliver on our promises to our customers. That is, we would like to exactly fill the monthly target capacity (*A*). We already have some business, the repetitive sales funnels. Deducting the capacity used by the repetitive sales funnels (*B*) from the target capacity available (*A*), we arrive at the monthly capacity available for the new business (*C*).

The amount of sales being pursued typically needs to be larger than the target monthly amount because of two factors: the length of the **sales cycle** and the **win ratio.** These factors are considered in part (*D*) of Exhibit 9.7. The length of the sales cycle is the average amount of time elapsed between starting an identified potential sales opportunity into the sales process funnel and placing the order on a drum production resource. If the length of the sales cycle is six months, then the funnel must have six times the amount of one month's sales to produce the single month's sales at the appropriate time. Therefore, the monthly capacity available (*C*) is multiplied by the length of the sales cycle (in months). The win ratio is the percentage of identified potential sales opportunities that are converted to actual sales. It is calculated as the sales opportunities closed divided by the sales orders placed into the sales funnel. Since not all sales opportunities pursued actually become firm sales, the target capacity is also divided by the win ratio in order to estimate the amount of sales opportunities that must be pursued in order to have the right number of actual sales. When the monthly target capacity has been expanded by these two factors, the result is the total size of the sales process funnel needed to fill the target capacity. This total amount of sales must be pursued at any given time to fill monthly capacity.

Section E: Existing Growth and Replacement Funnel

Some of the needed sales process funnel is already in process. For example, Chapter 6 considered the introduction of a new product, Haton. In Chapter 6 a target price of $192.65, which includes a target throughput of $112.93 per unit, was calculated for Haton as a free product.[11] The existing growth and replacement funnel is shown in Exhibit 9.8.

The existing growth and replacement funnel (E) in Exhibit 9.8 includes many specifically identified potential sales opportunities as well as the product offering of Haton to customer 03. If the sale to customer 03 is closed, then that offering will become part of the repetitive sales funnel in the future.

Section F: Needed Addition to Growth and Replacement Funnel

In order to bring the constraint to the desired strategic location (the polisher), it will be necessary to fill unused available capacity. How many additional sales opportunities must be added to the sales process funnel? Deducting (E) the existing growth and replacement funnel from (D) the expanded funnel needed to fill the target capacity, we arrive at (F) the needed addition to the growth and replacement funnel. These calculations are shown in Exhibit 9.9.

The organization needs to search in the cacophony of potential business to identify sales opportunities to fill this amount of capacity.[12] If (F) is negative, then it represents a larger sales funnel than the organization's production capabilities will be able accommodate. In this case, the company must either take action to control the rate of sales within the target capacity or it must elevate the capacity to accommodate the total sales funnel.

Exhibit 9.8   Existing Growth and Replacement Funnel

Example Company
Sales Funnel (months)

November 30, 20X2

E	**Existing Growth and Replacement Funnel**				Estimated Minutes Polisher	Cutter	
	Customer	Starter	Product	Quantity			Throughput
1	Cust 03	10/22/X2	Haton	46	736	552	$ 5,195
2							
3	*(Many other specifically identified*						
n	*potential sales opportunities)*			21,264	17,448	84,000
	Existing growth and replacement funnel				22,000	18,000	$89,195

Exhibit 9.9   Needed Addition to Growth and Replacement Funnel

Example Company
Sales Funnel (months)

		November 30, 20X2	
		Estimated Minutes	
		Polisher	Cutter
D	**Total Sales Process Funnel needed** (to fill target capacity)	27,260	53,464
E	**Existing Growth and Replacement Funnel**	22,000	18,000
F	**Needed addition to Growth and Replacement Funnel**	5,260	35,464

Section G: Score of Monthly Budgeted Throughput

At the bottom of Exhibit 9.1, the sales funnels coordinate in a harmonious score, representing the expected amount of throughput to be generated for the month. These are the sales orders that make it through the sales funnels and establish the production or shipping drum beat. As shown in Exhibit 9.10, these are also the sales orders that will provide the estimated (or budgeted) throughput for the month.

Sales Funnel Summary

The constraint management view of the sales funnels presented differs from the conventional view in several ways. Consider the various sales funnel elements, which are summarized in Exhibit 9.11.

The first difference is the focus on explicit consideration of tactical and strategic constraints. Second, the sizes of the funnels are measured by the capacity utilized or available rather than by sales dollars. Third, total sales dollars is not even calculated. The financial metric of interest is

Exhibit 9.10   Score of Monthly Budgeted Throughput

Example Company
Sales Funnel (months)

		November 30, 20X2
Repetitive Sales Funnels (*B*)		$72,965
Existing Growth and Replacement Funnel (*E*)	$89,195	
Multiply by win ratio and divide by sales cycle length	* 0.3 / 6	4,460
Budgeted throughput for next month		$74,518

Exhibit 9.11   Sales Funnels Summary

Example Company

November 30, 20X2

		Estimated Minutes		Throughput	
				Sales Process Funnel	Monthly Sales Funnels
	Element	Polisher	Cutter		
A	Target capacity available (monthly)	14,263	11,457		
B	Monthly Repetive Sales Funnel	12,900	8,784		$ 72,965
C	Monthly capacity available for Sales Process Funnel	1,363	2,673		
D	Expand (* cycle length; / win ratio) to Total Sales Process Funnel needed	27,260	53,464		
E	Existing Growth and Replacement Funnel	22,000	18,000	$ 89,195	4,460
F	Needed Replacement to Growth and Replacement Funnel	5,260	35,464		
G	Monthly budgeted throughput (Score)				$ 77,425

throughput (T), and T is a derivative of capacity usage. Fourth, rather than the pursuit of larger sales volume per se, the analytical purpose of the sales funnels is to coordinate, in a harmonious manner, the marketing and sales efforts with the strategic orientation of the organization.

SALES COMMISSIONS

In our data for the Example Company presented in Chapter 5, and especially in the pricing and throughput analyses contained in Chapter 6 and earlier in this chapter in the sales funnels discussion, we have assumed a sales commission that is calculated as a percentage of sales dollars. This is consistent with typical business-to-business sales management practice.[13] But does a revenue-based sales motivation model, which is designed to encourage greater sales volume in itself, make sense in a constraint management environment?

At first brush, it seems that the purpose of the sales function is to obtain more sales. But consider the following. As part of the constraint management focusing process, a strategic constraint has been identified. The exploitation decisions and supporting subordination actions should do two things:

1. Elevate—and break—tactical constraints that are not consistent with the strategic plan.

2. Result in the tactical constraint shifting to the strategic constraint location.

Within this framework, three possibilities exist. The tactical constraint is either internal (or external on the supply side) or (1) external in the market. If internal, the tactical constraint is either (2) the same as, or (3) different from, the strategic constraint.

When a *tactical* constraint appears as an internal physical constraint—but is *not* the same as the *strategic* constraint—additional current sales requiring the use of the tactical constraint cannot be accommodated. In this situation, greater current sales volume per se cannot be the desired result of the sales process.

When the *tactical* and *strategic* constraints are the same, the organization will have established a stable operating environment. Since the strategic constraint is also an active internal physical constraint, the organization does not have the capacity to handle additional sales volume at the present time. Once again, greater current sales volume per se cannot be the desired result of the sales process in this case.

The constraint is *in the market* for products that do not require use of constraint resources—the *free products*.[14] Even in this case greater current sales volume per se is not the desired result of the sales process. Rather, in each case the desired result of the sales process is to fill, *but not exceed,* the desired target capacity.

Let us consider the Example Company again. For our discussion of sales commissions we will return to the case in which there is a production constraint at the welder. The constraints accounting analysis of the relative profitability of the three products, Atex, Detron, and Fonic, was presented in Chapter 5, Exhibits 5.24 through 5.26. The price and profitability measures that we calculated in Chapter 5 are repeated in Exhibit 9.12.

When the welder is an active internal constraint, the company's preference for sales, and therefore the desired emphasis by the sales force, is established by the t/cu metric highlighted in Exhibit 9.12 and is as follows. First priority is Atex, which does not require use of the internal con-

Exhibit 9.12   Price and Profitability Data

	Atex	Detron	Fonic
Unit selling price	$ 175.00	$ 275.00	$ 180.00
Gross margin	$ 54.75	$ 123.50	$ 111.87
Gross margin as % of sales	31.3%	44.9%	37.8%
Throughput contribution (t) per unit	$ 101.25	$ 166.25	$ 106.00
t as % of sales	57.9%	60.5%	58.9%
Constraint (welder) minutes per unit (cu)	0	34	14
Throughput value of product in terms of constraint minute (t/cu)	**infinite**	**$ 4.8897**	**$7.5714**

straint at all. Second in terms of constraint desirability is Fonic, which returns a throughput of $7.5714 for each minute of welder time used. Finally, the lowest priority product is Detron, which returns $4.8897 for each welder minute.

If the Example Company pays a sales commission based on sales price or even gross margin, unit throughput, or the ratio of throughput to sales,[15] then the sales force is strongly encouraged to emphasize Detron, the *least* profitable product in terms of the production constraint. All of these incentive bases suffer from the same problem in that they fail to consider constraints and subordinate to exploitation decisions—in this case to emphasize Atex and Fonic over Detron—in decisions about how to manage the sales function. In fact, use of sales commissions as a sales incentive method is just another example of the segmented, local orientation of the cost world type of thinking discussed in Chapter 1.

A POOGI Bonus plan, intended to create congruence between the personal goals of individual employees and the global goal of the organization, was suggested in Chapter 4. That this plan, or some equally powerful means of obtaining goal congruence is indeed a necessary condition for successful constraint management will be shown in Chapter 11. The implication is clear: sales incentives must have goal congruence with the rest of the organization.

It would be difficult to overstate the importance of the culture changes required to implement the global approach of constraint management in most organizations. Almost all of the rules and training that we have grown up with have a cost world orientation. Yet, subordination is key. If we fail in subordination—if we fail to capitalize on its dynamic supportive nature—we will fail to establish a process of ongoing improvement.

LEVERAGING CONSTRAINTS TO CREATE COMPELLING OFFERS

The **business results premise** states that businesses buy products or services for the primary purpose of producing better business results.[16] The business results of a sales offering may be grouped into three categories:

1. Results from elevating a customer's Archimedean constraint.
2. Results from satisfying a customer's necessary condition.
3. Results from affecting a nonconstraint-related performance metric of the customer.

The first category of business results leads to an understanding of what is known as a **compelling offer.**[17] All organizations have constraints, regardless of whether they are implementing constraint management concepts. The implication is that a selling firm, knowledgeable in the thinking processes of the theory of constraints, can identify an Archimedean constraint within a customer organization that is either addressed by the seller's offering or that is caused by a policy within the selling organization. A sales offering[18] by the selling firm that addresses a customer's Archimedean constraint results in elevating the customer's constraint. As we observed in the discussion of the POOGI Bonus in Chapter 4, when an Archimedean constraint is elevated, a significant and measurable improvement in the organization's performance occurs. This situation leads to the possibility of pricing the offering based on the demonstrated value added to the customer's bottom line. Such a compelling offer is a true *win-win* situation providing significant bottom-line benefits to both the buyer and the seller.[19]

The second type of business result stems from satisfying a customer's necessary condition. Two potential situations exist for this scenario; either the necessary condition is currently satisfied or it is not. If the customer's necessary condition is being satisfied currently, then the customer has enough of it. A new offering relating only to a currently satisfied necessary condition cannot have a significant effect on the customer's bottom line. Therefore, a new seller must compete both with the existing vendor and with the current means of satisfying the necessary condition. However, if the necessary condition is not currently satisfied, then the customer's throughput objective is not currently being realized (after all, that's the meaning of a necessary condition). In this case, the unsatisfied necessary condition is also a tactical constraint, and the business result stemming from satisfying the necessary condition may provide a win-win opportunity for a compelling offer.

Finally, the customer's business results may be expressed in terms of conventional performance metrics related to the customer's efficiency in a local area of operations not currently holding an Archimedean constraint. Since the results do not relate to a constraint, the potential to increase the customer's bottom line is negligible at best. A customer who is not aware of—or not interested in—constraint management focusing concepts is likely to consider performance metrics from the *cost world* paradigm to be important. Most organizations fall into this category. To the extent that such customers are going concerns, they represent potential markets for the seller's goods and services.[20] Powerful offerings based on business results for this customer must typically result in reduced costs for the customer, as well as change in some other metric.

Cost world performance metrics dominate the business-to-business marketing landscape. There is also a strong desire within organizations implementing constraint management, and starting with *drum-buffer-rope* production scheduling or *critical chain* project management, to create compelling offers in order to fill the additional capacity exposed. Consequently, a frequent *false start* in creating a compelling offer combines shorter and more reliable quoted lead times with reduced prices. The lower price, justified internally by the seller through some sort of direct costing-based pricing, satisfies the need for measurable business results. The financial manager may be concerned about starting a price war. This concern is quite legitimate, and therefore the delivery aspect of the offer must be much better than that of competitors. Rather than a powerful win-win offer, this particular combination is likely to trade the seller's price for greater volume with only small marginal impact.

The constraints accounting challenge associated with a compelling offer is to prepare the convincing and correct financial analysis that must accompany thinking process analyses for the offer. This analysis must be presented from the customer's point of view using financial effects calculated using the customer's costing techniques.

SUMMARY

One may well ask, "How can we be expected to increase sales at a fast enough rate to feed the voracious appetite implied by a robust POOGI?" As this is being written, sales executives throughout the world are bemoaning the state of the economy. At a time when it seems to be difficult—if not impossible—to maintain sales at their current levels, panic prevails. But, as William Woehr and Dieter Legat observe, "reacting in the TOC frame of mind, we . . . instead state simply that when sales drop, the sales system is constrained. . . . Somewhere the system has run out of capacity. A bottleneck appeared and was caused by a lack of physical capacity or by a policy. That's all."[21]

Woehr and Legat offer a systematic *how to* approach—detailing the creation of compelling offers that touch customers' Archimedean constraints. Their approach, which they call **Delta T-Selling,** makes an **opportunity engine** the focal point for consolidating sales operating information. The opportunity engine classifies notes in the cacophony of potential business based on the perceived difficulty of resolving constraints to throughput-oriented offerings. The opportunity engine identifies those opportunities that have more favorable prognoses for both the organization's ability to build a throughput-based sales offering and to win the sale. These favorable opportunities are said to be in the *T-Zone* and are brought into the *Growth and Replacement Funnel* as needed to create the desired score of budgeted throughput. Sales management focuses on resolving constraints to opportunities that are not yet in the T-Zone. If there are not enough T-Zone opportunities to fill the Growth and Replacement Funnel, then not enough opportunity constraints have been removed. Thus, Woehr and Legat conclude, "It is not the economy [that limits our sales]. It is us."[22]

Recognizing that in addition to potential internal constraints, sales— or the **market** as it is frequently known in constraint management circles—is always a constraint. Filling the Growth and Replacement Funnel allows an organization to be in control of its own destiny. It is not a decision of "if" or "when," but a decision of how to exploit the market and subordinate the sales function to the full set of exploitation decisions that is a key to locking in a process of ongoing improvement.

NOTES

[1] Cost accountants sometimes refer to this as the practical, or full, capacity level.

[2] This one shift limitation is an example of a *policy* constraint.

[3] The Gregorian calendar has month lengths that vary by as much as 10% and as much as 15% (or more) in terms of working days. These differences distort data when used for comparative purposes. As a result, many organizations use artificial calendars, such as a 13-period year with four weeks per period, to divide time into more useful periods. We use the traditional Gregorian calendar here for ease of discussion.

[4] Recall that tactical constraints are identified through the buffer management process as discussed in Chapters 7 and 8. Tactical constraints often may be confirmed by mechanical calculation; strategic constraint identification always involves human specification.

[5] Specification of the level of protective capacity is another management judgment and policy matter.

[6] These classifications correspond to the *step-type* and *incremental* markets discussed in Chapter 6.

[7] The source of the repetitive business might be something such as a store or an Internet web site. Note that the repetitive nature of the sales reported might stem either from the individual customers, some of whom are repeat customers, or from the store or web site itself, which generates some amount of business each month from unspecified customers.

[8] The small amount of expected capacity usage above 100% is not of concern because protective capacity is available.

[9] This applies to a shift in either a tactical constraint or a strategic constraint.

[10] This is a particularly important point for organizations that are implementing constraint management in local areas only, such as production drum-buffer-rope (DBR).

[11] The target price for Haton established in Chapter 6 assumed that the welder was the strategic constraint. Therefore, we need to check that the target price established ($192.65) is also appropriate in the current situation where Haton is a free product and the polisher is the strategic constraint. The minimum and maximum target prices for Haton are calculated in the accompanying table. Lines K1 and K2 show that the minimum price is $99.63 per unit and the maximum price is $308.64 per unit. Since the previously established target of $192.65 falls within this range, it is consistent with the pricing requirements for the current situation and does not need to be changed.

Price Range for Haton as a Free Product: Prices Based on Pseudo-Constraint (Polisher)

A	Springboard base of Haton per unit (Chapter 6)	$73.69
B	Lowest throughput per pseudo-constraint unit (t/pcu) of products currently being sold (Chapter 9)	$3.07
C	Lower bound on target throughput per pcu (arbitrarily selected as the midpoint between zero and B)	$1.54
C1	Lower bound on target throughput (C * 16 minutes)	$24.64
D	Highest throughput per pseudo-constraint unit (t/pcu) of products currently being sold (Chapter 5)	$11.88
E	Scope of existing t/pcu above lower bound (D–C)	$10.34
F	Adjusted throughout per pcu scope (arbitrary premium of 20% applied to allow for price expansion) [E * (1 + .20)]	$12.41
F1	Upper bound on target throughput (F * 16 minutes + $24.64)	$223.20
F2	Sales commmission on upper bound throughput (F1 * 5/95)	$11.75
K1	Minimum target price for Haton (A + C1 + C2)	$99.63
K2	Maximum target price for Haton (A + F1 + F2)	$308.64

[12] The cacophony also includes the temporary free products discussed in Chapter 6. These may be identified and comprise a *fast fill-in funnel* (which would appear between parts F and G of the sales process funnel) from which free product sales may be acquired quickly to fill in otherwise undesignated capacity.

[13] Research over the last few decades consistently shows that revenue-based sales compensation methods are in use by about two-thirds of industrial companies. Other popular sales incentive bases are profit margin, new accounts, and units sold. Less frequently encountered methods are product mix (to save costs) and company or unit performance.

[14] When all products are free products, there is no internal physical constraint.

[15] The ratio of throughput to sales is known as the **contribution margin ratio** in the conventional direct costing literature.

[16] This business results premise is adapted and extended from three papers written by Bill Hodgdon, "How to Manage the Sales Process: Measuring and Managing the Business to Business Sales Force," "Strategically Winning Industrial Markets," and "Leveraging Distributors to Increase Product Sales" (Hodgdon Consulting Services, telephone: 724-935-0409). Hodgdon also discusses the Sales Touch premise and the Strength premise, which are beyond the scope of these notes.

[17] A *compelling* offer is also known as an *unrefusable* offer.

[18] The term *sales offering* or *offering* refers to the offer to sell product or service and includes all of the associated terms of the offer, such as payment terms, warranties, and shipping.

[19] If the customer's constraint is in the market, then it may be necessary to influence the customer's customer. As constraints are elevated at the customer and the customer's customer, a supply chain solution begins to emerge. The requirements for successful constraint management within a supply chain are the same three as for an individual entity: (1) knowledge about constraint management, (2) communication of tactical and strategic constraint location and exploitation decisions, and (3) a reason for people in each entity of the constraint management supply chain to subordinate appropriately.

[20] These customers also probably comprise the majority of the selling organization's existing business.

[21] William A. Woehr and Dieter Legat, *Unblock the Power of Your Sales Force!* (NWV Neuer Wissenschaftlicher Verlag, 2002), p. 29.
[22] Ibid., p. 48.

10

People: A Valuable Asset

EMPOWERMENT AND RESPECT: ALIGNING AUTHORITY, RESPONSIBILITY, AND LONG-TERM COMMITMENT

The single word *respect* summarizes the appropriate treatment of people within a constraint management environment.[1] Throughout the preceding chapters we have seen that constraint management applications involve shifts in paradigms and corresponding changes in the organizational culture. Decisions are made differently; subordination—as the term is used within the theory of constraints—is often a new topic; employee empowerment speeds the flow of operations, and many standard operating procedures must be changed. Systematic techniques are needed to identify when and where new procedures should be implemented and to establish appropriate replacement operating procedures.

In this chapter we first establish the environmental platform by reviewing the course of a hypothetical holistic constraint management implementation. Then we will look at an example of Goldratt's technique for aligning authority with the responsibility of an empowered employee.[2] The example presented deals with the unavoidable issue of responding to the unused capacity that is exposed in robust applications of constraint management. Finally, constraints accounting analytical procedures relating to personnel employment decisions—appropriate for the long-term commitment that is needed to allow the empowered employee to risk independent action—are considered.

Environmental Platform

Consider an organization implementing constraint management. The decision to adopt constraint management as an overall management philoso-

236

phy started with education and strategic analysis at a high organizational level. The balance of the implementation proceeds as outlined in management's strategic analysis.

Let us assume that the next step, as identified in management's strategic analysis, was to create the ability to budget and report internally on a constraints accounting basis (Chapters 3 and 4), including constraint identification and consideration of personnel costs as long-term fixed costs and aligning authority with responsibility (Chapter 10).[3] Management, understanding the significance of the complexity divide (Chapter 3), provided an opportunity for all employees to complete a POOGI Bonus Orientation Course and established a POOGI Bonus plan (Chapter 4). Future costs are being carefully controlled (Chapter 3). The necessary conditions for successful constraint management (Chapter 11) are satisfied, and, following the sequence of the strategic plan, the organization introduces the various constraint management theory applications such as constraints accounting pricing (Chapter 6), drum-buffer-rope scheduling (Chapter 7), buffer management (Chapters 7 and 8), simplified critical chain (Chapter 8), distribution and replenishment, sales funnel reporting (Chapter 9), and compelling offers (Chapter 9).

Some constraint management applications require employee empowerment to speed the decision processes, and even greater empowerment is possible when the complexity divide is crossed. If empowerment is given lip service only, then many people will recognize that their authority is not commensurate with their responsibility; they will begin to doubt the validity and sincerity of the entire process. The organization will need to adjust to the changes in managerial authorities that accompany the empowerment process. In a better situation, authority is appropriately aligned with responsibility. This alignment leads to employees knowing that the empowerment is real and that they are truly valued.

Aligning Authority with Responsibility

When employees perceive that something within their sphere of responsibility should be done, they may initiate actions. If employees do not have the authority to take the actions, then they go to their supervisor to request an immediate decision or action. In this case there is often perceived misalignment of the employee's responsibility and authority. The employee feels the responsibility but not the commensurate authority.

Such misalignments easily arise in conjunction with a constraint management empowerment process. The proclaimed empowerment charges the employee with greater responsibility, but the culture and standard operating procedures are legacies from an earlier environment. Changes come about gradually in a methodical manner, using the techniques of the constraint knowledge to identify points at which change is needed.

The following example illustrates a systematic technique for aligning authority with responsibility.[4] The technique has eight parts:

1. Dealing with the immediate situation.
2. Identifying the situation as a possible misalignment of authority and responsibility.
3. Defining the situation (documenting the storyline).
4. Creating the evaporating cloud.
5. Communicating the cloud and obtaining agreement.[5]
6. Surfacing assumptions.
7. Specifying injections.
8. Documenting the modified authority or responsibility.

Assume, for our example, that Charlie is an experienced nonexempt[6] hourly employee who operates a metal lathe for a company that is implementing constraint management as described. He has completed the company's POOGI Bonus Orientation course and understands that as a part of proper subordination within the DBR and buffer management implementation he is to be like a **relay-race runner**—working as quickly as possible, with top-notch quality, when he has work to do and displaying his availability when he does not have work to do.

When applications such as drum-buffer-rope scheduling are implemented, a significant amount of clearly identifiable unused time is exposed. The organization will need to decide how to handle this idle time. General objectives for handling idle time should be established and communicated before the application is implemented. Twenty percent idle time is a conservative estimate; a more realistic estimate might be 50% or more.[7] Employees must have the confidence to expose this idle capacity if it is to be made available to the system.

It is 2:00 P.M. on Thursday. Charlie does not have anything to work on right now and would like to leave work two hours early, before the end of the shift. Assume that you are Charlie's supervisor. Charlie comes to you and asks if he may leave early. What do you do?

First, deal with the immediate problem. If people have gained the confidence to implement the relay-racer behavior, then capacity that previously was hidden by the Parkinson's Law effect will be revealed as being available.[8] Questions such as the one Charlie raised are going to come up; in fact, such questions are exactly what is expected. As a supervisor, you handle the question or problem within the existing organizational policies as you normally would.

Second, determine whether the question or problem involves a misalignment of authority with responsibility. In this case, Charlie has initiated the action of going to his supervisor—showing that he perceives his responsibility—and requested an immediate decision, revealing that he does not have the authority to make the decision on his own. Therefore, this is an identified situation in which empowerment needs to be clarified.

Third, write the storyline for the situation. Briefly (a single paragraph) describe the situation in which the problem or question arose. In this case it might be as simple as:

Charlie, a lathe operator, does not have anything to work on right now and would like to leave work two hours early, before the end of the shift.

Fourth, build an evaporating cloud as shown in Exhibit 10.1.

The numbers in the small square boxes of Exhibit 10.1 indicate the sequence in which the cloud entities are completed:

1. **Box B** is the need of the system that is jeopardized by the potential misalignment. In this case, employees make decisions for their areas of responsibility.

2. **Box E** expresses a rule (or existing standard operating procedure) that prevents the employee (Charlie) from satisfying the need in B: absences from workstations must be approved by supervisors.

Exhibit 10.1   Responsibility: Authority Evaporating Cloud

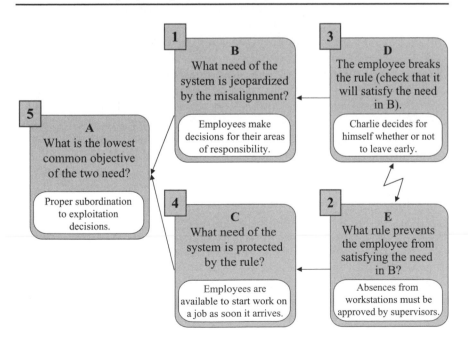

3. Next **box D** is completed. Here an action that breaks the rule is entered. We check to see that the action entered in D will, in fact, satisfy the need expressed in B. It does; Charlie decides for himself whether or not to leave early.

4. **Box C** is the need of the system that is protected by the rule as expressed in box E. In this case the rule is that employees be available to start work on a job as soon as it arrives at their workstation.

5. **Objective in box A** is the lowest common objective of the two needs. Both having employees make decisions for their areas of responsibility and having employees be available to start work on a job as soon as it arrives at their workstations have the objective of proper subordination to the exploitation decisions.

Fifth, review the evaporating cloud with the employee. The immediate effect of reviewing the cloud with the employee is to demonstrate that the employee is respected and taken seriously.[9] The initial purpose of this review is to obtain agreement on the nature of the misalignment of authority with responsibility. Box B specifies the employee's perceived responsibility, and box E details the employee's lack of authority.

Sixth, with the employee, surface the assumptions underlying the arrow between C and E. Although the immediate problem may be addressed in many different ways, Goldratt suggests that only by dealing with the linkage between C and E will the alignment of authority with responsibility accompanying the empowerment process be accomplished.[10]

The seventh step is to specify an injection or injections to invalidate one or more of the assumptions forming the linkage between C and E. Typically, this will require a change in a convention or policy at some level. In some cases, the needed change might be as easy as the supervisor verbally delegating—or clarifying—an additional authority. In other cases, the rule in E may be well entrenched in both formal (written) policy and/or convention. In such situations, the misalignment may affect many areas beyond the particular organizational unit in which the misalignment is first surfaced; the supervisor may not have the authority to make the desired change. What the supervisor does have, however, is a clear statement of the misalignment and a full quiver of injections with which to communicate the misalignment and suggest appropriate revised standard operating procedures. If all members of the organization have completed a POOGI Bonus Orientation Course (or its equivalent) and goal congruence has been obtained, then the presentation of the misalignment should receive a warm reception from the organizational level that has the authority to implement the necessary policy changes.

The eighth and final step in the process of aligning authority with responsibility is to document the modified authority or responsibility.

Empowerment represents delegated authority. But in a broader sense, empowerment is the effect of employees understanding the relationship between their actions and the bottom line, in conjunction with strong goal congruence.

PERSONNEL EMPLOYMENT DECISIONS

In Chapter 4 we saw that in most organizations seeking to implement constraint management as a management philosophy to drive a process of ongoing improvement, there is a need to change deeply seated paradigms about what individuals perceive their relationship with the organization to be.[11] The purpose of the POOGI Bonus is to confirm to employees that they are an integral and valued part of the organization. *Respect* for employees may involve a shift in the manner in which the financial analysis associated with hiring new employees is accomplished. We will examine two analyses. First, using a conventional T, I, and OE analysis, we will look at a typical request for budget revision. Second, we will check the application of the three characteristics of constraints accounting to the new employment hiring decision.

Conventional T, I, and OE Analysis

A typical *request for budget increase* form, as might be received by the POOGI Budget Committee, is illustrated as Exhibit 10.2. The content of the form (Exhibit 10.2) includes the five items suggested for review by the POOGI Budget Committee in Chapter 4.[12]

Assume that the proposal arose as an effect of the internal distribution of a performance report similar to the Constraints Accounting Earnings Statement illustrated in Chapter 3. That report was for the month of November 20X2 and was distributed internally during the first week of December. Note B to that report observed that a reduction in headcount of Class D labor had resulted in shipment of only two-thirds of the product that uses the Class D labor. There was a corresponding drop in throughput of $186,895, representing a decrease of about 20% in the performance profit. Note B further observed that about 75% of the customers representing the $186,895 of lost throughput would be permanently lost. However, $150,000 of untapped throughput remained in what we now understand is the Growth and Replacement Funnel.[13]

The first thing that we observe about the budget increase request is that it is dated December 18, 20X2. The background work—in this case consisting of investigating the reason for headcount reduction, evaluation of market wage rates, and determination that the organization is below

Exhibit 10.2　　Request for Budget Increase

Request for Budget Increase　　　Date:　　12/18/20X2

A Proposal is for (check one):　　**__**Elevating constraint
　　　　　　　　　　　　　　　　　____Satisfying necessary condition (NC)

B Specify constraint or NC:　　Class D labor

C Brief Description (attach additional pages if necessary):
　　Increase Labor Class D rate by 20% to market rate. Hire one additional person with
　　Labor Class D skills to replace employee who left at the beginning of November.

D Exploitation Decisions:
　　• Potential sales are evaluated by t/cu
　　• Class D labor to be used only for Gaton.

E Evidence of proper subordination:
　　• The Expansion and Replacement Funnel has $150,000 available work that
　　　has about 60% of the t/cu of the $140,000 permanently lost business.
　　• Labor Class D is not reassigned to other work.

F Impact on protective capacity: None.
　　　　This proposal will not create constraint capacity beyond that which previously
　　　　existed and was supported by sufficient protective capacity　　　　.

G Budget Revision: OE:　　$3,000 per month　　　**I:**　　None

　　Sources of future improvement ID (if I requested):　　Not applicable

H Estimated Cash Flow Change:

Monthly increase in Throughput:		$ 131,000
Monthly increase in cash OE:		
New hire	$ 6,000	
Increase for existing employees	2,000	8,000
Net Increase in Monthly Cash Flow		
		$ 123,000

I Recommendation Approval Actions:
　　　　　　POOGI Budget Committee (recommendation)
　　　　　　Managerial Authority (approval)
　　　　　　Controller (budget revision action)
　　　　　　Controller (implementation follow up action)

---

market for this category of labor—was completed in just a couple of weeks. This short period properly reflects the urgency that should exist when dealing with Archimedean constraints.[14] Because this single issue (Class D labor) accounts for about 20% of performance profit, it merits extraordinary attention.

Parts A, B, and C: General Description

Parts A and B of the request form unambiguously specify that the request is to elevate the Class D labor constraint, and part C provides a summary of the background data. Since the Class D labor has been designated as a constraint on the performance report, its constraint status does not need to be further verified. In some cases, the *request for budget revision* may be the first point at which a constraint is formally recognized. This latter situation calls for verification of the constraint and coordination with the accounting department for tracking purposes before increasing expenditures.

Parts D and E: Exploitation and Subordination

Parts D and E, relating to exploitation and subordination, are on the form to ensure that these steps have been considered before increasing the budget to elevate a constraint. As noted in Chapter 2, proper identification, exploitation, and subordination are often sufficient to break an apparent physical constraint. Our example assumes that the Class D labor has been recognized as a constraint and, in general, handled appropriately within the constraint management framework.

   Communication by the wide distribution of a Constraints Accounting Earnings Statement leads to general awareness of Class D labor as being identified as an active constraint. Two exploitation decisions were also made and communicated. First, since Class D labor is an internal physical constraint, otherwise desirable business is being turned away. The general exploitation decision rule is to use the throughput per constraint unit (t/cu) as a guide in accepting orders for Gaton. The $150,000 of potential throughput in unclosed business that is listed in the Expansion and Replacement Funnel provides evidence that there has been proper subordination to this general exploitation. These unclosed orders have a t/cu that, on average, is only 60% as great as the t/cu of the lost customers. In other words, the organization had been successful in obtaining the more profitable sales. The second general exploitation decision was to ensure that the scarce Class D labor was used only where other types of labor would not suffice.

Part F: Protective Capacity

Part F provides some assurance that the effect of the proposal on other areas has been considered because an increased level of activity frequently accompanies elevating a constraint. The form might also ask whether the proposal is expected to break the constraint and, if so, to state where the constraint is expected to shift as well as the strategic impact of such a shift.

Part G: Budget Revision

In part G, we finally arrive at the specific budget increase request. The request will be for an increase in either operational expense (OE) or inventory/investment (I), or both.[15] In Exhibit 10.2 the request is for an increase of $3,000 in OE. The $3,000 per month was calculated as shown in Exhibit 10.3.

If the budget revision request involved an addition to I, then the budget request form asks a short identification to be used in listings of the *sources of future improvement* (assuming that the payback allocation method is being used).[16] In the case of Exhibit 10.2, the requestor did not request additional I.

Part H: Estimated Cash Flow Change

In part H the anticipated cash flows are delineated. The cash flows in H differ from the budget revisions requested in G in two ways. First, the budget revisions in G deal only with OE and I costs, whereas the estimated cash flows in H include throughput changes as well. Second, although the amounts in G represent changes from the existing budget, the estimated cash flows in H represent changes from the currently existing cash flows.

Calculation of the monthly throughput increase started by taking the $186,895 of throughput lost in November and multiplying by 0.75 to arrive at an estimated $140,171 of throughput from permanently lost orders. This lost throughput was then multiplied by 0.6 (60%) to arrive at

Exhibit 10.3   Expected Change in OE Resulting from Proposal

Increased wages for the new hire (2,000 hours @ $25.71)	$51,429
Increased fringe benefits for the new hire (@ 40%)	20,571
Increased wage rate and fringe benefits for the two existing Class D labor employees:	
increase wages from $21.43 per hour to $25.71 per hour for 4,000 hours	17,120
increase fringe benefits @ 40%	6,848
Annual increase in cash OE	$95,968
Monthly increase in cash OE (divide by 12)	$ 7,997
Reduced by $5,000 per month already included in the OE budget (for the employee that left)	(5,000)
Net change in monthly budgeted OE	$ 2,997
OE Increase requested for budget revision (rounded to nearest $000 for budget estimate)	$ 3,000

$84,103, the throughput amount of the lower t/cu orders that would replace the same amount of constraint time required for the permanently lost throughput.[17] Although 75% of the $186,895 lost throughput, or $140,171, was permanently lost, 25%, or $46,724, was not permanently lost. The increase in throughput that may be expected when the Class D labor is restored to the pre-November capacity, then, is the sum of the throughput that was not permanently lost ($46,724) plus the replacement throughput ($84,103), or a total of $130,827. Since this is an estimate, it is rounded to $131,000.

Part I, Recommendation

In part I, there is a place to record the recommendation made by the POOGI Budget Committee. Since the actual spending authority is vested in an individual manager, space is provided to record appropriate managerial approval. This provides a clear audit trail of management's approval of spending. The controller makes a posting notation when the budget is revised to reflect the inclusion of the increased OE and/or I. Finally, provision has been made for a followup action by the controllership function to confirm that proposed actions are being taken in a timely manner.

The proposal outlined in Exhibit 10.2 appears to be quite desirable. For a $3,000 increase in monthly budgeted OE—reflecting an $8,000 increase in cash expenditures—throughput (T) is expected to increase by $131,000 per month.

Although the proposal appears to be desirable, we have not checked the application of the three characteristics of constraints accounting to the employment decision. The analysis shown in Exhibit 10.2 clearly meets the first two characteristics—explicit consideration of the role of constraints and specification of throughput contribution effects. But what about the third characteristic—decoupling of throughput from operational expense? The analysis implicitly assumes that the OE is coupled with the T.

T and OE Coupled by Decision Methodology

An unstated assumption inherent in the methodology of the foregoing conventional T, I, and OE analysis is that the time horizons for the $131,000 T increase and the $8,000 OE increase are the same. That is, for whatever the time horizon of the proposal is, both the T and the OE exist at the levels of $131,000 and $8,000 per month. At the end of the time horizon, the assumption is that both the throughput and the operational expense cease to exist. This can happen in either of two ways.

First, the assumption may be that the increase in employment-related OE is reversed (i.e., the employee is laid off or fired) at the time that the future nonemployment cash flows (net T) end. With this technique the increase in T is compared to the increase in cash OE to arrive at a net increase in cash flow. The decision rule, then, is to accept the proposal if the net increase in cash flow is adequate (a management judgment call). When we say that we like the proposal because it provides an additional net cash flow of $123,000 per month, we assume that the relationship is a continuing one. This approach is consistent with the conventional T, I, and OE analysis, shown in Exhibit 10.2 and, as we have seen, assumes that employment costs are variable. We reject this approach because it is inconsistent with the desired personnel policy of treating labor costs as fixed.

Second, the assumption may be that the increased T will continue as long as the increased OE continues. In this case, the assumption is that there will be sufficient sources of future T that are at least as good as the best opportunities now available. As a practical matter, if the future T is not available at the same level as the T used for the analysis, then pressure will mount to reduce the OE (i.e., lay off or fire employees) to match the lowered expectations for T. In this case the OE is again treated as variable, in spite of the professed desire to have it be fixed.[18]

Regardless of the assumption, since the product mix will be changing—perhaps rapidly—over time, the T increase is essentially transient. What about the OE increase? If the time horizons for the T and OE are the same, and the T increase is essentially transient in its nature, then the OE must also be assumed to be transient. *An implication of the conventional T, I, and OE analysis is that the commitment to employees is transient as well.*

Treating the increased OE for employee wages and fringe benefits as fixed in both the intermediate and long term is consistent with the necessary conditions for successful constraint management, which is discussed in Chapter 11.[19] The POOGI Bonus plan—with its attendant empowerment—is designed to bring individual and organizational goals into alignment, providing a secure and satisfying environment for employees as they pursue the global organizational goal. Part of the POOGI Bonus plan is that there is no incentive for reducing the current workforce. Rather than being an element of variable expense, people are viewed, in general, as valued permanent resources. As the perception of the relationship of employees with the organization changes, so also must the analytical methodology change.

If decisions are made routinely in a manner such that incremental cash inflows do not recover the investment costs (that is, the decisions do not result in improvement), then at some point it will become necessary to significantly reduce the expense level—and that means to lay off employees. Recovering an investment amount before claiming improvement recognizes that the organization has made a commitment to avoid making decisions in such a way that the actions put the employees' job security at risk in the future. This commitment implies a long-term OE expenditure that is separate from the immediate expected T gain realized when an employee is hired. What are the mechanics of breaking the linkage between OE and T?

Decoupling OE from T in the Decision Methodology

Decoupling the OE from the T is accomplished by explicitly recognizing that the planning time horizons for the T and the OE are different. Although the T is transient, the increased OE is comparatively permanent.

At the time of the decision to hire an additional person (in this case with Class D labor skills), the cost of the hire is associated with the identifiable throughput to be received due to elevating the labor constraint. However, after the employee has been hired, the employee and his skills are resources available for use in whatever way the organization might utilize them. The cost of the employee is no longer associated directly with specific throughput; instead, it is just another component of OE. This is an instance of the general rule, stated in Chapter 5, that once an expenditure for improvement has been made, the reality of the setting is changed and the resources acquired become part of the overall environment.

Investment in Employees

In discussing the nature of investment in Chapter 5, we observed that an investment is an expenditure made in the expectation of identifiable future improvement—the return on investment. We also saw in Chapter 4 that performance profit is the bottom line that summarizes operations in a manner consistent with the desired operating philosophy, and, in the discussion of the payback allocation method (Chapter 5), we saw that performance profit does not reflect improvement until the payback period has been reached and investment costs have been recovered.

Certainly the proposal under consideration meets the definition of an investment. The investment is the continuing stream of $8,000 monthly cash outflows associated with the employment costs. The return is the anticipated $131,000 monthly increase in nonemployment net cash inflow. Therefore, it will be appropriate to analyze the financial effects of the proposal in a manner consistent with the payback allocation method.

Applying the Payback Allocation Method to Employment Costs

The concept of computing a payback period for our employment example is easy. Simply determine how many years (or months) of nonemployment cash inflow of $131,000 are necessary to recover the required investment. But what amount of investment is needed for the proposal? In capitalizing the investment amount, we should recognize that the purpose of the analysis is to determine improvement. The question is, "How long will it take to recover the cost of the commitment to employees?" A problem arises in computing the payback data for employment decisions because the employment investment cost stream of $8,000 per month cash outflow is not completely specified. Two factors come into play when establishing an employment investment amount: the planning horizon (estimated length of time) over which the employment cost increase should be considered and the issue of the time value of money.[20]

Time Value of Money

Exhibit 10.4 illustrates two characteristics of the time value of money: the length of time into the future that the money is to be received and the discount (or interest) rate assumed.

The values shown in Exhibit 10.4 are the discounted present values of $1.00 received either 10 or 20 years into the future and discounted at either 10% or 20%. For example, the amount, $0.39, appearing at the intersection of the 10-year row and 10% column is the present value of $1.00 to be received 10 years from now when discounted at 10%. Another way of looking at this is that an investment of $0.39 made today and returning 10% compound interest would have a total value of $1.00 in 10 years ($0.39 principal plus $0.61 accumulated interest). Inspection of Exhibit 10.4 reveals the following:

- Given any selected discount rate, the further into the future an amount is expected to be received, the less value it has today.
- For a given future point in time, the higher the discount rate assumed, the less value the future amount has today.

When a high discount rate is combined with a long time horizon, present values of future expected cash flows are quite small. This is illustrated by the $0.03 at the intersection of the 20-year row with the 20% discount rate column.

Exhibit 10.4   Discounted Value of $1.00

	Discount Rate	
Years	10%	20%
10	$0.39	$0.16
20	$0.15	$0.03

Discounted values are calculated as $1/(1+r)^n$, where: r = discount rate and n = years in future

For our example we assume that the organization selected a 10% discount rate after obtaining the advice of an investment adviser who suggested that they could expect to earn 10% on financial investments as a long-run average. Other rates considered were the organization's cost of capital, which was thought to be about 20%, and 5% that they felt could be reliably earned on short-term cash investments.

Planning Horizon

We can identify two investment time frames that reach toward opposite depths of the potential planning horizon. On the far horizon, the organization might consider a lifetime employment cost approach, estimating the equivalent of the present value of lifetime employment cost. On a significantly shorter horizon, a financial reserve could be established as a *cost buffer* of adequate size to carry the organization over a length of time sufficient to prevent layoffs due to market turndowns.[21] In our example, we assume that the organization uses the lifetime employment cost concept for decisions about increasing the size of the payroll.

When considering the length of time to represent a *lifetime*, a question is whether the lifetime should be specific to the individual being hired, or a generic representative of the workforce as a whole. For our example, a generic lifetime was considered more appropriate because the commitment is to the workforce in general as opposed to specific individuals. The organization considered a number of time periods and discount rate possibilities in determining the stated employment investment.

Stated Employment Investment

Typical analytical results of these time values of money and planning horizon considerations are summarized in Exhibit 10.5.

Based on their understanding of data similar to that shown in Exhibit 10.5, the 20-year planning horizon and 10% discount rate were selected as the parameters for analyzing employment investment proposals. The actual median and mean lengths of employment of the organization's existing workforce were 11 years and 13 years, respectively, and it was thought that some employees might remain with the organization for more than 30 years. Nevertheless, the organization thought that a 20-year period was sufficient inasmuch as there was relatively little difference in the present values of the future cash flows between 20 years and 30 years.

The 20-year generic employment lifetime and 10% discount rate are combined to establish a stated employment investment amount of $820,000[22] to incorporate a level of commitment to employees into the decision process. Once an organization establishes the parameters, they are used for future analyses and are changed only in the event of significant environmental changes.[23]

Exhibit 10.5 Impact of Time Periods and Discount Rates on Stated
Employment Investment

Estimated Monthly Cash Flows	Employment OE ($8,000)	Non-Employment T and O E $131,000	Net Cash Flow $123,000
Discounted Value of Employment Operational Expense (Investment)			
Years	20%	15%	10%
30	$477,974	$630,336	$904,982
20	$467,974	$600,893	$817,306
10	$402,480	$481,805	$589,882
Limit of Internal Rate of Return (based on Investment above)			
Years	20%	15%	10%
30	329%	349%	174%
20	336%	262%	192%
10	391%	326%	266%
Miscellaneous Statistics			
	Minimum	Maximum	$820,000
Internal Rate of Return Range	174%	391%	Investment
Internal Rate of Return			192%
Payback Period			6.26 months

Payback Period

As shown in Exhibit 10.2, the estimated monthly net cash flow associated
with the proposal is $123,000. Therefore, based on the payback allocation
method, $123,000 will be charged to actual and budgeted OE (as a source
of future improvement[24]) until the payback period has been reached. In
this case, by dividing the stated investment amount of $820,000 by the
monthly net cash flow of $123,000, it is expected to take about seven
months to reach the payback period.[25]

Constraints Accounting Analysis

Whereas the decision criterion used in the conventional analysis essentially asks the question, "Is the increase in T greater than the increase in
OE?", the constraints accounting criterion is to ask, "How long is it expected to take for the increased T to recover the increased financial commitment to the employees?" Application of this revised analytical paradigm regarding human resources results in a different evaluation in parts
G and H of the *request for budget revision* form. Appropriate constraints ac-

counting modifications to parts G through J of the request form are shown in Exhibit 10.6; parts A through F remain the same.

Exhibit 10.6 differs from parts G, H, and I of Exhibit 10.2 (the conventional T, I, and OE analysis) in the following ways.

Part G, Budget Revision

In part G, $820,000 is shown as an increase in budgeted I. (The source of this amount is discussed in Part I, Analysis of Improvement.) Since additional I is requested, a short label is provided to tie the expected improvement to the financial statements as a source of future improvement.[26]

Part H, Estimated Cash Flow Change

Part H has been revised to categorize the estimates of monthly cash flows as being either employment related ($8,000 outflow per month) or non-employment related ($131,000 inflow per month).[27] The method of reporting does not change the reality of the net cash flow, which remains at $123,000 per month.

Part I, Analysis of Improvement

Part I in Exhibit 10.6 is a new section that analyzes the proposal in terms of improvement. *Real bottom-line improvement can be detected only after the en-*

Exhibit 10.6   Constraints Accounting Analysis Request for Budget Revision

	Employment	Non-employment
G. Budget Revision: OE: $3,000 per month **I:** $820,000		
Sources of future improvement **ID** (if I requested): Restore class D labor		
H. Estimated Cash Flow Change:		
Monthly increase in Throughput:		$131,000
Monthly change in non-employment OE		(0)
Monthly increase in cash employment OE:	($ 8,000)	
Net changes in monthly cash flows	($ 8,000)	$131,000
Net estimated monthly net cash flow	$123,000	
I. Analysis of Improvement:		
Approximate present value of financial commitment to employees:		
(See Exhibit 10.5. and related discussion)	$820,000	
Months to payback ($820,000 / $123,000)	6.67 months	
Approximate expected rate of return	180% (range: 160% to 360%)	
J. Recommendation, Approval, Actions:		

tire commitment has been recovered. Therefore, the payback period of 6.67 months is calculated in part I. The approximate rate of return of 180% for the proposal is displayed.[28] Since the analysis involves a very large amount of uncertainty with respect to both the length of commitment and the discount rate, the proposal's sensitivity to error in these estimates is expressed in terms of the potential range for the approximate rate of return estimate (160% to 360%).

Finally, the last change in the form is that the recommendation, approval, and actions section becomes part J.

As in the case of the conventional T, I, and OE analysis, the constraints accounting analysis shows the proposal to be quite desirable. Even though the conclusion reached in each case is the same, the mindset for the analyses is quite different. Therefore, we have not yet shown the constraints accounting approach to be significantly different from the conventional analysis.

MIXED MESSAGES

Let us modify the example so that the proposal is not so attractive. Assume that the increase in monthly throughput is $12,000 rather than $131,000 and that all other factors remain the same. We will again examine the conventional T, I, and OE and constraints accounting analyses, but now the former will indicate that the proposal is desirable and the latter that the proposal in undesirable.

Conventional T, I, and OE Analysis

The data for the revised example are shown in Exhibit 10.7. The data in this exhibit are the same as those in Exhibit 10.2 except that the monthly increase in throughput has been reduced from $131,000 to $12,000. This is a large change, and it is obvious that the proposal is not as attractive as it was before the assumption changed. But is the revised proposal desirable at all? The T increase of $12,000 is 50% more than the OE increase of $8,000 per month; I remains the same. The revised proposal clearly passes the conventional T, I, and OE screening criteria.

Constraints Accounting Analysis

Exhibit 10.8 shows the constraints accounting analysis—which treats the commitment to the employee as an investment—for the revised proposal. The commitment to the employees, and hence the investment commitment, is the same as calculated previously, $820,000. However, with only $4,000 per month of improved cash flow, the payback period is 205 months, or about 17 years. This yields an estimated rate of return of about

Exhibit 10.7   Conventional T, I, and OE Analysis: Revised Proposal

G. Budget Revision: OE:___$3,000 per month___ **I:**___None_____

Sources of future improvement **ID** (if I requested):___Not applicable_____

H. Estimated Cash Flow Change:

Monthly increase in throughput:		$ 12,000
Monthly increase in cash OE:		
New hire	$ 6,000	
Increase for existing employees	2,000	8,000
Net increase in monthly cash flow		$ 4,000

2%, well below the return that most business organizations would require for an additional investment.

Business of this type should be considered for the *fast fill-in funnel*. It would be desirable to fill in existing capacity, but not so desirable that the organization expand capacity in order to obtain the sale.

Exhibit 10.8   Constraint Accounting Analysis: Revised Proposal Reduced Throughput

G. Budget Revision: OE: $3,000 per month   **I:** $820,000

Sources of future improvement   **ID** (if I requested):   Restore class D labor

H. Estimated Cash Flow Change:

	Employment	Nonemployment
Monthly increase in throughput:		$ 12,000
Monthly change in nonemployment OE		(0)
Monthly increase in cash employment OE:	($ 8,000)	
Net changes in monthly cash flows	($ 8,000)	$ 12,000
Net estimated monthly cash flow		$4,000

I. Analysis of Improvement:

Approximate present value of financial commitment to employees:	
(See Exhibit 10.5 and related discussion)	$820,000
Months to payback ($820,000 / $4,000)	205 months
Approximate expected rate of return	2% (range: -9% to 3%)

SUMMARY

Employees at all organizational levels will be looking for signs that goal congruence exists among all four employee groups discussed in Chapter 4. When empowered by management, employees—who now have achieved incentive status by participating in the POOGI Bonus plan—feel a sense of ownership and personal commitment. They understand that an important purpose of the bonus plan is for them to be an integral part of the global organization, and they believe that they have the tools to make a difference. They feel the presence of respect. Now the organization is beginning to satisfy the employees' needs for belonging and acceptance. Trust among the diverse groups within the organization is built and is a key to locking in a process of ongoing improvement.

NOTES

[1] *Goldratt Satellite Program,* Tape 7, *Managing People—Respect.* Available from www.eligoldratt.com.

[2] Goldratt suggests that there will be about three to seven misalignments of authority with responsibility per person in the typical constraint management implementation (as well as in any typical organization).

[3] This internal reporting includes the reconciliation to the external GAAP reports.

[4] Goldratt presents the cloud technique for aligning authority with responsibility in *Managing People* (Tape 7) of the Goldratt Satellite Program (GSP) or the Self-Learning Program, *TOC on Managing People.* Available at www.eligoldratt.com.

[5] Of course, the cloud may be revised at this point if appropriate.

[6] *Nonexempt* is from the Fair Labor Standards (Wages and Hours) Act—a law in the United States that establishes minimum wage, hour limits, and overtime pay minimums. In general, salaried executive, administrative, and professional employees, as well as some inside salespersons, are exempt from the provisions of the Act.

[7] The failure to expose a significant amount of unused capacity throughout the organization is an indication that one or more of the necessary conditions for successful constraint management has not been satisfied.

[8] The relay-racer behavior is applicable to everyone in the organization, not just to those involved with drum-buffer-rope (DBR) or critical chain, and should be covered as a part of the common initial general training when implementing constraint management.

[9] Use of the evaporating cloud in this manner would have been covered as part of the POOGI Bonus Orientation Course (Chapter 4). The employee will be delighted to see this tangible sign that the constraint management implementation is proceeding and that the employee is an important part of the implementation.

[10] *GSP Tape 7, Managing People—Respect.*

[11] Chapter 4.

[12] Written cash flow estimates (H), specified constraint or necessary condition (A and B), exploitation (D), subordination (E), and protective capacity (F).

[13] The Growth and Replacement Funnel is discussed in Chapter 9.

[14] It is traditionally customary to allow two to four weeks for responses to

interdepartmental information requests in many organizations. However, since everyone is aware of the importance of the organization's Archimedean constraints, everyone in the organization gives top priority to matters dealing with or relating to constraints.

[15] The request could be for a *decrease*, but we doubt that that would happen very often. Nevertheless, before discarding the notion we might consider that such a procedure could present an avenue for obtaining agreement for budget decreases that could then be a component of a POOGI Bonus.

[16] The payback allocation method and the *sources of future improvement* are discussed in Chapter 5.

[17] Class D labor will still be an internal physical constraint. This is at variance with the analysis in Chapter 3 which suggested that the entire $150,000 of potential throughput listed in the Expansion and Replacement Funnel would be received. This discrepancy arises because in Chapter 3 we had not yet discussed the implications of different t/cus for accepting potential orders. Now, in Chapter 10, we add the assumption that the sales function has been exploiting and subordinating appropriately.

[18] This assumption about future T is discussed further in Chapter 11.

[19] The purpose of the commitment to employees is to continually satisfy the third necessary condition for successful constraint management: a reason for people to subordinate appropriately as discussed in Chapter 11.

[20] The *time value of money* refers to the fact that, as a rule, given a lump sum of money—say $100—we would rather have it sooner than later. However, probably at some point we would prefer a future amount. For example, we might prefer a reliable promise to receive $120 one year from today to receiving $100 today. Such a preference implies that there is some amount between $100 and $120 at which we are indifferent to having the money today rather than a year form now. If our indifference amount is $110, then we would say that our time preference for money is 10% per year ($100 plus 10% interest for one year = $110). Another way of stating this is that $110 one year from now has a *present value* of $100 when discounted at a discount rate of 10%. (*Discount* and *interest* are essentially the same thing. The term *interest* is used when calculating future values of present amounts, and the term *discount* is used when calculating present values of future amounts.) When cash flows occur over periods spanning several years, it is necessary to adjust the annual amounts to compensate for the time value of money. The techniques for doing this are known as *present value* or *discounted cash flow* methods and are discussed in most introductory management accounting and finance textbooks.

[21] We are indebted to Harvey Opps for this insight and for providing an example of a software company that attempted to establish a cost buffer equal to three years of wages and salaries for this purpose.

[22] Rounded from $817,306.

[23] The process for determining the stated employment investment described herein is intended to be a general example of how such a process might proceed rather than an established procedure for making such a determination. The concept is new and undoubtedly subject to substantial refinement in terms of actuarial assumptions and technique. Nevertheless, even the rough methodology presented accomplishes the purpose of setting an investment amount to recognize the impact of the decision process on the organizational commitment to employees.

[24] See Chapter 5 for a discussion of sources of future improvement.

[25] $820,000 / $123,000 per month = 6.67 months.

[26] The *Sources of Future Improvement* section of the earnings statement is discussed in Chapter 5.

[27] Section H, *Estimated Cash Flow Changes,* represents the cash flow analysis referenced in footnote 33 in Chapter 5.

[28] Recall that the reciprocal of the payback period (expressed in years) gives the upper limit on the internal rate of return and approximates the rate of return when the economic life is more than twice the payback period. In this case, [1 / (6.67 months / 12 months per year)] = 1.799 per year or approximately 180%.

11

Strategy and Conclusions

STRATEGY

The organization's **strategy** is its path to the future. Conventionally, we think of strategy as involving the creation of an elaborate and systemic plan. But we need to modify our conventional understanding of strategy for the constraint management environment. The elaborate nature of strategy implies planning with painstaking attention to numerous details. Instead of an elaborate plan, a constraint management strategy reflects the elegant simplicity lying on the far side of complexity (see Chapter 3). Focus on the relatively few constraints allows strategic planning to cross the complexity divide, resulting in just two aspects of a constraint management strategy—the overall management philosophy and the specification of **strategic constraints**—requiring the routine action of the corporate governance group.

In the first part of this chapter, we delineate responsibilities for strategic planning, distinguish between strategic and tactical constraints, specify potential attributes of strategic constraints, examine the role of markets in strategic planning, and resolve the short-run versus long-run dilemma.

Strategic Responsibilities

Strategy is the stuff of generals. The very highest organizational levels must be involved with both strategic considerations. The uppermost levels of the corporate governance group (the board of directors, executive management, and—sometimes—owners) establish the overall management philosophy, that is, the essential enabling rules for satisfying the three necessary and sufficient conditions for successful constraint management.

257

For example, the governance group might state that it is the policy of the organization to pursue a process of ongoing improvement through constraint management practices. In order to accomplish this policy, appropriate training is provided for all employees, all capital expenditures and requests for operating budget increases are evaluated with reference to constraints and necessary conditions,[1] the governance group would mandate that financial reporting at the executive level be accomplished on a constraints accounting basis (ensuring that Archimedean constraint location is reviewed periodically), and the governance group ensures that all employees have a reason to subordinate appropriately, such as the POOGI Bonus described in Chapter 4.

Top managers of individual independent business segments designate strategic constraints for their segments.[2] These strategically selected constraints typically should include a desired internal resource or capability and an element tying to the markets to be served by the organization.

Strategy versus Tactics

Whereas strategy provides the vision, tactics are the day-to-day actions taken in carrying out the strategy. Every organization has at least one tactical constraint. An organization may—or may not—have one or more strategic constraints. However, an organization *ought* to have tactical constraints and at least one strategic constraint.

The tactical constraints actively constrain current bottom-line performance. These are either actual physical constraints (materials, resources, markets) or are the manifestations of policy constraints. Tactical constraints exist as part of every system that has an open-ended goal. All open-ended systems have at least one tactical constraint.

Strategic constraints, on the other hand, are quite different. A strategic constraint is declared by management and therefore exists only if management establishes it. A strategic constraint is simply a statement of where management would like to locate a tactical constraint.

But the importance of a strategic constraint should not be underestimated. It is through designation of strategic constraints that the organization avoids a random walk into the future. The selection of a strategic constraint defines the future capabilities of the organization, which, in turn, define where the organization will go in the future. The selection also determines the pattern of future investment expenditures.

The selection of a strategic constraint is analogous to a young person making a career choice. Will the person be an auto mechanic, or perhaps a pharmacist, an accountant or a physician, a teacher or a professional athlete? The choice will define the capabilities that the individual needs to develop and thereby direct the expenditure of funds, time, and effort to develop those capabilities. The career choice itself is both a very important decision and a very personal decision. In similar fashion, the selection of a strategic constraint is a very important and very personal decision. The strategic constraint should be consistent with the pursuit of the organization's goal.

The TOC focusing steps apply to both tactical and strategic constraints but a little differently for each:[3]

1. *Identify* the constraint. For tactical constraints, find the existing active constraints; this is a reactive step. For strategic constraints, select the desired constraints. Note that because this step is important in defining the long-run course of the organization, this is a responsibility of senior management of the independent profit center; this is a proactive step.

2. Decide how to *exploit* the constraint. This step is similar for both tactical and strategic constraints. For example, consider a decision about pricing a new product. Assume that the product requires time on both Machine A, the current tactical constraint, and Machine B, a strategic constraint. Here we would examine two price ranges— one based on the active tactical constraint and the other on the strategic pseudo-constraint.[4]

3. *Subordinate* everything else to the exploitation decisions resulting from step 2. Strategic decisions typically have precedence over tactical decisions. For example, continuing the pricing example, if the price ranges overlap, there is no conflict—pick a price within the intersection of the ranges. However, if the price ranges do not overlap, then a conflict exists and the strategic decision "trumps" the tactical decision, with the price being set at the end of the strategic range closest to the tactical range.

4. *Elevation* is expensive and always has strategic implications.[5] If a tactical constraint is not also a strategic constraint, then the tactical constraint must be broken when causing the desired strategic constraint to emerge as an active constraint. Tactical constraints that are not also strategic constraints are either removed from the system or are expanded to a level where they have enough protective capacity to subordinate properly. Strategic constraints are elevated when the long-run increase in throughput contribution is expected to be greater than the long-run increase in costs (including the cost of commitment to employees).

5. We must constantly guard against the *inertia* of our thinking in identifying both tactical and strategic constraints. A change in the physical reality of the organization changes the environmental background. The changed background may lead to a different tactical Archimedean constraint. Here the organization has a choice. It may

accept whatever constraints emerge as the cyclical focusing process is followed, or it can decide the nature and location of its constraints. The fifth step applies equally to tactical and strategic constraints.

Appropriate selection of a strategic constraint assumes that a holistic approach to constraint management is being followed. Most organizations implementing individual applications of the constraint theory are not yet at that stage. Let us return to the analogy of a young person making a career choice. Many young people don't make a specific choice. They just go where luck draws them. Some of these youths will be quite successful, and others not so successful. So it is with organizations that do not select a strategic constraint. They will go where luck draws them. Some organizations will be quite lucky, and others less so. But rather than relying on the fickle nature of Lady Luck, an organization can take control of its destiny, a destiny that will continually reflect favorably on its bottom line.

Selecting a Strategic Constraint

Robert Newbold suggests several potential attributes, including the following, on which the selection of strategic constraints might be based:[6]

- A place that required a large capital expenditure to expand.
- A technology or concept to which the organization has exclusive rights, such as by a patent, that differentiates its products or services from those of a competitor.
- A resource that is difficult to elevate.
- A point to which it is easy for other areas to relate.
- Toward the beginning of the production process (to have lowest work-in-process inventory and production lead time).
- A currently active tactical constraint (or near constraint).
- A resource that is used only once for a significant portion of the organization's output (thus avoiding an interactive constraint).
- A resource within the organization's control.
- As the market (if all resources are easily elevated).

Strategic Constraints Relating to Markets

The constraint management philosophy is a growth strategy that relies on development of throughput from sales as an essential element of long-term success. At the time of this writing, most defined constraint management applications deal with the logistics of providing goods and services (operations, project management, and distribution). The sales expansion component has largely been addressed within constraint management circles by exhorting the organization to greater sales. It is assumed that the competitive edge factors (better quality, shorter quoted lead times combined with better due-date performance, and timely introduction of new features) resulting from the logistical applications—as well as reformulated prices—will produce the requisite sales. Segmentation of markets is recommended, and the *thinking processes* are applied. Nonetheless, such a process lacks the focus that one would expect from a constraint management implementation.

Recently, Bill Hodgdon has provided greater focus by suggesting that the organization's strategy must include both specification of the market(s) to be served and identification of the products and/or services that will be offered to those markets.[7]

Short Run versus Long Run

The failure to correctly identify the short-run versus the long-run dilemma can lead to much mischief in a constraint management implementation. For example, not considering this question may lead to the erroneous conclusion that *throughput accounting* should be used for the short-run financial decision making and *activity-based costing* should be used for long-run financial decision making.

If we assume that we are operating using a constraint management philosophy, then we will have a strategic plan that includes identification of strategic constraint(s). The long-run versus short-run question then reduces to the question of subordinating to the decisions about exploiting the strategic constraint (what we want the constraint to be—the long run) as opposed to exploiting a tactical constraint (where the constraint actually is today in the short run).

If the strategic constraint and the tactical constraint are the same, then there is no conflict. But if they are different, then the strategic constraint is also a pseudo-constraint, and there may be a conflict that can be expressed in the generic, or generalized, evaporating cloud portrayed in Exhibit 11.1.

For (A), the objective of the cloud, use your favorite statement of making money (or throughput, in the case of a not-for-profit organization). (B) is the need to *exploit* (decide how to get the most out of) the current tactical constraint, which means that you must (D) use the tactical constraint for higher t/cu (throughput per constraint unit) products or services. On the other hand, there is also the need to (C) *subordinate* to the exploitation decisions contained in the strategic plan, which means that you must (E) use the tactical constraint in a way that will cause (or

Exhibit 11.1   Short-Run versus Long-Run Evaporating Cloud

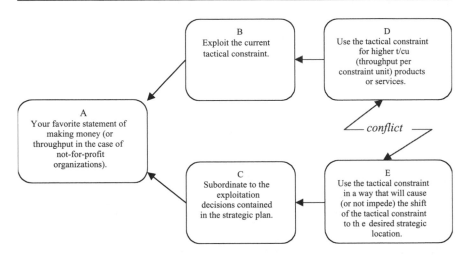

not impede) the shift of the tactical constraint to the desired strategic location. If (E) requires use of the tactical constraint in a way that is in conflict with (D), then the long-run versus short-run conflict exists.

Note that in need (B), the term *exploit* is a shortened form of *decide
how to exploit.* For the long run, the senior managers of the organization
select, as part of their strategic planning process, what and where the desired constraints are to be. The long-run strategy, then, is the set of decisions made about how to exploit those desired *strategic* constraints. The organization will subordinate to that strategy by elevating constraints in a
manner that will cause the desired constraints to appear. With a robust
constraint management process of ongoing improvement, then, the long
run is more directed than just a series of short-run actions strung together.
When the conflict has been resolved, and this is likely to involve management judgment, the set of exploitation decisions for the tactical constraint
will incorporate consideration of subordination to the strategic plan and
the conflict will be resolved.

SUCCESSFUL CONSTRAINT MANAGEMENT

One might well ask how an organization gets started on such a comprehensive route to a process of ongoing improvement, especially when it involves paradigm shifts and changes in the essential culture of the organization.

However compelling and seductive, implementations that focus on
autonomous local improvement are destined for ultimate failure. Defini-

tive success requires a companywide **holistic** approach. Constraint management defines the ingredients for that success. Understanding and using the dynamics nature of constraints, the poweful TOC generic applications, decoupling I from OE, and incorporating a constraints accounting measurement system that fully supports and provides motivation for everyone to act appropriately, constraint management propels organizations to experience a robust continuing process of ongoing improvement.

As shown in Chapter 4, successful constraint management implementations involve changing deeply seated paradigms held by individuals throughout the organizations. Such comprehensive culture change involves individual risk and comes neither easily nor quickly.

The implementation approach advocated here does not result in an immediate move to ultimate outcomes; rather, it concentrates on satisfying the necessary (and when all three necessary conditions are satisfied, sufficient) conditions for successful constraint management. After constraints have been identified and exploitation decisions made, the managerial focus shifts to controlling day-to-day operations. This step is known as *subordination* in the classic TOC focusing process (Chapter 2). The constraint management rule is to subordinate *everything* else—that is, to subordinate all of the nonconstraint operations—to the set of exploitation decisions. An excellent plan has been prepared. Now is the time to put the plan into action and ensure that actual operations achieve the intended results.

It is through subordination that constraint management realizes its dynamic potential. Let us reflect on the necessary conditions for a successful constraint management implementation, consider the role that organizational culture plays in subordination, and finally look at how doing constraints accounting changes data requirements.

Necessary Conditions

The three components necessary for successful constraint management are:

1. Knowledge about constraint management.
2. Communication of tactical and strategic constraint location and exploitation decisions.
3. A reason for people to subordinate properly.

The first component, knowledge about constraint management, consists of training or education that results in every member of the organization understanding the nature and significance of constraints. The second component, communication of tactical and strategic constraint location and exploitation decisions, when combined with the appropriate knowledge obtained in the first component, results in all members of the organization understanding how they should behave to subordinate their actions appropriately to the organizational exploitation decisions. When the first two components are in place, individual employees know what actions to take with respect to constraint management. The third component, a reason for people to subordinate appropriately, is distinct from—and complements—the first two components.

Current Status of Constraint Management

The general state of attempts to establish processes of ongoing improvement through constraint management is confusion. Since constraint management education is not widely integrated into general educational curricula, organizations desiring to implement constraint management concepts must themselves arrange for the education. Most organizations do a good job of making the training and knowledge available, but not necessarily evenly throughout the organization. This leads to the unavoidable result that the second necessary condition, communication of constraint location and exploitation decisions, is met in only some cases. The training tends to be uneven, and implementations reflect that unevenness.[8] Because individual TOC techniques (e.g., drum-buffer-rope scheduling, critical chain, and the thinking processes) offer extremely powerful results even when used independently, the techniques are frequently employed in local areas and are isolated from the dominant remainder of the organization. If TOC techniques are adopted on a local basis, neither identifying nor relating to global constraints, there is no constraint management. Such local applications typically do not incorporate the culture change that is requisite for bottom-line results in a dynamic process of ongoing improvement. The third necessary condition seems to be met only rarely. Since all three necessary conditions are seldom satisfied, one rarely finds organizations that have established robust POOGIs in association with constraints management.

Subordination

The third necessary condition, a reason for people to subordinate appropriately, directly addresses the point at which the theory of constraint management meets the real world of practical implementation. Given that exploitation decisions exist, organizational members must behave in such a manner as to subordinate their actions to the exploitation decisions.

There is a dictum in TOC that says, "Tell me how you will measure me, and I will tell you how I will behave."[9] Too often this dictum is misinterpreted as meaning that there ought to be a specific constraint management measurement that identifies the correct specific actions to be taken associated with each individual area of operations. Given that the correct action in terms of the organization's global goal is known, it is assumed that people will take that correct action. However, a measurement can be congruent with the organizational goal but still fail to motivate an individual to subordinate his or her actions appropriately. In fact, *there is no automatic congruence between the goals of individuals and the global goal of the organization.* In order for a measurement to be an effective determinant of behavior, (1) the measurement must result in expected significant desirable effects for an individual and (2) there must not be another, more powerful, measurement for the same action that leads in a conflicting direction.

Sullivan observes that the common characteristic of companies attempting to implement TOC without a culture change is that they

> *have skipped step 3 . . . Subordination. Most organizations are very good at identifying bottlenecks and after TOC clues them in to the special bottleneck known as the constraint, assuming they have an active, internal, physical constraint—they find it. They can exploit effectively, usually emulating what Alex did in* [The Goal: A Process of Ongoing Improvement]. *Then if there is not enough capacity increase, they elevate and go back to step 1 to identify their new constraint. They skip subordination.*[10]

Why is the subordination step skipped over? The other four focusing steps[11] relate directly to constraints and have parallel concepts in traditional cost world analysis. Changing the culture with respect to those four steps is incremental in that it involves extending an existing paradigm. The concept of subordination, however, does not have a shadow from the former cost world paradigm. Subordination involves an entirely new paradigm and, correspondingly, a far greater amount of culture change. The realizations that every system is constrained; more than 99% of the organization operates in a nonconstraint mode; and a nonconstrained area can influence global improvement only through its relationship with a constraint, are new to most of us. This newness makes subordination more difficult to comprehend fully and to adopt as a new paradigm. Tim Sullivan notes that "subordination involves changing the measures, and changes in behavior are necessary to achieve acceptable performance levels on the new measures. Changing what we compare ourselves to, and how we must behave is changing the culture."[12] Robust implementation of constraint management will require change in the collective attitudes and behaviors, or culture, of almost all organizations.[13]

Why is changing organizational attitudes and behaviors so difficult?

Subordination and Culture

Perhaps people do not change because the new measures offered do not provide motivational effect or congruence between individuals' and organization goals. Hence, there is no compelling personal reason to change behaviors. All too often people are given new measurements, but there are no clear connections among the new measurements, their own individual goals, and the global goal of the organization. The new measurements must contain a motive as to why it is in the employee's best interest to risk change.

Perhaps the inertia of data collection for legacy efficiency measurements (that are no longer used) gives the appearance that the old familiar measurements are still actually calculated and reported at some level, hanging like the **sword of Damocles,** ready for use with the next management flavor of the month.

Perhaps the reason people don't change is a control issue. In this context, *control* means the feeling of being in charge of one's own area of operations or the fear of being expendable. Comparison of performance to local measurements means that individuals can control their destinies somewhat by increasing or decreasing the local measurement and that they have an opportunity to demonstrate their worth, solidifying their employment. People intuitively understand the concept of, and need for, subordination (to the general interest). They perceive that to subordinate means to give up personal control and that the personal psychological risk associated with yielding control is too great. Eli Schragenheim and H. William Dettmer echo this view when they suggest that being assigned what may be viewed as an inferior position (a nonconstraint whose role it is to subordinate to decisions about another area) can create behavioral problems at every organizational level. According to Schragenheim and Dettmer,

> *It's very difficult for most people to accept that they and/or their parts of the organization aren't just as critical to the success of the system as any other. Consequently, most people in non-constraints will resist doing the things necessary to subordinate the rest of the system to the constraint. This is what makes the third step so difficult to accomplish.*[14]

When people cross to simplicity on the far side of the complexity divide, they recognize that the feeling of control arising from local measurements is an illusion. Casual understanding of the word *improvement* creates the illusion. As noted in Chapter 1, *improvement* must be measured with respect to the global goal of the organization. Since *improvement* with respect to the global goal is always limited by a constraint, local metrics can never reflect improvement unless the local actions affect a constraint. For a person who has moved to the far side of the complexity divide, a personally satisfying feeling of control arises from knowing that actions taken are appropriate for both the organization and themselves—that what they are doing contributes to the robust POOGI. That is, control results from appropriate subordination.

The local measurement for individual performance (i.e., the measurement that determines behavioral patterns) must establish congruence between individual goals and the open-ended global goal of the organization. This linkage is essential to establish the robust process of ongoing improvement. The POOGI Bonus—and its attendant empowerment—are designed to bring individual and organizational goals into alignment. When all three necessary elements are in place, the dynamic synergy of the forces of knowledge, focus, and motivation is allowed to produce their unavoidable improvement.

We had originally thought that, at this point in the book, we would need to have an extensive discussion of whether the strategically selected constraint should be located internally or externally. However, when we completed the personnel employment decisions analysis in Chapter 10, we were convinced that the strategically selected constraint ought to be internal. It could be in marketing, sales, production, or some other area. To locate the strategic constraint externally (i.e., "in the market") is to ensure that the organization's employment level must be adjusted for every market downturn. Layoffs are the order of the day, and employees will always need to be concerned about their job security. Such a work environment clearly fails to satisfy the third necessary condition, a reason for people to subordinate appropriately. Therefore, for an organization to be in control of its own destiny, and not at the mercy of market downturns and the fickle nature of Lady Luck, the answer to the strategic location question is clear—the constraint must be located at a clearly identified internal area. As we have prepared this manuscript over the last several years, we have not needed to make adjustments to our previous material, consistently reinforcing the strength of the logic of the TOC thinking processes embedded in constraints management.[15] When these necessary and sufficient conditions are in place, a process of ongoing improvement occurs, leveraging the simplicity on the far side of the complexity divide.

In the new environment, management has confidence in the logic of the constraint management philosophy. Managers then focus their attention on ensuring that the three necessary conditions for successful constraint management are being satisfied. Managers, rather than maintaining a busy type of control, support and encourage greater reliance on individual employees and employee groups. This leads to individual employees accepting greater responsibility, entailing greater empowerment, for their individual areas.

Changed Data Requirements

In the legacy cost world paradigm, local areas are decoupled through the provision of inventories at every step. Each relatively independent area is controlled in a manner seeking the greatest efficiency, least cost, and least unused capacity. In order to control an individual area, it is necessary to accumulate data about the area. Time clocks and time cards are used to document the physical presence of individual employees at work; time sheets, or their digital equivalents, show how employees spend their time in excruciating detail. For example, a typical software product advertises that it creates over 65 different, customizable reports showing time and labor cost information, including graphs in hours, costs, and percentages, all broken down by projects, team productivity, client billing, and so forth. Activity-based costing systems have become increasingly popular in recent years (although the persistence rate appears to be only about 20%). The cost accounting systems use multiple cost drivers, perhaps even hundreds, to assign costs to products. Detailed data about the specific work performed in each area of the organization, as it relates to each of the hundreds of cost drivers, is gathered. Consultants and providers of activity-based costing software applications often advertise that they provide the *true cost* of products and services. The availability of such detailed and apparently accurate data gives a feeling of comfort, power, and control to many managers. Performance reports highlighting efficiency are provided for each individual area of operations.[16]

When an organization has moved to the simplicity that lies on the far side of the complexity divide, its day-to-day operational control metrics are simplified accordingly. Much less data is required for day-to-day operations. It is not necessary to routinely gather microscopic detailed performance data relating to the more than 99% of the organization that comprises the nonconstrained areas of operations. The types of performance data needed for subordination control reporting in the simplified control environment are twofold:

1. Data that measure the quality of overall subordination.
2. Data that identify emerging constraints.

In the throughput world of constraint management, the organization pursues systematic elevation of Archimedean constraints. Subordination control reports relate to those constraints. The Constraints Accounting Earnings Statement having performance profit or the current value of POOGI Bonus pool as its bottom line (Chapters 3 and 4) illustrates reporting progress toward the global goal. This Constraints Accounting Earnings Statement shows the degree to which the planned exploitation has been achieved, which in turn is a measure of the quality of subordination. Control measurements of subordination in local areas—typically buffer hole reports combined with buffer management—provide ongoing identification of tactical constraints.

In the constraint management environment, nonconstraint areas are loosely coupled, as in a slack tangle of chains; unused protective capacity provides the slack between operations that are not constrained. Inventory held as a buffer (or a small amount of protective capacity) decouples constraint operations from nonconstraint operations. This means that each nonconstraint operation has a close relationship with its neighbors as well as with a buffer. The buffers associated with a nonconstraint area are sometimes called the **points of first visibility** for that area. If a nonconstraint area fails to subordinate adequately, or is otherwise at risk of becoming a tactical constraint, the danger will be reflected in a buffer. Buffer management includes techniques to identify emerging constraints by monitoring the contents of the buffers and identifying things that should be in the buffers but are not (the buffer holes), and those things that should not be in the buffers but are (the buffer piles).

Buffer analysis provides exception reporting for all operations comprising the tangle of chains leading to the buffer. Therefore, detailed planning, scheduling, and control for each operation along the chain segments are not required in most cases.[17] Accordingly, data requirements are significantly reduced relative to the legacy cost world model. Indeed, collection of unnecessary performance data can result in confused communication and distrust relative to the behavior desired of those persons being measured.

Constraints accounting leverages the simplicity that lies on the far side of the complexity divide. Whereas cost world accounting develops numerous local performance measurements concerning efficiency in each area, constraints accounting operational measurement focuses on the global system, reporting only when the exploitation plan is jeopardized. Solid information about emerging constraints that reveal when and how the exploitation plan is jeopardized is provided.

SUMMARY

The word *change* gives birth to a wide range of emotions. Some see change as essential to their survival. For others change is threatening and disquieting. It is time to take the myth and fear out of change and to bring logic and common sense into the decision-making process. In the preceding chapters we have identified a number of keys to locking in a process of ongoing improvement. These keys are summarized in Exhibit 11.2.

It is crucial that we modify our conventional understanding of strategy. The love affair with complexity weaves a web that promotes secrecy and tyranny and leaves organizations and individuals ripe for fraud and

Exhibit 11.2   Keys to Locking in a Process of Ongoing Improvement

Chapter	Chapter Title	Keys
1	Thinking Bridges	Understanding the impact of Archimedes points on the bottom line.
2	Constraints	Understanding the relationship of Archimedean constraints to the financial reporting system.
3	Internal Financial Reporting	Crossing the complexity divide by coordinating the internal financial reporting system with the desired management philosophy.
4	Motivation and the Budget	Having an effective budget revision process for a constraint management setting.
5	Constraints Accounting Terminology and Technique	Provision of internal reporting techniques that support exploitation analysis in a manner consistent with an organization's desired management philosophy.
6	Pricing	The establishment of a constraints accounting approach to setting target prices addresses an Archimedean constraint that exists in almost every profit-oriented organization.
7	Tactical Subordination in Manufacturing	Replacement of legacy operational control systems with buffer management, including buffer reporting.
8	Tactical Subordination in Project Management	Understanding the constraint management implications of critical chain and multi-tasking.
9	Tactical Subordination in Sales	Critical role of appropriate subordination and filling the Growth and Replacement Sales Funnel.
10	People: A Valuable Asset	Mutual respect and trust among owners and all employee groups, implying an internal strategically selected constraint.

defalcation. The merging of constraints accounting into the constraint management environment reflects the *elegant simplicity* lying on the far side of complexity (see Chapter 3). It allows organizations and individuals to conduct their affairs confidently in honesty and fairness, and it provides a platform to make sense out of thoughts, words out of sense, and actions out of words. Focusing on the relatively few Archimedean constraints breaks the stranglehold of the web of complexity and complicity and provides organizations with the ability to take control of their strategic planning logically. Using just two aspects of a constraint management strategy—the overall management philosophy and the specification of

Exhibit 11.3   A Final Key

11	Strategy and Conclusions	Corporate governance group inserts the *master key* into the global bottom-line lock, unleashing the dynamic power of constraint management.

strategic constraints—requiring the routine action of the corporate governance group will propel organizations and individuals to experience the powerful simplicity of crossing the complexity divide.

We have added a master key (Exhibit 11.3) for holistic constraint management implementations: the active and uninhibited involvement of the corporate governance group [owners (or owners' representatives), board of directors, and top management]. *Inserting this master key into the global bottom-line lock and unleashing the dynamic power of constraint management to realize a robust process of ongoing improvement is in their hands.*

NOTES

[1] As illustrated in Chapter 10.

[2] Independent business segments must be at least real profit centers (see discussion in Chapter 2).

[3] The focusing steps are discussed in Chapter 2.

[4] See the pricing example in Chapter 6. There should never be a flow that creates a conflict between strategic constraints. If such a situation were to be encountered, the issue would be sent to top management for establishing a priority between the designated constraints—that is, removing the strategic designation from one of them.

[5] Tactical constraints that can be removed quickly and inexpensively should be dealt with immediately and are not strategic issues.

[6] Robert C. Newbold, *Project Management in the Fast Lane: Applying the Theory of Constraints* (St. Lucie Press, 1998), pp. 152–155.

[7] Paper written by Bill Hodgdon, "To Stop Shrinking—Think Smaller! (A Strategy for Producing Growth from Limited Resources)," 2002, Hodgdon Consulting Services, tel. 724.935.0409.

[8] This unevenness of training and apparent independence of various TOC applications was strongly reinforced in the 1990s by a major provider of TOC education that licensed individual consultants, who were doing TOC training, to present a maximum of only two of the applications that had been fully developed.

[9] Eliyahu M. Goldratt, *The Haystack Syndrome: Sifting Information Out of the Ocean Data* (North River Press Corp., 1991), p. 28.

[10] Tim Sullivan, *Drivers of Cultural Change* thread, CMSIG Internet discussion group. November 7, 2000, cmsig@lists.apics.org.

[11] Identify the constraint(s), decide how to exploit the constraint(s), elevate the constraint(s), and, if a constraint is broken, start over—but be aware of inertia.

[12] Sullivan, *Drivers of Cultural Change* thread.

[13] Eli Goldratt suggests that six layers of resistance to change must be overcome in sequence in order to effect change. (See http://www.ciras.iastate.edu/toc/ or

Debra Smith, *The Measurement Nightmare: How the Theory of Constraints Can Resolve Conflicting Strategies, Policies, and Measures* [St. Lucie Press, 2000], p. 156.) These were expanded to nine levels by Efrat Goldratt (Richard Zultner, *9 Layers of Resistance*, 2/24/2001). Here we are dealing with the highest layer, #6, unverbalized fear, or #9, "Now we have to change what we are used to . . ."

[14] Eli Schragenheim and H. William Dettmer, *Manufacturing at Warp Speed: Optimizing Supply Chain Financial Performance* (St. Lucie Press, 2001).

[15] For a discussion of the thinking processes, see Lisa J. Scheinkopf, *Thinking for a Change: Putting the TOC Thinking Processes to Use* (St. Lucie Press, 1999); H. William Dettmer, *Breaking the Constraints to World-Class Performance* (ASQ Quality Press, 1998). Eric Noreen, Debra Smith, and James T. Mackey describe the thinking processes as potentially the "most important intellectual achievement since the invention of calculus" in their research study, *The Theory of Constraints and Its Implications for Management Accounting* (IMA Foundation for Applied Research, 1995), p. 149.

[16] The following sentence, used to illustrate the business use of the word *culture* is also a good short description of data accumulation in the cost world: "The new management style is a reversal of GE's traditional corporate culture, in which virtually everything the company does is measured in some form and filed away somewhere" (*The American Heritage Dictionary of the English Language* [Houghton Mifflin Company, 2000]).

[17] With respect to planning, Eli Schragenheim refers to this simplified concept as the principle of **minimal planning.** He discussed this concept on the Internet TOC-L list on October 4, 1996.

Appendix

Accounting System Structure

BRIEF HISTORY OF COST ACCOUNTING

Cost accounting has penetrated into the composition of the modern corporation to the extent that some people speak of *management by the numbers*. This discussion of accounting system structure begins with a short trip through history showing that modern cost accounting principles developed in response to needs that still exist today. When we change the methods of the accounting system, we must be careful to satisfy the needs that spawned the existing system.

Taxation and Protection of Assets

By the time of the Italian Renaissance,[1] recordkeeping was a well-established vocation. Taxes had been collected for many centuries, and absentee rulers required accountings for their assets. Just as the Pharaoh had his scribes, so Confucius thought long and hard about the purpose of accounting while serving the emperor of China as a keeper of the royal storehouses. The role of accountancy had been established as necessary for collecting taxes and protecting assets.

The Mediterranean Sea provided a liquid highway, enabling commercial activities and bringing prosperity to the region. A century had passed since the Venetian merchants of the Polo family had opened an overland route to Cathay. The balls of the Medici shone brightly in Florence. Four decades subsequent to the printing of the Gutenberg Bible, the first accounting text appeared.

Mercantile activities increased, and larger capital investment requirements emerged. The cost and risk of acquiring and outfitting a ship were spread among a small number of partners rather than a sole proprietor.

Cost Allocation Concept

At the end of a successful voyage, the residual assets of the voyage—representing both the return of investment and the profit or loss of the voyage—were split up among the several investors. The ship itself was refitted and sent upon another venture. There was a need to determine what part of the cost of the ship the investors should bear in the first venture and what part in the second. So the concept of cost allocation (dividing a cost by some arbitrarily selected base and spreading the cost to the elements of the base) arose to apportion the cost of the ship between the two ventures.[2] Having each venture bear a portion of the cost was fair and reasonable for the partners of each venture. As a result, the notion of a formally splitting the progress of a series of economic events among several investors had its dawning.

Double-Entry Bookkeeping

Renaissance trade, having a broad geographical base, prospered. The banking and commercial environment flourished and dealt with many different types of currencies, goods, and transactions. A single firm might have had many employees or agents. This created a need for a reliable and comprehensive bookkeeping system that would protect the assets created by commercial transactions. A *double-entry* bookkeeping system developed for recording each transaction in two different locations.[3] No attempt was made to "balance" the books—in the sense of the equality of debits and credits—for the entries consisted of various types of money and, in some cases, physical goods. This system satisfied the need to protect assets because the comparison of two sets of entries provided a check on each other. As a result, a double-entry accounting system existed for ensuring the comprehensiveness and accuracy of commercial data.

Corporate Form of Organization

The prosperity engendered by the Italian Renaissance expanded throughout Europe and Britain. In England, where the manor formed the heart of the economic system, a verbal (auditory) *charge and discharge* system developed into an accounting system that paralleled the treatment of accounts on the Continent. The Dutch contributed the name *ledger* for the big book. Sailing ships were larger, navigation was better, the earth was viewed as spherical, and European nations undertook the colonization of the world. Larger sums of capital than could be provided by just a few individuals were needed for financing global enterprises and extending national influences. The managers of these global enterprises desired to extract sums of money, on a voluntary basis, from many people. In response to this desire, joint stock companies with limited liability for shareholders were authorized.

Limiting the liability of individuals to the amounts of their investments reduced the risk to the individual investor.[4] As a result, many different individuals—with different individual objectives—invested in a single venture.

Accrual Basis of Accounting

A voyage frequently lasted several years, and some shareholders may have wanted to sell their shares prior to the conclusion of the venture. The economic progress (i.e., the change in wealth) due to the venture needed to be estimated before its conclusion. In response to this need, changes in asset values were estimated as of arbitrary dates. This worked because comparing total asset values at the outset and at a subsequent date allowed one to estimate the change in value (interim income or profit). As a result, the concept of profit from an enterprise or venture was extended to the concept of a profit associated with an interim period.

Perpetual Inventories

Calculating an interim profit requires knowing the value of the stock of goods owned—but the goods may have been located on the other side of the world. A way to determine the amount and type of goods owned, without physically surveying the goods, was needed. A current balance of goods was calculated by reporting all transactions of the venture (purchases and disposals of goods) to the home office. The transactions, reported by mail or overland courier, were recorded in the home office accounts, permitting up-to-date records that showed both the additions to stocks and the disposal of goods. The accounting system was being used to calculate the interim financial position of ventures.

Continuous Corporate Life

Dependencies developed among the various voyages. Several voyages overlapped, there was common usage of shore facilities, and the goods of one voyage were shipped with the ships of another voyage. A way was needed to associate the revenues, costs, and profits of the individual voyages with the owners of the ventures. The concept of a continuing business (a going concern entity), which had no fixed ending to its corporate life, was given life (in England) in 1658. The continuing business brought all the economic events of several voyages under a single entity. Corporations with limited liability for investors and continuous life now existed.

Periodic Dividends

These corporations had no end at which there was a payout of the accumulated assets (the original investment and profits). A means had to be devised to pay a return on investment to the shareholders, while at the same time maintaining a sufficient asset base to conduct ongoing operations and satisfy creditors' claims. Two concepts developed to fulfill this need. First, profits were calculated at regular time intervals rather than at arbitrary points. Second, a clear distinction was drawn between invested (or subscribed) capital and profits. Dividends were paid to shareholders only out of profits. This ensured that sufficient assets remained to satisfy creditors and conduct business. With the addition of these two concepts, organizations with the characteristics of the late twentieth-century corporation existed.

Stock Market Regulation

By the early 1700s, a stock market had been fully developed, thereby easing the raising of capital and the transferring of shares. Fraud and defalcation characterized these markets. Dozens of *bubbles* (undertakings of little substance) existed in England and France; investors happily turned over their money to unknown agents. What was perhaps one of the most outrageous bubbles was described as being an "undertaking of great advantage, but no one to know what it is."[5] It was apparent that the financial markets needed to be regulated. Because much of the fraud related to unchartered companies or companies that were using dormant charters, the English Bubble Act of 1720 was passed prohibiting the use of dormant charters or raising monies by subscription without a charter and generally making it difficult to establish a new corporation. As a result of the bubbles and the Bubble Act, investors become skeptical and there was little new corporate activity for more than a century.

External Auditor

In the late eighteenth century, an industrial revolution started in Great Britain and spread to the rest of the Western world by the late nineteenth century. The new industrial organization had a different resource—and hence cost—structure. There was a permanent factory and administrative staff; instead of putting out work to the home, as in cottage industries, laborers came to the factory. Whereas the British industrial organizations were closely held and focused on a single product, in America mass production techniques dominated the philosophy of the factory in the later part of the nineteenth century. Many organizations needed to raise funds because capital was required to acquire manufacturing, communication, and transportation resources on a large scale.[6] Investors wanted to feel a sense of security that their investments were sound. Demand for external corporate auditors (public accountants) grew because an independent auditor, skilled in the art of accountancy, lent creditability to an organization's financial reports. As a result, financial markets—now dependent on audited financial statements—were active again by the turn of the twentieth century.

Costs Attach: Accounting Product Cost

By the end of the eighteenth century, the characteristics of the Italian *two-book* system and the English *charge and discharge* system had been combined into the present-day double-entry system. This system contained both a journal (chronological book of original entry) and a ledger (collection of individual accounts). During the nineteenth century, the *accounting identity* (assets = liabilities + capital) became widely accepted as self-evident. The accounting system, then requiring balancing debit and credit entries for each transaction, evolved into a wholly contained mathematical entity. Product inventories were generally valued at market-value approximations. But estimates coming from outside the double-entry accounting system were neither objective nor verifiable by the external auditors. The auditors wanted unbiased—objective and verifiable—inventory valuations. So "the public accountants demanded that information in audited financial reports come from double-entry books that 'integrated' all cost and financial accounts."[7] The auditors had discovered that objective historical costs could be *attached* to products as they flowed through the manufacturing process. A predetermined overhead rate was used to allocate a portion of indirect manufacturing costs to each unit of product produced. Documenting the perpetual flow of products through the manufacturing process provided a convenient audit trail. As a result, a simple integrated system existed for attaching costs to products (a calculated or artificial *product cost*) for purposes of financial market reporting (we will call this *accounting product cost*).

Cost-Based Decision Making

In the United States, mass production techniques dominated the philosophy of the factory in the last part of the nineteenth century. There were many selling opportunities for new products, and management wanted to know whether the potential sales would be profitable. The projected price was compared to the accounting product cost because it was believed that a price greater than average unit cost would provide a profit. As a result, management began to use the product-cost concept for decision-making purposes.

Engineered Product Cost

The new cost structure of the industrial organization led engineers to classify manufacturing costs into two types, based on the purpose of the cost. First, the costs associated with the capability to produce during a given time period was a new category and was frequently referred to as *fixed cost*. Second, the costs of actually producing—the cost of resources consumed in the production process—were frequently referred to as *variable cost*. In firms with a single (or homogeneous) product, average cost may reasonably be calculated by dividing the total costs by the number of units produced. In the United States, however, metalworking firms had diverse product lines. These firms needed more than overall efficiency measurements to determine the effect of individual products.[8] Engineers therefore used complex procedures, based on assumptions about how costs behaved, to develop specific data about the cost of individual products. They believed that the cost behavior of each element of the manufacturing process would need to be fully specified in order to learn how the overall system would react to product mix and bid (pricing) decisions.[9] This resulted in a complex system, supplemental to the double-entry accounting system, which was designed for associating costs with products (another calculated or artificial *product cost*) for purposes of managerial decision making. (We will call this *engineered product cost*.)

Engineered Product Cost Not Used

Early in the 1900s, auditors and accountants were increasingly relying on accounting product costs, but use of the engineered product cost was short-lived. The conventional wisdom is that, prior to World War I, "existing information-processing technology made it costly to trace accurately the resources used to make each diverse product in a complex manufacturing plant."[10] Conventional wisdom suggests that, because of this costliness, managers did not request detailed engineering product costs after about 1914.[11]

Yet an *additional cause reservation* relates to this hypothesized cause-and-effect relationship;[12] that is, *complex costs are difficult to comprehend*. If a complex system, supplemental to the double-entry accounting system, existed for associating costs with products—for purposes of managerial decision making—and complex costs were difficult to comprehend, then it is easy to understand Thomas Johnson and Robert Kaplan's conclusion that "engineers who were attempting detailed product costing in the late 1880s found that they 'could not convince those on whose support they must rely' without tying into historical records."[13]

Either way, the engineering product-cost model was not used following World War I. Since the engineered product cost was not employed and the accounting product cost was, the accounting product cost was the only accepted methodology for attaching costs to products in an articulated set of financial statements at that time.

C. J. McNair and Richard Vangermeersch echo this conclusion in their discussion of Alexander Hamilton Church (the industrial engineer, who thought that managers would want to use different costs for different purposes) but only for the internal decision-making role of product cost. They state: "one cost was all that managers wanted, and full absorption costing [the accounting product cost] was their preferred choice."[14] As the United States entered World War I, there was a single accepted product-cost concept in use—accounting product cost.

Product Cost as Conventional Wisdom

The early twentieth century witnessed an expanding demand for public accountants, and the need arose to train a relatively large number of new public accountants in product-costing techniques. University curricula in accountancy that included only the accounting product-cost concept were established because following World War I accounting product costing because the only product costing available. As a result, many people were trained in the accounting product-cost concept during the period 1920–1950. Business organizations became increasingly large, diverse, and complex during the twentieth century. There was a demand for managers who had the ability to manage the large, diverse, and complex organizations *by the numbers* rather than by direct observation. People trained in accountancy during 1920–1950 became senior executives in the 1960s and 1970s,[15] reflecting the fact that learning the accounting system was a long apprenticeship process—both in the classroom and on the job—with an emphasis on doing rather than understanding. Many accountants and managers were trained to manage by the numbers and came to "believe that inventory cost figures give an accurate guide to product costs."[16]

During World War I, the *Uniform Contracts and Cost Accounting Definitions and Methods* of the United States War Department recommended using full cost plus a percentage of cost, with allocations based on direct labor, for establishing the price of goods sold to the government.[17] This was the closest approximation of an authoritative source for cost accounting principles that existed and was influential beyond the war. Following World War I, manufacturing firms in America began to experiment with cost-based pricing. There was little foreign competition and small and medium-sized American firms tended to be full-line producers. Henry Gantt suggested that full costing "undermines the capitalistic structure by rewarding both productive and unproductive uses of resources equally."[18] McNair and Vangermeersch observe that the "uniform costing model, with its substitution of cost for value in the creation of a market price, represented the first major effort by opponents of *laissez-faire* capitalism to reshape the economic structure of the United States."[19]

In 1929 stocks traded in the American stock market developed the characteristics of a stock market bubble and crashed. As had happened following the bubbles of the eigthteenth century, there ensued a demand for stock market regulation. The Securities and Exchange Commission (SEC) was created as part of the New Deal legislation of the 1930s. The SEC was given the legal authority to regulate accounting principles. The empty term, generally accepted accounting principles (GAAP), was coined and gained public acceptance.[20] The integrated cost attach concept, developed three decades earlier, increasingly became the product-cost standard.

The next socialization effort also occurred in the 1930s when cost-plus pricing became an American national policy as part of the New Deal legislation.[21] The idea was that companies should hire excess numbers of people, charge enough to recover their full (and inflated) costs and earn a reasonable profit, and sell their products to a public willing to buy at the inflated price as a patriotic duty.[22]

As the result of all these efforts, by the middle of the twentieth century, accountants, managers, and the general public all tended to believe that there was an objective, verifiable cost, which was the *true* cost of the product.

The Price-Cost Relationship Concept

When the cost of providing a product could be reasonably estimated, customers became unhappy if they were asked to pay a price they considered unreasonably high relative to the cost of the product. Often, there was a need to establish a price that could be justified to (or by) a customer. In this case, the accounting product costs were used as a starting place for pricing products to which a reasonable markup was added. A price determined in such a manner was acceptable because accounting product cost was an amount that both buyer and seller could generally accept as reasonable. As a result, in the minds of the vast majority of people in the society, revenues were linked to costs in terms of a desirable relationship.

Cost Coupled with Revenues for Control

Since investors invest in an organization in anticipation of profits leading to dividends or capital appreciation, managers needed to control expenses in a manner that produced a satisfactory profit. This was accomplished by linking expenses to revenues in many ways to ensure that a predictable relationship was achieved because managers considered expenses to be under control if they bore a reasonable (specified) relationship to revenues (that is, total revenues exceeded total expenses by a satisfactory amount).[23] As a result, twentieth-century control systems focused on the relationship of costs to revenues and attempted to ensure that long-run costs varied directly and appropriately with revenues.

Control by the Numbers

If managers needed to control expenses in a manner that produced a satisfactory profit and many managers had been trained to manage by the numbers, then the managers needed a way to ensure a profit while controlling operations by the numbers. American managers accomplished this by adopting *full cost (accounting product cost) plus a percentage of cost* pricing for controlling operations. If the price of each individual product was greater than the cost associated with the product, if the markup was sufficient to cover selling and general administrative expenses, and if all products were sold, then the firm would have a profit. In addition, the appellation of GAAP to the product cost gave the comfortable feeling and appearance of accuracy and reliability. As a result, American managers incorporated accounting data into the managerial control process, and accounting data became essential for making operating decisions.

Gross Margin Analysis

Sometimes, however, a product could not be sold for its asking price, and so there was a need to converge on a profitable product mix. Gross margin[24] rules were strictly enforced, and products that could not be sold for their asking price were discontinued or never offered, leading to a decreased allocation base and higher prices for other products. However, the potential market price of the remaining products was higher than the current asking price. There was quite a bit of slack here—provided the organization was fairly well isolated from effective competition (as was the case in America through the 1960s). Then the market accepted the price increases on most of the remaining products. As a result, American industrial corporations were profitable through the 1960s based on a *cost plus* pricing policy and management *by the numbers* as produced by the accounting system.

COST AND REVENUE FLOWS

Revenue represents the money that we receive from our customers through sales, fees, and so forth, whereas *costs* represent the amounts that we pay to acquire the resources needed to conduct our business. In accounting theory, costs are subdivided into the categories of *assets* and *expenses*. Costs assumed to be of benefit to future periods are held on the balance sheet as assets until the future period. Costs that are considered to have served their purpose during the current period are assigned to expense and matched with revenue of the current period. All costs are on their way to becoming expenses, either in the current period or in some future period.

Next, we will examine cost and revenue flows from the point of view of the conventional absorption-costing model in order to establish a base in the prevailing paradigm. This will also establish a link to required external reporting techniques. Then we will examine how the constraints accounting model departs from the conventional system.

Financial Statements

Two basic financial statements are the **statement of financial position (balance sheet)** and the **statement of earnings** (income statement). A balance sheet shows the financial position of an organization at a particular point in time. An earnings statement shows how much an organization earned or lost, that is, *profit or loss,* during a period of time. The amount of profit or loss is the amount by which the owners' equity changes during the period.

The structures of a balance sheet and an earnings statement are illustrated in the top portion of Exhibit A.1.

The balance sheet is summarized using the accounting identity (Assets = Liabilities + Owners' Equity).[25] Also shown are examples of classifications used by the accounting system. A *listing* of the classifications used by the firm is called a **chart of accounts.** The actual accounts are pages in a **ledger**—one page for each classification—or an electronic conceptual equivalent.

The earnings statement summarizes revenue and expense accounts. These accounts are sometimes called *temporary equity accounts* because they are used to collect transaction data during a **fiscal period** (such as a year) and then closed.[26] The net amount of all the revenue and expense accounts represents the profit, or earnings, for the period. At the end of the period, the balances of the revenue and expense accounts are transferred into the equity account, Retained Earnings.

Consideration of the balance sheet and earnings statement, taken together, reveals that the owners' equity of an organization can be determined in two ways. One way is to start with the estimated value of all assets

Exhibit A.1   Financial Statement Structure

Balance Sheet (the Accounting Identity)			Earnings Statement
			Revenue
Asset =	**Liabilities** +	**Owners' Equity**	
110 Cash in Bank			410 Sales
120 Accounts Receivable	210 Vouchers Payable		- Expenses
131 Materials	250 Long-Term Debt		590 Cost of Sales
132 Resources in Process			610 Selling Expense
150 Property, Plant & Equipment			710 General & Administrative Expense
151 Accumulated Depreciation		310 Common Stock	= Earnings
		320 Retained Earnings ←	390 Earnings Summary

owned at a given point in time.[27] Then the amounts owed to other people or organizations at the same point in time are deducted; these are the liabilities. Whatever isn't owed to someone else is the owners' equity at that particular point in time. Through this technique, the earnings may be determined by comparing the owners' equities of two successive balance sheets.

A second way is to start with the owners' equity at the beginning of the fiscal period and to add or deduct the revenues and expenses that occur during the period.[28] The result is the owners' equity at the end of the period. Exhibit A.2 illustrates the way in which costs and revenues flow through the accounts to determine the owners' equity in the latter manner.

Arrows, with coded shafts to show the nature of the account, indicate the flow of costs and revenues through the ledger in a conventional absorption-costing system as might be used for general-purpose financial reporting in conformity with GAAP.[29] Each arrow starts in one account and leads to a second account. The cost journey through the ledger starts at the vouchers payable account identified by the oval labeled "start here."[30]

Resource Acquisition

The organization acquires various resources to be used in producing and selling its products or services. When acquired, the cost of the resource is recorded in *Vouchers Payable,* as the first step in writing a check to the supplier. At the same time, the resource is classified as either an asset or an expense, or it is held in suspense until the classification can be made at a later time. Acquisitions may be broadly grouped into four categories: material, personnel services, other contractual services, and long-term assets.

Material

The company purchases material that becomes part of the product. The solid arrow starting in Vouchers Payable and leading to Materials represents this transaction. We own the material, but we have not yet paid for it. Therefore, we have both an asset (Materials) and a liability (Vouchers Payable).

Personnel Services

The next arrow on the right-hand side of the Vouchers Payable account represents the payroll, or purchase of personnel services. This narrow solid arrow leads to the Payroll Suspense account. A suspense account is simply a place where something is held until you decide what to do with it later. Two distinct issues are associated with payroll. The first is to get employees paid the right amounts and on time. This can be difficult because

Exhibit A.2 Cost and Revenue Flow in Conventional GAAP (Absorption Costing) System

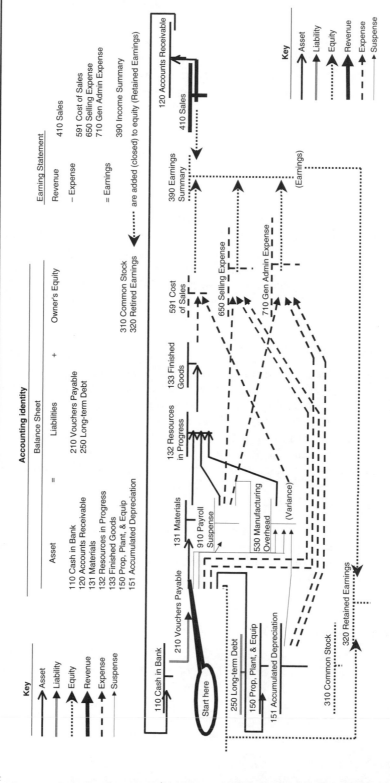

many calculations are involved and various deductions are different for different people. Payrolls are also the subject of various unemployment and pension laws and taxes that must be calculated at the same time. Once the payroll has been calculated and payroll checks have been distributed to employees and other recipients of the employees' earnings—which is an extremely time-sensitive task—the accountants can decide at their leisure where the costs of having employees should reside within the accounting system.

Other Contractual Services

The next three arrows originating on the right-hand side of the Vouchers Payable account represent costs incurred for other contractual services (such as supplies, utilities, insurance, and repairs). The costs represented by the light solid arrow relate to the manufacturing operations. These costs are assigned to Manufacturing Overhead, which is another suspense account, to be reassigned as an asset or expense later. The two heavy dashed arrows represent other contractual services classified as expense, either as Selling Expense or as General Administrative Expense, when acquired.

Long-term Assets

The heavy solid (asset) line from Vouchers Payable to Property, Plant, and Equipment represents the final category of resource acquisition. This is an asset for which the physical asset unit has an economic life of several years. Even though the physical unit is intact, the asset cost will be written off in a systematic manner as depreciation—a little each year—over the estimated economic life of the asset. The annual amounts of depreciation are recorded as an expense if the asset is used for selling or general administrative purposes. If the asset is used in manufacturing operations, then the depreciation is added to the Manufacturing Overhead account where the cost is held in suspense with other manufacturing overhead costs. A reduction in asset value in the same amount is recorded in an Accumulated Depreciation[31] account and is deducted from the Property, Plant, and Equipment account when displaying the balance sheet.

Dividends

The last (dotted) arrow originating in the Vouchers Payable account does not represent a cost. Rather, it represents the declaration of a cash dividend to the shareholders, and thus a reduction in Cash and Retained Earnings.

GAAP Cost Accounting Distribution

Now we turn our attention to the materials cost—the costs that have been put into the payroll and manufacturing overhead suspense accounts—and to the manufacturing process itself. Everything that happens in the factory is summarized in the Resources in Progress account.[32] The basic manufacturing process in many organizations is to take some materials of various types and convert the materials into finished products. The task for the conventional cost accounting system, then, is to attach the costs of resources used in production to the products produced.

Material

When materials are issued for use in production, the cost of the materials (an asset) is transferred from the Materials account to the Resources in Progress account. The heavy solid arrow originating on the right-hand side of the Materials account represents this transfer of cost. The materials in process are still classified as an asset.

Payroll

Four arrows exit the right-hand side of the Payroll Suspense account number 910 representing, in order, (1—heavy solid) direct labor wages, (2—heavy dashed) sales salaries and wages, (3—heavy dashed) general administrative salaries and wages, and (4—light solid) manufacturing overhead personnel cost.

The direct labor wage distribution from the Payroll Suspense account goes to Resources in Progress.[33] Here the cost of the people actually working on the product[34] is combined with the cost of the materials used in the product. Some of the personnel services cost is now classified as an asset and will not appear on the earnings statement until some time in the future.

The payroll costs of personnel working in the sales area as well as those of general administrative personnel are transferred from Payroll Suspense to the expense accounts, Selling Expense and General Administrative Expense, as shown by the heavy dashed arrows. These expenses will be deducted from revenues in computing the bottom-line amount earned this period.

The wage and salary costs of manufacturing supervisors, custodians, security guards, forklift operators, industrial engineers, warehouse people, factory cost accountants, and other indirect manufacturing people are reassigned from Payroll Suspense to another suspense account, Manufacturing Overhead, where they are to be combined with other manufacturing overhead costs and held until further assignment as asset or as expense is made.

Manufacturing Overhead

The Manufacturing Overhead account contains an assortment of costs. Some of the overhead costs tend to be incurred unevenly, such as property taxes that are assessed and paid only once or twice a year or insurance premiums that are revised and paid semiannually.

Since the total amount of overhead by the end of the period is not known, a predetermined estimate is used to allocate a portion of these overhead costs to Resources in Progress.[35] The nature of the manufacturing overhead costs is clear, for they are initially assigned to the Manufacturing Overhead account (wages, supplies, insurance, etc.), but they lose their individual characteristics as they are combined into an amorphous whole to be allocated.

The heavy solid arrow originating on the right-hand side of Manufacturing Overhead and extending into the left-hand side of Resources in Progress represents the flow of this overhead cost allocation.

Product Cost

The Resources in Progress account contains all of the costs associated with production of the organization's products. The Resources in Progress account is an asset account representing the partially complete production. In addition to materials, some of the payroll costs—the direct labor and some of the manufacturing overhead—have been classified as an asset.

Three arrows enter the Resources in Progress account on the left. The nature of the costs—materials, direct labor, and manufacturing overhead—represented by these arrows are clear as the costs enter the Resources in Progress account. But only one arrow exits on the right. When a product is completed, the physical units are moved to a finished goods holding area, and a cost per unit of those units is transferred from the Resources in Process account to the Finished Goods account. This cost per unit is the *product cost*, which has now been attached to the product. The product cost remains as an asset in the Finished Goods account until the goods are sold.

Sales and Cash

When a unit of product is sold, the product cost associated with the unit sold is transferred from the Finished Goods account into the Cost of Sales[36] account and the classification of the product changes from asset to expense. At the same time, the sale starts the revenue flow and gives rise to the account receivable represented by the revenue arrow from Sales to Accounts Receivable.

When the receivable is collected, the bank balance increases. The flow representing this is the long heavy solid arrow crossing the top of the flow diagram. This arrow starts on the right-hand side of the Accounts Receivable account and ends on the left-hand side of the Cash in Bank account.

Finally, the arrow between Cash in Bank and Vouchers Payable reflects the checks written for the vouchers that are due to be paid.

Reporting the Financial Information

At the end of an appropriate fiscal period, the temporary accounts (expense and revenue accounts) are closed. GAAP-based financial reports—the statements of earnings, financial position (balance sheet), and cash flows—are prepared for owners, management, and other interested parties. Performance report(s) based on constraints accounting are prepared for users within the organization.

Adjusting Accounts

Before preparing the reports, it is necessary to bring the accounts up to date. All of the flows we have examined (except depreciation) were entered as the result of an activity that took place—for example, purchase materials, move finished product, ship to customer, purchase equipment, receive payment in mail, and so forth. Depreciation occurs simply as a matter of the passing of time. Thus, before the statements are prepared, the depreciation for the period should be recorded.

A second adjustment that needs to be made has to do with the Manufacturing Overhead account. All of the manufacturing costs other than direct labor and materials were added to the account. Transfers out of the account were made using a predetermined, or estimated, overhead rate. At the end of a fiscal period it is unlikely that exactly the same amounts will have been added and removed from the account. Therefore, there will be a balance remaining in the Manufacturing Overhead account. An accepted way to handle this balance is to transfer it to the Cost of Sales account.

Calculating Earnings

In the closing process, the balances of the temporary expense and revenue accounts are transferred to the Earnings Summary. The four dotted arrows pointing into the Earnings Summary account represent these transfers.

The dotted arrow on the right side of the Earnings Summary represents the transfer of Sales. Then the balance of the cost of sales account is an expense that is deducted from sales when computing earnings. These are the product costs matched with revenues this period. Other product costs—held in the Resources in Progress and Finished Goods accounts—remain on the balance sheet as assets. The difference between the Sales and the Cost of Sales is the gross margin. The Selling Expense and General Administrative Expense are also transferred to the Earnings Summary. Finally, the net balance of the Earnings Summary is transferred to Retained Earnings as the earnings for the period.

Cost Accounting Evolution

Exhibit A.3 summarizes the way in which the evolutionary accounting concepts presented in our brief history of cost accounting are reflected in the accounting system cost and revenue flows illustrated.

CONSTRAINTS ACCOUNTING SIMILARITIES AND DEPARTURES

The revenue and cost flows are shown in Exhibit A.4 as they would appear if the accounting system were maintained on a double-entry constraints accounting basis. Comparing Exhibit A.2 with Exhibit A.4 reveals similarities and departures from the conventional GAAP system.

Chart of Accounts

The Chart of Accounts is revised to accommodate the constraints accounting approach by adding the following accounts:

136 Variable Cost in Process

137 Materials in Finished Goods

139 Allowance to Restate Inventory at Absorption Cost

160 Investment for Improvement (I)

161 Sources of Future Improvement

220 Liability for POOGI Bonus

Exhibit A.3   Evolution of Cost Accounting Reflected in Accounting System

Protection of assets	Voucher system to control cash payments; balance sheet
Cost allocation concept	Depreciation; predetermined overhead
Double-entry bookkeeping	Each event recorded in two accounts
Corporate form of organization	Separation of capital into the original stock amount and retained earnings
Accrual basis of accounting	Distinction between assets and expenses; sales recorded before cash received; materials recorded before cash paid, depreciation.
Perpetual inventories	Costs move with units of product as it is produced, completed, and sold
Periodic dividends	Dividend paid from retained earnings
Stock market regulation	Use of generally accepted accounting principles (GAAP)
Costs attach; accounting product cost	Manufacturing costs assigned to resources in progress and finished goods

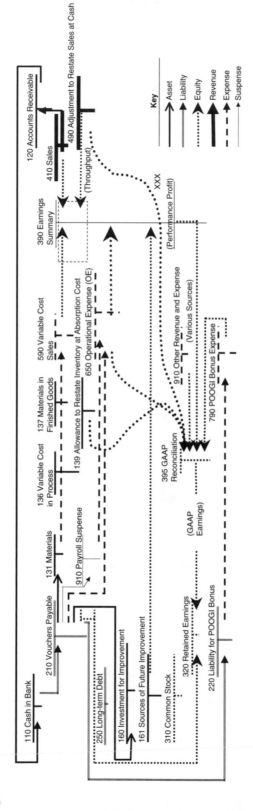

Exhibit A.4 Cost Accounting Flows in Constraints Accounting System

395 GAAP Reconciliation

490 Adjustment to Restate Sales at Cash

590 Variable Cost of Sales

650 Operational Expense

790 POOGI Bonus Expense

910 Other Revenue and Expense

These accounts are shown in Exhibit A.4 and are discussed in the following paragraphs.

Resource Acquisition

The positive control of expenditures provided by the voucher system remains in the constraints accounting system. Expenditures are still vouched and traced to their point of incurrence responsibility. Even though there is greater flexibility and room for managerial judgment within the limits of the existing budget authorizations, managers must be prudent in their expenditures. The Vouchers Payable account operates in exactly the same manner that it does in the GAAP-based system, controlling all cash disbursements.

Although the acquisition of materials, personnel, and other contractual services are accounted for in a manner similar to the GAAP system, the Cost of Sales line contains only the variable costs of production. The Payroll Suspense account is still used but with a single destination (Operational Expense). Note the first three closing entries (dotted lines) in the earnings summary, the credit from Sales and the debit from Variable Cost of Sales, when adjusted to Restate Sales at a Cash amount, provide a transparent throughput amount.

The treatment of long-term assets is different if either the direct write-off method or the payback allocation method is used. If the direct write-off method were used, then the acquisition of long-term assets would follow a path similar to other contractual services. Exhibit A.4 assumes that the payback allocation method is used. Expenditures representing specifically approved investments for improvement are vouched in the conventional manner and charged to the Investment for Improvement account. Of course, it is still necessary to maintain a record of, and accountability for, plant and equipment owned by the organization.

Constraints Accounting Cost Distributions

Materials used, whether drawn from the Raw Materials Inventory or acquired specifically for a particular job, result in the expenditure of funds that are variable with the production level. These are assigned to the individual job or product and are part of the throughput calculation when the goods are sold. There is an Allowance to Restate the Product Inventory at Absorption Cost.

In keeping with the philosophy of constraint management, conversion costs (direct labor and overhead) are not associated with specific orders or units of product produced. Instead, all personnel services and other contractual charges are assigned directly to Operational Expense. Even though there is only one destination for the personnel costs, the Payroll Suspense account is still used to ensure that the dictates of a subsidiary cost assignment system do not interfere with the important task of paying employees promptly.

Reconciling Items

A reconciling adjustment between the Constraints Accounting Performance Profit and the GAAP earnings transfer to Retained Earnings will be needed whenever the constraints accounting treatment of a revenue or cost item is different from the GAAP treatment.

The closing entry transferring the balance of the Operational Expense account to the Earnings Summary is shown as a dotted line because it is the larger of the actual or budgeted OE for the purpose of calculating the Performance Profit. If the budgeted OE is greater than the actual OE, then the difference is a GAAP Reconciliation item.

It will be necessary to associate some conversion cost to the product inventories to comply with GAAP for external reporting. If the organization has discontinued collecting conversion costs at the product level and has resisted the temptation to collect data regarding processing times, then it will need to establish new allocation bases to effect the association. Work-in-process may be valued using one-quarter of the production rope length.[37] For example, if the rope (production cycle time allowed) at the end of the period were 10 working days and there are 200 working days in the year, the rope would represent 5% ($10/200 = 0.05$) of the manufacturing time available. One-quarter of ($0.05/4 = 0.0125$) of the manufacturing portion of OE would be assigned to the Allowance to Restate Inventory at Absorption Cost for work-in-process.

The remaining balance of OE is associated with finished goods and the cost of sales. The ratio of the Materials in Finished Goods to the remaining OE balance may be used to allocate the finished goods portion of OE to the Allowance to Restate Inventory at Absorption Cost. The balance of the allowance account is added to the materials cost in inventory to arrive at an overall GAAP inventory valuation. If inventories increase, the effect will be to increase GAAP earnings by the amount of OE added to the allowance account.

An organization will likely want to accrue its receivables in the same manner that it does in a GAAP system in order to maintain positive control of amounts owed to it. The accrued amount may be converted to cash received from sales by adding (or deducting) the decrease (or increase) in Accounts Receivable from Sales during the period. The account, Adjustment to Restate Sales at Cash, serves this purpose. The receivables adjustment is closed to the GAAP Reconciliation.

Constraints Accounting Departures

Constraints accounting departs from conventional GAAP reporting in the same manner as direct costing does. Therefore, the conventional direct costing GAAP inventory adjustments would apply equally.

POOGI Bonus

The POOGI Bonus Pool is a liability to be paid in accordance with the provisions of the POOGI Bonus plan. Since the exact amount of the payment in a given month is not known until the current month's addition (or reduction) to the pool is known, the payment cannot be vouched until it is ready to be paid. Therefore, a current liability account will be established to hold the liability. This account, which we will call Liability for POOGI Bonus, could be either a general ledger account or a subsidiary ledger account under Wages and Salaries Payable.

The POOGI Bonus Expense is an Other (extraordinary) Variation and is reported as shown in Chapter 4 of this text. It is not included as part of operational expense (OE), and it is not deducted in the computation of Performance Profit.[38]

Assume the results for a POOGI Bonus plan that started in October 20X1 were as shown in Exhibit A.5. This exhibit shows that, in the first month of the plan (October 20X1), the wage and salary base is $300,000. Performance Profit increased by $60,000 over October 20X0 (the comparison month from a year earlier). Since the POOGI Bonus proportion is 50%, a POOGI Bonus amount of $30,000 (= 50% of $60,000 increase in Performance Profit) is shown in Exhibit A.3 as an addition to the bonus pool at the end of October. At the end of 12 months, the total of the differences for each month will equal the total difference in the 12-month amounts.

In the second month, November 20X1, there was actually deterioration in performance relative to the year earlier month. Performance Profit is $20,000 less than it was for November 20X0, which is reflected in the addition to the bonus pool of a negative $10,000. This type of situation is common when organizations implement TOC applications such as drum-buffer-rope. Production lead time is reduced, and some of the backlog of order is shipped, pulling orders forward. To the extent that the increase in orders shipped came from the backlog rather than an increase

Exhibit A.5   POOGI Bonus Pool and Base

(A)	(B)	(C)	(D)	(E)	(F)	(G)
	$C_{-1}/12$				(Total Gross Wages and Salaries for last 12 months or since plan inception)	D/F
	POOGI Bonus payments vouched During the	End of month Addition to POOGI	$D_{-1} - B + C$ End of month POOGI Bonus	Gross Wages and Salaries (excluding	POOGI Bonus Wage and Salary	POOGI
Month	month	Bonus Pool	Pool balance	POOGI Bonus)	Base	%
20X1	($)	($)	($)	($)	($)	
Sep	0	0	0	0-	0	0.0
Oct	0	30,000	30,000	300,000	300,000	10.0
Nov	2,500	-10,000	17,500	300,000	600,000	2.9
Dec	1,458	20,000	36,042	300,000	900,000	4.0
20X2						
Jan	3,003	72,429	105,467	300,000	1,200,000	8.8
Feb	8,789	94,158	169,107	300,000	1,500,000	11.3
Mar	14,092	122,405	249,172	300,000	1,800,000	13.8
Apr	20,764	159,127	350,813	300,000	2,100,000	16.7
May	29,234	206,865	480,705	330,000	2,430,000	19.8
Jun	40,059	268,925	647,510	380,000	2,810,000	23.0
Jul	53,959	349,603	862,474	380,000	3,190,000	27.0
Aug	71,873	454,484	1,140,202	380,000	3,570,000	31.9
Sep	95,017	590,829	1,499,666	363,334	3,933,334	38.1
Oct	124,972	768,078	1,965,027	333,333	3,966,667	49.6
Nov	163,752	90,725	1,892,000	333,333	4,000,000	47.3

in the rate of sales, the improved performance reported in October 20X1 was a timing difference, and is compensated for in a following period.

Recording the gross amount of the POOGI Bonus is part of the month-end adjusting procedures. When the plan is first established, the balance of the Liability for POOGI Bonus account is zero. The additions to the POOGI Bonus pool are credited to Liability for POOGI Bonus. The corresponding debit to POOGI Bonus Expense is an expense for the month of October 20X1, resulting in the entry (a) shown in Exhibit A.6.

Since one-twelfth of the balance in the POOGI Bonus pool is being disbursed monthly, the entry to record the vouchering of the bonus pay-

Exhibit A.6   Recording Gross Amount of POOGI Bonus

	20X1			
(a)	Oct 31	POOGI Bonus Expense	$30,000	
		Liability for POOGI Bonus		$30,000
		To record the liability for gross amount of POOGI Bonus earned in October 2001		

Exhibit A.7   Vouchering POOGI Bonus

	20X1			
(b)	No	**Liability for POOGI Bonus**	*$2,500*	
		Vouchers Payable *(Payroll)*		*$2,500*
		To voucher the November POOGI Bonus payments to employees of 1/12 of the pool balance.		

ments on November 10, 20X1, is as shown in Exhibit A.7. Individual checks are then distributed to employees on November 15 as with any other payroll (including the various deductions). The entry to record the November 20X1 POOGI Bonus reduction is as shown in Exhibit A.8.

The POOGI Bonus pool (Liability for POOGI Bonus) now has a balance of only $17,500 (= $30,000 − $2,500 − $10,000). On December 10, 20X1, the bonus payment to employees is again vouched, and checks are distributed on December 15 in a manner similar to entry (b) in Exhibit A.5. The entry for the December payment is shown in Exhibit A.9. Entries similar to (a) and (b) are then made each month.

At the end of October 20X2, the balance of the Liability for POOGI Bonus account is $1,965,027 as shown in the account illustrated in Exhibit A.10.

The $1,801,275 balance on November 10, 20X2, the November addition of $90,725, and the November ending balance of $1,892,000 are shown in Chapter 4 in the main text.

SUMMARY

As we walk back through the passages of time, it becomes apparent that humans have has an innate need to account for their belongings and the belongings of others. Moreover, the need to measure and be measured is

Exhibit A.8   Recording Reduction in Liability as Result of Negative Bonus Amount

	20X1			
(b)	Nov 30	**Liability for POOGI Bonus**	*$10,000*	
		POOGI Bonus Expense		*$10,000*
		To record the reduction in liability for negative amount of POOGI Bonus earned in November 20X1		

Exhibit A.9 Vouchering POOGI Bonus

	20X1			
(d)	Dec 10	*Liability for POOGI Bonus*	*$1,458*	
		Vouchers Payable (Payroll)		*$1,458*
		To voucher the November POOGI Bonus payments to employees of 1/12 of the pool balance.		

woven into the fabric of their lives in such a manner that it weaves a web within their minds that can prove to be a catalyst of change, for good and for bad.

When tracing transactions both yesterday and today, it is apparent that individuals who demonstrate an understanding of numbers are regularly considered to be more mentally agile and are frequently looked upon differently from those individuals who exhibit more artistic abilities. This impression, whether true or false, insidiously leads some people in positions of authority to abdicate their responsibility of checking the trail of numbers within an organization. Furthermore, knowing the great power of understanding that numbers can hold all too often leads some individuals to purposeful complexity, manipulations, distortions, and corruption. We must also recognize the ambiguity of some reporting financial systems laws and regulations, that in themselves promote manipulations within an organization. Such manipulative financial reporting systems serve as a catalyst not only in their quest to measure up to outside economical forces but also to ensure their survival.

There is a superior, more humane, and ethical way for an organization to realize a dynamic, robust process of ongoing improvement. Owners of the organization can demand an operating philosophy that unleashes the power of constraints, promotes and achieves global goal

Exhibit A.10 Liability for POOGI Bonus Account

				Liability for POOGI Bonus		
20X2				20X2		
				Oct 31	*Balance*	1,965,027
Nov 10	*November payment*	163,752				
				Nov 10	*Balance*	1,801,275
				Nov 30	*November Addition*	90,725
				Nov 30	*Balance*	1,892,000

congruence, and incorporates a supporting accounting system that both motivates appropriate behavior and is transparent and fluid in nature.

NOTES

[1] Roughly from the fourteenth through the sixteenth centuries.

[2] Richard Vangermeersch has suggested that the cost allocation concept is a nineteenth-century phenomenon. He points out that in Venice the problem was circumvented by vesting ownership of the ship itself in the city-state. Nevertheless, it is clear that by the seventeenth century ventures were being accounted for in a manner that apportioned, in one way or another, the cost of vessels between sequential undertakings. Thus the conclusion that the concept of cost allocation existed at the time of the Italian Renaissance is mine alone, and I leave it to the reader to draw his or her own conclusion.

[3] Perhaps one small and easily portable book was held by the banker or merchant and another, larger, book was the responsibility of an employee at the place of business; or perhaps one book was the banker's and one the customer's.

[4] As people saw their neighbors hoping to profit from investment in East India companies, they wanted to profit also—and the race was on.

[5] iTulip.com.

[6] H. Thomas Johnson and Robert Kaplan, *Relevance Lost: The Rise and Fall of Management Accounting* (Harvard Business School Press, 1987), p. 130.

[7] Ibid., p. 131.

[8] Ibid., p. 127.

[9] Ibid., p. 126.

[10] The quote is from Johnson and Kaplan, *Relevance Lost,* p. 128, but they attribute the idea to Robin Cooper, who is generally acknowledged as the driving force behind the popularity of the activity-based cost and activity-based management fads of the late twentieth century.

[11] Ibid.

[12] An *additional cause reservation* is one of about eight categories of legitimate reservation specified as part of the theory of constraints thinking processes. These categories of legitimate reservation provide a civilized way to disagree because they emphasize the logic and the system rather than individual personalities. The *additional cause reservation* says, "I see your point and I agree that the effect exists. However, I think that there is another cause that is so *much more important* than what you have cited that it should replace the causal relationship in your thinking."

[13] Johnson and Kaplan, *Relevance Lost,* p. 132. The internal quote is from Harrington Emerson.

[14] C. J. McNair and Richard Vangermeersch, *Total Capacity Management: Optimizing at the Operational, Tactical, and Strategic Levels* (St. Lucie Press, 1998), p. 136.

[15] Johnson and Kaplan, *Relevance Lost,* p. 135.

[16] Ibid., p. 145.

[17] McNair and Vangermeersch, *Total Capacity Management,* pp. 140–141.

[18] Ibid., p. 138.

[19] Ibid., p. 140.

[20] Generally accepted accounting principles (GAAP) is an *empty* term because there was no list of such principles until about 50 years later. Then, rather than having general acceptance, the GAAP principles were dictated by either the Financial Accounting Standards Board or the Securities and Exchange Commission. At the time of this writing the regulations have become so complex

that relatively few people can comprehend the full body of GAAP or the resulting financial statements. As a result, the public turns to the community of professional financial analysts to interpret the GAAP statements. That even this community of financial analysts routinely ignores the GAAP model in their interpretations is strong evidence that GAAP principles are, in fact, not generally accepted.

[21] McNair and Vangermeersch, *Total Capacity Management*, pp. 174–187.

[22] An interesting side issue that is rarely mentioned is the ethical question of whether cost plus pricing is appropriate for use when the objective is more or maximum profits, rather than reasonable profits.

[23] In addition to cost-based pricing, some techniques for linking expenses to revenues are (1) budgeting managed costs as a percentage of sales—the notion that all costs are long-run variable, and (2) budgeting all costs as a percentage of sales.

[24] Gross margin is the difference between the selling price and the GAAP product cost of a product.

[25] Assets are recorded on the left-hand, or debit, side of an account page; liabilities and equity are recorded on the right-hand, or credit, side. Thus, the rule stands that debits must equal credits.

[26] Closing an account involves transferring the entire balance to another account, leaving the closed account with a zero balance. The closed account is then ready to be reopened to collect and summarize data for the next fiscal period.

[27] The *assets owned* include monetary amounts that others owe us, which are shown in the illustration as *accounts receivable*.

[28] When the revenues and expenses are shown on a formal report, the report is an *earnings statement*. The *bottom line* of an earnings statement is the net earnings or profit, and that is the source of the general expression, bottom-line results.

[29] The key is shown in the lower right-hand corners of Exhibits A.2 and A.4.

[30] The Vouchers Payable account is similar to Accounts Payable, but all cash being paid out goes through the Vouchers Payable account and there is an implication that a process is in place to vouch for the appropriateness of the expenditure. A voucher is a place in the system to collect data about the transaction, such as authority for ordering, proof of delivery, agreement on terms, and approvals for account distribution and payment. When a transaction takes place that results in a cash payment, the transaction is vouchered.

[31] The Accumulated Depreciation account is a valuation, or contra-asset, account.

[32] The Resources in Progress account obviously summarizes a great deal of activity. The single account shown in Exhibits A.1 and A.2 may represent a summary of an entire subsidiary ledger having detailed cost flows through each department of the manufacturing plant.

[33] Resources in Progress (RIP) is also known as work-in-process or work in progress (WIP inventory).

[34] Sometimes direct labor is called touch labor.

[35] The allocation process is discussed in Chapter 5.

[36] Also known as Cost of Goods Sold. This is an expense.

[37] A *rope* is used with a constraint management drum-buffer-rope production scheduling system. It is the period of time allowed between when an order is released to production and the scheduled delivery date. The use of one-quarter of the rope length assumes that the work-in-process is 50% complete and that, on the average, orders are completed in one-half of the production rope length.

[38] The POOGI Bonus Expense will be included as part of the General Administrative Expenses on the external (GAAP) financial statements.

Glossary

Account classification, method of: A technique for classifying expenses into various categories (for routine financial reporting purposes) based on the general characteristics of another classification. For example, costs that are classified as raw **materials** might also have the derivative classification of **truly variable** for **constraints accounting** purposes. This technique allows routine financial reports of a specialized nature, such as constraints accounting, to be prepared automatically from the existing financial database.

Accounting identity: Assets = Liabilities + Owners Equity.

Activity-based costing (ABC): A system for allocating **costs** to products or other cost objectives using multiple measures of inputs used. The technique is similar to traditional service department allocations except that the activity base is an input measure, known as a **cost driver,** rather than an output volume measure. ABC also forms the basis for activity-based management.

Annual profit plan: See **budget.**

Archimedean constraint: A **constraint** that results in a dynamic change in system performance—either good or bad—when touched.

Archimedes point: A place to focus attention in order to get powerful results. Archimedes was a Greek mathematician in the third century before the Common Era. He is probably best known for running naked down the street and shouting "Eureka!," which was the way Greeks said "I found it!" He had discovered how to determine the weight of gold in the king's crown. As the story goes, he was bathing and noticed that he displaced his volume in water. He was then able to determine the weight of the gold in the king's irregularly shaped crown by determining how much water it displaced relative to an equal weight of gold of known purity. This business about the displacement of water is known as Archimedes' principle. But Archimedes was a man of many talents and also set about to move the entire world. He said that all he would need would be a firm place to stand, a lever of sufficient length, and a fulcrum against which to put the lever. That firm place to stand, which would allow the entire world to be moved, gives rise to what we call an Archimedes point. For more information about Archimedes, see the web site maintained by Chris Rorres at:

http://www.mcs.drexel.edu/~crorres/Archimedes/contents.html

Assembly buffer: A **buffer** placed on a nonconstrained path to ensure that parts, which do not require use of a constraint resource, that are to be combined with other parts, which do require the use of a constrained resource, are available when needed. Similar to a **feeding buffer** in **critical chain** applications.

Asset: A cost that is **capitalized** and allocated to expense over a number of fiscal periods.

Balance sheet: An accounting report, based on the **accounting identity,** showing the financial position of an organization at a specific point in time.

Bonus pool: The total dollars to be paid in the form of a bonus.

Bottom line: The summary position for a particular report. For example, an **earnings statement** might report net earnings or earnings per share as the bottom line. This summarizes the net effect of **revenues** and **expenses** during a fiscal period. The bottom line may be an accrual-based measurement, as would be calculated using generally accepted accounting principles **(GAAP),** or it may be a measurement of cash flow, such as cash flow from operations, using a cash basis for reporting.

Budget: A written estimate showing what an organization plans to do during a specified period, what resources are expected to be used, and the anticipated effects on the organization. The *budget* is an important component of the organization's internal control system as, when approved by management, it provides management's specific authorization for the expenditures delineated in the budget.

Budgetary control: Using reports that compare actual results achieved with the budgeted results expected in order to identify deviations from the plan and identify aspects of the operations needing management attention.

Budgetary planning: Decision making about expected future operations; *budgetary planning* results in the **budget** and its revisions.

Budgetary process: The overall process of **budgetary planning** and using the resultant **budget** in obtaining **budgetary control.**

Buffer: Time, inventory, space, or some other mechanism to decouple one part of an organizational tangle of chains from another part. See also specific types of buffers: **assembly buffer, capacity buffer, constraint buffer, drum-feeding buffer, drum resource buffer, (critical-chain) feed-**

ing buffer, planning buffer, project buffer, resource buffer, shipping buffer, space buffer, strategic resource buffer, and **time buffer.**

Buffer hole: An item of work that was expected to arrive in front of a constraint by a particular point in time but that has not yet arrived; a missing item that is needed soon or immediately.

Buffer pile: Items that are not expected in a **buffer** but that have been completed anyway. Goldratt refers to these as "doing what was not supposed to be done."[1]

Buffer management: Using the information provided by analysis of the contents of **buffers** to establish tactical priorities.

Buffer manager: An organizational function in **constraint management** implementations that has responsibility for monitoring and analyzing **buffers** for the purpose of extracting information for **buffer management.**

Buffer penetration: (1) The amount of time by which a **buffer hole** has penetrated into a **time buffer.** Frequently stated as a percentage of the **rope** or **time buffer** length; (2) a logical (yes/no) answer to whether an item is a **buffer hole** at some specified point in a **time buffer** (that is, entered a tracking zone or expedite zone).

Business results premise: The premise that businesses buy products or services for one primary purpose—to produce better business results.[2]

Cacophony: A combination of discordant sounds. In this book the term is used allegorically to represent the total set of potential business sales that are available to an organization as unorganized, and thus discordant, **notes.**

Capacity: (1) Capability to perform a given task or set of tasks; (2) the maximum quantitative amount that can be done within existing limitations.

Capacity buffer: A **time buffer** included in the **drum** schedule for a multiproject **critical chain** application. The *capacity buffer* prevents starting projects more frequently than the system can handle.

Capital expenditure: An expenditure that is expected to benefit several future periods and that is **capitalized** for accounting purposes.

Capitalize: To treat as an **asset,** as opposed to an **expense,** for accounting purposes.

CEO: chief executive officer.

Charging rate: A money amount per time period that is applied to products or other cost objectives to reflect the cost of using a particular resource or group of resources.

Chart of accounts: (1) A listing (including a data dictionary) of the predetermined classifications used by an organization for financial transactions; (2) a listing of the accounts contained in a general **ledger.**

Choopchick: A relatively unimportant action taken, in which pride and satisfaction are expressed, but which has diverted attention and energy away from more important matters.

Compelling offer: A sales offer that results in elevating a customer's **Archimedean constraint,** thereby significantly improving the customer's **bottom-line** measurement; an offer just too good to pass up. Also known as an **unrefusable offer.**

Complexity divide: The separation between two forms of simplicity.

Constraint: Anything that prevents an organization from achieving significant improvement relative to its goal.

Constraint buffer: (1) A **time buffer** that has its origin as a **constraint,** (2) a **drum-feeding buffer** in **critical chain.**

Constraint resource: A resource within an organization for which the demand for the use of the resource exceeds the amount of the resource's availability.

Constraint management: An overall management philosophy that views an organization as a single integrated entity connected by logical relationships rather than as a collection of relatively independent subunits. Such an integrated entity has relatively few points, known as **Archimedean constraints,** that control the performance of the entire system relative to its **global goal.** These **Archimedes points** are used to leverage the performance of the organization. Also known as **leverage-point** management.

Constraints accounting: An accounting reporting technique, consistent with a process of ongoing improvement and implementation of the **theory of constraints** and **constraint management,** which includes:
1. Explicit consideration of the role of **constraints.**
2. Specification of **throughput contribution** effects.
3. Decoupling of **throughput (T)** from **operational expense (OE).**

Contribution margin: An accounting term that refers to the difference between **sales revenue** and the **variable cost** associated with the **revenue.** The variable cost aspect has been defined as including raw materials, direct labor, and a variable portion of overhead so frequently that those cost elements have become accepted as a part of the meaning of "contribution margin." **Constraints accounting** uses the term **throughput** for the same concept but includes raw materials as the only obvious variable expense.

Contribution margin ratio: Contribution margin divided by **sales.**

Controlling: Obtaining action in conformity with plans.

Cost: The monetary amounts that are paid to acquire the resources needed to conduct a business. Costs are importantly classified as either **assets** or **expenses.**

Cost center: An organizational subunit headed by a manager who has responsibility for controlling costs but who has no responsibility for **revenues.**

Cost control: (1) Achieving actual expenditures that are in conformity with the budgeted expenditures; (2) spending only in accordance with management's general or specific authorizations; (3) **cost reduction.**

Cost driver: (In activity-based costing) a measure of inputs to a process that are assumed to create the demand for the process.

Cost reduction: (1) Reducing the amount of resources in the entity so as to reduce the acquisition cost of the resources; (2) reassigning resources from one cost objective to another and pretending that **costs** have been reduced.

Cost reimbursable contract: A sales contract for which the price to be paid by the customer is determined, at least in part, by the supplier's cost incurrence experience; such contracts include those for which supplier cost expectations are part of the negotiating process.

Cost world paradigm: A mindset that an organization consists of many relatively independent subunits and that maximizing the efficiencies in each individual subunit will result in the best performance for the organization as a whole.

Credit: A technical accounting term referring to the right-hand side of an account or statement of financial position (balance sheet); liabilities, shareholders equity, and revenues are recorded as credits. See also **debit.**

Critical chain: (1) The **theory of constraints** and **constraint management** applications for project management and the engineering function. **Critical chain** explicitly considers resource contention and using buffer management when managing projects (after the title of the book, *Critical Chain* by E. M. Goldratt)[3]; (2) the longest set of dependent activities from the start to the completion of a project that explicitly considers the availability of resources.

Critical-chain-feeding buffer: See **feeding buffer.**

Critical chain sequence: The sequence, or sequences, of tasks that lie on an unscheduled critical chain; used with **simplified critical chain (SCC).**

Current reality tree (CRT): The physical result of the **TOC thinking process** used to analyze and/or explain an existing situation.

Debit: A technical accounting term referring to the left-hand side of an account or statement of financial position **(balance sheet); assets** and **expenses** are recorded as debits. See also **credit.**

Decide how to exploit: See **exploit, decide how to.**

Delta-T selling: The systematic *how to* approach—detailing the creation of compelling offers that touch customers' **Archimedean constraints**—offered by Woehr and Legat. Their approach, which they call *delta T-selling,* revolves around an **opportunity engine** as the focal point for consolidating sales operating information.

Depreciation: An accounting allocation of part of the cost of a tangible **asset** incurred in a previous fiscal period to another asset (e.g., product) or to the current fiscal period as an **expense.**

Direct costing: (1) A product-costing method that assigns only **variable costs** to products (variable costs are traditionally considered to be **materials, direct labor,** and some portion of manufacturing overhead); (2) a method of income reporting in which the **earnings statement** is presented in two portions: (a) **revenues** less variable expenses = **contribution margin** (or **throughput contribution**), and (b) **fixed expenses.** When variable expenses are defined as only those that are truly variable, direct costing is similar to **throughput accounting.**

Direct labor: (1) Those persons working directly with the product, (2) the wages of those persons working directly with the product.

Drum: A resource schedule or other schedule (e.g., shipping schedule) that is used as the point from which a **rope** is tied (in **drum-buffer-rope** scheduling) or that is used to stagger projects to avoid resource contention in **critical chain.**

Drum-buffer-rope (DBR): A TOC production scheduling technique.

Drum-feeding buffer: A **buffer** inserted on a noncritical chain that feeds into a **drum resource** to ensure that the noncritical chain portion of the work does not delay the critical chain portion.

Drum resource buffer: A **buffer** that is placed before a **drum resource** (a resource that is used to establish starting times of projects) activity to protect the drum schedule.

Earnings statement: An accounting report that shows how much profit or loss resulted for a stated fiscal period.

Economic profit: The amount by which a person is better off as a result of activities accruing over a period of time or as the result of a particular undertaking.

Elevate: The fourth step of the TOC focusing process. Changing the physical reality of the organization by obtaining more of the constraining factor. Elevating a constraint often involves the expenditure of additional investment funds.

Entity: Something that has existence; the word *entity* is used in several ways, and its meaning is dependent on the context. (1) Used to refer to a node that is capable of being either true or false in a **theory of constraints thinking process** tree. (2) An organizational unit used as a focal point for accounting purposes. (3) The *entity concept* refers to distinguishing between a business (or other) organization and its owners. (4) An *analytical entity* is a management accounting entity that may be either broader or narrower than the legal organizational entity.

Evaporating cloud: (1) A **TOC thinking process** used to express a conflict; (2) a TOC thinking process used to break out of existing paradigms.

Exception reporting: A focusing tool; the policy of reporting only things that fall outside of specified control limits. This policy allows implementation of the principle of management by exception.

Expedite zone: The time in a **buffer** (typically about one-third of the buffer length) closest to the drum.

Expense: A **cost** that is matched with **revenue** in a particular **fiscal period.**

Exploit, decide how to: The second step of the TOC focusing process, getting the most out of the existing environment.

Exploitation plan: Operating budget.

Feeding buffer: A **time buffer** that protects a **critical chain** from statistical fluctuations in noncritical chain tasks; similar to an assembly buffer in **drum-buffer-rope** scheduling.

Final costing object: The last cost objective that **costs** are associated with before being transferred to **expense,** often units of product or a particular order or contract.

First-line supervisors: Managers who are directly responsible for supervising the people who engage directly in the productive processes and operations.

First visibility: See **point of first visibility.**

Fiscal period: A length of time used for reporting financial matters.

Fiscal year (FY): A **fiscal period** that is approximately 365 days in length. Designated by the calendar year in which the fiscal year ends. For example, an arbitrarily selected fiscal year beginning on July 1, 2004, and ending on June 30, 2005, would be known as FY05.

Five focusing steps: The cyclical focusing process of **TOC.**

Fixed expenses: Costs that remain relatively constant over a relevant range of activity. These costs are often related to the passage of time.

Flexible budget: A **budget** that can be adjusted to reflect different expectations when volumes are at different levels; contrasts with **static budget.**

Free product: A product that does not require time on an internal physical constraint.

Full cost: (1) An accounting costing technique in which all costs become a part of the **final cost object;** (2) absorption costing.

Future reality tree (FRT): A **thinking process,** verbalized by E. M. Goldratt, used for checking the logical connection between a proposed action and its inevitable effects. Often used to describe how anticipated results of implementing a particular strategy are to be obtained.

GAAP: Generally accepted accounting principles required by the U.S. Securities and Exchange Commission (SEC) for use in external, or public, financial reporting by publicly held companies.

Gating operation: An operation that signals the start of a production process. Often the gating operation in a **drum-buffer-rope** system is the release of raw material to production process. Like a gate, this operation restricts the flow of work orders into the production process.

Global goal: The single, open-ended reason for an organization's existence.

Goal congruence: The policies of the organization create an environment in which people enthusiastically pursue the organization's operating philosophy. When managers and other employees work to improve performance relative to the organizational global goal, they are automatically pursuing improvement relative to personal goals.

Going concern assumption: The assumption that a business **entity** will remain in business and operate in a similar manner indefinitely into the future.

Green curve: The green curve refers, within **TOC,** to a diagram that Dr. Goldratt drew in the early 1990s. The color had no significance other than the color of the pen that Goldratt happened to pick up at the time. The *green curve* portrays desirable change in a local area of operations, such as manufacturing, that results in exposing excess capacity. When further improvement becomes impossible without the participation of other areas of the organization, there is a tendency within the cost world paradigm to capture **bottom-line** results by reducing the number of people employed in the area that displays the excess capacity. Of course, the employees quickly learn that they will be penalized for displaying idle time. The effect exists even when a particular organization has not had such layoffs, but they are endemic in the society. The green curve diagram is shown below in Exhibit G.1.

Gross margin: The difference between sales **revenue** and **product costs.** Gross margin is a key metric in cost-based pricing strategies. Also known as *gross profit.*

Holes: See **buffer hole.**

Holistic: The view that the power of the whole of the entity is greater than the sum of individual parts; the organization taken as global whole.

I: See **inventory/investment.**

Identified potential sales opportunity: Something (product, service, offering) that a salesperson is attempting to sell to a specific customer and that the customer is not currently buying.

Identify: First step of the **TOC** focusing process, identification of the constraint.

Improvement: Always measured in terms of the **global goal** of the organization in **constraint management.**

Income statement: See **earnings statement.**

Incremental market: Many customers, each being asked the same price and each having a relatively small share of the overall throughput mix.

Exhibit G.1   Green Curve

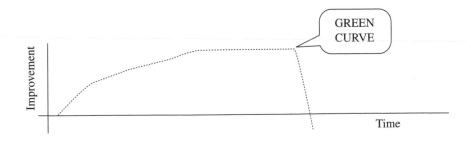

Inertia: The fifth step of the **TOC focusing process** provides a warning—we must protect against the comfortable complacency of our thinking. For example, whenever the **constraint** of a system is **elevated** sufficiently to cause a different resource to become an active constraint, the operating characteristics of the system change. In the changed environment, both the decisions about **exploiting** the former constraint and the policies established for **subordination** to the former constraint are no longer appropriate. We must return to step 1 and identify the new constraint.

Intermediate cost objective: A temporary resting place for **costs** within an accounting system.

Internal physical constraint: A resource that limits the organization's ability to improve.

Internal rate of return: The rate of return expected to be realized from a particular investment proposal. Used in capital expenditure analysis to rank the desirability of proposals.

Intervention expediting: Expediting that involves a change in plans and requires managerial intervention. Intervention expediting is contrasted with routine expediting (giving priority to tasks based on relative buffer consumption or penetration).

Inventory: See **inventory/investment.**

Inventory/investment (I): Costs incurred that have not yet been assigned to expense.

Inventory profits: Apparent profits reported when more units are produced than sold and absorption-costing methods are used. Absorption costing assigns some **costs** that relate to time periods to product inventories. If the products are not sold, then the costs are held on the balance sheet to be released to **expense** at some later date. Thus, it is possible to have higher **periodic reported net profit** by producing more, even if there are not greater sales.

IO map (intermediate objectives map): A network of entities, graphed by time sequence that must exist before a desired objective can be achieved. Often used to describe the means of implementing a particular strategy. See also **prerequisite tree (PRT).**

Just-in-time (JIT): A production technique in which work-in-process inventories are distributed in small quantities throughout the production process. Often misconstrued as a raw material inventory stocking policy that pushes the responsibility for maintaining inventories down the supply pipeline.

Labor: (1) The group of people who routinely engage directly in the productive processes and operations, (2) a general term applying to the human resources used by an organization.

Least product cost: A **thinking bridge** that is frequently used to span the gap between a proposed action and its expected bottom-line result. The assumption is that reductions in costs *assigned* to products or services will ultimately result in *actual* cost reductions. This is one of the assumptions challenged by constraint management.

Ledger: A book that holds the physical collection of an organization's accounts.

Legacy system: An inherited system that is in use at the present time.

Leverage point: See **Archimedean constraint.**

Liabilities: Monetary amounts owed to other people or organizations.

Long-term capacity: Capacity expected to benefit a number of fiscal periods (e.g., equipment that we purchase today and can use in future years as well as in the current period).

Market: A general term referring to the customers and potential customers of an organization.

Master production schedule (MPS): The short-term production schedule from which other schedules are derived in a MRPII production scheduling system. The MPS may serve as the **drum** schedule in a **DBR** scheduling system when the drum is at the market.

Material or **materiality:** Being of such magnitude as to be likely to influence or change a judgment or decision.

Middle management: Managers, other than **top management,** who are not **first-line supervisors.**

Minimal planning: The concept that, when an organization has moved to the far side of the **complexity divide,** complex and detailed performance data are not required for the vast majority of the organization.

Monte Carlo simulation: A method using heuristic techniques, such as repetitive random number generation, to develop an understanding of mathematical or physical problems (named after the casino at Monte Carlo, Monaco.)

Multitasking: The practice of assigning two or more tasks to one individual with the understanding that those tasks are to be performed during the same calendar period and that progress is to be shown on all assigned tasks during the period. This practice frequently results in a resource attempting to work on two tasks or activities at the same time, switching back and forth from one to the other.

Murphy: A general term, based on mutations of Murphy's Law, referring to the unpredictable nature of operations. Routine cases are frequently referred to as statistical fluctuations, and more serious disruptions as Murphy.

Near-constraint: A physical resource that is in danger of becoming a **constraint** if loaded more heavily than it currently is.

Necessary condition: A condition that must be met in order for an organization to achieve its purpose. If a necessary condition is not met, then the organization will be thwarted in its pursuit of the organizational **global goal.** Hence, an unmet necessary condition is a special type of **constraint.** Necessary conditions may be imposed by the physical operating environment, governmental action (laws and regulations), power groups (such as labor unions and special interest groups), market forces and competitive pressures, and management (through organizational policies).

Net profit: A general term referring to some measure of sales **revenues** less **expenses.**

Noninstant availability: A resource needed for the completion of a job or contract that is not available to work on the job or contract because the resource is currently being used for a different purpose or for a different job or contract.

Notes: Identified potential sales opportunities.

Operating budget: See **budget.**

Operational expense (OE): The **period costs** of the organization not included in **T.** Defined in *The Goal* as all the money the system spends in turning **inventory (inventory/investment, I)** into **throughput.** Frequently referred to as *OE.*

Opportunity cost: Profits that would be available from a particular course of action but that are lost when a second course of action is taken instead.

Opportunity engine: Classifies **notes** in the **cacophony** of potential business based on the perceived difficulty of resolving **constraints** to throughput-oriented offerings.

Opportunity gap: The amount above the **target price** asked that a customer would be willing to pay for a product. May be expressed by customer, contract, product, or as an aggregate amount.

Out of POOGI expenditure: An expenditure made for a purpose other than obtaining improved performance relative to the goal.

Owners: Group (or person) holding legal or rightful title to a business organization; in the case of a corporation, the holders of common stock.

Paradigm:[4] A patterned way of thinking within a person's mind that:

- Blocks the ability to see possibilities that are not part of the paradigm.
- Establishes boundaries on our thinking.
- Instructs how to behave within those boundaries to be successful.

Paradigm shift: A change in the pattern of thinking from one **paradigm** to another. The movement into a new (or different for the individual person) paradigm involves an acute awareness of the person's revised understanding of the subject.

Pareto analysis: See **Pareto principle.**

Pareto principle: J. M. Juran coined the phrase *the vital few and trivial many* to apply to the phenomenon that when there is a common effect resulting from a population containing many different sources, relatively few of the sources account for most of the effect. He also recognized that the phenomenon was applicable to so many fields as to be a general principle. Juran used the name *Pareto principle*, after an economist who had observed the phenomenon in income distribution in his writings.[5]

Parkinson's Law: The general principle that work expands to fill the time available for its completion.[6]

Payback allocation method: A capital write-off technique in which the periodic charge to income is prescribed by the anticipated cash flows, as specified in the capital expenditure analysis, associated with taking on the project. As a result, periodic net profit does not reflect improvement until the estimated cash flows exceed the investment costs.

Performance profit: An operating profit metric that is the difference between throughput and the greater of the actual or the budgeted OE.

Performance report: A report designed to be used as a basis for evaluating the performance of an organization, organizational subunit, or individual.

Period cost: A cost that is associated with a particular period of time; a cost that is matched with revenue in a particular time period; an expense.

Periodic reported profit: The amount of **net profit** shown on an **earnings statement** that is a function of both actual economic events and the accounting principles and techniques used to prepare the report.

Permanent product: A product that the organization intends to provide to the market, or a specific customer, on a reliable long-term basis; a product that is part of the core business of the organization.

Planning buffer: A buffer associated with a task dedicated to detailed planning of a **critical chain** project at the beginning of the project. Penetration into this buffer may be interpreted as a statistical fluctuation but also might be representative of inadequate planning to achieve the benefits of critical chain. (Developed by the Product Development Institute.)

Point of first visibility: The buffer in which failure of a nonconstraint area to subordinate properly, or inadequate **protective capacity** in an area, will first create a **hole** and be identified.

POOGI (Process of Ongoing Improvement): The subtitle of the book, *The Goal: A Process of Ongoing Improvement.*[7]

POOGI bonus: Money distributed to all employees in recognition of the achievement and maintenance of a **POOGI.**

Prerequisite tree (PRT): A **thinking process,** verbalized by E. M. Goldratt, used for checking the logical connections existing among obstacles and intermediate objectives that must be achieved to overcome the obstacles. Used to create a plan to achieve a difficult objective or to develop a plan to implement a particular strategy that has been described in a **future reality tree (FRT).**

Process of ongoing improvement: See **POOGI.**

Product cost: The **cost** assigned to a unit of product by the cost accounting system. If done in accordance with **GAAP,** this cost includes the cost of raw **materials** as well as value added costs associated with **direct labor** and manufacturing overhead. U.S. tax law also requires that a portion of selling, distribution, and general administrative expenses be assigned to product inventories for purposes of computing taxable income even though they must be excluded from product cost under GAAP.

Profit center: An organizational subunit headed by a manager who has responsibility for both generating revenue and controlling costs. Such a responsibility center is measured by its profits.

Progress payment: A partial payment made to a supplier as work on a contract is completed.

Project buffer: A **time buffer** that is scheduled between the last task of a project and the promised completion date.

Protective capacity: Reserve capacity distinguished from idle capacity because it is necessary to the system.

Pseudo-constraint: A local, generally internal, resource treated as a constraint and used for scheduling or other decision purposes when the real constraint is not perceived as being under the control of the local area of operations.

Pseudo profit center: A nominal **profit center;** a profit center in name only; either the **revenue** or the **expense** portion of the profit measurement is contrived. Contrasts with a **real profit center.**

Quoted lead time (QLT): The length of time between when an order is received and its promised delivery date.

Real profit center: A **profit center** in which both the **revenues** and the **expenses** are the result of arm's length transactions with external entities.

Relay race behavior: See **roadrunner work ethic.**

Relay race runner: Displaying the characteristics of a roadrunner. See **roadrunner work ethic.**

Representational faithfulness: Correspondence or agreement between a measure or description and the phenomenon it purports to represent.[8]

Resource buffer: An early warning device to notify resources in advance of when they will be needed for critical chain tasks.

Responsibility budget: An operational expense budget that has been broken down into segments, classified by the individual managers having cost incurrence authority for segment costs.

Return on investment (ROI): Decision analysis tool for ranking alternative investment proposals in terms of economic desirability.

Revenue: The monetary valuation of products sold or fees earned. *Revenue* is an accounting term and has different interpretations depending on the accounting principles employed. *Synonym:* sales.

Revenue center: An organizational subunit headed by a manager who has responsibility for revenue generation; **revenues** and **costs** are tracked but not compared in such a way as to calculate a **net profit.**

Roadrunner work ethic: Work as fast as you can, while maintaining excellent quality, when you have something to work on. If you do not have something to work on, wait patiently; something will come for you to work on. Expect a fair amount of idle time. The work ethic (or mentality) that replaces the efficiency (keep everybody working all the time) model. Also known **relay race behavior.**

Rope: Is measured in units of time and ties the **drum** to the **gating operation** where material is released to initiate the production or other process. The time that material is started into process is a rope length in time before the item is scheduled to be worked on at the drum resource.

S, G, & A or **(SGA):** Selling, general, and administrative (or selling and general administrative) expenses.

Sales: An accounting term that refers to the gross revenue received from providing goods or services for a fee. *Synonym:* revenue.

Sales cycle, length of: The average amount of time elapsed between starting an **identified potential sales opportunity** into the **sales process funnel** and placement of the order on a **drum** resource.

Sales funnels: The flows of sales orders into the organization.

Sales process funnel: The portions of the **sales funnels** that relate to replacing existing customers or sales that may be lost in the future and for providing growth of sales.

Scheduling period: (1) A segment of time, less than or equal to the budget period, that is the shortest period for which a plan exists, (2) the shortest period for which a control report may be reasonably prepared.

Score: A combination of closed sales **note** opportunities that results in a harmonious sales mix.

Secondary constraint: A resource having not only some characteristics of a physical constraint, but also characteristics of a pseudo-constraint.

Shipping buffer: A time buffer that has the shipping schedule as its origin; used to buffer the market constraint.

Short-term capacity: Capacity, which if not used during the current fiscal period, must be purchased anew, to be used in a future period (e.g., personnel services or rent on a month-to-month lease).

Simplified critical chain (SCC): Critical chain using only a **project buffer** (and a **rope** from a **drum** resource in a multiproject environment).

Sources of future improvement: Initiatives, appropriately capitalized, that will propel the process of ongoing improvement to the next levels.

Space buffer: A physical space to allow products to pile up either before or after a **constraint.** Space buffers are placed both before and after internal physical constraints.

Springboard base: (In pricing analysis) the lowest **target price** that would allow a product to be sold without reducing the organization's overall profitability.

Standard cost: (1) A carefully engineered estimate of what a component of product **cost** ought to be; (2) an engineered estimate of what the cost of a product ought to be; (3) an estimate of what the cost of something should be; (4) often used within **TOC** circles to refer to absorption-costing systems.

Static budget: A **budget** that is prepared for only a single estimated level of activity, contrasts with a **flexible budget.**

Statistical fluctuation: Routine variation in the duration needed to complete a task; large variations of a less frequent nature are sometimes known as **Murphy.**

Step-type change: A change in the level of operations that jumps to a new, quite different, level. Step-type changes often require significant levels of additional investment—such as a new plant or expensive machinery and employees.

Step-type market: Characterized by relatively few customers accounting for the major portion of the throughput mix; changes take place in lump-sum amounts relating to a relatively broad range of activity.

Strategic constraints: Locations selected by top management as being strategically desirable places to have constraints. May or may not be active as constraints.

Strategic plan: A plan for the direction of an organization established by strategically selecting constraints and allowing the elegant simplicity of constraint management to lead to an unavoidable process of ongoing improvement.

Strategic resource buffer: See **drum-feeding buffer.**

Strategy: Focusing on the relatively few **constraints** that allow strategic planning to cross the **complexity divide.**

Subordination: The proper behavior for unconstrained activities to support global improvement through an appropriate relationship with constrained areas.

Sword of Damocles: A sword hanging over a person's head, ready to fall at any moment. Damocles was a courtier to Dionysius the Elder, the wealthy tyrant of Syracuse. Damocles told Dionysius that he would like to try his life-style for a day. As part of his "King for a Day" fantasy, Damocles enjoyed a magnificent banquet. But Dionysius had caused a sword to be hanging over Damocles' head, suspended by a single horsehair and ready to fall at any moment. In this way, Damocles was able to experience the precariousness of kingship as well as the spoils.

T: See **throughput.**

Target price: (1) The asking price for a product or service, (2) the price that an organization would like to receive for its products or services.

Target throughput contribution: (In pricing analysis) the throughput that a product or order would provide if it were sold at the **target price.**

Task focusing: The practice of completing one task before switching to work on another task.

Temporary free product: A product offered for sale in a market to which the organization does not make a commitment.

Theory of constraints (TOC): The thinking processes verbalized by Eliyahu M. Goldratt and their known applications.

Thinking bridge: The mental tools and patterning techniques that we, as individual humans, use to assess the potential consequences of our actions.[9]

Thinking processes: See **TOC thinking processes (TP).**

Throughput (T): The rate at which the system generates money through **sales.** Equivalent to the **variable** (or direct) **costing** concept of **contribution margin** when contribution margin is calculated using a cash basis and only **truly variable costs;** sales **revenue** less truly variable expenses associated with the sales revenue. Also known as **throughput contribution** and **throughput value added.** See also **throughput world paradigm.** A number of other uses of the word *throughput* are discussed in Chapter 5 of the text.

Throughput accounting (TA): (1) The accounting procedures implied by *The Goal: Excellence in Manufacturing*[10] early in the constraint management accounting literature and consisting of the T, I, and OE metrics, (2) an extreme form of **direct costing** in which only **materials** are considered to be variable operating cost.

Throughput contribution: See **throughput.**

Throughput expense: Truly variable cost; a **cost** included as part of the **throughput** calculation.

Throughput mix: The proportions of **throughput** provided by the organization's various offerings.

Throughput per constraint unit: A metric designed to reveal the relative profitability of an organization's offerings.

Throughput premium: (In pricing analysis) a target amount of **throughput** to be added to the **springboard base** in establishing a **target price.**

Throughput value added (TVA): See **throughput.**

Throughput world paradigm: An owner and employee mindset that views the organization as a single group of interconnected activities, the profit of which is determined by a relatively few constraints.

Time buffer: A length of time—taking into account the existence of **statistical fluctuations**—allowed for activities to take place; acts as a decoupling mechanism. See also, and contrast with, **space buffer.**

TOC: See **theory of constraints.**

TOC thinking processes (TP): Processes for logical analysis of historical, current, and future cause-and-effect relationships—and the necessary condition structures used to expose underlying assumptions—that lie at the heart of the **theory of constraints.** These processes currently consist of (1) sufficiency trees (**current reality tree, future reality tree, transition tree**), (2) necessary structures (**evaporating cloud, prerequisite tree,** or **IO map**), and (3) the categories of legitimate reservation.

Top management: The group of managers responsible for establishing the overall strategic initiatives of the organization and for ensuring execution of plans in a manner consistent with the expressed goal of the organization's owners.

Total quality management (TQM): The management philosophy of W. Edwards Deming emphasizing the needs of internal and external customers and seeking continuous improvement in local area metrics through statistical process control.

Tracking zone: A point in time in the middle of a **time buffer** at which the location of the physical product representing a **buffer hole** is recorded.

Transfer price: An artificial price associated with the internal transfer of goods or services between two units or divisions of the same overall **entity.** The transfer price is used for internal control. For internal reporting the transfer price amount is treated as a **revenue** or sale by the "selling" unit and as an **expense** or purchase by the receiving unit. These entries are backed out or "eliminated" when the overall entity financial statements are prepared in accordance with **GAAP.**

Transition tree (TT): A **thinking process,** verbalized by E. M. Goldratt, used for checking the logical connection between a proposed action and its inevitable effects. Often used to detail the specific steps to be taken to achieve an intermediate objective in a prerequisite tree or an injection in a **future reality tree.**

True cost: A fantasy. The expression is frequently used by consultants to sell their particular flavor of a cost allocation technique by suggesting that a competing flavor does not provide the *true cost* of products, with the listener or reader left to derive the unstated—and erroneous—conclusion that the consultant's flavor *does* provide the *true cost.*

(TVC) truly variable costs: Costs that vary directly and proportionately with sales volumes. The traditional approach to determining cost variability is to treat a cost as variable "when in doubt." The TOC suggests that in most cases raw materials costs are the only variable costs. The revised rule is to treat cost as nonvariable if in doubt.

Unit-coupled cost: A **truly variable cost** that varies with the number of units sold (or, in some cases, units produced) or with a block of units produced taken as a group.

Unrefusable offer: See **compelling offer.**

Value-coupled cost: A **truly variable cost** that varies as a percentage of sales value.

Variable Costing: See **direct costing.**

Win ratio: In selling, the percentage of identified potential sales opportunities that are converted to actual sales. Calculated as the sales opportunities closed divided by the sales orders introduced into the sales funnel.

NOTES

[1]Eliyahu M. Goldratt, *Haystack Syndrome: Sifting Information Out of the Data Ocean* (North River Press Corp. 1991), p. 146 (emphasis removed).

[2]This business results premise is adapted and extended from three papers written by Bill Hodgdon, "How to Manage the Sales Process: Measuring and Managing the Business to Business Sales Force," "Strategically Winning Industrial Markets," and "Leveraging Distributors to Increase Product Sales." (Hodgdon Consulting Services, telephone: 724-935-0409). See Chapter 9, footnote 16.

[3] Eliyahu M. Goldratt, *Critical Chain* (North River Press Corp., 1997).

[4] This definition is based on Joel Barker's book, *Paradigms: The Business of Discovering the Future* (HarperBusiness, 1993). Barker also has a videotape, The Business of Paradigms, that I recommend viewing.

[5] J. M. Juran, *The Non-Pareto Principle, Mea Culpa,* http://www.juran.com/research/articles/ SP7518.html.

[6] C. N. Parkinson, *Parkinson's Law* (Cambridge, MA: Riverside Press, 1957).

[7] Eliyahu M. Goldratt and Jeff Cox, *The Goal: A Process of Ongoing Improvement,* 2nd rev. ed. (North River Press Corp., 1992).

[8] SFAC No. 2, *Qualitative Characteristics of Accounting Information,* ¶63.

[9] Eliyahu M Goldratt and Robert E. Fox, *The Race* (North River Press Corp., 1986), pp. 20–23.

[10] Eliyahu M. Goldratt and Jeff Cox, *The Goal: Excellence in Manufacturing* (North River Press Corp., 1984).

Index